Educational Research

EDUCATIONAL RESEARCH

Edward L. Vockell

Purdue University Calumet

MACMILLAN PUBLISHING CO., INC.
New York

COLLIER MACMILLAN PUBLISHERS
London

*To my father, Ray Vockell, who first taught me
to think scientifically.*

Macmillan Publishing Co., Inc.
866 Third Avenue, New York, New York 10022

Collier Macmillan Canada, Inc.

Library of Congress Cataloging in Publication Data

Vockell, Edward L.
  Educational research.
  Includes index.
  1. Educational research. I. Title.
LB1028.V88   370'.7'8   82-15345
ISBN 0–02–423070–7   AACR2

Printing: 7 8   Year: 9 0 1 2 3 4 5

ISBN   0-02-423070-7

Contents

Preface

PURPOSE AND SCOPE OF THE BOOK

An educator is a person whose responsibility it is to help people to learn. Most educators are professional teachers, but there are others who function as educators in helping people develop skills or insights. This book is written for all educators. The purpose of this book is to enable educators to apply research skills to their professional responsibilities and therefore be able to do a better job at promoting learning.

Research deals with the application of the scientific method to problem solving. It has not always been obvious to teachers and other educators that scientific methodology is of importance in education. Very likely this neglect of scientific methodology has occurred because research has been considered irrelevant to educators. Teachers have too many practical problems to worry about ivory tower research—or so the belief goes.

This book approaches research from a perspective different from that taken in other educational research textbooks. The goal is to show educators that the application of research principles can make them more effective in their job of promoting learning. The basic point is that you do not have to stop teaching to do research; research is something you can do *while* teaching. And if you do good research, you will do better teaching.

The book covers most of the topics treated in traditional educational research books, but in a different order and with a different emphasis. The major topic *not* discussed in the text is the distinction between various types of research and evaluation. I have deliberately omitted a discussion of such distinctions because I find that students who have this topic thrust at them wind up focusing on it to the neglect of the important content of a research course. The important content consists of using research ideas in a way that will promote effective teaching and learning.

ACKNOWLEDGMENTS

This book had its birth in the frustrations I faced in trying to make educational research relevant to the in-service teachers I taught in northwestern Indiana. They often expressed their thanks for making the research course "painless," but I was still left with the impression that not many of them found the traditional approach very relevant to their daily responsibilities. It was the encouragement of these students that led me to embark upon the new line of presentation that became the basis for the book.

During the writing of the book several people were extremely helpful. Sam Paravonian, Jim Gaffney, and Bill Asher read each chapter carefully and offered important comments that led to substantial improvement and reorganization of the material. Frank Labmeier and Mark Breitenstein made valuable suggestions regarding the style of composition. Pete Chojenski offered considerable assistance with the Library Usage chapter. Theresa Perry, Paula Wells, Pat Spudic, and Mildred Blosky competently typed the major part of the manuscript.

As the deadline for this book drew near, my wife, Alice, understood why authors thank their wives and children. As I became increasingly invisible and irritable under the pressure of completing the various tasks, Alice became increasingly helpful.

Finally, I want to acknowledge the contribution of the students in my educational research course who took the course during 1980 and 1981, when the major portion of the book was written. Their willingness to offer constructive criticism eliminated numerous ambiguities and forced me to think along lines that are likely to be useful to similar educators who will read this text.

Edward L. Vockell
Hammond, Indiana

1   The Four Levels of Research

Teachers do research every day. If they do not, they should. It would make their lives much easier, but most teachers do not believe this is so. They usually dislike research, and they feel that they lack the technical competence to carry it out.

This is primarily because research has been presented as something that scientists do and that nonscientists do from time to time when they want to use scientific methods. Conventionally, in order to do research a teacher temporarily or partially stops teaching, and most teachers either do not want to do this or cannot afford to. (Unless, of course, they can pick up three hours of graduate credit for doing research. In such cases they might even enjoy doing research, for doing research on something interesting is more rewarding than taking a course on something uninteresting. But even here, research is viewed as something that the teacher does *besides teaching or instead of teaching,* not as *part of teaching.*)

Without watering down the concept of research, I would like to approach it from a different point of view and demonstrate that research is something you can do *while* teaching. By behaving at all times in the classroom at least partially as a researcher, you can become a much better educator.

FOUR LEVELS OF RESEARCH

Research is performed at four levels. These levels are hierarchical in the sense that a higher level presupposes the techniques employed at lower levels. Most research textbooks speak of research as if everyone who does research is working at only the higher levels. This is not only a wasteful approach; it is positively destructive, for it discourages teachers from doing research on the countless occasions that arise for them to do lower level research. The four levels are summarized in Table 1–1.

1

Level I is an authentic mode of research.[1] It is something that teachers should be doing all the time. In college I took a philosophy course in which we studied Spinoza for about a week. The professor was an intelligent and friendly person who wanted to teach us to "appreciate" Spinoza. He wanted us to have a feeling for what the man was saying, to become excited about his significant ideas. I got a 95 on the test and did not "appreciate" Spinoza at all. I do not think anybody in that class of sixty people appreciated Spinoza. The professor had no idea that this was the case. He was not doing his research. Had he found an appropriate way to measure our appreciation of Spinoza, it is quite likely that he would have modified his teaching strategy—and today Spinoza would have a few more followers.

Level I, then, consists of finding good ways to measure what is happening. All subsequent levels depend on a sound basis at Level I. This is a good reason for discussing Level I research strategy at the beginning of the book instead of near the end (as most textbooks do). First, it is something we can do when we have no intention of doing any further research. And second, it gives us a firm basis for going on to the more sophisticated cause and effect levels of research.

Quite often educators doing Level I research will discover that something is not happening the way it should be, and they will try to make improvements. After they try to make improvements, they will check again to see what is happening after their intervention. In many cases, such educators have not gone beyond Level I research at this point. They have merely performed Level I research on two separate occasions. There is nothing wrong with this; it is something we all should do. But in other cases, educators should want to go one step further and determine *why* a change has occurred. They should want to find out if their intervention has *caused* the differences they have observed.

To take the example discussed above, let us assume that my philosophy teacher has found a valid way to measure appreciation of Spinoza and has discovered that we all dislike Spinoza. After thinking it over, he comes up with what sounds like a better way to help us appreciate the philosopher. He tries his new idea. Then at the end of the course he measures us again, and finds that our appreciation has increased. In terms of Level I research, he has found out what he wanted to find out; he knows that he has not been wasting his time and ours. But at Level II, has he shown that his new method caused the improvement? No! For reasons which will be discussed later, he has not demonstrated a causal effect. Other factors could have accounted for the change. One is that another teacher (say, in history class) might have demonstrated

---

[1] A strong argument can be made that Level I research is not research at all. It can legitimately be considered *pre-research*. If research is defined as "the process of establishing scientific relationships," then only Levels II, III, and IV fit this definition. However, the concepts and principles described in this text under the label of Level I research (Chapters 2 through 7) provide the foundations upon which cause-and-effect conclusions must be built. If a reader wishes to adhere to a pure definition of research, therefore, it might be best to regard these chapters as describing *measurement strategies* or the *tools of research*, rather than as dealing with research itself. However, the application of the concepts and principles discussed in these chapters involves the use of scientific methodology. This methodology enables the teacher to step beyond haphazard management of learning and makes it more likely that desired results will occur. Even if a teacher declines to advance to higher levels of research, the use of the principles described at this first level will enhance teaching. Because of this, I have chosen to "dignify" this set of concepts and principles by labeling them Level I research. The distinction described in this footnote is not essential to understanding this textbook. It is intended for readers who are jarred by an apparently nontraditional use of the term *research*. If you feel this footnote has dealt with a nonproblem, you should feel free to ignore it. Read on!

TABLE **1–1.** The Four Levels of Research.

Level I
(Data Collection)

What is happening? (What is the problem? Is this what I want to happen? Is this what should happen?)
Examples: Can Johnny read?

Does Roberta enjoy Shakespeare?

Is Wanda more anxious now than she was in September?

Are only a relatively few students participating in class discussion?

Level II
(Internal Validity)

What is causing this to happen? (Am I causing it? Can I change it?)
Examples: Johnny does read better this year. Is this because of my program? Or is it because he grew a year older? Or because his dad said he'd pound the heck out of him if he flunked?

Wanda is no longer anxious. Is this because of my self-concept program or because of something else?

Is the fact that my questions are directed at only a small minority of pupils causing others to "turn me off"?

Level III
(External Validity)

Will the same thing happen under different circumstances? (How far can the results be generalized?)
Examples: Will the same program that taught Johnny how to read help him with math?

Will the self-concept program that helped Wanda also help Jeanette?

If I change to a different set of questions, will I still get intensive participation in class discussion? If so, how widely can such new sets of questions differ from those previously used?

Level IV
(Theoretical Research)

Is there some underlying principle at work?
Examples: Did Johnny improve because I supplied him with an appropriate interaction of optimal discrepancy and reinforcement schedule?

Do children learn better if they organize the material themselves than if they receive the information in a highly structured format?

Does intrinsic reinforcement result in more effective learning than extrinsic reinforcement?

---

that Spinoza had a valuable contribution to make, and this could have accounted for the differences.

Has the professor done a bad job on his research? That depends on what he thought he was accomplishing through his little project. If he thought he was proving that the new method worked, then he did a bad job of it. On the other hand, if his main interest was to make sure that he was not turning loose on the world a group of Spinoza-haters, then his research was quite successful. He knew that a degree of appreciation existed among his students at the end of the unit. He did not especially care why the students had this attitude. The important thing was that it existed.

What should his intention be? Again, that depends. Certainly, he should have done at least Level I research. He seriously weakened his course by not doing so. But was Level II necessary? If he spent a great deal of time or money on his new method and it would be expensive to continue this method, then knowledge of causality would be important. If the new method was inexpensive, however, then establishing causality would be much less crucial. If causality can be established with little or no effort, then why not? On the other hand, there might be better things on which to spend one's time. Stopping short at Level I is not necessarily bad or watered-down research. It's often the wisest possible use of one's resources.

Once causality has been demonstrated at Level II, there is still room for increased sophistication. If we have demonstrated that something has produced an effect in one isolated situation, we still don't know that it will work somewhere else. At Level III, we examine the *generalizability* of research findings. It should be obvious that Level II is a prerequisite for Level III; for if we have proved nothing, then we have nothing to generalize.

In the case of the philosophy professor, assume that he has established that his new method probably caused the improved attitudes toward Spinoza. He then goes to the annual meeting in Canton, Ohio, of the International Association for the Advancement of the Appreciation of Spinoza. There he finds a speaker bemoaning to a sleeping audience the fact that college students just do not appreciate Spinoza. My professor jumps to his feet and excitedly proclaims that he can help solve their problems. What the other professors should do is implement his program in their classrooms! What is the probability that his program will work in the other classrooms? If all he has done is good Level II research, we do not know. There are numerous factors which might have been operating in his classroom which might have been unique to his situation. The most obvious is his personality. He thought of the new idea and really liked it, and so it is possible that other professors using someone else's idea which only mildly turns them on will have much less successful results. Level III research controls these numerous other factors and helps the researcher declare that it is the treatment *independent of the experimental situation* which caused the observed results.

Level III research is not performed by classroom teachers as often as Level II. This is because they are most frequently concerned about solving unique problems in their own classrooms. Level III research becomes important when we want to share our results with someone else or adapt someone else's results to our own situation. If we are going to publish the results of a research grant, for example, and someone else plans to make use of these results, we need Level III research.

Although educators do not often do Level III research, this does not mean that they do not need to understand it. A good way to get new ideas is to read journals and talk to other teachers about what they're doing. When a project has worked somewhere else, teachers must make a decision about whether or not it will work in their own situations. This becomes especially important if it is expensive in terms of effort or money. A working knowledge of Level III research will help teachers make wiser decisions and avoid wasting time on inefficient changes.

Finally, there is Level IV research. This is the kind of research that scientists do when they discover, for example, that a new behavior is learned most rapidly if it is reinforced continuously but that it is maintained longer if the schedule is eventually switched to an irregular reinforcement schedule. Likewise, when Jean Piaget differentiated between concrete-operational and formal-operational thought, he was doing Level IV research. At this level the researcher not only demonstrates that a generalizable outcome will reliably occur, but he gives theoretical reasons why it occurs. This in turn suggests other related situations in which similar results are likely to occur.

Let us return once more to our philosophy professor. He has now done Level III research. He knows that he has caused an improvement in attitudes and that this is not unique to his isolated situation. Now he might wonder why the dramatic improvement has occurred. Let us assume that his method was to give the students moral dilemmas and then to have them role-play, with students taking turns adopting a Spinoza viewpoint. At Level IV, he might draw a conclusion that "examining ethical concepts from the philosopher's viewpoint in a lifelike situation enhances the college junior's appreciation of that philosopher." He would have to work hard to demonstrate this, probably replicating the study in more situations with a wide variety of philosophers; but if he could successfully perform this research, he would have a principle with extremely wide generalizability. This principle could be applied through role-playing, movies, interviews, and so on. It could be applied to areas outside of philosophy, such as to literature, history, and psychology. As you may have noticed, Level IV is really an extension of Level III with the results generalized *at a conceptual level* and much farther beyond the original situation.

Your first reaction might be that you will never do Level IV research. Of course, I can fall back on the valid reply that you will need to understand it so that you can intelligently read the results of scientists who do this kind of research. But there's actually an even better reason for knowing how to do Level IV research. At Level IV we apply what John Dewey has called the *scientific method*. Many writers of research books have started their books with a chapter on the scientific method, treating it as if Dewey were primarily describing a good way to do scientific experiments. Actually, this is not what Dewey was doing. Rather, he was writing about how people in general develop complicated thoughts and advance their understanding of concepts. Hence he called his book not *How to Do a Scientific Study* but *How We Think*. The point I am making is that if this is how we think, then a careful analysis and application of the principles of Level IV research will make us not only better researchers but better thinkers—whether we are thinking about how to get Johnny to read or about how to achieve world peace. Furthermore—although this may sound grandiose—since Levels I, II, and III are hierarchical prerequisites for Level IV research, it seems clear that learning to do these things will not only help us to solve specific problems but may eventually make us better overall thinkers.

The essential ingredient that distinguishes educational research from an educator's other professional activities is that it uses the scientific method to solve problems. This means that at all four levels educational research is *systematic, logical, data-referenced* and *replicable*. These characteristics of educational research will be discussed throughout this book.

It is important to note that educational research is not the *only* endeavor in which the professional educator must engage. There are many problems that must be solved through recourse to strategies other than research. For example, a decision to include or exclude sex education from a school curriculum must be based largely on philosophical considerations rather than on research information. School boards, principals, teachers, and parents who discuss this problem and make the decision are likely to be concerned about such issues as the right to privacy, personal ethical convictions, the dangers of overpopulation, and the nature of the social contract between the individual and the state as it applies to the educational setting. None of these issues focuses primarily on empirical data, and therefore the contribution of research will not be dominant.

Educational research would likewise probably not be the primary factor in decisions about how much emphasis to give to team sports in the local school, about whether there should be prayers in public schools, and about whether busing should be employed to achieve racial integration. Each of these may be important questions, but in each case the issues are going to be settled primarily on the basis of philosophical and legal considerations, rather than on the basis of research information. However, the primary emphasis on non-research considerations does not mean that research is completely irrelevant to such issues. For example, even though the debate over prayer in public schools focuses on philosophical and legal issues, research can still play an important supportive role. For instance, if during a discussion on this issue someone raises the point that a particular solution (such as permitting a period of silence for private meditation at the beginning of the school day) makes non-participants feel isolated and develops a negative self-concept among such pupils, then it *would* be possible (and desirable) to employ research strategies to determine whether undesirable isolation and negative self-concepts really do occur. The empirical data arising from such an investigation could usefully influence the outcome of such a discussion.

Educational research strategies should be interwoven with other professional capabilities in an integrated fashion to promote successful problem solving and intelligent decision making. By understanding the principles of each of the four levels of research, you can become more professionally competent both by emphasizing your research skills when such emphasis is specifically called for and by integrating these skills into your other professional endeavors.

THE ORGANIZATION OF THIS BOOK

Chapters 2 through 7 of this book focus on Level I research. They discuss how to define outcomes in terms that can be measured, how to construct and administer instruments to measure these outcomes, and how to record and interpret the scores obtained from these measuring instruments.

Chapters 8 through 12 focus on Level II research. They describe how to establish cause and effect relationships. To perform such cause and effect research it is necessary to apply not only the principles discussed in Chapters 8 through 12, but also the principles discussed in Chapters 2 through 7.

Chapter 13 focuses on Level III research. This chapter describes the principles which must guide us in making generalizations from a research setting to the other settings in which we intend to apply the research findings. Level III research depends on the principles discussed in Chapter 13, and also on the principles discussed in Chapters 2 through 12.

Chapter 14 attempts to integrate the information discussed in Chapters 2 through 13. It shows how all the parts fit together into a "formal" research project.

Chapter 15 focuses on Level IV research. It provides guidelines for studying the theoretical principle that are at the basis of the cause and effect relationships we observe. Level IV research depends on the principles described in Chapter 15, and on those principles discussed in Chapters 2 through 14.

Chapters 16 and 17 deal with the use of the computer and the library to solve research problems. These tools can be employed at any of the four levels of research.

Chapter 18 describes the appropriate strategies for carrying out and reporting upon a formal research project. It includes a discussion of both practical and ethical guidelines.

This book is intended primarily for in-service educators—teachers, counselors, administrators, and others who are actively responsible for helping learners acquire new skills. It has been arranged in its present format to make it as useful as possible to this audience. Nevertheless, it will also be useful to those who are interested in doing formal research—that is, for educators who are willing and able to devote time specifically to a research project. Chapter 14 will be especially helpful to readers who fall into this category. As Chapter 14 will show, researchers pursuing formal research projects will often follow a chronological sequence that does not correspond to the ordering of chapters in this textbook. Nevertheless, the logical sequence of the levels of research is still quite valid. In other words, even if a person starts by first stating a theoretical hypothesis at Level IV, such a hypothesis cannot be usefully examined without a firm understanding of the lower levels of research.

Understanding each level of research in the order in which it is presented here will enable you (1) to solve problems that are appropriate at that level and (2) to develop understandings that will enable you to progress to higher levels of research as the need arises.

PUTTING IT ALL TOGETHER

A section like this will appear near the end of each chapter. This section will pursue a common problem throughout the book and will point out the relevance of each chapter to the common problem. This will help you to integrate and apply the information as it accumulates throughout the text.

These sections will focus on the activities of Eugene Anderson, a mythical humane educator. Mr. Anderson works for a humane education organization, and his job is to help humane organizations and schools develop strategies for implementing humane education programs in schools throughout the country. When humane education programs come into schools, they should have the impact of changing the children's attitudes toward animal life. Mr. Anderson read this textbook before he took his job, and then he was shocked to discover that nowhere in the field of humane education literature was there a single piece of research to demonstrate that any particular strategy for conducting humane education actually accomplished anything.[2] Mr. Anderson realized that humane education would probably be more effective if it were pursued in a more scientific spirit, and so he entered upon the activities described in these "Putting It All Together" sections of this book.

Of particular relevance to the present chapter is the overall plan of action that Mr. Anderson developed. He realized that if he was going to accomplish anything constructive, he would have a better chance of succeeding if he followed these steps:

First, he would find a way to determine what outcomes were actually occurring among the children he dealt with (Level I research). He needed to find a way to define and measure humane attitudes. When he went into a school classroom, he always

---

[2] Mr. Anderson and his exploits are fictional. However, the examples are based on my own research in humane education. Interested readers can find further information in Vockell and Hodal (1978, 1980). See ERIC microfiche ED196 799 and ED199 118.

hoped something good was happening; but in reality he had no idea what the children's attitudes were either when he came into the classroom or when he left. He needed a way to find out what was going on.

Second, he wanted to find out whether his efforts were causing anything important to happen. This was Level II research. He wanted to find this out right away, but he realized that he couldn't logically do this until he had first done his Level I groundwork. But once he found a way to measure what was going on in those classrooms, it was quite important for him to find out what cause and effect relationships existed between his own work and those outcomes. After all, his job was costing his organization several thousand dollars a year, and it would be desirable to spend that money as efficiently as possible.

Third, if he did establish cause and effect relationships, he wanted to know whether the same effects would occur elsewhere. If something worked in one of the schools he dealt with, would it work in another school?

In addition, Mr. Anderson went to state and national conventions quite often, and he wanted to be able to share his results with others and to learn from them. Thus, Level III research was also quite important to Mr. Anderson.

Finally, Mr. Anderson was concerned with underlying principles that might be at work. In his highly speculative mind, he mulled over such questions as *What is a humane attitude anyway? How do such attitudes develop and how do they change? Is it possible that there's no such thing as a humane attitude, but merely humane behavior?* Such problems filled his conversations at conventions and frequently brought him wide awake in the middle of the night. Now, he realized, after he did his Level I, II, and III research, he would be able to dip into Level IV research and make an original contribution to the theory of developing humane attitudes.

The adventures of Eugene Anderson will be continued in this same section at the end of the next chapter.

SUMMARY

In this book we are going to examine research in a hierarchical fashion. The first level of research consists of collecting data to find out what outcomes are occurring in an educational setting. At the second level, we attempt to establish cause and effect relationships. The third level concerns itself with determining how far the conclusions of a research study can be generalized. Finally, at the fourth level we examine the theoretical principles which explain the results which we observe in a research study.

These levels are hierarchical in two ways: (1) they become increasingly complex, and each succeeding stage presupposes the previous one, and (2) the probability that the teacher will actually perform the research decreases as the level increases. A teacher should almost always be doing some kind of research in the classroom. This book will help to determine what kind of research is needed and will demonstrate how to perform it as efficiently and productively as possible.

2   Measuring Outcome Variables

Chapter Preview

The purpose of Level I research is to find out what outcomes are occurring in the educational setting about which the teacher is concerned. This chapter is devoted to techniques for developing operational definitions of these outcomes. Operational definitions are the evidence a teacher is willing to accept to indicate that an outcome is occurring. In some cases this evidence is quite direct, and in other cases it is indirect. In addition to discussing strategies for developing operational definitions, the chapter suggests strategies for making this evidence as solid as possible.

After completing the chapter you should be able to

- Define and identify examples of outcome variables.
- Identify examples of well-written operational definitions of outcome variables.
- Write an operational definition of a given outcome variable.
- Identify strategies for making the evidence acquired through the operational definition as solid as possible.

MEASURING OUTCOMES IN EDUCATION

Level I research consists of collecting data regarding an outcome which is occurring or which is supposed to be occurring. There are two main reasons why teachers collect such data: they need to know whether they are accomplishing what they want to accomplish, and they need to know whether things are happening that they do not want to happen. The outcome being measured is referred to in this book as the *outcome variable*. The term *variable* and the relationship of outcome variables to other kinds of variables will be discussed later. The following are examples of outcome variables:

Reading ability.
Spelling errors.
Rate of speech.
Student anxiety.
Teacher anxiety.
Tardiness.
Parental satisfaction.
Moral behavior.
Number of suspensions.
Number of arrests.
Attitude toward English.
Extent of voluntary pupil
   participation in class
   discussion and class
   activities.

Many of the problems that teachers encounter in education occur because they neglect to measure outcome variables. For example, the philosophy teacher's failure to inculcate in us an appreciation of Spinoza (discussed in Chapter 1) was a direct result of his failure to measure our attitudes. Had he known what was happening, he could have attempted to change the state of affairs. Many teachers have discipline problems in their classrooms because they fail to assess the level of anxiety among their pupils. Other teachers accidentally require their students to become uncreative because their tests measure conformity rather than insight. Many social studies teachers release into the world students who receive A's but who will never vote; and these teachers could have taken steps to overcome this apathy, if they would have measured their students' attitudes toward the democratic process. Principals often preside over a school filled with apathetic teachers, thinking that all is going well because no one complains. Counselors sometimes waste weeks or months while they overlook the observable indications that a client needs a different type of treatment. In each of these cases a problem exists and the problem is going untreated because an outcome variable has gone unmeasured. The simple act of measurement would help us become aware of such difficulties and focus our energies on solving such problems.

The first step in measuring an outcome variable is to devise an *operational definition* of it. This operational definition states precisely what observable events we should record in order to say that we have collected data regarding the outcome variable.[1]

In a few cases, the behaviors we want to develop or change are completely external and easily observable. In such cases, stating the operational definition is merely a matter of becoming precise, of focusing on what we really want to observe and eliminating irrelevancies. Such instances are rare. Examples include in-seat behavior, frequency of tantrums, and tardiness. These are all completely observable events, and all we have to do to measure them is be in the proper place at the proper time and look for the appropriate behavior.

---

[1] This chapter discusses operational definitions of *outcome variables*. The general topic of operational definitions is covered in detail in Chapter 13.

Most of what we try to accomplish in schools, however, involves an *internal* change, often referred to as learning. Learning cannot be observed directly. All we can do is collect evidence by observing external behaviors performed by the learner.

A major misfortune in recent years has been the confusion instigated by emphasis on behavioral objectives, which are really specific types of operational definitions. Many people have misread the behavioral objectives literature and have come away with the impression that they should merely teach trivia—things that can be observed directly. "If it can't be stated as a behavioral objective, don't teach it." This is nonsense. Behavioral objectives are helpful—extremely helpful—but not essential. It is emphatically *not* wrong to want to teach understanding, appreciation, and attitudes. What the behavioral objectives literature says is do not naively believe that these internal changes are occurring. Collect evidence. That is all a behavioral objective or an operational definition is: *the evidence that you are willing to accept as an indication that an internal change has occurred.* We collect evidence (with varying degrees of accuracy), and then we *infer* that this observable evidence is correlated with the presence or absence of an internal change in the learner.

In a few cases, the inference is quite direct, and there is no reason whatsoever to doubt the validity of the inference. This is because the external behavior is almost synonymous with the internal learning. This is the case when we want a person to learn how to perform a behavior. If we want to teach students to saw a board in half, we can ascertain that learning has occurred by giving the learners a board and asking them to saw it in half. If the physical evidence shows that the board is in fact sawed in half, we can pretty well assume that they have learned how to do this. The slight remaining uncertainty can be eliminated by having them repeat the task several times, thus eliminating the likelihood of a chance success. (**Note:** Even here we have not demonstrated that we have *taught* them anything, but only that they have learned. They may have learned the behavior previously.) Likewise, we can directly observe that a child has stopped being tardy or that a child is throwing a tantrum. No inference is necessary.

In other cases, the evidence is not so clearly related to the learning, and hence the inference that learning has occurred is more remote and needs to be buttressed by further reasoning and additional evidence. If we want to teach a child to understand a passage in a book, for example, can we ascertain this from his correct answers to questions about the passage? Not really; for there is a good chance that he is merely guessing well, incorporating information from other sources, or reacting to subtle cues from the question. By carefully structuring the testing situation, we *can* still make an accurate assessment of what the child has learned; but the point is that the evidence is much less direct, and we have to rely much more heavily on logical inferences and supporting evidence than in the case of the more external behavior.

Even more remotely connected with observable behaviors are the *affective* goals of education. Affective goals are quite important. Unless a student appreciates or understands the value of something, he is unlikely to take it with him beyond the classroom. But because of the very remote connection between the internal affective change and any observable evidence, the inferential leap becomes considerable. Does this mean we shouldn't bother to collect evidence? Of course not; evidence is even more important here than in the other cases. The solution is to collect more evidence and to collect it more carefully. The precise methods for collecting such information will be discussed later. Here I shall simply point out that the problems of collecting data on these extremely internal outcomes are often best surmounted by (1) using unobtrusive forms of measurement, and (2) by collecting more than a single form of evidence.

WRITING OPERATIONAL DEFINITIONS OF COGNITIVE OUTCOME VARIABLES

In this chapter I shall talk about operational definitions as though they were synonymous with behavioral objectives. This is technically not quite accurate. Actually, a behavioral objective is a specific type of operational definition, but there is little point in making an issue of the distinction here. (Operational definitions are more fully covered in Chapter 13.) If you can write good behavioral objectives, you can write good operational definitions of outcome variables, and vice versa. The treatment here will be brief. If you are interested in more detailed information on writing operational definitions, the behavioral objectives literature (see end of chapter) provides excellent help.

In writing an operational definition, state the *observable activity* which you are willing to accept as evidence that the outcome is occurring. An observable activity is one about which two or more observers would almost certainly agree with regard to its occurrence or nonoccurrence.

Spot Quiz

According to this definition, which of the following is an observable activity?

a. Understanding a reading passage.

b. Paraphrasing a reading passage.

Answer:

b. Since *understanding* involves no observable activity, you cannot tell from purely objective, observable data whether or not a person understands something. You have to make an inference. However, it *is* possible to tell whether or not a person has paraphrased a passage merely by listening to him.

No inference is necessary to say, "That child is paraphrasing the passage I just told him to read!" Note, however, that if we conclude that a person who paraphrases a passage must therefore understand it, we are making an inference. Accurate paraphrasing is the objective, observable data that we are willing to accept as evidence to support our inference that understanding is occurring within the learner. Hence "paraphrasing a reading passage" is one of many possible operational definitions of understanding a reading passage. (Inadequacies of this operational definition will be discussed later.)

Note that I am not saying that paraphrasing is more useful than understanding. I am not suggesting that the teacher should stop teaching students to understand passages and teach them to paraphrase instead. In a few rare cases it might be important to teach a student how to paraphrase, but in most cases paraphrasing is a relatively trivial activity. What we really want is understanding. But even though it's trivial, paraphrasing is observable; and as Sherlock Holmes was wont to tell Dr. Watson, trivial evidence can support important inferences.

Spot Quiz

Try another one. Which of the following are observable activities?

a. Understanding Boyle's law.

b. Identifying correct applications of Boyle's law.

c. Distinguishing between correct and incorrect applications of Boyle's law.

d. Solving problems that require Boyle's law.

Answers:
b, c, d.
By observing a student we cannot tell what he understands. Understanding is all in his head. We can tell by simple, direct observation, however, whether or not he can identify correct applications, distinguish among them, and solve problems based upon them. And from this observable data, we can infer that the student understands how to solve them.

If you got both of these examples wrong, you probably do not yet understand what operational definitions are, and likewise you do not know how to write them, and therefore probably need remedial help. Right? Not necessarily. All we have really established is that you cannot distinguish between well written and poorly written operational definitions. Before you despair, read the next section. (If you got them both right, we still are not certain that you understand and know how to do everything expected of you. You might have merely broken my system or psyched me out or been just plain lucky.)

DEAR RESEARCHER: I am a 12-year-old girl with a great personality. I'm pretty good-looking too. My problem is Dwayne, a great-looking guy in my class. I'm madly in love with him, but he doesn't care about me. I asked him to kiss me yesterday, but all he did was let out the grossest belch I've ever heard. I asked him to carry my books home, but he stuck them up in a tree, and I had to get an ugly 14-year-old to get them down. All Dwayne ever does is throw snowballs at me and my friends. Why won't Dwayne return my love? Why does he hate me? (signed) YOUNG LOVE IN PEORIA

DEAR YOUNG: Your problem here is one of operational definition. You're interested in receiving Dwayne's affection, and you operationally define this as kissing, holding hands, and carrying books. Guys like Dwayne often operationalize affection by throwing snowballs at girls they like and sticking their books up in trees. It's also likely that Dwayne's misreading *you*. You're trying to show your affection by kissing, book-carrying, etc.; but it's likely that Dwayne might view these activities as an operational definition of "weirdness." If I were you, I'd tie his coat in knots or hit him in the face with a pie. On second thought, don't. I just noticed your letter was postmarked 14 years ago. (signed) THE LONELY RESEARCHER

MAKING THE EVIDENCE MORE SOLID

If students can perform the observable activity inolved in our operational definition, can we say that the outcome variable is occurring? Conversely, if they fail to perform it, can we say that it is not occurring? In both cases, the answer is no, not unless we can rule out other likely explanations for the occurrence or nonoccurrence of the activity.

Look at the paraphrasing example. Assume that some reading students have paraphrased correctly. For what reasons, other than actually understanding the passage, might they paraphrase it correctly? The list of alternate explanations could be almost endless, but here are a few:

- They could have guessed wildly but accurately.
- They could have guessed from context clues (such as pictures).
- Other students could have whispered the paraphrase to them.
- They could have memorized the paraphrase the night before.
- They could have noticed that you grimaced when they started out inaccurately and then smiled slightly when they changed to an accurate paraphrase.
- They might have deliberately worded their paraphrase in such vague terms that it would cover almost any of the possibilities.

You can probably think of many more possibilities. In collecting evidence, your job is to rule out as many as possible of the alternative explanations. In the above example, this actually isn't very hard. Here are some simple ways to eliminate each of these alternative explanations:

- Give them three or four passages. Wild guessing is no more likely to hold up over time than is luck at the roulette wheel.
- Eliminate the context clues (such as pictures), or ask questions about things not referred to in the context clues.
- Have the students sit where they will not hear whispers.
- Give them a new passage, so that they won't have any idea what to memorize the night before.
- Do not include "test-wiseness" clues in your testing format.
- If they give you a vague paraphrase, ask them specific questions about it, or in some way require them to become more specific.

By doing these things we would increase the accuracy of our inference that students who paraphrase a passage actually understand it. But what if they failed to paraphrase? Would this mean that they didn't understand the passage? No, there are many explanations for not paraphrasing, including the following:

- They might have good receptive skills but poor expressive skills.
- They might not like to talk to you.
- They might be shy or anxious.
- They might feel that the original passage said the thought well enough and see no reason to paraphrase it.

You can probably think of more reasons. As the evidence collector, your responsibility is to rule out these alternative explanations. Here are some possibilities:

- If they lack expressive skills, teach them some.
- If they do not like you, either make an effort to befriend them or have someone else whom they do like ask them to paraphrase the passage.
- If they are shy or anxious, make the situation as non-threatening as possible.
- Make a deliberate effort, if necessary, to convince them that paraphrasing is a useful skill, if for no other reason than that this skill will enable them to communicate to you whether or not they have understood the passage.

By doing all these things, we maximize the probability of accuracy in our inference that a non-paraphraser is a non-understander. In many cases, validating evidence that learning has *not* occurred is much more difficult than validating evidence that learning has occurred.

In addition to eliminating alternative explanations for the existence of evidence, there is a second route that the researcher should pursue, namely, *collect a second type of evidence*. For example, we could have our students who have read the passage attempt *each* of the following things:

1. Paraphrase the passage.
2. Answer questions about the passage.
3. Follow directions contained in the passage.
4. Tell us whether or not they feel they understand the passage.

If students cannot do 1, but can do 2, 3 and 4, we would probably conclude that they did understand the passage, especially if there was a plausible explanation for their failure to paraphrase. When there is a conflict in the evidence, we simply evaluate what evidence we have. Then we either make an inference based on how we reconcile the conflicts or we seek further data. Such further evaluation often becomes quite detailed and can lead to useful diagnostic data which will help the learner in the future.

In actual practice, while it is often useful to use more than one approach to collecting evidence when you are first working with students, you will eventually find out which approaches are valid and which are invalid and be able to use one valid method of collecting evidence at a time. For example, an experienced teacher can find out if high school students understand a passage by asking questions which previous experience has shown to provide good evidence. And with college students, most professors simply ask the students whether or not they understood the passage. When the college students nod *yes*, this is *evidence* that they did understand. But the professors would do well to remember that the nods are *only evidence*. (The students may nod because they may be reluctant to reveal their ignorance to their peers and to their professor. Or they may know the professor will talk longer if they don't nod.)

In summary, there are two good ways to make the evidence more solid:

- Reduce the number of alternative explanations.
- Collect more than one type of evidence.

Neither of these methods actually succeeds in making the evidence foolproof, of course, but their combined use increases the probability that we are making accurate inferences.

DO YOU MEET THE OBJECTIVES OF THIS CHAPTER?

Let us stop to see if we are accomplishing what we are supposed to in this chapter. That is, do you understand what operational definitions are, and do you know how to write good ones? An operational definition of this goal is as follows:

- Given an undefined outcome variable and set of several suggested operational definitions of this variable, you should be able to distinguish between those which state observable activities and those which do not.

To determine whether or not you have met this objective, take Test 1 in the Review Quiz. But before doing so, think. If you get 90% or 100% on this test, does that really mean that you understand what operational definitions are and know how to write them? No; without knowing anything else about you, I really cannot say that for certain. For one thing, it would be easy to guess correctly on Part 1. However, if I have designed a good test, I can say that for most people success on this test is a good indicator that the goal has been met. But there will be many people for whom this statement will not hold true, and I have no idea whether or not you are one of them. Two reasons why you might get all the answers in Test 1 correct without having reached the goal are that you may have learned only to recognize good work in others and not be able to do it yourself, and that you may have noticed subtle clues inadvertently included in the test items that tip you off. In the second case, success on the test would actually be a good operational definition of test-taking ability, not understanding operational definitions or knowing how to write operational definitions.

Moreover, what should you conclude if you missed three or four of the items in Test 1? I am assuming that this means that you do not understand and do not know how to write operational definitions. Is my assumption correct? Again, I cannot tell without knowing anything about you. If I have written good test items, then the vast majority of people who miss these items will miss them because they have not met the goals of this chapter. But there are other reasons for errors. For example, perhaps you might get an item wrong because you read into it something that I did not intend to say (and perhaps most people might read the item exactly the way I intended it to be read). In such a case, your failure would not be an operational definition of not understanding operational definitions, but rather of failing to perceive things from my point of view.

To get around the above problems, here is a second operational definition of understanding and knowing how to write operational definitions:

- Given an undefined outcome variable, you should be able to write a clearly expressed operational definition of it.

Test 2 was devised to determine whether or not you are successful according to this operational definition. Before you take it, pause for a moment. What will success or failure on this test mean? If you succeed by matching my answers quite closely, that might be pretty good evidence that you have met the goal. But what if your answers do not match mine very closely? Then you have to decide on your own whether or not you are right, and if you have not met the goal, how can you possibly answer this question? In this case, "success" might be a good operational definition of a lax conscience rather than understanding how to write operational definitions.

To further circumvent uncertainties, I consider a third operational definition of understanding operational definitions. It is as follows:

- You should be able to restate in your own words the definition of "operational definition."

Your success according to this operational definition is tested in Test 3. This test obviously has problems similar to the first two tests. But it is a third piece of evidence, quite different from the other two.

If I were dealing with you on a one-to-one basis, I might find many other ways to collect evidence. Here is just one more operational definition:

- You should say that you feel that you understand what this is all about.

This is tested in Test 4, simply by asking you if you are satisfied. Note that this statement is often not a good operational definition of understanding in a classroom lecture. Under those circumstances, asking the whole class "Do you understand what I'm saying" is often a good way to operationally define eagerness to get out of the classroom. But in this book you are under no pressure, and you probably really do want to understand, and so you can validly use it as an operational definition for yourself.

The above are four plausible operational definitions of "understanding and knowing how to write operational definitions," and four ways to test for their attainment. If you do well on all the tests based on these operational definitions, it is probably safe to assume that you have met the goal of this chapter. If you do poorly on all of them, you probably have not met the goal. If you do well on some and poorly on others, then the evidence is ambiguous; and it becomes your job to evaluate the evidence (as described elsewhere in this chapter)—to determine which evidence is contaminated and which is actually a valid measure of understanding how to write operational definitions. If your evaluation of the evidence indicates that you have met the goal, go on to the next chapter. If the evidence shows that you have not met the goal, either reread the information or refer to the more detailed sources listed in the bibliography at the end of the chapter.

This detailed description of how to take these tests is intended as a model for collecting evidence in an instructional program. It follows these steps:

1. Decide what outcome variable you want to attain.
2. Devise enough operational definitions of that outcome variable to enable you to collect adequate evidence to determine whether or not you have attained that outcome.
3. Test (before, after, or during your program) to collect evidence.
4. Evaluate your evidence.

Use these steps in your own instructional programs. Now take the tests and see how you are doing.

Review Quiz: Test 1

Part 1
Choose the best operational definition of the underlined term in the general goal.

1. General goal: to teach children to *appreciate* poetry.
   a. The students will value poetry.
   b. When given a list of topics and asked to choose which ones they value, they will choose poetry.

2. General goal: to teach children to *understand* how smoking causes cancer.
   a. The students will identify on a chart the parts of the body that are influenced by smoking-related carcinogens.
   b. The students will thoroughly know what does and does not cause cancer in smokers.

3. General goal: to enhance children's *self-concept*.
   a. The students will come to a better understanding of themselves as self-actualizing human beings.
   b. The students will verbalize accurate self-assessments of their successes in school work.

Part 2
Put an X next to all of the following proposed operational definitions of *rapport with other students* which actually state an observable activity.

a _____ Identifying each of the other students by name.
b _____ Having a good sense of humor.
c _____ Having a respect for the opinions of others.
d _____ Making no remarks to other students which are perceived by the observer as derogatory.
e _____ Valuing the other students as persons.
f _____ Naming one hobby that each other student is interested in.
g _____ Being chosen frequently by other students on a "who's your friend" questionnaire.
h _____ Having other students smile when they talk to him.
i _____ Initiating conversations with other students.

Answers:
Part 1
1. b
2. a
3. b
Part 2
a
d
f
g
h
i

Review Quiz: Test 2

Below are several undefined outcome variables. Write a clearly expressed operational definition for each.

Goal 1: to teach the children *how to do long division.*

Goal 2: to teach the student driver *how to parallel park.*

Goal 3: to eliminate *disruptive outbursts.*

Goal 4: to have the students *develop moral standards.*

Answers:
(Note that these are only sample answers. Other answers which state definite clearly observable behaviors are also acceptable.)

Goal 1: Given a series of problems set up in long division format, the children will obtain the exact answers.

Goal 2: The student driver will parallel park the practice car within a 25-foot boundary without bumping the barriers or the curb. He/she will do this within one minute. When the car is parked, it will be no more than one foot from the curb.

Goal 3: The child will stop engaging in the following behaviors: shouting, hitting, throwing objects in class. (*Note:* If you envisioned a different sort of child, your answer could be quite different and still correct.)

Goal 4: The students will verbalize reasons for their behavior which reflect increasingly higher levels of moral reasoning according to Kohlberg's theory of moral development.

The students will stop engaging in behaviors which the teacher and other objective observers agree are selfish.

Given hypothetical situations in which moral choices are possible, the students will increasingly base their decisions on a social-benefit rather than a personal-good standard.

(Goal 4 is highly internalized. Many operational definitions are possible. In actual practice, it would be desirable to use more than one operational definition.)

Review Quiz: Test 3

In your own words, explain what an operational definition is.

Answer:
Your answer should paraphrase the following sentence:
An operational definition is the observable evidence you are willing to accept that an (internal) outcome is occurring.

Review Quiz: Test 4

Do you feel that you understand the term "operational definition" and know how to write operational definitions of outcome variables of your own?

Answer:
Your answer should be "yes."

PUTTING IT ALL TOGETHER

Eugene Anderson, the mythical humane educator, presents programs in school classrooms with the goal of developing favorable attitudes toward animal life. He recognizes this as an affective outcome, which needs to be operationally defined. He therefore asks himself what evidence he would be willing to accept to indicate that this internal, affective change has taken place among the students he visits.

He draws up the following tentative list of behaviors which he feels would indicate that a child has a favorable attitude toward animal life:

1. The child talks enthusiastically about animals.
2. The child protects animals from harm.
3. The child appropriately reports stray or injured animals.
4. When others are talking about things which are harmful to animals, the child will present arguments to persuade these others to be kind to the animals.
5. When presented with a list of statements, the child will agree with those showing a value for animal life.
6. If the child has a pet, he will care for it properly.
7. The child will show a great deal of interest during Mr. Anderson's presentation.
8. The child will ask Mr. Anderson to come back and talk about animals some other time.

Moreover, Mr. Anderson comes up with the following list of behaviors which would indicate an unfavorable attitude toward animal life:

9. The child will needlessly attack animals.
10. The child will verbalize support for positions which are harmful to animal life.
11. If the child has a pet, he will neglect it.

Mr. Anderson reasons that children could be operationally defined as having a favorable attitude toward animal life to the extent that they engage in the first set of behaviors and avoid the second set.

As he looks over his list, Mr. Anderson realizes that it has inadequacies. Taken alone, some of them are not very good operational definitions; but combined, they should at least provide him with better evidence than he has been receiving regarding what happens in his classrooms. In fact, he realizes that the operational definition he had implicitly been using up to this time consisted of a combination of Numbers 7 and 8. It has now occurred to him that these might be better operational definitions of "desire to escape ordinary schoolwork" than of a favorable attitude toward animal life.

Eventually, Mr. Anderson will shorten his list and select only a few of these operational definitions as a basis for collecting data. His choice will be based largely on the validity of each operational definition and his ability to collect the evidence suggested by each definition. For that reason, we'll leave Mr. Anderson now and return to this topic in the following chapters, where specific attention will be given to validity.

SUMMARY

An outcome variable is an event of interest to the teacher which is occurring in the classroom or other educational setting. Many of the events we are concerned about in education involve learning, which is an internal and unobservable event. Therefore, operational definitions become necessary if we are going to ascertain whether or not such outcome variables are occurring. An operational definition is the evidence we are willing to accept as an indication that the outcome variable is occurring. In some cases the evidence is almost synonymous with learning; and in such cases, the operational definition is quite easy to devise. In other cases (such as with regard to affective outcomes), the evidence is by no means nearly synonymous with the learning, and in such cases strenuous efforts have to be made to make the evidence more solid. The evidence can be made more solid by (1) ruling out contaminating factors and alternate explanations, and (2) using more than one operational definition.

Annotated Bibliography

MAGER, R. *Preparing Instructional Objectives* 2nd ed. (Belmont, Cal.: Fearon, 1975). This book deals with instructional objectives, which are a specific type of operational definition—the most common type of concern to teachers. The book is written in a highly enjoyable, programmed format.

MAGER, R. *Goal Analysis* (Belmont, Cal.: Fearon, 1972). This book is a sequel to *Preparing Instructional Objectives*. It deals with useful strategies for operationalizing affective outcomes.

Professional Journals

The following journal articles contain good examples of operational definitions of outcome variables. You may find it useful to see how someone else has dealt with the problem of operationally defining an outcome which needs to be measured.

MCHALE, S.M., and SIMEONSSON, R.J. "Effects of interaction on nonhandicapped children's attitudes toward autistic children," *American Journal of Mental Deficiency* 85 (1980):18–24. The authors use multiple operational definitions of attitudes toward autistic children in order to collect valid evidence regarding this characteristic.

MOYER, S.B. "Readability of basal readers and workbooks: A comparison." *Learning Disability Quarterly* 2 (1979): 23–28. The author uses three separate variables as an operational definition of readability.

SMITH, W.H. "What they didn't tell you about Jack and Jill: An aspect of reading comprehension," *Journal of Reading* 24 (1980): 101–108. This article uses the nursery rhyme "Jack and Jill" as a basis for a discussion of the operational definition of reading comprehension. (The article also provides a delightful discussion of epistemological problems in comprehension.)

TORGESEN, J.K. "What shall we do with psychological processes?" *Journal of Learning Disabilities* 12 (1979): 514–521. This author argues for the value of collecting *several* pieces of evidence to verify that a child has a deficiency in a psychological process and to determine the nature of this deficiency.

3 Reliability

Chapter Preview

Once you have decided upon an operational definition of an outcome variable, you will want to collect data to see whether or not that outcome is occurring. Chapters 3 and 4 describe some essential characteristics of good data collection techniques. Chapter 5 describes how to design and use specific types of data collection instruments. The present chapter defines reliability in terms of how consistently an instrument measures what it purports to measure. It discusses ways to increase the probability that you can make consistent decisions based on your observations.

After completing this chapter you should be able to

- Define reliability.
- Identify examples of reliable and unreliable measuring instruments.
- Identify factors which contribute to the unreliability of measuring instruments.
- Identify effective ways to increase the reliability of an instrument.
- Identify appropriate statistical procedures for estimating the reliability of an instrument and identify appropriate situations in which each of these procedures would be appropriately employed.
- Identify the weaknesses and limitations of these statistical procedures for estimating reliability.
- Describe how to use the concept of reliability in selecting and improving techniques for measuring outcome variables.

Reliability addresses the question of whether or not a measuring instrument is consistent. An instrument or test[1] is *unreliable* if the results are influenced by

---

[1] The terms *test* and *instrument* are used in this book to indicate any sort of data collecting device or technique. Classroom tests and questionnaires are some of the most obvious ways that teachers collect data. However, there are other good ways to collect data (such as the unobtrusive observation techniques described in Chapter 6). The information on reliability in this chapter and validity in the next chapter apply to these techniques as well as to the more traditional techniques. Likewise, the words *student* and *respondent* are used in this chapter, but they should also be understood to refer to anyone who is giving data to the data collector.

irrelevant factors which cause the results to fluctuate when they should not fluctuate. It is reliable to the extent that the results are the same every time they *should* be the same.

If a mother wants to measure the temperature of a sick child, she will want the measurement to be reliable. If she measures his temperature once, and the temperature is 102.4, then tries it again two minutes later and gets a temperature of 99.9, she has an unreliable thermometer. If she gets 102.4 both times, she has a reliable thermometer. (Of course if she gives him aspirin and then takes his temperature an hour later and discovers a large drop, this would have nothing to do with reliability. The temperature would not be expected to be the same on the second occasion, since the medicine is supposed to have an effect.)

Reliability can be applied in the same way to an instructional situation. If you ask a child a question and conclude on the basis of her answer that she has achieved an educational outcome, you would hope that if you asked her again a few minutes later you would still conclude that she had achieved the outcome. To the extent that the result is the same, you are dealing with a reliable method of measurement. However, if you concluded the second time that she had *not* achieved the outcome, then you would be dealing with an unreliable measuring device.[2] (Obviously if a week goes by and it is plausible that she might have forgotten something in the intervening week, then a different result on the second occasion would have nothing to do with reliability, any more than a difference in temperature after the child is supposed to be cured would have anything to do with the reliability of a thermometer.)

Review Quiz

Examine the following brief descriptions and indicate whether the description shows good reliability, shows poor reliability, or provides no information about reliability.

1. _____ Ralph got a B when Mrs. Washington scored his essay test. However, he got a D when Mr. Lincoln scored the same test.

2. _____ Both witnesses independently told the police that the suspect had been carrying a violin case when he got off the train.

3. _____ Thelma got a C in third grade reading, but a B in fourth grade reading.

4. _____ The students filled out a rating sheet on Mr. Rivers on Monday, and on it they rated him as an overall good instructor. On Wednesday, they filled out the same rating sheet and rated him as a mediocre instructor.

5. _____ On Tuesday, the counselor concluded that the client had a severe neurosis. On Friday, she concluded that he was probably as sane as anyone else. On the next Tuesday, she concluded again that he had a severe neurosis.

6. _____ Steve didn't know anything about reliability, and so when he took this test he guessed wildly. The first time he got six right. He tried it again, without any further studying, and this time he got three right.

7. _____ Mr. Monroe's class had to study a list of 1000 spelling words. His exam consisted of two 50-word subtests. The average score on both halves was about 85%.

---

[2] It is not really the instrument that is reliable, but rather the use of the instrument. The use of the "Apple-Counting Arithmetic Test" might be reliable for certain groups of pupils, but not for others. Keep in mind, therefore, that the statements about the reliability of an "instrument" in this chapter more accurately refer to the *use* of an instrument.

24

8. _____ Mr. Roth's new novel was rated Number 1 in the *Chicago Tribune* poll, but it didn't even make the list in the *Time* magazine poll.

Here are the answers with brief explanations:

1. **Unreliable.** If they are measuring Ralph's ability consistently, they should be able to agree on the score. Obviously, the score Ralph gets depends on who scores his test, not on what he wrote down. This is like having two parents read the thermometer and one conclude that the child is sick while the other concludes that he is healthy.

2. **Reliable.** Of course, you may need more than two witnesses to convince the jury. Their testimony could even be *invalid* (to be discussed later), if they had conspired to lie about the violin case. However, in the sense we're using the word here, their testimony is reliable.

3. **No information about reliability.** It is quite plausible that her performance could have changed during the intervening year. There's no reason to expect the two grades to be identical.

4. **Unreliable.** If the students are rating his overall ability as a teacher, there does not seem to be any good reason why this should change between Monday and Wednesday. The results should be similar on each occasion. (Note that if they were rating him on how well he taught a specific lesson, then it might be plausible to say that he did well one day and much less well the other. In this case, the inconsistency would have to do with his actual performance, and it would not be evidence of unreliability.)

5. **Unreliable.** Neuroses are supposed to be relatively permanent personality characteristics. They do not come one day and go the next. Neurosis is a vague term, and the counselor is probably having trouble defining what she is talking about.

6. **Unreliable.** The test should prove him equally ignorant both times. Wild guessing is one of the most frequent causes of unreliability on "objective" tests.

7. **Reliable.** Mr. Monroe has essentially measured them twice and has come up with the same result. That's consistency. (This measurement of the *class* is apparently reliable. It still may be an unreliable way to diagnose individual students. This distinction is treated later in this chapter.)

8. **Unreliable.** If the pollsters are both trying to measure popularity of novels, then their results should be very much alike. However, if one is measuring nationwide popularity, and the other popularity in Chicago, then discrepancies are plausible, provided there's an actual reason (other than inaccuracy of measurement) for the differences. For example, if the novel was first introduced in Chicago or was about Chicago, then a reliable test might indeed show that it was more popular among Chicagoans than among readers in the rest of the country.

If you got most of the preceding questions right, or if you easily saw the logic of the explanations, then you probably have a good basic grasp of the concept of reliability. If not, reread the chapter to this point, check the chapter in the workbook, refer to the recommended readings, or ask your instructor for help. Be sure that you understand the summary in the following paragraph, so that you will profit from the rest of this chapter.

In summary, reliability refers to whether or not a measuring instrument is consistent. If the scores on an instrument vary when they should not, then the test is unreliable. If the test produces consistent results, then it is reliable.

WHY IS RELIABILITY IMPORTANT?

Who cares about reliability? If you have heard of reliability before, you have probably heard that it has to do with the computation of correlation coefficients or with something even more mysterious sounding called the Kuder-Richardson-20 formula.

You have probably never computed them unless you were required to do so for a course. If you possess the spirit of the true skeptic, you have perhaps even wondered whether the people who teach education courses actually compute them. The answer is, most of them do not. The ones who do it are usually teachers of statistics or measurement courses, who do it to provide examples for their students. The only other people (besides students) who frequently compute reliability coefficients are researchers who are going to publish the results of their research and designers of published tests. These researchers and test designers are not wasting their time on mere technicalities; they have good reasons for what they are doing, and these reasons will be explained later in this chapter. However, not counting students in my measurement classes, I have rarely met a classroom teacher, a school principal, a college professor, or an angry parent who has ever made an intelligent decision about a teacher-made test based on a reliability coefficient.

If almost no one uses reliability coefficients, then why am I writing this chapter on reliability? If it is irrelevant, why not skip it? Actually reliability is far from irrelevant. The reliability coefficients described in the preceding paragraph are often irrelevant, unnecessary, or at least more trouble than they are worth. The important point, however, is that *reliability is not synonymous with reliability coefficients*. Even if you do not feel an urgent need to compute reliability coefficients, you should feel an urgent need to make sure your tests and observations are reliable—to make sure that when you make a decision you are making it on the basis of consistent data rather than on the basis of fleeting information which will change if you simply take the trouble to collect the data a second time.

Elsewhere in this chapter you will see that it is important to know how to interpret the technical kinds of reliability coefficients and even to know how to compute them yourself with the help of a computer or calculator. However, for the present, let us forget about correlation coefficients and focus on the important topic of making our measurements reliable—of reducing the probability that we will be making decisions based on inconsistent data.

SOURCES OF UNRELIABILITY

The best way to increase the reliability of our measuring instruments is to determine what causes unreliability, and then to make sure that these causes of inconsistency are not present in the data-collection strategies we employ. The following are the major sources of unreliability:

1. Faulty Items

Items on a test or questionnaire can be ambiguous, tricky, or presented in a confusing format. When people are presented with such faulty items, it is hard for them to respond reliably. If you are presented with a poorly written multiple-choice item, you are likely to guess; and if you had to take the same item again another time, you might guess differently. The same thing is true on an essay exam. If the question is vague, you will have to guess at what you are expected to say in response, and you might guess differently if you had to do it again. Likewise, if an attitude question is so complex that you cannot figure out what your task is, it would be hard for you to respond reliably. Under one set of circumstances you might merely guess at what you should do; under another you might patiently try to figure it out and give accurate answers; and under another you might get frustrated and give hostile answers because you are upset at having to put up with such a foolish questionnaire. The point is that if the respondent does not know what he is expected to do, it will be hard for him to respond reliably.

2. Excessively Difficult Items

If a test item is too difficult, the test-taker will guess at the answer, and the resulting problems are the same as those discussed in the previous paragraph. Some types of test items promote guessing on difficult items more readily than other types. For example, if a true-false item is too difficult, the student still has a 50–50 chance of getting it right; whereas on a short-answer test, the probability of blindly guessing correctly is considerably smaller.

3. Excessively Easy Items

If I ask you a question that is extraordinarily simple for you to answer, I may learn nothing about what you really know. This is especially true if the correct answer is obtained from extraneous clues that are unrelated to the learning task. Asking an excessively easy question is often like not asking any question at all. This becomes a problem of reliability when I am asking a student to answer several questions on a test and plan to add the responses up in some way to get a total score. If I ask you ten questions, and nine of them are absurdly easy, then I am really basing my decisions about you only on the one good question that was not excessively easy. I might *think* I have a ten-item test, but it is really a one-item test camouflaged by nine non-items. The problem of length of test is discussed in the next paragraph. The point here is that excessively easy items often contribute nothing to the length of the test—to the sample of questions you are asking. The same effect occurs with questionnaires. If you ask everyone in your class to fill out a ten-item agree-disagree questionnaire, and if nine of the items are written in such a way that almost everyone is practically guaranteed to answer "strongly agree," then you really have a one-item questionnaire.

4. Inadequate Number of Items

The shorter the measuring instrument, the greater the opportunity for chance factors to operate, and the more likely that unreliability will creep in. For example, assume that I give you a one-item exam on how well you understand the material in this book. You may know the material quite well—with 95% accuracy—but if I happen to choose the one question you don't know, you'll look as though you know nothing. The opposite is also true. If you know almost nothing about what is in this book, I might happen to ask you the one question to which you know the answer, and you'll look as though you've mastered the material. A short test, therefore, provides an inadequate sample of items. The test is likely to be unrepresentative of the many items that could have been included on it. In addition, a short test or questionnaire increases the probability that many of the other reliability-reducing factors on this list will operate. For example, a single faulty item will have a great impact on a short test, but will be outweighed by the many good items on a longer test; and a proclivity to guess will have a serious impact on the reliability of a short test, whereas the accurate and inaccurate guesses will even out on a longer test.

5. Dissimilarity of the Items

If all the items on a test are measuring the same characteristic, then the reliability will be quite high; whereas if the items are measuring greatly different characteristics, the reliability will be quite low. In fact, when the items are measuring different characteristics, you really have a large number of very short tests (which are therefore likely to be inconsistent) rather than a single longer test.

Assume that you are taking an English test, and the teacher asks you 25 questions. Five of the questions deal with punctuation, five with spelling, five with poetry, five with the plot of a novel, and five with vocabulary from the same novel. This test is likely to be quite unreliable, because it is measuring several different abilities, rather than a single ability. If you took an alternate version of this particular English test— again with five items from each of the areas—your score would be quite likely to vary. The precise reasons for this inconsistency are subtle, and they will not be discussed in detail here; but it comes down to the fact that five different abilities are required to take this test, and chance is operating in different ways on each of these abilities during the test. On the other hand, if all 25 items would have been on one topic—say, vocabulary—then the reliability would have been much higher, since only one basic ability would have been involved.

Not all examples of dissimilarity of items are as obvious as the case of the above English test. A person trying to measure attitudes toward Communists might discover that his test is inconsistent because it is actually trying to measure several conceptually different attitudes on a single questionnaire. A respondent might have one set of attitudes regarding Communists as athletic competitors, another set regarding Communists as military aggressors, and a third set regarding Communists as philosophical theorists. Instead of a single lengthy questionnaire this person would in reality have three shorter subquestionnaires.

The point is this: if you are going to add your scores up and think that you are measuring a single characteristic (such as English ability or attitude toward Communists), then you have to be certain that all the items are measuring the same thing. To the extent that all the items are measuring the same thing, then you are taking steps toward consistency of measurement. To the extent that the items are dissimilar, then unreliability is creeping in.

6. Characteristics of the Respondents

Reliability is reduced by any temporary characteristic of the respondents which causes them to respond differently than they would respond under normal conditions. Such characteristics include inability to concentrate at a given time, fluctuations in mood, and inconsistent recall of information. For example, if a student has acquired a certain attitude, we would expect him to be able to express this attitude on a questionnaire. However, because of changes in his mood, he might decide to reveal his attitude on one occasion but to conceal or falsify it on another. Such inconsistency in moods is a source of unreliability. Another example would occur if a student knew enough to get an 80% on a spelling test, but she might get a mere 40% on a given occasion because she was sitting in front of someone who kept poking her in the back with a pencil while she was taking the test. Such factors make it likely that if we measured the students on different occasions, we would get different impressions of their knowledge or attitudes.

7. Faulty Administration of the Instrument

The way a test is administered can render the results inconsistent. If a test is given in a room which is extremely hot or full of distractions, the results will be affected. If the teacher gives one set of instructions to one class, and a more carefully stated set to another class, performance will be less consistent and comparisons will be based on unreliable test scores. In addition, the mannerisms, idiosyncracies, and other characteristics of the person administering the instrument can make a difference. For example, a white respondent will perhaps display different attitudes toward blacks if a black person is interviewing him than if a white person were the interviewer. Inconsistencies arising from the administration of the instrument are especially likely to arise when several different people administer it, as when each classroom teacher administers the instrument to her own class.

8. Faulty Scoring Procedures

After the student or respondent has done his share of responding, inconsistency can still creep in when the scorer tries to assign values to the respondent's performance. The scorer could simply be inaccurate and count the correct answers incorrectly. If the answer sheet was at all ambiguous, it might be hard to determine what the respondent meant. Extended-answer essay tests are notorious for the inconsistency with which they are scored. Research has shown that it is possible for one grader to give a paper an A while another grader would give the same paper an F. Furthermore, even after the instrument has been accurately scored, it is possible to introduce inconsistency by faulty record-keeping.

HOW TO INCREASE RELIABILITY

The way to increase reliability, of course, is to minimize the sources of unreliability cited in the previous section. There are statistical procedures for determining a "coefficient of reliability," and one of the desires of professional test constructors is to get this coefficient as high as possible. The use of these coefficients will be discussed in the next section of this chapter. However, it is quite possible (and important) to take steps to improve reliability even if you never intend to compute a reliability coefficient outside an assignment for a college course. The following are specific guidelines for improving reliability.

1. Use Technically Correct, Unambiguous Items

Make sure the respondent is able to give the answer he really wants to give. There are excellent textbooks available on educational measurement, and these contain specific guidelines on how to write technically correct items. Teachers frequently collect data with instruments they have not even proofread, and such laxity is quite likely to lead to unreliability. A very simple procedure for improving the technical quality of an instrument is to have someone else look it over or take the test before the students see it.

2. Standardize the Administration Procedures

Give the test in such a way as to promote consistency. Eliminate distractions. Don't make yourself a part of the testing situation, unless you plan to define yourself as a permanent part of the instrument. If more than one person will administer the instrument, make sure they are using precisely the same instructions.

3. Standardize the Scoring Procedures

Develop systematic strategies for being consistent in scoring. This is easy with objective instruments such as true-false and multiple-choice tests and Likert questionnaires. It becomes harder with extended-length essay tests and open-ended interviews. The idea here is that you want to leave to the respondent as much of the decision as possible regarding what the response is. Otherwise, you will have two sources of error—yours and the respondent's. For this reason, it is often best to use the more objective type item when you have a choice. Design the instrument in such a way as to let the respondent make the choices. When you do have to make decisions about what a respondent knows or meant to say, make them according to a structured format. One piece of evidence that your format is structured enough to be considered consistent would be to let someone else examine the respondent's answers using the same format and see if that person comes up with the same decisions about the outcome as you did.

4. Be Alert for Respondent Irregularities

Do not give tests when students are in atypical moods. If everyone is giggling, if someone is extremely anxious, if half the class is sick—such temporary characteristics will get you an unrepresentative (and inconsistent) sample of the students' performance. If you are trying to measure a student's typical performance, be sure he feels typical while you are sampling that performance. If you want to measure a student's maximum performance, be sure that he is working at his maximum while taking the test.

5. Make the Test Long Enough to Include a Good Sample of Items

The difficulties presented by a short (e.g., one-item) test were discussed in the previous section. Overcome these difficulties by making sure that you include enough items so that you are confident that you are measuring a stable performance, not a chance result. Be sure to include a good sample of items for every outcome you are trying to measure. This brings us to the next guideline.

6. Be Certain Each Item on the Test Measures the Same Outcome or Set of Outcomes

If you have a ten-item test which measures ten separate outcomes, you really have ten separate one-item tests. Consequently, any decision you make based on any one of these items is likely to be unreliable; and a decision based on the whole test is both unreliable and meaningless. If you have several outcomes, develop appropriate subtests of sufficient length. On each test or subtest your goal should be to make each item measure the same outcome.

7. Construct Items of an Appropriate Level of Difficulty

Be sure you are measuring what the person actually knows and not his luck at guessing answers or figuring out what your questions mean. Also remember that excessively easy items often add nothing to the length of the test.

Review Quiz

Write *R* next to each sentence which describes a factor which contributes to the reliability of the measuring technique. Write *U* next to each sentence which describes a source of unreliability.

1. _____ Mrs. Stallings decides to base the spelling grades on a 100-item test rather than on her previous 10-item test.

2. _____ Mr. Carol is proud of his 10-item English test, because it contains 5 "mind-benders" that nobody got right.

3. _____ Miss Harmon gives a fifty-item test every two weeks. Previously she has tried to base her tests on a common set of objectives, but now she has decided to save time and test on five distinctly different sets of objectives on the same fifty-item test.

4. _____ Mrs. Rogers has decided to measure Curt's creativity by giving him a highly imaginative problem and asking him to solve it.

5. _____ Mr. Peters considers each of the ten subscales of a 100-item standardized test to be more useful than the entire test, and so he bases his decisions entirely on these subscales.

6. _____ Miss Adams planned to give a test on Friday, but she postponed it when she heard that the biggest pep rally of the year would occur during the period immediately after her class.

7. _____ Mrs. Wolf likes to promote informality with her students, because she feels that this makes them work to the best of their ability. Therefore she sets aside the instructions for the standardized test and instead explains in her own words what the students should do when taking the test.

8. _____ There is a wide range of mastery of skills in Mrs. Johnson's Spanish class. On the test, most of the items are gotten right by 40–70% of the students.

Answers:
1. **R.** She is increasing the length of the test and getting a better sample of student behavior.
2. **U.** He is using excessively difficult items.
3. **U.** She is making the items more *dis*similar. Items which are to be added into a single score should be on a common topic.
4. **U.** This is an excessively short (one-item) test.
5. **U.** Each of these subtests is very short. Mr. Peters *would* be on solid ground if he knew that each of the subscales had adequate reliability.
6. **R.** Miss Adams is avoiding the chance that temporary characteristics of the students will lead to inconsistency.

7. **U.** Mrs. Wolf is adding an additional source of inconsistency (the chance that she will make a mistake in the instructions) to the sources that the students themselves bring to the test.
8. **R.** Mrs. Johnson is using items of medium difficulty in a situation in which it is plausible to expect less than perfect mastery.

If you missed several of these items, refer back to the appropriate sections of this chapter for clarification. It is important to understand this information before proceeding. If you are a true skeptic, you might by now realize that this quiz may itself be somewhat unreliable. If that worries you, check out the appropriate exercises in the Workbook. A longer test will enable you to make a more reliable (consistent) judgment regarding your knowledge of this material.

STATISTICAL PROCEDURES FOR ESTIMATING RELIABILITY

Reliability coefficients are statistical procedures for estimating how consistent a test is. These are important tools, but they are merely tools. Even if you do not feel a particular urge to compute these statistics, you should still be quite concerned about reliability. These procedures are described here because they are easy to understand and can be quite helpful to you. In addition, you will often want to administer professionally prepared tests, interpret the results of such tests in your school, or interpret the results of tests in the professional literature. Understanding the meaning of these procedures can be extremely helpful in such cases.

The following are the basic types of statistical reliability coefficients:

1. Test-Retest Reliability

To compute this reliability coefficient, you would administer your test, let some time pass, and then administer it again to the same people. Then you compute a correlation coefficient between the two sets of scores.[3] A high correlation coefficient indicates that the respondents performed about the same on both tests, whereas a low coefficient indicates that their performance was inconsistent.

A frequent misapplication of this concept of reliability is to give a pretest, then instruct the students, then give the same test as a posttest, and finally compute a reliability coefficient. Actually, this coefficient often has nothing to do with reliability, because the two sets of scores are not necessarily supposed to be related. If instruction has been successful, there is no reason why a person's score on the posttest should be at all similar to her pretest score.

A further subtle distinction is worth mentioning in passing. A low reliability coefficient indicates either that the test is unreliable or that the person being tested does not possess a stable pattern of behavior with regard to the characteristic. For example, a low reliability coefficient for a test of Preference for Color Among Infants might mean either (1) that the infants possess a reliable characteristic which can be labeled Preference for Colors, but the test has failed to identify this characteristic

---

[3] Simplified procedures for computing correlation coefficients are given in Appendix D. The topic of correlation is treated in Chapter 11.

consistently, or (2) that the infants have not yet developed a consistent preference for colors.

2. Equivalent-Forms Reliability

To compute this form of reliability, you would administer one form of the test to a group and then administer a different form of the same test to the same group. A high correlation between the two sets of scores indicates that the respondents performed about the same on both tests; and this means that the forms are equivalent, which is a sign of consistency.

This form of reliability is especially useful when you want to determine the effectiveness of instruction by using one form of a test as a pretest and the other as a posttest. If you have a reliable test, you can attribute any improvements in performance between pretest and posttest to the intervening instruction; whereas if you have an unreliable test, the improvements (or absence of improvements) can be the result of chance fluctuations due to the inconsistency of the test.

3. Test-Retest with Equivalent Forms Reliability

To compute this coefficient, you would administer one form of the test, let some time pass, and then administer the other form of the test. A resulting high correlation coefficient indicates that there is a stable characteristic of some sort which both forms of the test are measuring. This coefficient is obviously a combination of the first two types.

4. Split-Half Reliability

To compute this coefficient, you would administer the test to a group of respondents. Then, after collecting the responses, you would randomly split the test in half and score each half of the test separately. This is usually done by scoring the odd numbered items as one half and the even numbered items as the other half. Then you would compute a correlation coefficient between the respondents' scores on the two halves of the test.[4] A high correlation indicates that the respondents performed very similarly on each half of the test. This is a measure of what is called *internal consistency reliability,* and a high internal consistency coefficient means that all the items on the test appear to be measuring about the same thing.

5. Kuder-Richardson Reliability

This coefficient is similar in principle to the split-half method, but it is based on a mathematical formula which does not require splitting the test in half. It is easily computed by computer, and is therefore readily available with most test-scoring services. It is a measure of internal consistency, and therefore a high coefficient indicates that all the items on the test are measuring about the same thing. For technical reasons, the Kuder-Richardson coefficient can be computed only for tests that are scored on a right-wrong or yes-no basis. For other measures, such as five-point agree-strongly to disagree-strongly scales, there is a similar procedure called Coefficient Alpha, which accomplishes the same thing.

---

[4] The resulting coefficient is also "corrected" by the Spearman-Brown formula. See Appendix D.

6. Interscorer Reliability

In using this procedure, you would have two different persons score the same test, and then you compare the two sets of scores. A high correlation coefficient indicates that both persons were scoring the test similarly. A low coefficient would indicate that differences between persons on the test might be the result of the way the test was scored rather than the result of real differences in the respondents. (The objection that many Olympic events which are based on ratings by judges are inconsistently judged is actually a statement about poor interscorer reliability.)

With many educational tests, interscorer reliability is irrelevant. There is little chance that two scorers will differ significantly in their scoring of a multiple-choice or true-false test. With more subjective tests, such as essay tests and ratings of personality characteristics, an evaluation of the consistency of the scoring process is quite important. Interscorer reliability sets an upper limit on all the previously discussed forms of reliability. Whatever the interscorer reliability is, the other forms will always be lower. This is because the scoring process provides chances for error in addition to whatever inconsistencies are inherent in the respondent's own performance on a test.

7. Interobserver Agreement

This estimate of reliability differs from the others in that it involves a percentage rather than a correlation coefficient. It is used when a rater is trying to observe someone else and determine whether or not a behavior is occurring. The interobserver reliability is determined by having a second person simultaneously make the same observation. After this has been done on a certain number of occasions, a percentage is computed to determine how often the two raters agreed. For example, if the two observers are watching a kindergarten child to determine how often he is out of his seat, the two raters would make their ratings of out-of-seat behavior independently. They might each watch the child for ten fifteen-second intervals and mark him as being in-seat or out-of-seat during each interval according to some preestablished criteria. Afterwards, they would compute their percentage of agreement. If they agreed during 8 out of the 10 intervals, their interobserver reliability would be 80%. Interobserver reliability is quite important in situations (such as behavior modification programs) where the test consists of observing a child to determine whether or not he is performing some predefined behavior.

WHAT KIND OF RELIABILITY COEFFICIENT DO YOU NEED?

In a very real sense, you do not need any reliability coefficient. What you need is reliability, because you want your measurement to be consistent. The question, therefore, is what kind of reliability is going to be helpful to you in determining whether or not your instruments are consistent.

Some textbooks make the statement that teachers should most often use the split-half method, "because that's the easiest to compute by hand." Some likewise suggest the Kuder-Richardson method, because it is so easily generated by computer. I've even had one professor who recommended the split-half method "because it's usually

35

higher." All these suggestions miss the point. The correct procedure is to compute *the kind of coefficient you need* to help you determine whether or not your instrument is consistent.

For example, if you have two tests on the same unit and want to give one of them to your 9:00 English class and the other to your 10:00 class, you might be concerned about whether or not the two tests are really equivalent. A computation of split-half or test-retest reliability is irrelevant to this question. What you want is equivalent-forms reliability.

In this case does the teacher really need equivalent-forms reliability? Computation of this form of reliability would require administering both forms of the test to the same group and then computing a correlation coefficient for the scores. How many teachers really do this? Is there any other way to assure equivalent-forms reliability. The answer is yes, there is another way. Even without computing the correlation coefficient the teacher can maximize her chances of having equivalent forms of the test by either (1) carefully determining that each item on both tests is based directly on a specified set of common objectives, or (2) making up all the items for both tests and then randomly assigning each of the items to one or the other of the tests. Teachers can assure themselves that their tests are likely to be equivalent by following both of these guidelines. In fact, these are the guidelines followed by professional test constructors in designing highly effective, standardized tests. An important consideration, however, is that even if you follow these guidelines, you are not sure that your two forms are equivalent. As a general rule, every teacher should at least sometimes compute the actual equivalent-forms reliability coefficient. A good idea would be to check yourself every once in a while, whenever you are in new territory, when you do not have enough experience with a topic to rely heavily on your own judgment. Of course, if you are doing research that you expect someone else to examine, then it would be most unwise to expect that person to rely on your intuition. Common sense dictates that you should provide that person with the more objective estimate of reliability provided by a correlation coefficient.

This discussion of equivalent-forms reliability has been rather detailed so that it can serve as an example. The same principle applies to all the statistical procedures for determining reliability. Use them if they provide the information you want, otherwise skip them. Table 3–1 summarizes the purpose and computational procedure for each of the types of reliability. By understanding the rationale behind each procedure, you can make intelligent determinations about which procedure can be helpful to you. In addition, such information will help you in making useful decisions about purchasing tests for your students and in reading the research literature more carefully. For example, you will know enough to challenge a researcher who proclaims that he knows his pretest and posttest were equivalent "because they both had Kuder-Richardson reliabilities of .90 or better."

The guidelines discussed earlier in this chapter will enable you to increase each of the types of statistical reliability. Note that each of these guidelines can be followed even without computing the statistical coefficient. In fact, even if you do compute the coefficients, you still have to follow these guidelines to increase reliability. Statistics do not produce reliability—they merely verify it. However, do not conclude that the statistics are irrelevant. You should probably back up your judgment about the consistency of the tests with the appropriate statistic at least occasionally; and if you expect someone else to believe you when you say your instrument is reliable, you should always back up your judgment with the appropriate statistic.

TABLE 3–1. Statistical Methods of Estimating Reliability.

	Purpose	*Procedure*	*Statistic*
Test-retest reliability	To assure stability; to rule out the possibility that results fluctuate widely on different administrations of same instrument to same people.	Administer the same test twice to the same group with a time interval in between; then compute the correlation.	Correlation coefficient
Equivalent-forms reliability	To assure that two forms of a test are actually equivalent.	Administer two forms of the same test to the same group in close succession; then compute correlation.	Correlation coefficient
Test-retest with equivalent forms	To assure both stability and equivalence (combines first two methods).	Administer one form; let time pass; administer second form; compute correlation.	Correlation coefficient
Split-half reliability	To determine the extent to which the items on a test are measuring a common characteristic (to assure internal consistency).	Administer test only once; score each half separately; compute correlation between two halves; apply Spearman-Brown correction formula.	Correlation coefficient
Kuder-Richardson reliability	To determine the extent to which the items on a test are measuring a common characteristic (to assure internal consistency).	Administer test only once; apply Kuder-Richardson formula to results.	Kuder-Richardson coefficient
Interscorer reliability	To determine the extent to which the results are objective; i.e., will be the same no matter who scores the test.	Administer the test once; have two different persons score the test; compute correlation between the two sets of scores.	Correlation coefficient
Interobserver agreement	To determine the extent to which different observers can agree whether or not an outcome is occurring.	Have two observers watch for the occurrence of an event during a designated number of intervals; compute the percentage of intervals during which they agree.	Percentage of agreement

One additional statistical procedure is helpful in increasing reliability. This technique is referred to as *item analysis*. It is discussed in detail in most measurement books. In this book it will be described just briefly in this paragraph. The item analysis procedure enables you to examine each individual item on a test and see how that item relates to the overall score on the test. For example, on an objective English test, an item is a good item if people who got it right tend to be the ones who scored high on the whole test. If most of the students who got it right were those who scored poorly on the test, there is a good chance that it is not measuring the same characteristic as the rest of the test. By selecting and retaining only those items which fare well in such an item analysis, a teacher is able to revise and improve the internal consistency of the test. And improving the internal consistency often results in an improvement in the other forms of reliability as well. Refer to the Annotated Bibliography at the end of this chapter for sources of information on item analysis.

Review Quiz

Identify the type of statistical reliability which would be helpful in determining whether or not the designated measurement technique is consistent.

1. Mr. Perkins had decided to help Jamahl control his aggressive behavior. He has defined aggressive behavior as any attempt to inflict physical harm on another person. He plans to count how often such attempts occur.
   Type of statistical reliability: _____

2. Ms. Wilkes is going to give her music students a test of tonal discrimination. She doesn't want to waste her time with a test which will give her one result today and a different result next week.
   Type of statistical reliability: _____

3. Mrs. Johns is a vocational education supervisor. She has developed a rating scale for each student to determine how ready that student is to take a full-time job in an out-of-school situation. She plans to have each of the teachers use this instrument, and she expects that the scores will reflect the students' capabilities, not the eccentricities of the teachers.
   Type of statistical reliability: _____

4. Mr. Byrd teaches Freshman Composition. He has developed an end-of-the-year test which he claims gives a good indication of an overall skill which he labels "Proficiency in the Basics." Students are required to get at least a score of 80 on this test before they can take more advanced courses.
   Type of statistical reliability: _____

5. Miss Gordon wants to find out if her new method of teaching speed reading works. She wants to give one test of speed and comprehension at the beginning of her course and another at the end. She hopes to be able to demonstrate that speed will increase while comprehension stays about the same.
   Type of statistical reliability: _____

Answers:
1. Interobserver reliability.
2. Test-retest reliability.
3. Interscorer reliability.
4. Split-half or Kuder-Richardson reliability (internal consistency).
5. Equivalent-forms reliability.

SOME DANGERS IN THE BLIND USE OF STATISTICS

The statistical procedures for estimating reliability are tools originally developed for use by psychologists for writing standardized tests. There are some dangers in blindly adapting these procedures to the different needs of classroom teachers. There are two closely related difficulties which occur when educators use such statistics:

1. When Scores Are Not Spread Out the Reliability Coefficients Go Down

This is because most reliability coefficients are designed for norm-referenced tests. A norm-referenced test is one which is designed to measure how a person compares to other persons, rather than to compare a person's performance with a specific criterion. On a few occasions, such comparisons between students are what classroom "teachers have in mind; and on such occasions norm-referenced tests are appropriate. But in most cases, when you want to find out what outcomes are occurring in your classroom, you should be using criterion-referenced tests.

The differences between norm-referenced and criterion-referenced tests are discussed briefly in Chapter 5. At this point it is necessary merely to point out how these two types of tests relate to correlation coefficients. Norm-referenced tests are designed to spread the scores out; and for mathematical reasons, this results in higher correlation coefficients. With criterion-referenced tests, the concern is with whether or not the test items match the objectives; and so whether or not the scores are spread out depends on how well the students have mastered the objectives. For this reason, you can have a good criterion-referenced test and still get a low correlation coefficient, if a large number of students achieve mastery.

2. A Large Number of Perfect Scores on a Test Lowers the Correlation Coefficient

On standardized, norm-referenced tests developed by large testing companies, items which are gotten right by either a very large or a very small number of respondents are discarded from the test. This is appropriate on a norm-referenced test, since if everyone gives the same response to an item, that item is providing no new information on how the respondents differ. However, if you try to do this on your classroom tests, you will come up with the ironic result that you'll be discarding the very items that relate to the objectives which you have done the best job teaching and which your students have learned the most thoroughly! If you teach well and your students study carefully, the only items which will be gotten right by a medium number of respondents are those which have not been covered in the course but rather relate to some outside characteristic, such as intelligence or ability to psych the teacher. This does not seem to be an educationally appropriate procedure, and some would consider such a practice unethical.

The above problems are easily circumvented by recalling that the statistical procedures are merely tools; and as tools, they can be used only to the extent that they are appropriate. If you use these tools only in conjunction with the other strategies for improving reliability, you will not be led astray. For example, assume that you want to give a 50-item pretest on some topic in English, then teach a unit on that topic, and then give a posttest. You might design your tests by constructing 100 items based on the objectives and randomly assigning 50 items to each form of the test. If the students scored about 50% on the pretest and then about 90% on the posttest, it would be quite possible to get split-half reliabilities of .90 for the pretest and .40 for the posttest. It would be utterly absurd to interpret these results as meaning that the test was less reliable (consistent) in determining each student's mastery of the objectives on the posttest than on the pretest. The more appropriate interpretation in this case would be to conclude that because the items were carefully matched to the same set of objectives and randomly assigned and because the reliability was high at the time when the scores were spread out, then both forms of the test are probably quite reliable.

Note that criterion-referenced tests do not automatically render statistical procedures irrelevant to estimating reliability. In the above example, for instance, the statistical reliability coefficient from the pretest was quite useful in estimating the reliability of the test given after the students had mastered the material. In addition, statistical procedures are often relevant even on posttests after teachers have carried out effective instruction. This is because students do not, in fact, always master everything teachers try to teach them. For reasons of interest, capability, and study habits, you often do get a wide spread of scores, and you often do have items which are appropriately missed by a large number of students who simply haven't met the objectives. In such cases, the use of reliability coefficients can assist you in estimating and improving the reliability of your tests.

Use the statistical reliability coefficient as one of several tools in making your observations and conclusions reliable. For example, if 95% of your students get an answer right on a test or express a certain attitude on a questionnaire, this will lower the statistical reliability of the instrument. The best idea is to look at the item and try to determine why so many gave the same answer. If the item is a good operational definition of a desired educational outcome or attitude, and if it is quite plausible that a large number of persons might have mastered the subject matter or acquired a certain attitude, then you should keep the item and realize that its impact on the reliability coefficient is merely a statistical anomaly resulting from the nature of that statistical tool. You have better information than that provided by the statistic, and so you should make your judgment accordingly. If you use the statistical coefficients appropriately and in conjunction with the guidelines discussed earlier in this chapter, you will discover that you will actually be doing a better job of measuring outcome variables.

HOW RELIABLE DO TESTS HAVE TO BE?

Whether you use statistical procedures or not, it is obvious that some tests are more reliable than others. It is also obvious that the reliability of almost any given test could be improved if you worked on it a little harder. How reliable is reliable enough? The answer is that the necessary degree of reliability depends on what you plan to do with the results of your observations.

If you are giving a weekly arithmetic test, and you happen to make an inaccurate decision based on it, there is probably no serious problem. If you gave a child credit for mastering the topic and you discover a day later that she had not mastered it after all, then you can simply change your decision and offer her some more instruction.

Although you would not want to make frivolous decisions even in such cases, it is obvious that you could settle for a less reliable instrument in these cases than you would require if you were deciding whether or not the same students should embark upon the college preparatory curriculum in mathematics. Therefore, the first answer to your question is that the test needs to be more reliable to the extent that the decisions based on that test are likely to be permanent or irreversible.

A second, closely related factor is whether or not the results of the test will be the only source of information in making a decision or whether they will be supplemented by several other sources of information. To the extent that a test is supplemented by other sources of data, lower reliability is tolerable. The inconsistencies in one set of data will be counterbalanced by information from the other sources of data.

The point is this. The more confidence you want to be able to place in the score an individual attains, the greater the reliability you should require from your instrument.

The situation is somewhat different when you are examining group performance rather than diagnosing the performance of an individual. The factors that lead to unreliability (inconsistency) on a test are random factors, and they tend to average out over the long run. In other words, if one student improves his score significantly by guessing accurately on a test, it is probable that someone else's score has been hurt substantially by poor guessing on the same test. Therefore, a chance factor like guessing is likely to contribute less to inconsistency when group evaluations rather than individual evaluations are being considered. For this reason, substantially lower reliabilities are acceptable for comparing group scores than for comparing individual scores.

Although it would often be absurd to evaluate an individual's performance in a history course based on her answer to a single question, it would nevertheless make sense to evaluate the performance of a group based on the group's answer to that same question. In fact, this is exactly what the highly reputable National Assessment of Educational Progress (NAEP) is attempting. The NAEP is asking several questions to carefully selected groups of respondents in schools throughout the country. On the basis of the NAEP results, it will be possible to conclude something like, "In 1975, 80% of the fifth graders knew who Christopher Columbus was; whereas in 1985, only 15% of the fifth graders knew who he was." On the other hand, it would not be appropriate to use one child's answer to that same question to draw any conclusions about his knowledge of history.

PUTTING IT ALL TOGETHER

As you will recall, Eugene Anderson, the humane educator, had written several operational definitions of attitudes toward animal life. Several of these will be discussed in the next few chapters, but here we will focus on one of them. Based on his second operational definition ("The child will protect animals from harm"), he devised the following instrument. He reasoned that a person with a favorable attitude would choose to save animals rather than objects from the fire. (The validity of this belief will be examined in Chapter 4.)

Mr. Anderson planned to give each respondent a score between 0 and 3, depending on how many animals the child selected on this test. Of course, he wanted to be reasonably certain that the score a child received on any testing occasion would actually represent that child's feelings toward animals, not some irrelevant factor. In

---

Johnny and the Fireman

Johnny is a boy about your age. One night his house catches fire. He and all the members of his family escape, but they have time to bring nothing with them. A fireman comes up to Johnny and says, "The house is going to be a total loss. Is there anything you would like us to try to get out of the house before it burns down?"

Here is a list of some of the things in the house. Choose the three things that Johnny should tell the fireman to try to save if there is time. Then explain the reasons for your choice.

Color portable TV (brand new; cost $450).
Father's wallet ($75 and credit cards).
Johnny's dog (1 year old; cost $30).
Johnny's stamp collection (worth $75).
His sister's cat (she got it free a year ago).
Dad's car keys (car is safely parked on the street).
Mother's expensive coat (worth $300).
CB radio (worth $210).
Little brother's pet gerbil.
Dad's checkbook.

What is the first thing to save? _____
What is the second thing to save? _____
What is the third thing to save? _____

FIGURE 3–1. Mr. Anderson's Humane Attitudes Test.

addition, he wanted to have two forms of the test; and so he devised a second test (Billy and the Fireman—not shown here) which contained a different set of animals and objects. Mr. Anderson needed to ascertain that both tests really were equivalent forms of the same test. If they were really equivalent forms, then he could give one as a pretest and the other as a posttest, to determine whether attitudes had really changed as a result of his visits.

Mr. Anderson tried to follow all the nonstatistical guidelines listed in this chapter to make the test as reliable as possible. As he completed his task, the only guideline that actually caused him any concern was the one about making the test long enough. Was a range in scores of 0 to 3 a big enough range? On the one hand, he thought it might be a good idea to increase the number of choices; but on the other hand, he felt that the larger number of choices might needlessly confuse his respondents, since many of them would be in only the third or fourth grade.

Because of his doubts about the length of the test, he decided to use statistical techniques to check its reliability. If the test was really too short, he would get a low reliability coefficient; if he got high coefficients, he would know that the brevity of the test was not a serious problem. In addition, the statistical procedures were necessary to establish the equivalence of the two tests. He had tried to assure equivalence by randomly assigning items from a larger pool, but he would feel more secure if he had statistical evidence to prove they were equivalent. Finally, the statistical evidence would be quite helpful to Mr. Anderson when he presented his results to his colleagues at meetings. With the statistical reliability data, he would not have to persuade them of his personal capability as an item writer. He could simply show them the numbers to prove that the tests were consistent.

He found several schools in which he was allowed to field-test his instrument. In some cases, he had the same students take the same test with an interval of a week or

TABLE 3–2. Reliability Data on the Fireman Tests.

Test	Grade Level	Test-Retest Reliability	
		Time Interval	Correlation
Johnny	5th (n = 20)	1 week	.63
Johnny	4th (n = 24)	1 week	.75
Johnny	6th (n = 25)	2 weeks	.70
Billy	5th (n = 20)	1 week	.69
Billy	4th (n = 23)	1 week	.70
	Equivalent-Forms Reliability		
	Grade Level	Time Interval	Correlation
	4th (n = 47)	1 week	.70
	4th (n = 26)	2 days	.64
	3rd (n = 35)	1 day	.73
	4th (n = 24)	4 days	.55
	5th (n = 65)	1 day	.71
	5th (n = 65)	1 day	.73

two in between (test-retest reliability). In other cases, he had them take the alternate forms after intervals of only a day or so (equivalent-forms reliability). In two cases, he gave the alternate forms with two weeks between the two testing sessions (test-retest with alternate forms reliability). The results are summarized in Table 3–2. As Mr. Anderson looked at his results, he was quite satisfied. The reliability coefficients showed that he had devised a reasonably consistent instrument. In addition, the alternate forms of the test really did appear to be equivalent. When one of his colleagues pointed out that his correlation coefficients weren't as high as the correlation of .90 often reported for standardized tests, Mr. Anderson replied that he was not concerned about that. The standardized tests were intended for diagnosing *individual* abilities, and a higher reliability was necessary for that. All Mr. Anderson wanted to do was examine *group* attitudes, and his statistical reliabilities were more than sufficient for his purposes. Mr. Anderson had indeed developed a consistent test. His next problem was to demonstrate that the trait he was consistently measuring could legitimately be called "attitude toward animal life." That problem will be discussed in Chapter 4.

SUMMARY

Reliability refers to whether or not a measuring technique is *consistent*. Reliability is important because you will want to make decisions about your students based on consistent data rather than on fleeting information which would change if you simply took the time to collect the information a second time.

Unreliability (inconsistency) enters into measurement procedures when any of the following factors are present:

- Faulty items.
- Excessively difficult items.
- Excessively easy items.
- Too few items.

- Dissimilar items.
- Irregularities of respondents.
- Irregularities of instrument administration.
- Irregularities of scoring procedures.

Unreliability can be reduced (and consistency increased) by following these guidelines:

- Use technically correct, unambiguous items.
- Standardize the administration procedures.
- Standardize the scoring process.
- Be alert for respondent irregularities.
- Make the test long enough to include a good sample of items on the designated topic.
- Be certain each item on the test measures the same outcome or set of outcomes.
- Construct items of an appropriate level of difficulty.

In addition to the above guidelines, statistical procedures can be useful tools to help assure reliability. This chapter describes several techniques. You should regard these statistical procedures as useful tools, should select an appropriate technique when you feel that technique will be helpful, and should avoid the blind use of these procedures.

Knowledge of the principles of reliability will help you make more appropriate decisions regarding outcome behaviors in the classroom. In addition, reliability is a useful concept in selecting appropriate commercially designed tests and in reading the professional research literature.

A final consideration is how high reliabilities should be for commercially available, published tests. If we're paying the pros to come up with good tests, shouldn't we expect them to have highly reliable tests? Here again, it depends on what kind of test you're looking for. Commercially available intelligence tests often report reliabilities of .90 or higher. On the other hand, some personality tests used for group research report reliabilities of only .60. The correct procedure is to determine what you want to use the test for, and then to look for information regarding the specific type of reliability you want. (Look for alternate-form reliability, not internal consistency, if you are interested in using one form for a pretest and the other for a posttest.) A good idea is to look in a source like the *Mental Measurement Yearbook* to find out what levels of reliability are available for tests of the sort you're looking for. If there are five tests of the same sort, and four of them report reliabilities of .85 or better, then the fifth one with a coefficient of .60 is substantially less reliable.

Annotated Bibliography

The following sources provide more detailed information on the general topic of reliability:

ANASTASI, A. "Reliability," Chapter 5 of *Psychological Testing* (4th ed.) (New York: Macmillan, 1976), pages 103–133. This chapter gives a clear statement of traditional reliability theory from the viewpoint of a psychological test designer. Remember, the psychologists are the ones primarily responsible for norm-referenced testing, and so a psychological viewpoint can provide useful insights.

EBEL, R.L. "How to estimate, interpret, and improve test reliability," Chapter 14 of *Essentials of Educational Measurement* (3rd ed.) pages 274–295. This chapter presents a clear statement of the theoretical rationale behind the traditional methods of assessing reliability with a special emphasis on how to apply these methods to educational practice.

GRONLUND, N.E., "Reliability and other desired characteristics," in *Measurement and Evaluation in Teaching* (3rd ed.) New York: Macmillan, 1976), pages 105–131. This chapter takes the traditional methods of establishing reliability and gives concrete advice on how to apply these methods to improving classroom tests.

LEVINE, S. and ELZEY, F.F. *A Programmed Introduction to Educational and Psychological Measurement* (Belmont, Cal.: Brooks/Cole, 1970). Part III (Chapters 6 to 10) provides a good review in programmed format of the important principles of reliability.

SAX, G. "The reliability of measurements," Chapter 7 of *Principles of Educational Measurement and Evaluation* (Belmont, Cal.: Wadsworth, 1974), pages 172–204. This chapter presents a clear statement of the theoretical rationale behind the traditional methods of assessing and establishing reliability.

The following sources are useful for those readers who are interested in more theoretical information on reliability:

MAGNUSSON, D. *Test Theory* (Reading, Mass.: Addison-Wesley, 1966). Chapters 4–9 deal with reliability. They are quite technical, but clear. They provide excellent insights into the derivation of the important mathematical formulas for assessing reliability.

STANLEY, J.C. "Reliability," Chapter 13 of R.L. Thorndike, ed., *Educational Measurement* (2nd ed.) (Washington, D.C.: American Council on Education, 1971), pages 356–442. This is an extremely comprehensive review of all the major theoretical issues relating to reliability.

The following sources provide more detailed information on the specific topic of reliability as it relates to criterion-referenced tests.

POPHAM, W.J. "Reliability, validity, and performance standards," Chapter 7 of *Criterion Referenced Measurement* (Englewood Cliffs, N.J.: Prentice-Hall, 1978), pages 142–174. This chapter discusses the unique problems of reliability with regard to criterion-referenced tests. This is a new field, and Popham's is probably the most comprehensive treatment currently available.

POPHAM, W.J. "Traditional measurement practices," Chapter 2 of *Criterion Referenced Measurement* (Englewood Cliffs, N.J.: Prentice-Hall, 1978), pages 23–41. This chapter discusses "traditional" approaches to reliability and points out some of the problems that are likely to occur when we try to apply these same approaches to the kind of tests that teachers should be using to evaluate student performance.

An important technique that has the effect of increasing the reliability of a test by identifying weak items and promoting internal consistency is *item analysis*. The following are good, practical guides on how to perform an item analysis on a classroom test.

EBEL, R.L. "How to improve test quality through item analysis," Chapter 13 of *Essentials of Educational Measurement* (3rd ed.) pages 258–273.

GRONLUND, N.E. "Appraising classroom tests," Part of Chapter 11 in *Measurement and Evaluation in Teaching* (3rd ed.) (New York: Macmillan, 1976), pages 263–276.

LEVINE, S., and ELZEY, F.F. *A Programmed Introduction to Educational and Psychological Measurement* (Belmont, Cal.: Brooks/Cole, 1970). Part IV (Chapters 11–13) provides a good review of the principles of item analysis.

SAX, G. "Item analysis procedures and applications," Chapter 9 of *Principles of Educational Measurement and Evaluation* (Belmont, Cal.: Wadsworth, 1974), pages 228–254.

Item analysis of psychological tests (questionnaires, personality tests, attitude assessments, etc.) has some peculiarities which do not show up in educational textbooks. The following source is especially useful for psychological tests:

Anastasi, A. "Item analysis," Chapter 8 of *Psychological Testing* (3rd ed.) (New York: Macmillan, 1976), pages 198–226.

Professional Journals

Articles dealing exclusively with reliability are rare and are usually of a technical nature which is not in keeping with the practical orientation of this book. For articles dealing with reliability's more practical aspects, refer to the articles dealing with validity (Chapter 4) and with specific types of measurement strategies (Chapter 5). In addition, reliability of measurement is essential for higher levels of research. For this reason, many of the articles given as references for Chapters 8 through 15 also include discussions of reliability.

4 Validity

Chapter Preview

Validity refers to the extent to which an instrument really measures what it is designed to measure. This is an extremely important concept, since it determines the confidence we can place on the decisions we make regarding the outcome variables we are trying to measure. This chapter will discuss factors which influence validity and methods of establishing validity. Some technical methods of passing interest to the classroom teacher will be briefly described.

After completing this chapter you should be able to

- Define validity.
- Identify factors which introduce invalidity into measurement techniques.
- Describe the process for establishing validity of classroom measurement techniques.
- Identify guidelines for enhancing the validity of measurement techniques.
- Describe the role of content validity, criterion-related validity, and construct validity in measuring outcome variables.

Validity addresses the question of whether or not a measurement technique is really measuring what it purports to be measuring. An instrument is *invalid* to the extent that the respondent's scores are influenced by irrelevant characteristics rather than the outcome the instrument is intended to measure. An instrument is *invalid* to the extent that the respondent's score is actually a measure of the characteristic it is designed to measure, free from the influence of these extraneous factors.[1] *Validity is the most important characteristic of a test.* If a teacher gives a reading test and the test does not really measure reading ability, the test is useless. There is no logical way that particular test can help her measure the outcome she is interested in. If she gives a

---

[1] Actually, it is the *use* of a measurement instrument that is either valid or invalid. This distinction is more completely treated in measurement textbooks. It will be useful to keep the distinction in mind as you read this chapter.

AN OBVIOUSLY INVALID TEST

A TEST THAT MAY BE INVALID IN A MORE SUBTLE WAY.

self-concept test that is so hard to read that the third graders taking it cannot understand it, the test cannot measure self-concept among those third graders. It is invalid for that purpose. It cannot help the teacher to make decisions about the outcome variable labeled "self-concept." In designing and carrying out any sort of measurement, therefore, validity is of paramount importance.

SOURCES OF INVALIDITY

What makes a test valid or invalid? Before answering this question, let us first look at some examples of invalid tests. Assume that a researcher wants to design an intelligence test. He operationally defines intelligence as follows: "A person is intelligent to the extent that he agrees with me." He then makes up a list of 100 of his opinions and has people indicate whether they agree or disagree with each of the opinions. A person who agrees with 95 of the opinions would be defined as more intelligent than the person who agrees with only 90. And so on. This is an invalid measurement of intelligence. It is invalid because the operational definition has nothing to do with intelligence as any reputable psychologist has ever defined it.

Not all invalid tests are so blatantly invalid. For example, one of the most heated arguments in educational psychology today is over the question of what intelligence tests actually measure. This whole question is one of validity. The advocates of such tests argue that intelligence can be defined as a general problem-solving ability. They operationalize this definition with something like, "A person is intelligent to the extent that he can solve new problems when they are presented to him." Then they give a child a series of problems and count how many he can solve. A child who can solve a large number of problems is more intelligent than one who can solve only a few. The opponents of such tests argue that such tests are often invalid. These opponents argue that such general problem-solving ability is not the only quality—or even the most important quality—required to do well on such tests. The tests, they argue, really measure how well a person can adapt to a specific middle-class culture. Success on such tests, therefore, is really an operational definition of "ability to adapt to middle-class culture." Since the test is *designed* to measure general problem-solving ability but really measures ability to adapt to middle-class culture, the test is invalid. The argument over the validity of intelligence tests is far from settled. Important theorists continue to line up on both sides, and others continue to recommend compromises—such as recommending new tests or redefining the concept of intelligence.

Consider a third hypothetical intelligence test. Assume that I ask the child *one* question directly related to a valid operational definition. This is an excessively short test, and my result is likely to be unreliable. My result is also likely to be invalid, because my conclusion that this child is a genius for answering 100% of the test correctly is about as likely to be based on chance factors (unreliability) as upon any real ability related to the concept of intelligence.

Hence, there are three factors that determine the validity of a measuring instrument: (1) the logical appropriateness of the operational definition, (2) the match between the tasks on the instrument and the operational definition, and (3) the reliability of the instrument. These factors are diagrammed in Figure 4–1. The first test cited above was invalid because the operational definition was inappropriate. The second was argued to be invalid because the tasks the respondents perform are alleged to be different from those included in the operational definition. The third was invalid because the test was unreliable. A test is valid to the extent that it meets all three of these criteria. It can fall short in validity by failing seriously in one of these criteria or by failing to lesser degrees in some combination of these criteria.

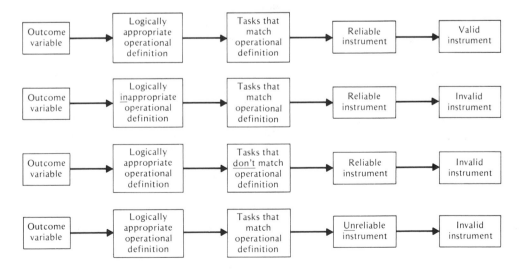

FIGURE **4–1.** Factors Leading to Test Validity or Invalidity.

ESTABLISHING VALIDITY

From the preceding discussion, it can be seen that there are three steps in establishing the validity of an instrument designed to measure an outcome variable:

- Demonstrate that the operational definition upon which the instrument is based is actually a logically appropriate definition of the outcome variable under consideration.
- Demonstrate that the tasks which the respondent has to perform to obtain a score on the instrument match the task suggested by the operational definition. '
- Demonstrate that the instrument is reliable.

Each of these steps will be discussed briefly in the following paragraphs.

1. The strategy for demonstrating that an operational definition is actually a logically appropriate definition of the outcome variable under consideration has been discussed in detail in Chapter 2, Measuring Outcome Variables. In that chapter it was pointed out that the operational definition is not actually synonymous with the outcome variable, but is rather the *evidence* you are willing to accept to indicate that an internal behavior is occurring. The important consideration in establishing validity is to demonstrate that the occurrence of the behavior in the operational definition is actually evidence that the outcome variable is occurring. You have to rule out the possibility that the behavior is actually evidence that some other internal behavior is occurring.

TABLE **4–1.** Some Examples of Logically Inappropriate Operational Definitions of Outcome Variables.

Assumed Outcome Variable	Operational Definition	Conceivable Real Outcome Variable
Ability to understand reading passages.	The pupil paraphrases a passage he/she has read silently.	Ability to guess from context clues.
Love of Shakespearean drama.	The student will carry a copy of Shakespeare's plays with him to class.	Eagerness to impress prof.
Appreciation of English 101.	The student will indicate on a questionnaire that she liked the course.	Anxiety over alienating instructor.
Knowledge of driving laws.	The candidate will get at least 17 out of 20 true-false questions right on license test.	Ability to take true-false tests with subtle clues present in them.
Friendliness toward peers.	The pupil will stand near other children on the playground.	Anxiety over being beat up if he stands alone.
Appreciation of American heritage.	Child will voluntarily attend the Fourth of July picnic given by the American Legion.	Appreciation of watching fireworks explode.

Table 4–1 lists some cases where the operational definition is to varying degrees logically inappropriate. For example, if the instructor of English 101 gives an anonymous questionnaire at the end of the semester to evaluate the course, she might *think* that the students are responding to questions regarding how much they appreciated the course. However, it's possible that the students who are filling out the questionnaire might think, "If we tell her what we really think, she'll be upset and come down hard on us when she grades the exam. Let's play it safe and give her favorable ratings for the course." If this is actually how the students are thinking, then the favorable comments on the instrument are not an operational definition of "Appreciation of English 101," but rather of "Anxiety Over Alienating the Instructor." Similar discrepancies between assumed outcomes and actual outcomes being measured can be seen in the other examples listed in Table 4–1.

In many cases, the logical connection is quite easy to establish, and hence the logical inappropriateness found in Table 4–1 is often easy to avoid. For example, the connection between the operational definitions and the outcome variables in Table 4–2 are much more obvious than the connections in Table 4–1. It's still possible for a person to perform the behavior described in the operational definition without having achieved the outcome variable, but it is much less likely than was the case in Table 4–1.

TABLE 4–2. Some Examples of Operational Definitions that Are Almost Certain to Be Appropriate for the Designated Outcome Variables.

Ability to add single-digit integers.	The student will add single-digit integers presented to him ten at a time on a test sheet.
Ability to tie one's own shoes.	The student will tie her own shoes after they have been presented to her untied.
Ability to bench press 150 pounds.	The student will bench press 150 pounds.
Ability to spell correctly from memory.	The student will write down from memory the correct spelling of each word from dictation.
Ability to spell correctly on essays with use of dictionary.	The student will make no more than two spelling errors in a 200-word essay written during class with the aid of a dictionary.
Ability to type 60 words per minute.	The student will type a 300 word passage in 5 minutes.
Ability to raise hand before talking in class.	The student will raise his hand before talking in class.
Ability to recall the quadratic equation.	The student will write from memory the quadratic equation.
Ability to apply the quadratic equation.	Given the quadratic equation and ten problems that can be solved using the equation, the student will solve at least nine.

Logical inappropriateness is most likely to occur when the outcome variable under consideration is a highly internalized one. Affective outcomes provide particularly difficult problems, because the evidence is much less directly connected to the internal outcome than is the case with behavioral, psychomotor, and cognitive outcomes. The guidelines presented in Chapter 2 are applicable here, namely, (1) rule out as many alternative explanations as possible, and (2) use more than one operational definition.

To the extent that you are specific in stating your operational definition and keep it present in discussing your outcome variables, it becomes less likely that you will make invalid conclusions based on a logical incompatibility between your operational definition and the outcome variable.

2. The advantage of selecting an appropriate operational definition or set of operational definitions can be completely nullified if the tasks the respondent is asked to perform in achieving a score on the instrument do not match the tasks stated in the operational definition.

TABLE **4–3.** Some Examples of a Mismatch Between the Operational Definition and the Task the Respondent Has to Perform on the Instrument.

Operational Definition	Task on Instrument
The student will add single-digit integers presented to him ten at a time on a test sheet.	"If I have 3 apples and you give me 2 more apples, how many do I have?"
The student will solve problems using the quadratic equation.	"Explain the derivation of the quadratic equation."
The student will use prepositions correctly in his essays.	"Write the definition of a preposition."
The student will apply the principles of operant conditioning to hypothetical situations.	The student first has to unscramble a complex multiple-choice thought pattern and then apply the principles.
Given a (culturally familiar) novel problem to solve, the test-taker will be able to solve the problem.	The student is presented with a problem which is entirely foreign to his cultural background to solve.
The student will describe the relationship between nuclear energy and atmospheric pollution.	The student will write, in correct grammatical structures, a description of the relationship between nuclear energy and atmospheric pollution.
The student will circle each of the prepositions in the paragraph provided.	The student will first decipher the teacher's unintelligible directions and then circle each of the prepositions.
The respondent will place herself in the simulated job situation provided to her and will indicate how she would perform in that situation.	The respondent has to first ignore that the situation is absurdly artificial and highly different from the real world and still respond as she would perform in the hypothetical situation.

Table 4–3 provides examples of such mismatches. The first three are not included to be facetious. Mismatches this obvious actually do occur on teacher-designed tests. The others are more subtle. In these cases, the teacher has one behavior in mind; and in fact, many of the persons responding to the instrument will perform the behavior that the teacher expects. But the mismatch occurs whenever a respondent is required to perform the different or additional tasks indicated in the column to the right of the table.

When questions arise concerning various sorts of bias, it is often the match between task and operational definition which is being called into question. For example, with regard to bias in intelligence testing, the argument is essentially that middle-class youngsters who take the test are taking a test where there is a match between the task and the operational definition; whereas when people of lower socioeconomic status take the same test there is a discrepancy between the task and the operational definition.

A good way to assure a match is to have several different persons examine the same instrument and state whether they think the task matches the operational definition. In addition, it is important to be aware of the various kinds of biases and other contaminating factors which could be causing the discrepancies, and to carefully rule these out. Such sources of mismatching include cultural bias, test-wiseness, reading ability, writing ability, ability to put oneself into a hypothetical framework, tendency to guess, or social desirability response bias. The preceding list is not to be considered exhaustive. There are other factors unique to specific individuals which produce a similar impact.

3. Reliability was discussed extensively in the previous chapter. Here it is necessary only to demonstrate how reliability affects validity. The contribution of reliability to validity was mentioned in Figure 4–1 and in the accompanying discussion. The relationship between reliability and validity is diagrammed more specifically in Figure 4–2. As this diagram suggests, a certain amount of reliability is essential if a test is going to possess validity. In other words, a test cannot measure what it's supposed to measure if it measures nothing consistently. In demonstrating that their tests are valid, professional test constructors often first demonstrate that their tests are reliable—that they measure *something* consistently; and then they demonstrate that this "something" is the characteristic which the tests are supposed to measure. In other words, they first demonstrate reliability, and then validity.

One caution is necessary in discussing the relationship between reliability and validity. It is crucial to realize that it is possible (but undesirable) to increase reliability *while simultaneously decreasing the validity of an instrument*. This can be done by either (1) narrowing or changing the operational definition to a less valid definition or (2) changing the tasks based on the operational definition to less directly related tasks, and then (3) devising a more reliable test based on the new inaccurate definition or tasks. This is obviously a bad idea, because the result is that the instrument now measures the wrong outcome "more reliably."

Such an increase in reliability accompanied by a decrease in validity occurs, for example, if a teacher introduces unnecessarily complex language into a test. A test which had previously measured "ability to apply scientific concepts" might now instead measure "ability to decipher complex language and then apply scientific concepts." The resulting reliability might be higher; but if the teacher thinks he's still

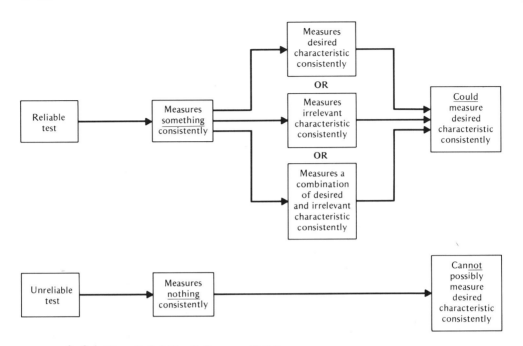

FIGURE 4-2.   How Reliability Influences Validity.

measuring the original outcome, his test has become less valid. This is one of the arguments against culturally biased norm-referenced tests. Their detractors argue that such tests become more reliable when cultural bias is added, because such cultural bias is a stable (consistent) factor, which is likely to work the same way on all questions and on all administrations of the test. However, the cultural bias detracts from the validity of the test. It is important to be alert to the tendency to accept such spuriously high reliabilities as evidence of validity. The fact that a certain amount of reliability is a necessary prerequisite for validity does not provide any sort of guarantee that the test with the highest statistical reliability coefficient is the most valid test. Statistical reliability is far from the most important factor in establishing validity. Another way to state this is to say that reliability is a necessary but insufficient basis for validity.

In summary, the above three steps should be followed in ascertaining whether a test is valid. Establishing validity is largely a logical process.

When you read Chapters 9 and 10 dealing with experimental design and internal validity, you will see a similarity between the strategies discussed there and this discussion of test validity. In a sense, the use of a test to measure an outcome variable represents a little experiment. The tester wants to be able to declare that the outcome variable in question (and *only* that outcome variable) is the *cause* of the respondent's unique performance on the test. The process of validation of the test consists of demonstrating this cause and effect relationship by ruling out other factors which could plausibly explain the respondent's performance. The tester wants to be able to say that the student did well on the test because she has displayed the outcome variable of which the test is supposed to represent an operational definition. Readers who wish to come to a more thorough understanding of the concept of test validity might be wise to reread the present section after completing Chapter 10.

A final note is called for before leaving this section on establishing the validity of tests. It is important to note that an instrument which provides valid data for group decisions will not always provide valid data for individual decisions. On the other hand, a measuring instrument that provides valid data for individual decisions will always provide valid data for group decisions. This is not as complicated as it sounds. To take an example, I might operationally define appreciation of Shakespeare as "borrowing Shakespearean books from the library without being required to do so." It would not be possible to diagnose Janet Jones specifically as either appreciating or not appreciating Shakespeare using a test based on this operational definition. There are too many competing explanations for her behavior, and these would invalidate the test as a measure of her appreciation. (For example, she might hate the subject but need to pass the exam; and so she has to borrow vast quantities of books to do burdensome, additional studying. Or she might like Shakespeare so much that she owns copies of all the plays and never has to borrow a book from any library except her own.) Nevertheless, it would still be valid to evaluate the *group* based on this operational definition. If you teach the Shakespeare plays a certain way one year and only 2% of the students borrow related books from the library, and the next year you teach it differently and 50% of the students spontaneously borrow books, it is probably a valid inference to conclude that appreciation of Shakespeare has increased. The group decision, at any rate, is more likely to be valid than is the individual diagnosis.

Review Quiz

Part I
Identify the item from each pair which is most likely to be an *invalid* measure of the outcome variable in question. (The outcome variable is given in parentheses.)

PAIR 1
A. _____ The child will correspond intelligibly with an assigned French-speaking pen pal. (Understands French)

B. _____ The child will correspond intelligibly with the French-speaking pen pal assigned to him/her. (Appreciates French culture)

PAIR 2
A. _____ The student will identify examples of the principles of physics in the kitchen at home. (Understands principles of physics)

B. _____ The student will choose to take additional courses in the physical sciences. (Appreciates physical sciences)

Part II
Write *I* next to statements that indicate an *invalid* instrument. Write *V* next to those which indicate a *valid* instrument. Write *N* if no relevant information regarding validity is contained in the statement.

1. _____ The questions were so hard I was reduced to flipping a coin to guess the answers.

2. _____ This test measures mere trivia, not the important outcomes of the course.

3. _____ To rule out the influence of memorized information regarding a problem, only topics which were entirely novel to all the students were included on the problem-solving test.

4. _____ The only way he got an A was by having his girl friend write the term paper for him.

5. _____ The length of the true-false English test was increased from 30 to 50 items to minimize the chances of getting a high score by guessing.

6. _____ The teacher ruled out the likelihood of cheating by giving the students at the same table a different form of the test.

7. _____ Since the personality test had such a hard vocabulary level, it probably came closer to measuring intelligence than any personality factors.

Answers:
Part I
PAIR 1: **B**
PAIR 2: **B**
In both cases, the second item requires a greater inferential leap to assume that it is evidence that the outcome variable is occurring. The first item in each pair is more direct evidence.

Part II
1. **Invalid.** The test is unreliable and therefore invalid.
2. **Invalid.** The tasks do not match the desired outcome variable.
3. **Valid.** The selection of topics is designed to rule out a source of bias.
4. **Invalid.** *Copying* the assignment is a different task than *writing* the assignment on one's own.
5. **Valid.** This would increase reliability and hence validity—provided the true-false items are all appropriate for the outcome variable.
6. **Valid.** Ruling out cheating increases the likelihood that the students will, in fact, respond to the correct tasks.
7. **Invalid.** Intelligence and personality are different outcomes.

SPECIFIC, TECHNICAL TYPES OF VALIDITY

If you read a test manual or look up the citation of a test in the *Mental Measurements Yearbook*, you will find references to three basic types of validity. These have been defined by the American Psychological Association.[2] Distinctions based on these three types of validity are not especially useful to classroom teachers in daily test construction. However, they are important to teachers when they select standardized tests for their classroom or schools, when they read the professional research literature, and when they attempt to measure psychological or theoretical characteristics beyond those that are normally covered by classroom tests. These three types of validity are (1) content validity, (2) criterion-related validity, and (3) construct validity. Each will be considered briefly here.

Content Validity

Content validity refers to the extent to which a test measures a representative sample of the subject matter or the behavioral changes under consideration. Of the three technical types of validity discussed in this section, content validity is the most relevant to the classroom teacher. A high school English teacher's midterm test lacks content validity, for example, when it focuses on what was covered in the last two

---

[2] For details, refer to *Standards for Educational and Psychological Tests*, American Psychological Association (Washington, D.C.: APA, 1974).

weeks and ignores the first six weeks of the term. Likewise, a self-concept test would lack content validity if all the items focused on school situations, ignoring the impact of home, church, and other outside-the-school factors on the self-concept. Content validity is assured by the process of logically analyzing the domain of subject matter or behavior which should be included on the instrument and examining the items to make sure a representative sample of this subject matter or behavior is included. In classroom tests, a frequent violation of content validity is to write test items which focus on the knowledge and comprehension levels (because such items are easy to write), while ignoring the important higher levels, such as application and synthesis (because such items are difficult to write).

Criterion-Related Validity

Criterion-related validity refers to how closely performance on a test is related to some other measure of performance. There are two types of criterion-related validity, predictive and concurrent validity.

Predictive validity refers to how well a test predicts some future performance. If my university uses the Graduate Record Exam (GRE) as a criterion for admission to graduate school, for example, the predictive validity of the GRE would be worth knowing. This predictive validity would have been established on a group of graduate students similar to those in my school. It would be expressed as a correlation coefficient, and a high coefficient would indicate that persons who did well on the GRE tended to do well in graduate school, while those who scored low on the GRE tended to do poorly. A low correlation coefficient would indicate that there was little relationship between GRE performance and success in graduate school.

Concurrent validity refers to how well a test correlates with some current criterion. It "predicts" the present. At first glance it sounds like an exercise in futility to predict something one already knows, but more careful consideration will suggest two important uses for concurrent validity. First, it is a useful predecessor for predictive validity. If the GRE, for example, does not even correlate with success among those who are succeeding right now, then there is little value in doing the more expensive, long-term, predictive validity study that might take a number of years. Second, concurrent validity enables us to use one instrument instead of another instrument. If a university wants to require that students either (1) take freshman composition or (2) take a test to demonstrate that they know the subject matter of freshman composition, concurrent validity would enable the English department to demonstrate that success on the test measures the same thing as success in the course. Like predictive validity, concurrent validity is expressed by a correlation coefficient.

Construct Validity

Construct validity refers to the extent to which a test can be interpreted in terms of underlying psychological constructs. (A construct is a psychological quality—such as self-confidence, motivation, or intelligence—which we assume exists to explain some observed behavior.) Construct validity often necessitates an extremely complicated process of validation. To state it briefly, the researcher develops a theory about how people should perform on the test if it really measures the alleged construct and then collects data to see if this is the way things actually happen. The process is complicated by the fact that often the researcher is doing two things: (1) proving that the test possesses construct validity, and (2) proving that the construct exists or refining the theory about the construct. Construct validity often deals with the intervening variable (discussed in Chapter 14), and it is of greatest relevance to Level IV research (discussed in Chapter 15).

Although validity itself is of tremendous importance to teachers, these three technical types of validity are not of great use to most educators in their daily work. They are relatively simple to understand. The difficulty is in carrying out the procedure. The information provided here should be enough for you to deal with these concepts short of doing Level IV research. If you find that you need further information (for example, if your job requires that you be able to select people accurately for various programs), consult the more technical references in the Annotated Bibliography.

Review Quiz

Indicate the type of technical validity required for each of the following situations. Choose from this list:

a. Content validity.

b. Predictive validity.

c. Concurrent validity.

d. Construct validity.

1. _____ The test designer has developed an Anxiety Measurement Scale and wants to verify that it really measures a characteristic which can be labeled anxiety.

2. _____ The counsellor wants to select students into his school's college preparatory program based on the likelihood that they will succeed in college, and he wants to know whether a certain test can help him accomplish this selection process.

3. _____ The test designer has developed a new, ten-minute IQ test and wants to demonstrate that it measures about the same thing as the Stanford-Binet IQ Test.

4. _____ The dean wants to make sure all the exams in the English composition courses cover all the objectives they are supposed to cover.

5. _____ The teacher wants to find out if the students who fail her final comprehensive exam really are the ones who will have trouble with related materials the next year.

Answers:
1. d
2. b
3. c
4. a
5. b

PUTTING IT ALL TOGETHER

One of Eugene Anderson's primary concerns was that his humane attitude tests should be valid. He was concerned about the validity of *all* his measuring instruments, but in this section we will focus exclusively on how he established the validity of his Fireman Test.

In establishing the validity of the Fireman Test, Mr. Anderson followed the guidelines suggested in this chapter. First he looked at his operational definition to ascertain that it was really a valid one. The operational definition had been revised to state, "Given a hypothetical situation in which animals might undergo pain and suffering, the respondent will choose to save the animals from that pain and suffering." He talked this over with several of his colleagues, and they agreed that saving the animals was what they would expect a humane person to do.

Next, he ascertained that the children taking the test would actually be doing what the operational definition said they should be doing. At this point, he had to rule out such irrelevant tasks as reading or tendencies to give socially desirable answers. The reading variable he ruled out by consulting some reading specialists. They agreed that for most third to seventh graders, the vocabulary would not be excessively difficult. They suggested that in case of uncertainty, Mr. Anderson should simply read the test to the respondents. Next he ruled out the social-desirability possibility by reasoning that all the objects in the house were socially desirable. In addition, the test would be presented in such a way that the children would not even know that it had anything to do with attitudes toward animals.

Finally, he noted that he had already established the reliability of the test through methods discussed in Chapter 3.

Mr. Anderson decided to use some statistical procedures to further authenticate his validity. The procedures he employed were a combination of criterion-related (concurrent) and construct validity. (It is not very important for you to distinguish precisely between the various techniques he used.) What he did was to ask, "If my test is valid, what can I predict about the results?" He answered this question with three predictions:

- If the test is valid, it will correlate rather strongly with other tests of humane attitudes.
- If the test is valid, people who are known to have good attitudes will score higher on the test than those who are known to have poor attitudes.
- If the test is valid, it will *not* correlate very strongly with irrelevant factors, such as reading ability or IQ.

He set out to check each of these predictions.

Mr. Anderson found it hard to check his first prediction. This was because he couldn't find any other good tests of humane attitudes anywhere in the country. What he did, therefore, was to compare the results of his Fireman Tests with the results of some of the other measuring techniques he had derived from his own set of operational definitions. (Some of these other tests are described in the next chapter.) He found a definite pattern. Those who did well on the Fireman Test also did well on these other instruments. This information seemed to verify his first prediction.

His second prediction was much easier to check. He knew from his professional reading that one specific geographic region of the country was noted for its humane attitudes. The largest humane organizations were in that part of the country, and the incidence of pet and animal abuse was very low there. He also knew of another area which was generally considered by the experts to be populated by much less humane people. He arranged to have his test given at the same grade levels in comparable schools in each of these communities. The results overwhelmingly supported his prediction. The students from the part of the country where the attitudes were known to be favorable scored significantly higher on the test than the other students. (The idea of significance will be discussed in Chapter 12.) This provided very strong support for the validity of his test.

Then Mr. Anderson checked his third prediction. He correlated the test scores with scores on reading tests, math tests, and intelligence tests. The Fireman Test did not correlate significantly with any of these other scores. This is what he had hoped for. If the Fireman Test *had* correlated strongly with reading ability, for example, this might have indicated that the test was really a measure of reading ability rather than of humane attitudes.

Mr. Anderson was quite happy with his validity data. He had demonstrated both logically and statistically that his test really did seem to measure attitude toward animal life. He still intended to supplement the Fireman Test with other measuring techniques (described in the next chapter), but at least he knew he was off to a good start.

SUMMARY

Validity refers to the degree to which a measurement technique really measures what it purports to measure. This concept is of extreme importance to educators, since they are interested in knowing what outcomes are occurring among learners. The validity of measurement technique is established through a three-step process:

- Demonstrate that the operational definition upon which the instrument is based is actually a logically appropriate definition of the outcome variable under consideration.
- Demonstrate that the tasks the respondent has to perform to obtain a score on the instrument match the tasks suggested by the operational definition.
- Demonstrate that the instrument is reliable.

To the extent that the instrument fails significantly at one of these steps or fails partially at some combination of them, the instrument lacks validity.

There are some specific, technical procedures for establishing the validity of an instrument. These are content validity, criterion-related validity, and construct validity. Although these types of validity are extremely important for psychological and theoretical research, they are not of great practical relevance to classroom teachers in their daily work.

Annotated Bibliography

EBEL, R. L. "The Validity of Classroom Tests," in *Essentials of Educational Measurement,* (Englewood Cliffs, N.J.: Prentice-Hall, 1979). This chapter de-emphasizes the traditional psychological concepts of content, criterion-related, and construct validity and instead insists that teachers can best enhance the validity of their tests by making sure they are appropriate for the purposes for which they are intended.

GRONLUND, N.E. "Validity," In *Measurement and Evaluation in Teaching* (3rd ed.) (New York: Macmillan, 1976). While staying within the traditional, psychologically-oriented framework of content, criterion-related, and construct validity, this chapter provides some very useful guidelines for teachers to follow in order to increase the validity of their classroom tests.

LEVINE, S. and ELZEY, F.F. "Behavior Sampling and Test Validity," Part III of *A Programmed Introduction to Educational and Psychological Measurement* (Belmont, Cal.: Brooks/Cole, 1970). These chapters provide a programmed introduction to the concepts of content, concurrent, and predictive validity. The discussion is straightforward and uncomplicated.

MAGER, R. *Measuring Instructional Intent* (Belmont, Cal.: Fearon, 1973). This book addresses the very important problem of matching test questions to behavioral objectives (operational definitions of outcome variables). Although Mager does not use the specific term *validity*, this little programmed text provides an excellent guide to one of the most important validity-related problems the classroom teacher faces.

POPHAM, W.J. "Reliability, Validity, and Performance Standards," Chapter 7 of *Criterion-Referenced Measurement* (Englewood Cliffs, N.J.: Prentice-Hall, 1978). This chapter provides the most comprehensive treatment yet available of the application of validity theory to criterion-referenced tests.

Professional Journals

The following journal articles contain good examples of attempts to establish the validity of specific measurement strategies. You may wish to examine the descriptions of these articles to see if any of them deal with problems similar to those you yourself have to deal with. (As you will notice in later chapters, validity of measurement is essential for higher levels of research. For this reason, many of the articles given as references for Chapters 8 through 15 also include discussion of validity.)

FELDSTEIN, J.C. and GLADSTEIN, G.A. "A comparison of the construct validities of four measures of empathy," *Measurement and Evaluation in Guidance* 13 (1980): 49–57. The researchers list six criteria of good tests of empathy (based on sound counseling theory) and examine how thoroughly each of four tests which purport to measure empathy actually adhere to these criteria.

GANNAWAY, T.W., SINK, J.M., and BECKET, W.C. "A predictive validity study of a job sample with handicapped and disadvantaged individuals," *Vocational Guidance Quarterly* 29 (1980): 4–11. This study determines how accurately a job sample (performance on a job-related task rather than a psychological test) predicts eventual performance on a real job.

HOFFMAN, R.A. and SMITH, D.L. "The use of the Test of Everyday Writing Skills in a college screening program," *Journal of Educational Research* 73 (1980) 168–171. The authors examine the validity of using the Test of Everyday Writing Skills as a screening device to identify students who possess satisfactory writing skills.

HYND, G.W., QUACKENBUSH, R., KRAMER, R., CONNOR, R. and WEED, W. "Concurrent Validity of the McCarthy Scales of Children's Abilities with Native American primary-grade children," *Measurement and Evaluation in Guidance* 13 (1980) 29–34. This study suggests that although the McCarthy Scales of Children's Abilities may be valid for other purposes, it should not be used as a valid way to determine the intelligence of Native American primary-grade children.

MCINTYRE, D.J. "Administrator's Dilemma: Teacher evaluation and the observer effect," *NASSP Bulletin* 64 (1980):36–40. The author examines the validity of observation by an administrator as a method for evaluating teacher performance in the classroom.

ROSZKOWSKI, M.J. "Concurrent Validity of the Adaptive Behavior Scale as Assessed by the Vineland Social Maturity Scale," *American Journal of Mental Deficiency* 85 (1980):86–89. This study demonstrates the validity of a new test (the Adaptive Behavior Scale) by comparing it to an old test (the Vineland Social Maturity Scale) and showing that correlations appear where they should appear and are absent where they should be absent.

5 Test Scores and Their Meaning

Chapter Preview

Once you have designed and administered a measuring instrument, the scores have to be computed, summarized, presented, and interpreted. This chapter deals with the basic principles of score use and interpretation. The topics are approached in a conceptual rather than mathematical manner. By understanding these concepts, you should become able to make better use of your own results, as well as more capable of interpreting the data which others present to you.

After completing this chapter you should be able to

- Identify examples of nominal, ordinal, and interval scale data.
- Define the mode, median, and mean and identify situations in which each is used.
- Describe and interpret examples of the standard deviation.
- Distinguish between norm-referenced and criterion-referenced measurement techniques.
- Interpret examples of percentiles and derived scores.

MEASUREMENT SCALES

Examine the questionnaire in Figure 5–1. The person who completed it has given the answer "2" to Questions 1, 2, 4, 5, 7, 9A, and 9E. Does the number 2 have the same meaning in each of these statements? For example, does "2" always mean twice as much as "1" and half as much as "4"? Actually, it has this meaning only in Question 5. There is no logic behind the assumption that a female is twice a male, that single is twice married and half widowed, or that "disagree" is twice "strongly disagree" and half "agree." The number "2" is meaningful in these answers; but the meaning is different from that in Question 5, where a person who has two children

Questionnaire

1. What is your sex?
    1 _____ male
    2 ___X___ female

2. What is your personal annual income?
    1 _____ under $5000
    2 ___X___ between $5001 and $10,000
    3 _____ between $10,001 and $20,000
    4 _____ between $20,001 and $30,000
    5 _____ over $30,000

3. What is your present age? ___29___

4. What is your marital status?
    1 _____ single
    2 ___X___ married
    3 _____ divorced
    4 _____ widowed
    5 _____ other (Explain) _____

5. How many children do you have? ___2___

6. What is your estimated IQ? ___145___

7. Did you vote in the last presidential election?
    1 _____ Yes
    2 ___X___ No

8. How old do you think American citizens should be before they are allowed to vote?
    ___21___ years old

9. Record your reaction to each of the following statements. Use this scale:
    1—Strongly disagree
    2—Disagree
    3—Uncertain (In between)
    4—Agree
    5—Strongly Agree

    A ___2___ Anyone who pays taxes should be allowed to vote.
    B ___1___ Six-year-old children should be allowed to vote on any issues that concern them.
    C ___4___ Only those who have graduated from high school should be allowed to vote.
    D ___4___ Inmates in prison should not be allowed to vote.
    E ___2___ Absolutely all Americans over age 18 should have an equal vote in all issues
        which concern them.

FIGURE **5–1.** Illustrations of the Three Scales of Measurement.

does have twice as many as a person with one child and half as many as a person with four children. These differences in meaning are related to the concept of scales of measurement.

There are three levels of meaning (scales) of measurement which are relevant to educators.[1] These are nominal scale, ordinal scale, and interval scale.

---

[1] Actually, there are four levels. The fourth is *ratio* scale. This scale is similar to the interval scale, but it is based on a true zero, whereas the interval scale is not. However, since there are few instances in educational research where the difference between ratio and interval scale data makes a difference, this text will classify both interval and ratio data under the label *interval*.

In *nominal scales*, the number merely attaches a label to a piece of information. The response "2" in Question 1 is nominal scale data. The nominal scale does not indicate rank, nor do the sizes of the intervals between the numbers mean anything significant. It would be just as appropriate to classify males as "1" and females as "2," or even to classify males as "2" and females as "7." All the number does here is attach a label to the respondent's answer.

In *ordinal scales*, the number not only attaches a label, but it also indicates a rank ordering. For example, in Question 2, the answer of "2" indicates that a person had a level of income between the levels indicated by a number "1" or "3." The ordinal scale "2" attaches a label and assigns a rank, but this rank is *only* a rank. The size of the interval between ranks is not constant, nor is it meaningful to multiply and divide the ranks. For example, it is not accurate to assume that a person answering "2" is as much more affluent than a person answering "1" as a person answering "5" is more affluent than a person answering "4." If this last part confuses you, just remember, ordinal data indicates *only* rank. It is more than nominal, but less than interval data.

In *interval scales*, the number not only attaches a label and indicates a rank, but also the intervals between the various numbers are meaningful. A person who has 2 children has one more child than a person with 1 child; and likewise a person with 5 children has one more child than a person with 4 children. Of the three scales, therefore, interval scale provides the most complete information.

At this point, you may ask, "Who cares?" In a moment I'll show you what difference this all makes, but first try this little quiz.

Review Quiz

Indicate which scale of data is provided by the underlined number in each statement.

John had the <u>second</u> highest score with <u>14</u> correct.
Mary wore the number <u>2</u> during her varsity days.
<u>Fourteen</u> players wear the number <u>12</u> in the NFL.

1. <u>Second</u> is _____ scale.

2. <u>14</u> is _____ scale.

3. <u>2</u> is _____ scale.

4. <u>Fourteen</u> is _____ scale.

5. <u>12</u> is _____ scale.

_____

Answers:
1 ordinal scale
2. interval scale.
3. nominal scale.
4. interval scale.
5. nominal scale.

If you got items wrong, check back to see if you can find out why you are confused.

There are two reasons why understanding scales of measurement is important. First, since the higher levels of measurement convey more information, you should choose instruments that employ the highest levels whenever possible. For example, if you construct a questionnaire with Question 2 written the way it appears on the questionnaire on page 63, then you would be losing information and would not be able to compute a precise average of the incomes. However, if you asked the respondents to indicate their exact income, then you would have interval data, and your analysis could be more precise. Second, some statistics can be used only when the data fit the proper scale, and so you can do better analyses if you know what the scales mean.

Having said this, I nevertheless will not use the terms nominal, ordinal, and interval scale data anywhere except in footnotes and parentheses in the rest of this text. I *do* intend to use the concepts, but I intend to work around the labels in the chapters where these concepts are relevant. I have chosen to do this because I find that many perfectly intelligent people have a sort of classically conditioned anxiety reaction whenever they hear these words, and the rest of this book can be understood without using these terms. Nevertheless, if you have understood this section, this is evidence that you understand the concepts, and this will help you with the subsequent concepts.

WAYS TO REPORT SCORES

When you have one score on one person, it is easy to report that score. You just state what the score was. However, when you have either a single score on a large group of people or a large number of scores on a single person, it is overwhelming and confusing to list all these scores at once. A much more convenient way to do this is to report a single score which summarizes the whole set of scores. One of the most common ways to do this is to use a measure of *central tendency*. A measure of central tendency is what we loosely refer to as a typical or average score. There are three kinds of central tendency scores: the mode, the median, and the mean. Each will be discussed briefly.

The *mode* is the most frequently occurring score. When what you want to report is what category occurs most frequently, the mode is what you report. (You *have* to use the mode to indicate the average when all you have is nominal data. Any other average would be meaningless.) If you wanted to know what color eyes the average American has, the answer would be expressed in terms of a mode. A certain color would be the most frequently occurring color of eyes. If we would say that the average American is a white female 23 years old, white and female are modes. They indicate that more Americans are female than male and more are white than any other race. The 23-year-old part, however, is not a mode. It would be either a median or a mean.

The *median* is the middle score. Half the other scores fall above and half below the median.[2] When you want to focus on the midpoint, the median is what you report. (You have to use the median instead of the mean when you have ordinal data; but with interval data, you can take your choice of the mean or median, depending on which gives the better picture.) If there are 15 runners in a race, the median finisher will be in eighth place. Half will finish before her and half after her. In the 23-year-old white female example given above, the age would probably be given in a median, since the person with the middle age is a reasonable representation of what is typical.[3]

The *mean* is the arithmetic average. The mean is obtained by adding all the scores together and dividing by the number of scores that went into getting that total. The mean is popular because it is easy to compute. In statistics, it's also popular because it can be used as the basis for a vast number of useful statistics.

Table 5–1 presents some salaries and the averages computed by each of the above methods of computing central tendency. The mode is not very meaningful. Although more employees had that salary than any other salary, it is hardly logical to argue that that is the typical salary. Likewise, the mean is inappropriate, because it is distorted drastically by the extreme salary of the owner of the company. The median salary, on the other hand, is a reasonable approximation of the typical salary. Half the people earn that amount and half earn less. When you present your results, determine which measure of central tendency will give the most accurate picture, and use that statistic. In Table 5–1, this would be the median.

TABLE 5–1   Salaries of Employees in a Small Company with Ten Employees.

Employee A	$ 6,500
Employee B	17,450
Employee C	12,400
Employee D	6,500
Employee E	22,500
Employee F	22,000
Employee G	13,750
Employee H	21,000
Employee I	19,450
Employee J	18,000
Employee K (owner)	1,500,000

Mode = $6,500.
Median = $18,000.
Mean = $150,868.

When the data meet the mathematical specifications of the normal distribution (discussed later in this chapter), the mode, median, and mean all come at the same score; and in such cases the mean is most frequently reported. Even when the data deviate slightly from the normal curve, the mean is still the most popular measure of central tendency. The general practice appears to be that when it is possible to do so

[2] Actually, the median is computed by a slightly more complex formula, which will not be discussed here.

[3] Technical note: Many people mistakenly consider the geographic middle score to be the median. This would be F in Table 5–1. This is incorrect. The scores must first be ranked from highest to lowest and then the middle score is identified.

(that is, when you have interval data) compute and report the mean, unless there is a good reason (such as extreme scores) to recommend a different method of reporting central tendency.

Review Quiz

What is the mode, median, and mean of each of the following sets of scores?

A. 45, 35, 48, 39, 41, 44, 45
    Mode _____
    Median _____
    Mean _____

B. 25, 18, 17, 18, 27, 18, 23, 17, 14
    Mode _____
    Median _____
    Mean _____

Answers:
A. Mode: 45
    Median: 44
    Mean: 42.4
B. Mode: 18
    Median: 18
    Mean: 19.7

In addition to knowing the typical score from a measure of central tendency, it is helpful to know how much spread there is among the scores. This can be done very crudely by stating the *range*, which is merely a statement of the highest and lowest scores. If I told you that the scores on the test averaged 45 with a range of 3 to 95, you would conclude that they were more spread out than if I told you the average was 45 with a range of 40 to 50. The range is actually a crude and clumsy estimate, and a better method is to report the standard deviation. This is not a statistics text, and so the computation of the standard deviation will not be discussed here. (A computational formula is provided in Appendix D.) As its name implies, the standard deviation is merely a statement of a type of average spread among the scores. The larger the standard deviation, the wider the scores are spread out. For example, you were told that a test had a mean of 45 with a standard deviation of 12.3, you would know that the scores were further spread apart than if the average were 45 with a standard deviation of 2.3. The standard deviation requires interval data and accompanies the mean, and so this is another reason why the mean is preferred over the mode or median.

Review Quiz

In each of the following descriptions, write *Most* before the description where the scores are most spread apart. Write *Least* before the description where the scores are most closely clustered together.

A. 1 _____ The test had a mean of 60 with a standard deviation of 6.3
    2 _____ The test had a mean of 60 with a standard deviation of 16.3.
    3 _____ The test had a mean of 60 with a standard deviation of 1.3.

B. 1 _____ The test had a mean of 50 with a standard deviation of 5.4.
   2 _____ The test had a mean of 60 with a standard deviation of 9.5.
   3 _____ The test had a mean of 70 with a standard deviation of 17.5.

Answers:
A. Most spread out   2
   Least spread out   3

B. Most spread out   3
   Least spread out   1

It's also useful to graph the data so that a person reading the report has a visual represesntation of the data. Although graphs will be used in the later chapters of this book, specific graphing strategies will not be discussed here. Useful specific instructions can be found in the measurement and statistics books referred to in the Annotated Bibliography at the end of this chapter.

In presenting your data, use whatever statistics and graphs give a meaningful picture. By using the wrong statistic or a badly drawn graph, you can seriously mislead your reader. This information is also helpful to you as a reader of reports written by others. Watch for misleading presentations of data. In *How to Lie with Statistics,* Huff (New York: Norton, 1954) demonstrates some grotesque falsifications that can be achieved by simply using the wrong statistic or graph.

DESCRIBING AND COMPARING TEST PERFORMANCE

There are three basic ways to describe a person's performance on a measuring instrument. A person's performance can be compared to a norm-referenced standard, to a criterion-referenced standard, or to an absolute standard. Some examples from physical measurement may make this clear:

Absolute standard: He is 5'10" tall.

Criterion-referenced standard: He is tall enough to dunk the ball in the basket.

Norm-referenced standard: He is the third smallest and second fattest player on the squad of fifteen.

The same standards can be applied to educational outcomes:

Absolute standard: He spelled 43 out of 50 words right.

Criterion-referenced standard: His score of 43 out of 50 put him past the cutoff point to go on to the next lesson.

Norm-referenced standard: His score of 43 out of 50 words right put him in only the 25th percentile in his class.

The use of such standards can be summarized as follows:

Absolute scores simply state the actual outcome.

Criterion-referenced scores compare the person's performance to a standard or "criterion."

Norm-referenced scores compare the person's performance on the test to the performance of other persons who took the same test.

All three types of scores are useful, depending on the purpose for which you are conducting the measurement.

Much of measurement theory has been developed by persons whose main job has been to devise ways to determine differences among people. In other words, these developers of measurement theory have been primarily interested in norm-referenced test theory. Because of this, many teachers have come away with the impression that norm-referenced tests are the only way, or at least the best way, to interpret educational outcomes. This has been an unfortunate emphasis. In reality, norm-referenced tests are of importance to classroom teachers on relatively rare occasions.

On the other hand, criterion-referenced measurement is of considerable importance to teachers, because this is a concrete way to determine whether our students are making the progress we expect them to make. To put it another way, knowing that half the children in the nation are below average in mathematics achievement is of utterly no importance. It has to be that way by the very definition of the term *average*. Knowing that the children in our school are below average in the same abilities really means nothing significant, unless we have reason to believe that they are capable of performing better. On the other hand, knowing that we have set realistic goals and knowing that 90% of our students have met these realistic outcomes is a worthwhile piece of knowledge. The simple fact is that criterion-referenced information is more likely to lead to constructive actions on the part of teachers than is norm-referenced information.[4]

The preceding paragraphs have been written to provide a counter emphasis both to what has been emphasized in teacher education programs and to what will come next in this text. Since absolute and criterion-referenced scores are extremely easy to interpret, there is very little to write about them in a chapter like this. After all, what is difficult about interpreting the statement that a child can spell only 35% of the words on his sixth-grade spelling list or that 90% of the sixth-graders in Ohio know that Columbus is the state's capital? The difficulty with these scores is giving them a meaning by establishing that the criterion is a valid criterion, and this is a problem of reasoning, not of measurement theory. On the other hand, norm-referenced scores are often more difficult to interpret. Because of this greater complexity, it is necessary to spend more space in this chapter discussing such scores. This greater space should not be taken as an indication that these scores are more important or more useful than criterion-referenced scores. As an educator, you should determine what it is that you wish to accomplish and choose your testing strategies accordingly. Unless there is something unusual about your situations, you will discover that this means that most of your tests should be criterion-referenced. Nevertheless, for the 10% of your testing activities which involve norm-referencing, the following information will be helpful.

Percentiles

A percentile is a score that indicates the percentage of scores which a raw score exceeds. (Percentiles are ordinal data.) A percentile must necessarily be based on a

---

[4] An excellent case for the more widespread use of criterion-referenced tests can be found in the reference to Popham (1978) in the Annotated Bibliography at the end of this chapter.

reference to some specific group. Thus, if I score in the 75th percentile on the final exam in a course, this means that I finished above 75% of the rest of the students who took that exam. Finishing in the 75th percentile does not mean that I got 75% of the questions right on the test. If the rest of the students did well, it might take a percentage correct of 95% to be at the 75th percentile, whereas if everyone else did poorly, a score of 60% might put me at the 75th percentile.

Percentiles are often used in the interpretation of standardized tests. For example, a person might take the Graduate Record Exam (GRE) and discover that he scored at the 80th percentile with regard to the overall norm group, at the 50th percentile compared to School A students, and at the 95th percentile compared to School B students. This means that when compared to all the students who typically take the GRE, his score exceeded 80% of them. When compared to the students at School A, however, his score exceeded only 50% of them. On the other hand, his score exceeded 95% of the students at School B. In practical terms, this means that if the skills measured by the GRE are important at both School A and School B, he will have an easier time competing with those at School B than those at School A.

Derived Scores

The normal distribution (normal curve) is a graph of a mathematical probability formula. Its derivation and theory will not be discussed in detail here, except to say that many chance occurrences (including the distribution of genes) approximate the normal curve. It is a mathematically very convenient probability formula. It turns out that many human abilities (such as intelligence, spatial ability, and manual dexterity) are correctly represented by this theoretical distribution. Because of the mathematical convenience and because of the fact that many educational abilities do fit this curve, the normal curve has become popular as a means of interpreting educational and

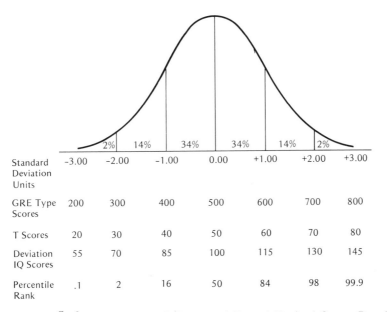

	2%	14%	34%	34%	14%	2%	
Standard Deviation Units	−3.00	−2.00	−1.00	0.00	+1.00	+2.00	+3.00
GRE Type Scores	200	300	400	500	600	700	800
T Scores	20	30	40	50	60	70	80
Deviation IQ Scores	55	70	85	100	115	130	145
Percentile Rank	.1	2	16	50	84	98	99.9

FIGURE 5–2. The Normal Curve and Several Derived Scores Based on It.

psychological tests. When test designers began designing achievement tests and other tests which did not happen to fit this pattern of occurrence, they artificially forced them into this probability format. This may sound illogical, and sometimes it is. But to the extent that student learning is influenced by random factors, the normal distribution is perfectly logical. Whether we approve of the logic or not, the results of many standardized tests are still presented in terms based on the normal curve; and so an understanding of these terms will be helpful to you as an educator.

The normal curve is diagrammed in Figure 5–2. In the normal curve, 68% of the scores fall within plus or minus one standard deviation of the mean (34% above and 34% below the mean). Try reading the percentages yourself. What percentage of the scores fall below 2 standard deviations above the mean? The answer is 98%.

By applying some relatively simple mathematical procedures, it is possible to compute *derived scores*. These are scores with an arbitrarily assigned mean and standard deviation. That may sound complicated, but the use of such scores is actually rather simple. For example, a *standard score* is a derived score with a mean of 0 and a standard deviation of 1. Standard scores are not particularly important, except as a basis for computing practically all other derived scores. A more popular derived score is the IQ score, which usually has a mean of 100 and a standard deviation of 15.

Spot Quiz

With this information, answer the following questions:

1. What percentage of people have an IQ below 100?

2. What percentage of people have an IQ above 100?

3. What percentage of people have an IQ between 85 and 115?

4. What percentage of people have an IQ below 115?

5. What percentage of people have an IQ below 85?

Answers:
1. 50% (34% + 14% + 2%)
2. 50% (34% + 14% + 2%)
3. 68% (34% + 34%)
4. 84% (34% + 34% + 14% + 2%)
5. 16% (14% + 2%)

Another common type of score is the T Score, which has a mean of 50 and a standard deviation of 10. Another derived score, popular on standardized achievement tests is the GRE-type score, which has a mean of 500 and a standard deviation of 100. The interpretation of all these scores is exactly the same, and they serve as a good way to compare performances of different people on the same test or even of the same person on different tests.

Note that it is always possible to convert a standard score to a percentile. This can easily be done from the diagram or from more detailed tables based on the formula from which Figure 5–2 is derived. For example, a person with an IQ of 100 is at the 50th percentile, and one with an IQ of 115 is at the 84th percentile.

Review Quiz

1. What percentage of T scores fall below 60?

2. What percentage of T scores fall between 30 and 40?

3. What percentage of GRE scores fall above 600?

4. What percentage of GRE scores fall between 400 and 600?

Answers
1. 84% (34% + 34% + 14% + 2%)
2. 14%
3. 16% (14% + 2%)
4. 68% (34% + 34%)

A technical note is in order here. For mathematical reasons, a slight change in raw scores near the mean (near the 50th percentile) results in a greater shift in percentile ranks than does a shift of the same size near either extreme of the distribution. Because of this irregularity, it is not appropriate to average or to do most other statistical computations with percentiles. This is important to remember. A frequent error that teachers make is to average the percentiles on the pretest and posttest and compare the differences in score. This is *not* appropriate. The correct procedure is to use the raw (absolute) scores for the mathematical computations. Then if you wish to do so for comparison purposes, you can convert to percentiles after the math is finished. Many readers will understand this quite easily if they simply reread this paragraph and look at Figure 5–2. Others will find this whole concept mystifying. It is not worth losing sleep over. Just remember, do not average percentiles—average raw scores instead.

More specific details on the computation and use of various derived scores can be found in a good measurement textbook. When interpreting such scores, remember that they are often artificially distributed scores based on a specific norm group. If this artificiality is not theoretically incompatible with your goals, then the use of such scores provides an easy mode of comparison with a norm group. Also remember that the *validity* of the norm group is a separate consideration. Only to the extent that the norm group resembles your own group do you really want to compare your scores to theirs.

PUTTING IT ALL TOGETHER

When Mr. Anderson had the teacher administer his Fireman Test a week before he gave a program in a school, he found a mean of 1.2 with a standard deviation of .63. Since the scores were pretty well spread out (much like a normal curve), he decided that the mean was an appropriate way to report the data. This average meant that in the class of 30 children, they chose an average of 1.2 animals to save from the fire.

A week after the pretest, Mr. Anderson visited the school and gave what he considered to be a good program. The children responded happily and enthusiastically. A week later, the teacher gave the alternate form of the Fireman Test. This time the students chose an average of 1.3 animals with a standard deviation of .71. Mr.

Anderson was somewhat discouraged, because these results showed that the children had not changed much at all as a result of his efforts. He resolved to try some new strategies the next time he visited a classroom.

When Mr. Anderson told the teacher about the results, she was amazed. She remarked, "How can my kids be so cruel? Where have I gone wrong?" Mr. Anderson agreed that it would have been nice to see higher scores, but he pointed out that the pupils' performance was actually typical of how most pupils throughout the country responded.

During his validation process, the test had been administered all over the country. He had gotten averages as low as .6 and as high as 2.3. The performance of the present children was typical, according to these informal norms.

Although he was somewhat reassured by his awareness that these scores were typical, Mr. Anderson was still concerned. After all, it was not exactly inspiring to know that the typical child would save only one out of three animals from the fire. Several children had chosen none—preferring to save credit cards, TVs, and stereos instead of living animals. The fact that several humane schools had averaged so much higher suggested to him that it was possible (and desirable) to develop attitudes which would persuade children to be more concerned about animal life. Mr. Anderson resolved to keep working at his project.

SUMMARY

When collecting or interpreting data, it is important to know that numbers can have different levels of meaning. For example, a number can be used merely to label or categorize a person. This sort of number (nominal scale) has a very low level of meaning. A higher level of meaning comes with numbers that rank a person (ordinal scale.) An even higher level of meaning (interval scale) is present when numbers attempt to present scores, such as by stating that a person got a score of 17 out of 20. Although even the lowest scale is useful, higher level scales give more precise information and are more easily adapted to many statistical procedures.

Scores can be summarized with either the mean (arithmetic average), median (midpoint), or mode (most frequent score). When reporting data, you should choose the measure of central tendency which gives the most accurate picture of the typical score. In addition, it is possible to indicate how widely spread out the scores are by stating the standard deviation.

Scores can be either absolute, criterion-referenced, or norm-referenced. An absolute score simply states a measure of performance without comparing that performance with anything. However, scores are not very useful unless they are compared with something. Criterion-referenced scores compare test performance with a standard. Such a comparison enables the tester to know whether or not the performance is what it should be according to established standards. Norm-referenced scores compare the test performance with the performance of other people who have taken the same test. Teachers are usually more interested in knowing how a child compares on the basis of a useful standard than how he compares with other children; but norm-referenced comparisons often provide useful insights.

Criterion-referenced scores are quite easy to understand because they are usually straightforward raw scores or percentages. Norm-referenced scores are often converted to percentiles or derived scores. A student's percentile on a test indicates what percentage of the other persons who took the same test fell below that student's score. Derived scores are often based on the normal curve. They use an arbitrary mean. Such comparisons state how the respondent compares with other persons who took that same test.

Annotated Bibliography

BERTRAND, A. and CEBULA, J.P. *Tests, Measurement, and Evaluation: A Developmental Approach* (Reading, Mass.: Addison-Wesley, 1980). Chapter 7 provides an innovative presentation of most of the topics covered in this chapter.

BRADLEY, J.I. and MCCLELLAND, J.N. *Basic Statistical Concepts* (2nd ed.) (Glenview, Ill.: Scott, Foresman and Company, 1978). This is a programmed (self-instructional) textbook which introduces the basic statistics which are useful in interpreting test scores.

EBEL, R. *Essentials of Education Measurement* (3rd ed.) (Englewood Cliffs, N.J.: Prentice-Hall, 1979). Chapter 11 provides Ebel's clear and concise treatment of most of the topics covered in this chapter.

SAX, G. *Principles of Educational Measurement and Evaluation* (Belmont, Cal.: Wadsworth, 1974). Chapter 6 provides a good discussion on the topic "Summarizing and Interpreting Measurements."

Professional Journals

The following article uses the terms and concepts discussed in the present chapter. In addition, these same terms and concepts are found in many of the examples of higher level research cited at the end of Chapters 8 through 15.

WILKINS, R.A. "If the moral reasoning of teachers is deficient, what hope for pupils," *Phi Delta Kappan*, *61* (April 1980): 548-549. The author compares normal curves of teachers, senior high students, and junior high students and shows that many teachers are likely to think at lower levels of moral reasoning than the pupils they teach.

6 Data Collection Instruments

Chapter Preview

Chapters 3 and 4 dealt with the technical characteristics of a good test. These characteristics are general. They can be applied to any specific measurement technique. The present chapter deals with the many different formats within which data can be collected. These formats range from very open-ended to very structured approaches. Different formats have different purposes. Each solves one set of problems while opening the door for other problems. Your goal in designing or selecting a data-collecting instrument is to devise a combination of these various techniques which will enable you to collect valid and reliable information about the outcome variable upon which you wish to focus your attention.

After completing this chapter you should be able to

- Identify examples of well-constructed instruments of each of the following types:
  - Classroom achievement tests.
  - Questionnaires.
  - Interviews.
  - Observational techniques.
  - Unobtrusive techniques.
  - Standardized tests.
- Identify the purposes of each of the above techniques.
- Identify the strengths and weaknesses which can occur with each of the above techniques.
- Devise strategies for integrating several of the above formats into a useful data-collection strategy.

TEACHER-DESIGNED ACHIEVEMENT TESTS

Educators spend a great deal of time promoting cognitive outcomes. They therefore spend a great amount of time developing and administering classroom tests to measure these cognitive outcomes. Most teacher education programs have at least one special course devoted to the construction and interpretation of such tests, and so the present text will not attempt to duplicate that important effort. Therefore, the present section will make no attempt to tell you everything you always wanted to know about classroom test construction. Only a few important, general guidelines will be presented here. If you are interested in further information, the selected references in the Annotated Bibliography are excellent sources.

The logic behind designing a classroom test is the same as that behind any other instrument. Your goal is to develop a valid way to find out whether or not your students have mastered an educational outcome. There are three simple steps in developing a good classroom test.

The first step is to *determine exactly what it is that you are trying to measure*. If your course objectives are stated in specific, observable terms, this will be easy to do. Chapter 2, Measuring Outcome Variables, provided useful guidelines for stating operational definitions of course goals. One caution is to avoid the tendency to test only low level learning, such as knowledge and understanding, while ignoring such higher levels as application and synthesis. Teachers often have a tendency to do this because lower level objectives are easier to write. Teachers who have clearly stated, valid objectives of worthwhile outcomes find it relatively easy to design valid tests.

The second step is to *match the testing technique to the operational definition*. The goal of a colleague who teaches psychology courses is to teach students to understand the important principles of psychology. When he was asked what this meant, he agreed that being able to identify concrete instances of important concepts and principles would be a valid operational definition of about 95% of what he is trying to teach. And yet he always uses essay tests. When he was asked the reason, he answered, "Multiple choice tests are multiple guess tests. They measure trivia." The truth of the matter is that well-written multiple-choice tests are probably the best way to measure what he is trying to teach. In a valid multiple-choice format, the student would be able to focus on exactly what the teacher has in mind and identify the concept or principle involved. The multiple-choice format has two major advantages for a course such as the one described in this example: (1) such tests are designed to measure the recall, understanding, and application of specific concepts or principles, and (2) because a student can answer a large number of such questions in a short time, a large sample of items can be incorporated into the test. The essay test, on the other hand, is an inadequate way for this instructor to evaluate his students. The essay test would be weak in this case (1) because essay tests measure higher-order processes, such as the ability to organize and integrate information, whereas this instructor is interested in measuring mastery of concepts; and (2) because of the time needed to answer each question, only a few topics can be covered. This instructor should either change his objectives or modify his testing technique to match the objectives.

The point of the preceding paragraph is not to argue for a wider use of multiple-choice tests, but rather to point out the illegitimacy of deciding *a priori* what kind of test is best in all situations. The correct procedure is to determine the appropriate operational definition of the outcome variable, and then to match the testing technique to the operational definition.

The third step is to *write good items based on that testing technique*. My colleague's dissatisfaction with multiple-choice tests probably arose either because he himself wrote terrible multiple-choice tests or because as a student he was subjected to bad multiple-choice tests by his own teachers. Several of the books cited in the Annotated

Bibliography provide useful guidelines on how to write good items of a designated type.

In designing your tests, avoid falling into a rut. Be creative. Look for new ideas in writing or selecting good tests. The book by Bloom, Hastings, and Madaus (1971), cited in the Annotated Bibliography, presents innovative ways to write items in several different subject areas. If you administer a good standardized test, look through it to see if there are new ideas. For example, many good standardized tests now use the testing format referred to as an interpretive exercise. Such interpretive exercises use the multiple choice format to test higher order abilities much more efficiently than can be accomplished in an essay format. Many of the exercises in the Workbook that accompanies this textbook are interpretive exercises.

In designing your classroom tests, find the most valid way to measure the outcome you're interested in observing. Then devise good items within that format.

QUESTIONNAIRES

As its name implies, a questionnaire is a device which enables the respondent to answer questions. In this section, the term will refer to any data-collecting instrument, other than an achievement or ability test, where the respondent directly supplies his or her own answers to a set of questions. This definition is not intended to be technical; it is merely stated for convenience. Other sections in this chapter discuss achievement tests, interviews, and observation techniques.

The answers the respondent will give on a questionnaire are determined by (1) the nature of the questions, and (2) his or her reactions to these questions. Your job is to design the questionnaire in such a way as to facilitate rather than impede the respondent's ability to provide exactly the information you want. In the case of specific demographic or factual information, writing a good questionnaire item is largely a matter of using language clearly and concisely. However, if you want the respondent to reveal an attitude, personality trait, or other internalized characteristic, the job becomes much more difficult. In this case you have to write the item in such a way as to help the respondent reveal what you really want him to reveal, rather than revealing some alternate characteristic, such as how eagerly he wants to please you or how he feels society would want him to answer the question.

Figure 6–1 presents six ways to ask essentially the same question. Note that the way each question is stated imposes a somewhat different task upon the respondent, and therefore the answer obtained by each item is likely to be somewhat different.

Question 1 asks the respondent to make up her own list of sports. This has the advantage of imposing no artificial constraints upon her selection. If we supplied her with even an extremely long list, it would still be possible that we would leave off her favorite sport. A major disadvantage of this way of asking the question is that we give the respondent little information about the framework within which we want her to respond. For example, she has to make up her own definition of what a sport is. It's possible (and quite likely) that different persons answering this same question will define the term differently. Is jogging a sport? Perhaps someone would consider jogging to be a sport if done with someone else, but merely an exercise if done alone. And what about exercise? Am I engaging in a sport if I do fifty sit-ups every morning as soon as I get out of bed? How about chess—is that a sport? A closely related problem is that some people would focus only on sports in which they've participated during the last month or so, and they might ignore favorite sports which occur during a different season. Indeed, it is possible that a person might enjoy skiing immensely, but has never had a chance to participate in it since he moved to Hawaii. What is he supposed to put down? Many of these problems could be solved by rephrasing the question more carefully: "List the five sports in which you would most like to participate, if given a chance. In writing this list, consider a sport to be any athletic activity in which a person participates for enjoyable competition. Be sure to consider all possible sports from all seasons of the year." This would solve some problems, but others would still emerge. The major difficulty with open-ended questions is that different respondents are likely to supply different frameworks for answering the questions; and if our intention is to compare these different respondents to one another, we need a common framework.

Questions 2 through 6 solve this framework problem by presenting a list of sports. Since language is not perfectly precise, it's still possible that respondents will understand the nature of their tasks differently, but the likelihood of this happening in Questions 2 through 6 is considerably less than in even the revised version of Number 1. The major difficulty with these questions, however, is that the respondents' favorite sports may not even be on the list. This problem can be partially solved by lengthening the list, but this has other difficulties. A longer list makes the task more time consuming, and it adds complexity. Just imagine Question 3 with fifty sports matched up in a two-by-two pairing! Even if the list is lengthened, there's still the possibility that a favorite sport will be omitted. Adding an additional space marked "other (specify) ____"is not a perfect solution, because this involves the same sort of problems inherent in Question 1.

Question 2 differs from Questions 4 and 6 in that it requires a ranking of the sports. A person who likes both tennis and volleyball for instance, has to choose between one or the other. There's a certain validity in requiring this forced choice, because in fact most people probably would prefer one over the other. On the other hand, what if this same person doesn't care at all about bowling or jogging? Is it valid to force the person to decide which he is least unconcerned about? Another problem with the ranking method is that it is quite difficult to rank large numbers of items. Young children cannot handle more than 3 to 5 items to rank. Even sophisticated adults dislike being asked to rank more than 9 or 10 items.

Question 3 is similar in principle to Question 2. In a sense, the ranking task is simplified, because the respondent never has to consider more than two sports at a time. If a person is logically consistent, the rank ordering resulting from Number 3 would be the same as the ordering derived from Number 2. A disadvantage of this approach is that respondents often find it irritating to have to make so many comparisons. Since it is necessary to match up each of the sports with every other sport, the number of comparisons becomes quite large as the number of sports increases. For example, if 25 sports were included on the list, it would be necessary to have 300 comparisons. For 50 sports, 1225 comparisons would be needed.

Question 4 has the advantage of not requiring the artificial forced choices found in Numbers 2 and 3. In addition, it's usually not considered fatiguing or frustrating to go through even a very long list like this and mark choices. The respondent simply checks what she likes and passes by those she doesn't like. Of course, a severe

1. List the five sports you enjoy participating in the most.
   a.
   b.
   c.
   d.
   e.

2. Rank the following sports in order of preference. Give a ranking of "1" to the sport you would like to participate in the most, "2" to the one you'd next like to participate in, etc.
   _____ tennis
   _____ bowling
   _____ baseball
   _____ basketball
   _____ volleyball
   _____ swimming
   _____ jogging

3. In each of the following pairs of sports, circle the *one* that you would prefer to participate in. You should circle 24 sports altogether—one from each pair.

tennis-bowling	volleyball-basketball	swimming-basketball
basketball-jogging	swimming-baseball	tennis-basketball
jogging-tennis	bowling-basketball	volleyball-baseball
swimming-jogging	baseball-basketball	bowling-jogging
jogging-baseball	volleyball-swimming	tennis-swimming
bowling-volleyball	swimming-baseball	swimming-jogging
volleyball-jogging	tennis-baseball	tennis-baseball
baseball-bowling	volleyball-tennis	jogging-basketball

4. Check all of the following sports that you enjoy participating in:
   _____ tennis
   _____ bowling
   _____ baseball
   _____ basketball
   _____ volleyball
   _____ swimming
   _____ jogging

5. Rate each of the sports below on the following scale:
   1—I enjoy participating in this sport very much.
   2—I enjoy participating in this sport.
   3—I'm rather indifferent about this sport.
   4—I dislike participating in this sport.
   5—I hate participating in this sport.

   _____ tennis
   _____ bowling
   _____ baseball
   _____ basketball
   _____ volleyball
   _____ swimming
   _____ jogging

6. Assume that you have to spend all of your recreation time for the next year participating in some combination of the following sports. Indicate the percentage of time you would spend in each sport. (The total should add up to 100%.)
   _____ % tennis
   _____ % bowling
   _____ % baseball
   _____ % basketball
   _____ % volleyball
   _____ % swimming
   _____ % jogging

FIGURE 6–1. Six Ways to Determine Sports Preference.

disadvantage of this approach is that from the results it's impossible to tell which sports are liked more than the others. All of the "likes" look the same.

Question 5 is similar to Number 4, except that it allows the respondent to state a degree of preference. (Actually, Question 4 is just Question 5 with only two choices: 1 = like, and 2 = dislike.) It takes only slightly more effort to fill out this sort of ranking, with a lot of tied ranks. However, allowing tied ranks (for example, by allowing a respondent to rate all three of his favorite sports "like very much"), often gives a false impression, because there probably *is* some difference in the rater's actual preference.

Question 6 tries to get the best of all worlds. It enables the respondent to rank the sports (by giving greater amounts of time to more preferred sports), while deliberately allowing ties if the respondent wishes (by giving an equal amount of time to each of two sports), and while allowing her to give different weights to different rankings. A serious shortcoming, however, is that this sort of rating is a complex activity, requiring patience and intelligence. Young children and even unmotivated adults will not use it to its full potential. A further problem which occurs specifically with regard to applying this format to sports is that a person might spend eight hours a week jogging (which he does not particularly like) in order to train for his Saturday tennis match (which he dearly loves). This last problem is less likely to occur when this technique is applied to nonsport activities.

In summary, each of the formats in Figure 6–1 has both advantages and disadvantages. The disadvantages can often be minimized. For example, if it is necessary to have a respondent rank 15 items (as in the Question 2 format), it's possible to give helpful directions to the respondent. For example, the instructions might say, "It's often a good idea to find your two or three top choices, and mark these. Then find your two or three bottom choices, and mark these. Continue until you have ranked all the items." An even more helpful idea for younger respondents is to have each of the items written on cards; it is easier to stack cards in order of preference than it is to rank ideas which cannot be concretely manipulated. A similar idea with regard to the Question 6 format is to give the respondent a certain amount of play money and have her put amounts into different envelopes, corresponding to the amount she would like to spend on each activity.

Aside from the advantages and disadvantages of each format, it is important for the tester to know what the answers actually mean. Assume that a physical education teacher is trying to promote jogging among his students. The results of Question 1 would enable him to conclude that "35% of the students spontaneously mentioned jogging as one of their favorite sports. This was more than any other sport." Question 2 would enable him to conclude that "jogging received an average ranking of 3.5 among the seven sports listed. This ranked it third among the seven." Question 3 would enable him to say, "Jogging received an average of 2.5 out of a possible 6 choices. Three sports ranked higher." Using Question 4, he could say that "80% chose jogging as a sport they would like to participate in. This was more than any other sport." With Question 5, he could find that "jogging received a ranking of 2.7 on a scale of 1 to 5. Two other sports were rated higher." Using Question 6, he could discover that "the respondents were willing to spend an average of 30% of their time on jogging. This was the highest amount for any sport on the list." It seems apparent that there are subtle differences in these statements. In some cases, these subtle distinctions may not make any difference to the tester, and in such cases the decision about which format to use would be based on which one could be used most efficiently. In other cases, the tester will want to focus on the nuances uncovered more effectively by one format than the others; and then the decision will be to use that format as effectively as possible. As will be pointed out later in this chapter, many of the shortcomings of questionnaire strategies can be overcome by supplementing them with data from nonquestionnaire techniques. You don't have to limit yourself to any single method.

Open-Ended vs. Structured Formats

When we were examining Figure 6–1, it was obvious that Question 1 differed more from the other five than these others did among themselves. This was because Question 1 is an open-ended question, whereas the others all used a structured format. The major advantage of the open-ended format over the structured format is that in the open-ended format it is the respondent himself or herself who takes the initiative in deciding what answer to supply; whereas with structured formats the respondent merely selects from among answers supplied by the writer of the questionnaire. On the other hand, the structured format has the advantage of requiring all the respondents to answer within the same framework; with the open-ended format it is possible for two respondents to adopt such divergent frameworks that it is hardly accurate to view their responses as replies to the same question.

Let us pursue this difference a little further. For our example, we will use one of the most frequent situations in which the teacher uses questionnaires—course evaluation. An open-ended format might consist of asking the students to write on a sheet of paper how they felt about the course. With a structured format, the teacher might come in with a set of 25 questions and ask the students to rate each on an agree-disagree scale. The type of information the teacher will get could differ considerably, depending on which method is used. For example, what would the teacher conclude if three students out of the twenty-five in her class indicated that "the teacher has an irritable habit of talking about her own family too much." On an open-ended questionnaire, respondents can only put down what comes into their minds. How can this teacher tell how all the other students in the class felt about this problem? How likely is it that another student in the same class will write down on an open-ended format, "It doesn't bother me one way or the other whether the teacher talks about her family or not"? Not very likely. Chances are, the topic would not even enter this respondent's mind. The students in this example are all responding to their own separate questionnaires, and it is impossible to know what the consensus is on most questions.

An alternative would be to use a structured format. The teacher could come in with her 25 questions, and let the students respond to each. Then she would know how each one of them felt about each of the topics on the questionnaire. The trouble with this approach is that there may be things on the students' minds which she didn't happen to put on the questionnaire. She might feel quite good about her performance, because she did quite well at the things *she* was concerned about; whereas the students might be quite dissatisfied, because she did poorly at things *they* were concerned about but which did not appear on the teacher-designed questionnaire.

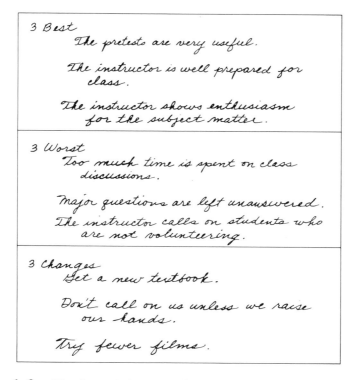

FIGURE **6–2.** The Open-Ended Part of a Two-Step Procedure to Obtain a Valid Course Evaluation from Students.

One way to solve the dilemma this teacher faces would be to give the structured questionnaire and ask the students to add additional comments at the end. This is an inadequate solution, because the open-ended part of the questionnaire faces the same problems of interpretation as a completely open-ended format. A better solution to the dilemma is presented in Figures 6–2 and 6–3. The teacher follows a two-step process. First she asks the students to write down the three things they like best, the three things they like least, and three changes they'd like to see in the course. She takes these open-ended responses with her; and from these responses she generates the questionnaire. Part of the questionnaire generated in this manner is presented in Figure 6–3. The teacher next asks all the students to respond to this structured questionnaire. She therefore has a questionnaire generated by the students (the major advantage of the open-ended format) which is completed by all the students (the major advantage of the structured format).

Similar strategies are useful in developing questionnaires for purposes other than classroom evaluation.

Computer Generated Questionnaires

One of the advantages of structured questionnaires is that they are easily adapted to computerized scoring. Specific advantages of such computerization will be explored

---

Indicate how strongly you agree or disagree with each of the following statements. Use the following scale.

1 = Strongly agree
2 = Agree
3 = (In between)
4 = Disagree
5 = Strongly disagree

1. _____ The required texts are interesting and practical.
2. _____ The point system adapts easily to individual needs.
3. _____ The class is too long.
4. _____ There is too much generalization and not enough application to specific situations.
5. _____ There is not enough variety during classes.
6. _____ The pretests serve a useful review function.
7. _____ The instructor is well prepared for classes.
8. _____ The instructor shows an interest in the students.
9. _____ The instructor shows enthusiasm for the subject inappropriately.
10. _____ The instructor calls on students who are not volunteering.
11. _____ The instructor tries to cram too much into each class session.
12. _____ Too much time is spent on class discussions.
13. _____ Major questions are sometimes left unanswered.
14. _____ The instructor allows an isolated individual or small group of individuals to side-track discussion.
15. _____ The outline and assignments supplied at the beginning of the year are useful.
16. _____ Objectives for individual units are useful.
17. _____ Students should be required to submit questions in writing rather than merely raising hand in class.
18. _____ The course is geared toward practical applications.
19. _____ There is too much emphasis on *elementary* level work.
20. _____ Work turned in by students should be discussed in class.
21. _____ The class has an informal atmosphere.
22. _____ Too much time is required on out-of-class activities.
23. _____ The unit on educational research was irrelevant.
24. _____ The guest lecturer on learning disabilities was good.

FIGURE 6–3. Part of the Structured Half of a Two-Step Procedure to Obtain a Valid Course Evaluation from Students.

in Chapter 12. Figures 6–4 through 6–6 demonstrate a technique for using the computer to simplify the process of questionnaire usage. This Cafeteria format was developed by the Center for Instructional Services at Purdue University. Figure 6–4 shows part of a form the instructor uses to select the items he wants on his course evaluation questionnaire. (The mark-sense sheet on which he would enter these coded numbers is not presented.) This procedure enables the instructor to select up to 40 items which he feels are uniquely adapted to his course. Figure 6–5 shows that the questionnaire is generated by the computer from the instructor's request. Figure 6–6 presents the results of one such evaluation. The results include the number of persons who gave each response, the median (average) response based on a 1 to 5 scale, and a percentile which indicates how the instructor compares with other instructors at the university. Further programming of the computer would enable the instructor to do a cross-tabulation. For example, he could find out what percentage of the students who thought he had clearly stated objectives also felt the course was intellectually fulfilling.

CAFETERIA is a computer-assisted, course and instructor appraisal system developed and administered by the Measurement and Research Center, Purdue University. CAFETERIA is intended to serve faculty and all information pertaining to individual instructors, courses and departments is treated confidentially.

Directions

To initiate CAFETERIA service, an instructor should obtain an *item selection form* for each class to be evaluated. From the following 200-item catalog, the instructor may select *up to 40 items.* Selections are recorded on the item selection form by darkening the numbered space which corresponds to the number of the desired catalog item. In addition to the selected catalog items, each rating form will contain demographic questions and 5 University core items which are added automatically when the rating forms are printed. The University core is not considered part of the 40 items an instructor is permitted to choose.

If your department has requested that you select certain specific items as part of the 40 items you may choose, commonly referred to as departmental core, please mark those items on your item selection form.

Item Catalog

Clarity and Effectiveness of Presentations
001 I understand easily what my instructor is saying.
002 My instructor displays a clear understanding of course topics.
003 My instructor is able to simplify difficult materials.
004 My instructor explains experiments and/or assignments clearly.
005 Difficult topics are structured in easily understood ways.
006 My instructor has an effective style of presentation.
007 My instructor seems well-prepared for class.
008 My instructor talks at a pace suitable for maximum comprehension.
009 My instructor speaks audibly and clearly.
010 My instructor draws and explains diagrams effectively.
011 My instructor writes legibly on the blackboard.
012 My instructor has no distracting peculiarities.

Student Interest/Involvement in Learning
013 My instructor makes learning easy and interesting.
014 My instructor holds the attention of the class.
015 My instructor senses when students are bored.
016 My instructor stimulates interest in the course.
017 My instructor displays enthusiasm when teaching.
018 This course supplies me with an effective range of challenges.
019 In this course, many methods are used to involve me in learning.
020 My instructor makes me feel involved with this course.
021 In this course, I always felt challenged and motivated to learn.
022 My instructor motivates me to do further independent study.
023 This course motivates me to take additional related courses.
024 This course has been intellectually fulfilling for me.

Broadening Student Outlook
025 My instructor has stimulated my thinking.
026 My instructor has provided many challenging new viewpoints.
027 My instructor teaches one to value the viewpoint of others.
028 This course caused me to reconsider many of my former attitudes.
029 In this course, I have learned to value new viewpoints.
030 This course fosters respect for new points of view.
031 This course stretched and broadened my views greatly.
032 This course has effectively challenged me to think.
033 The class meetings helped me see other points of view.
034 This course develops the creative ability of students.
035 My instructor encourages student creativity.

FIGURE **6-4.** Page 1 of Cafeteria Item Catalog for Course Evaluation

Class	School	Sex	Expected Grade	Course Required

Please read each statement carefully, then select one of these five alternatives: Strongly Agree (SA), Agree (A), Undecided (U), Disagree (D), Strongly Disagree (SD).

My instructor has an effective style of presentation.	SA A U D SD
This course supplies me with an effective range of challenges.	SA A U D SD
My instructor motivates me to do further independent study.	SA A U D SD
My instructor has provided many challenging new viewpoints.	SA A U D SD
In this course I have learned to value new viewpoints.	SA A U D SD
My instructor emphasizes relationships between and among topics.	SA A U D SD
My instructor emphasizes conceptual understanding of material.	SA A U D SD
This course builds understanding of concepts and principles.	SA A U D SD
My instructor is actively helpful when students have problems.	SA A U D SD
My instructor suggests specific ways I can improve.	SA A U D SD
My instructor returns papers quickly enough to benefit me.	SA A U D SD
My instructor adjusts to fit individual abilities and interests.	SA A U D SD
I am free to express and explain my own views in class.	SA A U D SD
I feel free to challenge my instructor's ideas in class.	SA A U D SD
My instructor relates to me as an individual.	SA A U D SD
My instructor readily maintains rapport with this class.	SA A U D SD
The objectives of this course were clearly explained to me.	SA A U D SD
I was able to set and achieve some of my own goals.	SA A U D SD
This course contributes significantly to my professional growth.	SA A U D SD
There is sufficient time in class for questions and discussions.	SA A U D SD
This course provides an opportunity to learn from other students.	SA A U D SD
My final grade will accurately reflect my overall performance.	SA A U D SD

FIGURE **6–5.** Sample Cafeteria Format Evaluation.

Summary Regarding Questionnaires

There are several other specific strategies for generating, administering, and scoring questionnaires. For example, sociometric techniques, the semantic differential, and the Q-sort are all examples of specific techniques for allowing respondents to provide information. These more specialized techniques are not discussed in this book. If you need more detailed information, the reference to Kerlinger in the Annotated Bibliography will supply you with useful information on such strategies. The important thing to remember in designing a questionnaire is to determine what it is you want the respondents to tell you, and then make it as likely as possible that the questionnaire will actually enable them to provide that information. The general strategies and specific examples presented in this section should help you accomplish this goal.

INTERVIEWS

Like a questionnaire, an interview is designed to enable the respondent to answer questions. The interview, however, differs from the ordinary questionnaire because of the personal presence of the interviewer while the respondent gives his or her answers. This personal presence of the interviewer has both advantages and disadvantages. One of the disadvantages is that this one-to-one approach takes much longer than an ordinary questionnaire. Another disadvantage is that the personal presence of the

```
STUDENT DEMOGRAPHICS -          A604 ED VOCKELL  ED 570-51              01/25/78

      CLASS              SCHOOL            SEX          EXPECTED          COURSE
      ---------          ---------         -------      GRADE             REQUIRED
      FRESHMAN   1       AGR      0        FEMALE  26   ----------        ----------
      SOPHOMORE  0       BAS      0        MALE     4   A/PASS   26       YES    26
      JUNIOR     0       HOME EC  1                     B         3       NO      3
      SENIOR     4       HESS     2                     C         0
      GRADUATE  28       COMM CLGE 2                    D         0
      OTHER      0       GRAD    26                     F/FAIL    0
```

CATALOG NUMBER		SA (5)	A (4)	U (3)	D (2)	SD (1)	MEDIAN	PER CENTILE
3	1. MY INSTRUCTOR IS ABLE TO SIMPLIFY DIFFICULT MATERIALS.	23	10	1	0	0	4.8	96
6	2. MY INSTRUCTOR HAS AN EFFECTIVE STYLE OF PRESENTATION.	20	11	3	0	0	4.7	90
7	3. MY INSTRUCTOR SEEMS WELL-PREPARED FOR CLASS.	24	9	1	0	0	4.8	84
8	4. MY INSTRUCTOR TALKS AT A PACE SUITABLE FOR MAXIMUM COMPREHENSION.	8	12	6	7	1	3.8	21
10	5. MY INSTRUCTOR DRAWS AND EXPLAINS DIAGRAMS EFFECTIVELY.	15	16	2	1	0	4.4	79
12	6. MY INSTRUCTOR HAS NO DISTRACTING PECULIARITIES.	7	15	5	7	0	3.8	21
13	7. MY INSTRUCTOR MAKES LEARNING EASY AND INTERESTING.	22	8	2	2	0	4.7	89
14	8. MY INSTRUCTOR HOLDS THE ATTENTION OF THE CLASS.	22	9	3	0	0	4.7	91
15	9. MY INSTRUCTOR SENSES WHEN STUDENTS ARE BORED.	20	8	6	0	0	4.7	98
17	10. MY INSTRUCTOR DISPLAYS ENTHUSIASM WHEN TEACHING.	28	6	0	0	0	4.9	94
21	11. IN THIS COURSE, I ALWAYS FELT CHALLENGED AND MOTIVATED TO LEARN.	9	17	6	2	0	4.0	74
24	12. THIS COURSE HAS BEEN INTELLECTUALLY FULFILLING FOR ME.	13	12	5	4	0	4.2	67
25	13. MY INSTRUCTOR HAS STIMULATED MY THINKING.	12	17	3	2	0	4.2	68
30	14. THIS COURSE FOSTERS RESPECT FOR NEW POINTS OF VIEW.	16	14	3	1	0	4.4	79
35	15. MY INSTRUCTOR ENCOURAGES STUDENT CREATIVITY.	20	10	2	2	0	4.7	78
44	16. MY INSTRUCTOR IS ACTIVELY HELPFUL WHEN STUDENTS HAVE PROBLEMS.	20	10	2	2	0	4.7	77
45	17. MY INSTRUCTOR RECOGNIZES WHEN SOME STUDENTS FAIL TO COMPREHEND.	13	16	3	1	0	4.3	89
51	18. MY INSTRUCTOR IS READILY AVAILABLE FOR CONSULTATION.	18	11	3	1	1	4.6	82
56	19. EXAMS ARE USED TO HELP ME FIND MY STRENGTHS AND WEAKNESSES.	21	10	2	1	0	4.7	99
58	20. THIS COURSE SHOWS A SENSITIVITY TO INDIVIDUAL INTERESTS/ABILITIES	14	13	5	1	0	4.3	69
61	21. MY INSTRUCTOR TAILORS THIS COURSE TO HELP MANY KINDS OF STUDENTS.	17	11	4	2	0	4.5	90
68	22. I AM FREE TO EXPRESS AND EXPLAIN MY OWN VIEWS IN CLASS.	22	7	3	1	0	4.8	86
79	23. THIS INSTRUCTOR ENCOURAGES DIVERGENT THINKING.	20	10	2	2	0	4.7	86
81	24. THIS COURSE HAS CLEARLY STATED OBJECTIVES.	29	4	1	0	0	4.9	98
84	25. I UNDERSTAND WHAT IS EXPECTED OF ME IN THIS COURSE.	29	5	0	0	0	4.9	99
90	26. THIS COURSE MATERIAL IS PERTINENT TO MY PROFESSIONAL TRAINING.	21	11	2	0	0	4.7	80
105	27. MY INSTRUCTOR DEVELOPS CLASSROOM DISCUSSION SKILLFULLY.	15	16	3	0	0	4.4	84
114	28. EXAMS ARE FAIR.	30	3	1	0	0	4.9	99
131	29. LENGTH AND DIFFICULTY OF ASSIGNED READINGS ARE REASONABLE.	19	13	1	0	0	4.6	94
151	30. MEDIA (FILMS, TV, ETC.) USED IN THIS COURSE ARE WELL CHOSEN.	20	11	3	0	0	4.7	96
CORE 1	31. MY INSTRUCTOR MOTIVATES ME TO DO MY BEST WORK.	14	13	6	1	0	4.3	85
CORE 2	32. MY INSTRUCTOR EXPLAINS DIFFICULT MATERIAL CLEARLY.	16	15	3	0	0	4.4	85
CORE 3	33. COURSE ASSIGNMENTS ARE INTERESTING AND STIMULATING.	15	12	6	1	0	4.3	90
CORE 4	34. OVERALL, THIS COURSE IS AMONG THE BEST I HAVE EVER TAKEN.	15	13	3	3	0	4.3	87
CORE 5	35. OVERALL, THIS INSTRUCTOR IS AMONG THE BEST TEACHERS I HAVE KNOWN.	18	10	5	1	0	4.6	84

```
       REPORT BASED ON  34 STUDENTS.        01/25/78      COPYRIGHT 1975 PRF.
```

FIGURE 6-6. Sample Printout from Cafeteria Evaluation.

interviewer often reduces the respondent's spontaneity. Anonymity is gone, and so the willingness to be completely frank and honest might be reduced.

The major advantage of the interview over the ordinary questionnaire lies in its flexibility. For example, it is possible to combine both open-ended and structured formats in a single interview. This could be done, for instance, by asking the respondent an open-ended question and then following up with one of several different sets of structured questions, depending on the answer to the first question. In addition, it is possible for either the interviewer or the respondent to ask for clarifications.

There are two basic types of interviews, exploratory and structured interviews. An exploratory interview is designed to elicit good ideas for subsequent data collection. It is informal and quite unstructured. The researcher merely asks leading questions, notes the answers, and decides on the basis of one question what to ask next. Such exploratory interviews are usually of little direct usefulness for evaluation and decision making purposes. In fact, it is difficult even to make a comparison between two different persons' responses to such interviews, because in many cases the two don't even answer the same set of questions. For the exploratory interview to provide useful data, it usually has to be followed by a more structured technique. This follow-up could be a structured interview, but it could also be a questionnaire or an observation strategy.

A section from such a structured interview is shown in Figure 6–7. This is part of a 19-page schedule.[1] This interview schedule was developed after a series of exploratory interviews. The schedule was devised in such a way that fifteen people were in the field administering it at one time, and yet the researcher had reasonable assurance that all of them were gathering the same sort of information. This assurance was derived from the fact that the schedule had been carefully devised to take into consideration any possible answer which could be given. At places where unusual answers *could* come up, the interviewers were instructed simply to make a note of the unusual event and continue or stop as appropriate.

Notice that with the interview schedule in Figure 6–7, the interviewer has to do very little writing during the interview. As much as possible, he merely listens to what the respondent says and circles appropriate items. Such pre-coding is an important feature of a good interview schedule. Respondents usually do not enjoy pausing during the interview while the interviewer slowly and deliberately takes a verbatim transcription of every word they utter. Also notice that the interviewer hands the respondent a card when he asks the second question. This is a good idea, since it avoids both the ambiguity of requiring the respondents to memorize a list as the interviewer reads it to her and the uncomfortableness which often results when the respondent actually looks at the schedule with the interviewer while they fill it out jointly.

This 19-page questionnaire was easily completed in 20 to 40 minutes by pet owners and in less than 5 minutes by non pet owners. The variations in time occurred primarily because of differences in how much the respondents felt like elaborating upon details during the interviews. The interviewers asked each question, noted the responses, and then did whatever the schedule instructed them to do next. Such structured interviews provide useful information upon which to base intelligent comparisons and decisions.

A major disadvantage of the interview compared to the simple questionnaire is that the interview is much more time consuming. If you are going to have fifty persons answer a set of questions, you can usually have the entire group fill out a questionnaire in the time it takes to do a personal interview with just one or two people from the same group. If there is an advantage to be gained by spending the additional time, then do not hesitate to use the interview format; otherwise the more efficient questionnaire format may be desirable. Therefore, interviews are more appropriate (1) if the questions cannot be easily asked and answered and they must be accompanied by a personalized explanation, (2) if the nature of a follow-up question can be determined only after the respondent has answered a first question, or (3) if it is unlikely that the respondents will return the questionnaire if left on their own. In most other situations, the simple questionnaire is preferable.

A second major disadvantage of the interview is that the interviewer becomes a part of the instrument, in the sense that the respondent reacts to the interviewer as well as to the questions he asks. Anonymity is lost, and this loss can result in a reduction in spontaneity, frankness, and honesty. In addition, such irrelevant factors as the physical appearance of the interviewer can interfere with some types of interviews.

---

[1]*Schedule* is the term applied to the written questionnaire the interviewer uses to conduct the interview.

Section Two: In this section I have a series of questions about pets.

1. Do you own any pets such as dogs, cats, rabbits, gerbils, birds or fish?

   YES . . . . . . 1⃝ (Ask A & C)   NO 2   (Ask B)

   A. What animals do you own?
      What others do you own?

   B. During the last 3 years have
      you owned any pets?

   Code all animals mentioned; then
   for each type, ask:

   Yes _____ No_____ (Go to next sec.)
   **
   If Yes, ask: WHY do you no longer
                have these pets?

   How many ___*1*___ do you own?

   RECORD RESPONSE verbatim:

   Type of animal (code) No. of animals

   _____

Dog	1	① 2 3 4 5 6 7 8
Cat	2	1 2 3 4 5 6 7 8
Rabbit	3	1 2 3 4 5 6 7 8
Gerbil	4	1 2 3 4 5 6 7 8
Bird	5	1 2 3 4 5 6 7 8
Snake	6	1 2 3 4 5 6 7 8
Fish	7	1 2 3 4 5 6 7 8
Other		
(Specify)	8	1 2 3 4 5 6 7 8

   Then code all that apply:

Too costly to keep	1
Pet needed more care than expected	2
Pet was noisy, destroyed property	3
Pet attacked people (bit, dangerous to children)	4
Pet was very sick	5
Pet was very old	6
Not enough space to keep	7
Pet died	8
Other (Specify) _____	9

   C. During the last 3 years have you
      owned any pets which you no
      longer have?

   YES _____   NO   X

   IF YES, GO TO **

2. This card lists some reasons people give for owning pets and small animals. Of the things listed on this card, which come closest to your reasons for owning a pet/pets? PROBE AS DIRECTED.

   IN COLUMN A, CODE "1" FOR ALL REASONS MENTIONED: CODE "2" for reasons not mentioned. Then, if more than one reason is mentioned, ask which of the given reasons is the most/more important and code response in column B. (If more than one reason is given in A, ASK: "WHICH ONE OF THESE REASONS WOULD YOU SAY IS THE MOST IMPORTANT TO YOU?" and code.)

		A YES	NO	B Most Important
HAND	a. companionship	①	2	1
CARD	b. recreation (sport, hunting?)	1	②	1
1	c. protection	1	②	1
	d. educational for children	①	2	1
	e. enjoy animals	①	2	①
	f. no special reason	1	②	1
	g. other (Specify)	1	②	1

   GO ON TO NEXT PAGE

FIGURE **6–7.** Example of a Structured Interview Format.

For example, the typical person on the street might respond differently to an interview regarding racial prejudice if the questions are being asked by a six-foot-four-inch, militant-appearing black man than if the same questions were asked by a five-foot-four-inch, gentle-looking white coed.

OBSERVATIONAL TECHNIQUES

The techniques discussed so far ask the respondents to write down or to describe the outcome variables occurring within them. With the observational techniques, however, an observer watches someone else's behavior, judges that behavior in some way, and records this judgment. Therefore, it differs from the strategies discussed previously in that the respondents are much more remotely involved in actually recording their scores. There are two manners in which an observation can be conducted. First, the observer can merely look for the occurrence or non occurrence of some designated behavior. Second, the observer can make some attempt to evaluate (rate) the quality of the performance she is observing. These two strategies will be discussed separately.

Observing the occurrence or non-occurrence of a behavior. The first of these strategies has become quite important because of the recent emphasis on behavior modification and data-based instruction. It is important to note, however, that the use of behavioral observations is quite important, even if a teacher has no urge to implement a behavior modification program. With this first strategy, the observer identifies a specific behavior and watches during a designated time period to see if that behavior occurs. In making such observations, it is often useful to distinguish between discrete and continuous behaviors.

A discrete behavior is one which can be counted. Examples include a child raising her hand in class, a player swinging at a bad pitch in a baseball game, a teacher making a sarcastic comment. Such events can be counted over a designated period of time, and then the rate per unit of time can be computed. For example, it would be possible to say that a child raised her hand an average of 3.1 times per hour, that a child swung at bad pitches about three out of ten times, or that a teacher made an average of 49.6 sarcastic comments per hour. Discrete behaviors are quite easy to observe. It is merely a matter of defining the behavior clearly enough and then counting how often that behavior occurs.

A continuous behavior is one which cannot be meaningfully recorded by merely counting it. Attending behavior, on-task behavior, and out-of-seat behaviors are all examples of continuous behaviors. It is not meaningful to count how often these occur. For example, if one child sat down at 8:30 and paid attention continuously until 12:00, this child would get credit for attending once, if we merely counted the behavior. On the other hand, a child who was continuously distracted might get a count of attending 95 times, if we recorded each time he started paying attention. Rather than counting the occurrence of such behaviors, it is necessary to determine a number of equal sized time intervals, to observe the child during these intervals, and to determine the percentage of time intervals during which the behavior occurs. A child could be defined as attending, for example, either if he paid attention during the whole period, if he paid attention at all, or if he paid attention according to some other criteria. It is up to the observer or researcher to set the standards. Based on such observations, it might be possible to conclude that a child was paying attention during 35% of the intervals. An example of a continuous-behavior recording sheet is provided in Figure 6–8.

Such observation techniques will be reliable to the extent that they are clearly defined. It is often a good idea to check the interobserver reliability of the observers, using the guidelines described in Chapter 4.

Name of child ___Jane Doe_____ Date ___March 14, 1980___

Time Started ____9:10 a.m.____

Time Finished ___9:19 a.m.____

Directions: 1. Watch the child for 10 seconds.
2. During the next five seconds, record whether or not he was out-of-seat at all during that period. (Consider the child out-of-seat if his/her posterior is not in contact with the chair.)
3. Repeat this process until you have done this for ten minutes.

X = In seat   O = Out of seat

MINUTE				
1	X	X	X	O
2	O	O	O	O
3	O	O	X	X
4	X	X	O	O
5	X	O	X	O
6	X	X	X	X
7	X	X	O	O
8	O	O	O	O
9	X	X	X	X
10	X	X	O	O

Total number of intervals ___40___
Number of intervals in seat ___21___   Percentage in seat ___53%___
Number of intervals out of seat ___19___   Percentage out of seat ___47%___

FIGURE **6–8.**   An Example of a Recording Sheet for Observing Continuous Behavior.

Rating the Quality of the Behavior Observed

A rating scale differs from the observational techniques described previously in that the observer attempts to assign a qualitative value to the observed behavior. Some examples of rating scales are shown on Figure 6–9. Question 1 is one of the simplest sorts of rating scales. All the rater has to do is write a number in the space provided before each behavior. Question 2 is also quite simple. The rater merely circles one of the numbers. Question 3 presents the same questions in a graphic format. The lower numbered questions are easier to devise, whereas the higher numbered ones are often easier for a rater to employ with little practice.

The reliability of the rating scale can be estimated using the interscorer method described in Chapter 3. Rating scales will be reliable to the extent that they refer to observable behaviors with clearly defined criteria for the various quality levels. Since the rating scale involves a certain amount of subjectivity, however, the reliability of such scales will usually be lower than the reliability of the purely observational strategies discussed previously. However, the question of *validity* must also be taken

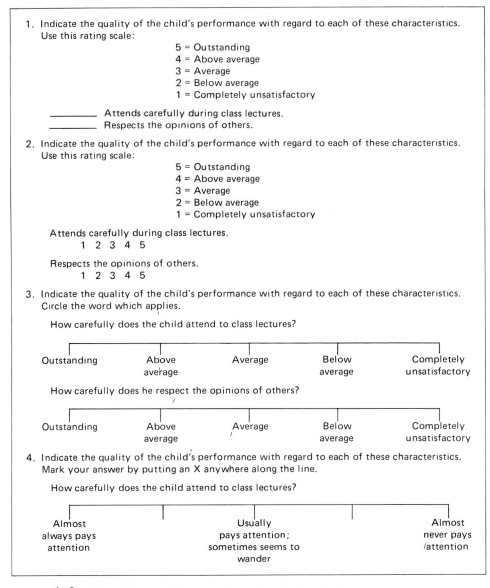

FIGURE **6–9.**   Four Ways to Phrase an Item in a Rating Scale.

into consideration. For example, is it possible to consider a person to be either paying attention or not paying attention? Are there not varying degrees of attention? If there *are* varying degrees of attention, then concluding that he received an average rating of 3.1 on a 1 to 5 scale during the past week is more useful than stating that he attended during 35% of the intervals. As with all measuring instruments, the important consideration is to determine what it is that you want to know, and then find a way to measure that outcome.

The reliability of rating scales can be increased by becoming familiar with and trying to minimize certain rating errors. One set of such errors is referred to as *personal bias errors*. Some people rate everyone high. They display a *generosity error*. Others rate everyone low. This is referred to as a *severity error*. Still others have a tendency to rate everyone about average and this is referred to as a *central tendency error*. Another type of error is referred to as the *halo effect*. When this error is operating, it leads a rater to rate specific traits of an individual on the basis of an overall impression of that person. For example, a teacher might rate a student as extremely motivated or intelligent because the student is a generally friendly person rather than because the student has shown any degree of motivation or intelligence. By knowing about these errors and instructing raters specifically to avoid them, their influence on reliability can be reduced.

Concluding Remarks Regarding Observational Techniques

The discussion in this section has focused on observing *people*. It is also possible to observe *products*. For example, it would be possible to examine a sample of a student's writing to observe how many times per 100 words she commits a spelling error or to rate her on the quality of her penmanship. The following section, dealing with unobtrusive measures, will provide some useful suggestions on how to increase the validity of observational techniques by using some unusual approaches.

UNOBTRUSIVE MEASUREMENT

A potential problem with most of the popular data-collection techniques arises because the person about whom data is being collected often knows that this data collection is taking place. In some cases this awareness makes no difference. In other instances, however, the person whose behavior is being measured reacts to the measurement. The data collector, therefore, is often uncertain whether the measuring device is collecting information on the real outcome variable or on a version of the outcome variable that has been altered because of the person's reaction to the measurement device. The alterations in the observed outcome variables that result from such reactions are obviously a significant source of invalidity. To the extent that a measurement device promotes such reactions, the device can be referred to as a *reactive measuring instrument*. A major effort has been made in recent years to use nonreactive or unobtrusive measurement techniques to offset the threats to validity which arise from reactive measurement.

A measurement technique is unobtrusive to the extent that it precludes the likelihood of the respondent's reacting to it and thus reducing its validity. For example, if a researcher asks someone how much alcohol he consumes per week, he might react to the question and give an answer that he thinks might at least maintain the researcher's esteem for him. On the other hand, if the researcher goes through his garbage each week and counts the empty liquor bottles, he will not even know his behavior is being measured, and therefore he can't react to the measurement. The book *Unobtrusive Measures* by Webb et al. cites numerous examples of effective ways to collect unobtrusive data. Table 6–1 lists several suggestions that may help you generate some ideas for your own use.

A reasonable caution is in order here. Unobtrusive measurement, like all forms of measurement, should not be undertaken in a frivolous or unethical manner. It would be possible to measure attitudes toward school, for example, by placing microphones in the towel dispensers in the restrooms and monitoring the students' conversations there; but this would certainly be an inappropriate invasion of privacy. In fact, the

TABLE 6–1. Some Examples of Unobtrusive Measurement Techniques.

Outcome to be Measured	*Measurement Technique*
Number of cigarettes smoked per hour.	Let respondents have a discussion in lounge for an hour and then count the cigarette butts in the ashtray after they leave.
Preference for a political candidate.	Leave some postcards around with a message relevant to one or the other candidate on one side and a standard address on the other. People are more likely to pick up and mail the ones for the candidate they prefer and throw away the ones for the candidate they dislike.
Feelings toward a film shown in class.	Watch to see how often the students turn around to see how close the film is to being over.
Extent to which physical education students actually clean themselves while taking shower after gym class.	Weigh the soap before and after the shower session (or obtain its volume by immersing it in a measurement device.)
Appreciation of Shakespeare.	Count number of books about Shakespeare borrowed from library.
Child's favorite color.	Measure size of crayons. Favorite colors will be shorter.
Favorite radio station.	Turn car radio on and see what station it's tuned to. Also see where the buttons are set.
Children's bedtime.	Ask them what TV shows they watched last night. Then check to see what time the shows were on.
Racial prejudice.	Watch whether the students sit in racially isolated or mixed groups at various activities.

garbage-can example cited above is mentioned facetiously, and not as a recommended invasion of your neighbor's privacy. Common sense and appropriate ethical codes should regulate all forms of data collection.

It is apparent from Table 6–1 that while unobtrusive techniques often reduce one source of invalidity (arising from reacting to the instrument), they often introduce other sources. For example, when the nosy garbage collector examines a garbage can and discovers 10 liquor bottles and no soft drink containers, his conclusion that the owner of that garbage can had been engaging in a particularly wild party consisting of all alcohol and no soft drinks might be invalid. The most obvious source of invalidity in this conclusion is that liquor often comes in throwaway bottles, whereas soft drinks often come in returnable bottles. All the unobtrusive techniques noted in Table 6–1 are susceptible to similar sources of invalidity. For this reason, unobtrusive measurement techniques are recommended as *supplemental* strategies. In most cases, it is desirable to collect more than one sort of data. For example, you could give a questionnaire about prejudice and also watch to see where people sit in the lunchroom. The strategies are quite different and control different sources of invalidity. It is often useful to supplement more formal strategies with several different unobtrusive techniques.

It is not correct to say that an instrument must be either obtrusive or unobtrusive. Measurement techniques actually exist along a continuum ranging from extremely obtrusive to not at all obtrusive. By being aware of this factor and selecting less obtrusive techniques whenever possible, you can reduce a significant source of invalidity in your measurement efforts.

STANDARDIZED INSTRUMENTS

Sometimes you may want to measure a rather complex characteristic. Either for that reason or for some other reason, you may want to use a standardized or professionally prepared device rather than one which you construct yourself. In such instances, your task is to select a correct instrument rather than to develop it yourself. The strategy for selecting a device is the same as the instrument construction strategies described in the various sections of this chapter. Decide what it is that you want to measure, and then look for a device that will do that.

Information on professionally developed tests is available in many professional journals. In addition, two excellent sources are *Tests in Print* and the *Mental Measurements Yearbooks*. By consulting these sources you can determine basic information about the contents of the test, the type of respondents for whom the test is intended, and its reliability and validity. You can also find competent reviews by specialists in the appropriate field. Another source of useful information is to write to the test publishers for information about the test in which you are interested.

Standardized tests have the advantage of being designed by persons who are experts in an appropriate field. When you want to measure complex behavior, such expertise can lead to more reliable results than your own efforts at measuring that outcome variable. In addition, standardized tests provide normative data that will compare the scores of your respondents to the scores attained by other relevant groups of respondents. Such normative data is often important in interpreting the results. However, the fact that standardized tests are designed by an *outside* specialist is sometimes a disadvantage. There is often a less-than-perfect match between what the standardized instrument measures and what you want it to measure. For example, the designers of standardized achievement tests want to sell their tests to as many school systems as possible, and so they cover content that is likely to be covered in as large a number of schools as possible. In addition, for reasons of reliability specified in Chapter 4, designers of normative tests omit items which are answered correctly by a large number of respondents. For these reasons, it is likely that the content covered by the standardized achievement test will not perfectly match the unique content of your course or curriculum. Therefore it is wise to use standardized tests largely as a useful supplement to your own evaluation strategies.

CHOOSING AND USING A MEASUREMENT TECHNIQUE

Measuring instruments are useful ways to collect information about whether or not an outcome variable is occurring. The present chapter has reviewed several specific measurement strategies. The principles discussed in Chapters 2, 3, and 4 have to be carefully integrated with those covered in this chapter to select and develop instruments useful for your own purposes.

The most important quality of any instrument is its validity. Therefore, validity should be a factor in choosing the type of instrument you want to administer as well as in determining the contents of that instrument. There are four steps in constructing a valid measurement technique:

1. Identify the outcome variable you want to measure.
2. State a valid operational definition of that outcome variable.
3. Select a data collection format that matches the requirements of your operational definition.
4. Within the requirements of that format, design an instrument that matches your operational definition as closely as possible.

Chapter 2 has provided direction with regard to the first two steps. Chapters 3 and 4 have focused on the final step. The present chapter has dealt primarily with the third step. The information from all four of these chapters has to be fused and integrated to

TABLE **6–2.** Purposes and Accompanying Weaknesses of Various Measurement Formats.

Format/Technique	Purpose of Format	Weaknesses of Format
Classroom achievement tests	Estimate academic achievement.	Really only an indirect measure of internal learning; ignores affective outcomes.
Questionnaires	Enable respondent to provide answers without personal presence of data collector.	Less flexible than interview; rely on respondent to state accurately what he/she feels or will do.
Interviews	Enable respondent to provide answers with personal presence of data collector.	Interviewer often increases reactivity to instrument.
Observational techniques	Focus on actual performance rather than introspection or accuracy of respondent.	Data is recorded by outsider (observer), who provides an additional source of error; only completely external behaviors can be recorded.
Unobtrusive techniques	Minimize tendency for responses to be reactions to the instrument rather than true indications about the outcome variable.	Often only indirectly connected to outcome variable.
Standardized tests	Designed and field-tested by professionals with a great deal of experience with regard to a given outcome variable.	Often the content of the standardized instrument matches up imperfectly with the data collector's goals.

develop useful strategies to help you determine what outcome variables are occurring in your educational settings. This is the essence of Level I research.

Table 6–2 summarizes the purposes and accompanying weaknesses of each of the formats discussed in this chapter. These principles can be readily understood from reading the table, and all have been discussed in appropriate sections of this chapter. The important point is that each of the formats serves a certain purpose and solves certain problems; but at the same time, any single technique has certain basic weaknesses. For this reason, it is often a good idea to use more than one format for measuring an outcome variable. The full process for developing or selecting appropriate data collection techniques is graphically presented in Figure 6–10. An important feature of this diagram is the feedback loop, which indicates that the second through fourth steps should be repeated as often as necessary to assure a valid measurement process. For example, it might be a good idea to (1) give a child an achievement test on scientific concepts and (2) unobtrusively observe the child to determine whether or not she really applies the information in situations in which it can be applied. Likewise, it might be appropriate to (1) ask an adolescent boy questions regarding his attitudes toward females and (2) observe him to see how he really interacts with girls. By using the various formats in this supplementary fashion, you can retain the strengths of each measurement technique while canceling out the weaknesses.

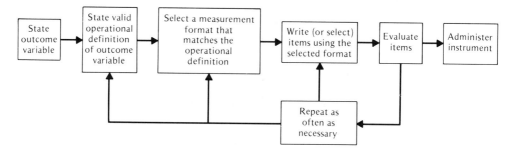

FIGURE **6–10**. The Complete Process for Developing Valid Strategies for Measuring an Outcome Variable.

Before concluding this section, it is important to note that no attempt has been made to discuss all possible data collection techniques. For example, there has been no discussion of many of the specific types of achievement tests, such as short-answer essay tests, completion items, and true-false tests. Likewise, there has been no discussion of specific techniques such as the semantic differential or of the use of checklists for evaluation purposes. Nor has there been a detailed discussion of many of the various nuances that could occur within any of the formats discussed here, such as the differences between telephone interviews and other kinds of interviews. Rather, this chapter has attempted to point out the important guidelines to use in selecting and implementing a measurement format. The principles discussed in this chapter can be applied to any of the additional techniques that have been passed over. Readers interested in specific guidelines regarding these other techniques should consult current issues of measurement journals (such as the *Journal of Educational Measurement*) and the references in the Annotated Bibliography at the end of this chapter.

Review Quiz

Match the data collection format on the right with the appropriate description on the left. Each format can be used once, more than once, or not at all.

1. _____ Minimize the likelihood that the respondent will react to the instrument rather than giving his true response.

2. _____ Provide the greatest amount of flexibility during the actual administration of the instrument.

3. _____ Designed primarily to determine academic achievement.

4. _____ Useful for measuring complex outcomes which you personally feel incapable of assessing for yourself.

5. _____ Provide a basis for comparison with the performance of other respondents on the same instrument.

6. _____ Rely on the respondent to *state* what he/she feels or will do, with no opportunity to probe.

7. _____ Examining the actual performance of a behavior rather than the respondent's statement about what he/she feels or will do.

8. _____ The most likely to have the results influenced by the person administering the instrument.

a. Classroom Achievement Tests
b. Questionnaires
c. Interviews
d. Observational Techniques
e. Unobtrusive Techniques
f. Standardized Tests

Answers:
1. e
2. c
3. a
4. f
5. f
6. b
7. d
8. c (d is also acceptable, if you interpreted it to mean that it is the observer, and not the respondent, who actually records the score.)

PUTTING IT ALL TOGETHER

Eugene Anderson, the humane educator, followed the steps suggested in Figure 6–1 when he was developing his data collection strategies. His use of these steps will be summarized here.

To begin with, he knew that the outcome variable he wanted to measure was "attitude toward animal life." He had previously drawn up a list of operational definitions (Chapter 2). From this list, he selected one that he thought was especially good; "Given the opportunity to either let an animal experience pain or save the animal from pain, the student will choose to save the animal." He examined this operational definition, talked it over with a few colleagues, and decided that this was indeed a good operational definition of favorable attitude toward animal life.

Next, he looked for a format with which he could assess the occurrence of this operational definition. He decided against observational techniques, because he felt it would take too long to wait for such events to occur in a natural setting, and ethical considerations militated against inflicting pain on animals just so Mr. Anderson could get his data. Therefore, he decided to use the questionnaire format. Specifically, he decided to use the hypothetical situation of the burning house and ask each respondent how he or she would respond in that situation. (See Chapter 3, page 42, for a copy of his instrument.) He incorporated some ideas from unobtrusive measurement into this instrument, because he reasoned that most students filling out the questionnaire would have no idea that the questionnaire had anything to do with animal life, and therefore they would be unlikely to react to the instrument.

Next, he wrote the first version of the Fireman Test. He revised the items based on several trial runs, reliability coefficients, validity information, and item analysis, as discussed in Chapters 3 and 4. He eventually came up with two valid forms of the Fireman Test, so that he could use one as a pretest and the other as a posttest, if he wished to do so.

At this point, he started using the Fireman Tests to evaluate some of the presentations he gave. At the same time, he went through the feedback loop in Figure 6–10. He asked himself if he needed any further data. Was his evidence already strong enough to require no further data collection, or should he look for more evidence? He decided he needed more evidence; and so he returned to the second step in the diagram and selected another of his operational definitions from the list he had previously devised in Chapter 2. He then went through steps 3 and 4 and the feedback loop as often as he felt he needed still more evidence. He continued this process until he had the following set of measurement techniques:

- Two versions of the Fireman Tests.
- A questionnaire that he administered to the student after he gave presentations, asking them to give their feelings about animal life.
- An observation sheet that he left with the teachers, asking them to record specific sets of behaviors that the children might display which would reveal different attitudes toward animal life.
- A values rating scale that listed a whole set of worthwhile values, one of which was attitudes toward animal life, and asked the children to rank these in order of importance.
- A form that he submitted to veterinary clinics and animal control programs to ascertain whether or not certain animal related behaviors increased or decreased after his presentations.

He could have developed more measurement strategies, but he decided it would be best to do a good job with what he had rather than run the risk of overwhelming himself with too much information. He felt these strategies would get him some fairly good evidence, and he knew he could always resort to additional operational definitions and new measurement strategies if he found he needed them.

Mr. Anderson did not always use all the above measurement techniques in every school he visited. In some cases, circumstances prohibited him from collecting any data at all. However, whenever possible he collected what evidence he could. This information made it possible for him to change certain methods of presentation and to evaluate the effectiveness of some of his new ideas. He developed new confidence that his programs were actually accomplishing useful goals.

SUMMARY

With well-designed measuring instruments, we can collect reliable and valid evidence concerning the outcomes of interest to us in educational settings. This chapter has discussed the major types of data collection instruments. Table 6–2 summarized the purposes and weaknesses of each of these major strategies. Many specific strategies for collecting data have not been discussed in this chapter, but the guidelines presented here will help you evaluate these other strategies as the need arises.

In order to measure an outcome variable, it is necessary to follow these steps: (1) identify the outcome variable; (2) state a valid operational definition of the outcome variable; (3) select a measurement format that matches the operational definition; (4) write (or select) items using the selected format; (5) evaluate the items and make changes as necessary; and (6) administer and score the instrument.

Annotated Bibliography

BLOOM, B.S., HASTINGS, J.T., and MADAUS, G.F. *Handbook of Formative and Summative Evaluation of Student Learning.* (New York: McGraw-Hill, 1971). Part I provides overall strategies for test achievement construction and evaluation. Part 2 provides specific guidelines for constructing good items in specific subject matter areas.

EBEL, R.L. *Essentials of Measurement* (3rd ed.) (Englewood Cliffs, N.J.: Prentice-Hall, 1979). Chapters 6 through 9 provide specific guidelines on how to write good items for the various types of classroom achievement tests.

GRONLUND, N.E. *Measurement and Evaluation in Teaching* (3rd ed.) (New York: Macmillan, 1976). Part II provides useful guidelines on constructing classroom tests. Chapter 9 presents especially good information on the interpretive exercise. Part IV provides useful guidelines for observational techniques and rating scales.

KERLINGER, F.N. *Foundations of Behavioral Research* (2nd ed.) (New York: Holt, Rinehart and Winston, 1973). Chapters 28 through 34 present detailed and sometimes complex information on the use of specific methods of data collection.

WEBB, E.J., CAMPBELL, D.T., SCHWARTZ, R.D., and SECHREST, L. *Unobtrusive Measures* (Skokie, Ill.: Rand McNally, 1966). This book presents in detail the theory behind unobtrusive measurement, as well as numerous specific strategies and examples of the successful use of such strategies.

Professional Journals

The following journal articles contain good examples of measurement instruments or strategies designed to measure specific outcomes. (Many of the research studies described in chapters 8 through 15 likewise include descriptions of measurement strategies. You may wish to consult them for further examples.)

BECKER, H.A. "The assertive job-hunting survey," *Measurement and Evaluation in Guidance* 13 (1980): 43–48. This article describes the process of developing and revising an instrument to measure the job-hunting skills of college students. The instrument was then used to evaluate the effectiveness of an assertiveness training program.

BOWEN, S.M. and MILLER, B.C. "Paternal attachment behavior as related to presence at delivery and preparenthood classes: A pilot study " *Nursing Research* 29 (1980): 307–311. This study uses observational strategies to operationally define and measure the attachment of fathers to newborn infants.

DERICCO, D.A. and NIEMANN, J.E. "*In vivo* effects of peer modeling on drinking rate," *Journal of Applied Behavior Analysis* 13 (1980): 149–152. These authors were able to observe and record another person's rate of consumption of beer (with 100% reliability!) without having that person even realize that she was being observed.

FELDHUSEN, J.F. and WYMAN, A.R. "Super Saturday: Design and implementation of Purdue's special program for gifted children," *Gifted Child Quarterly*, 24 (1980): 15–21. The authors used a simple questionnaire to evaluate the effectiveness of a program for gifted children. This is a good example of Level I research.

OSWALD, M.T., KATZ, B.M., and KREKELER, K. "Knowledge and health practices of high school students with respect to heart disease risk factors — A pilot study," *Science Education* 64 (1980): 269–278. The authors report on the development and use of a questionnaire to determine the knowledge and habits of high school students with regard to heart disease. The results lead to recommendations for curriculum change.

7 Sampling

Chapter Preview

The preceding chapters have described strategies for operationally defining and measuring various outcomes. In most cases, when we assess such outcomes, we identify the group of people whose performance is of interest to us and then measure the performance of each individual within that group. However, when the numbers of people become very large or measurement strategies become complex, it is practical to use the performance of a subgroup to estimate the performance of the overall group. This can be accomplished through the sampling procedures discussed in this chapter.

After reading this chapter you should be able to

- Describe the purpose of sampling and identify situations where sampling would be useful.
- Identify examples of each of the major sampling procedures.
- Identify the major sources of bias in sampling.
- Identify the major strengths and weaknesses of each of the sampling procedures.
- Given a sampling situation, specify how to use each of the major sampling techniques in that situation. Evaluate the relative strengths and weaknesses of each.
- Determine how large a sample is needed to estimate population characteristics at a designated level of accuracy.

THE IDEA BEHIND SAMPLING

As every baseball fan knows, the only really perfect way to find out how the 600 major league baseball players feel about the designated hitter rule is to ask all 600 of them for their opinions. Only then can we conclude with perfect accuracy, for example, that 84% (but only 63% of the nonpitchers) are opposed to the designated hitter rule. Even here, however, our conclusions would be inaccurate if there would have been anything ambiguous about our question or about the responses of the players. But what if you want to know the answer to this question but cannot afford (because of lack of time or money) to contact all 600 players? Obviously, if you asked *some* of the players, you would have a better idea of what their opinion was than if you asked none of them. If you asked 10 players, it seems obvious that your results would be better than if you asked only two. Likewise, 50 would probably be better than 10. In addition, if the 50 players were evenly split between the National and American leagues, would that not make your conclusions better? And certainly it would be better to have players from several different positions, rather than all pitchers or all designated hitters. How big does the group of players have to be before you can make useful decisions? How can you make sure to get proportionate representation from all positions and from both leagues? What does *better* mean when we talk about finding players to whom we can ask our questions?

The problems dealt with in the preceding paragraph focus on sampling. The term *sampling* refers to strategies which enable us to pick a subgroup from a larger group and then use this subgroup as a basis for making judgments about the larger group. In order to use such a subgroup to make decisions about the larger group, the subgroup has to resemble the larger group as closely as possible.

In discussing sampling procedures, the term *sample* is employed to refer to the *subgroup*, and the term *population* refers to the *larger group*. Thus in the example at the beginning of this chapter, the 600 major league baseball players represent the population (assuming that this is the whole group); whereas a group of 50 players to whom we might ask our questions would be a sample. The terms *sample* and *population* will be used in this sense throughout this chapter.

There are many situations in education where sampling is not necessary at all. If I want to know how many of the 30 graduate students in my course plan to enroll in an advanced course the next semester, the easiest way to find this out would be to ask the whole class this question. Likewise, if a third-grade teacher wanted to know how many of her students could add two-digit numbers, the best way to find this out would be to give all of them a valid test involving two-digit addition. Sampling techniques are useful only when there is some reason why it would be difficult to ask everyone in the target population the desired questions. If I wanted to find out how many graduate students in my entire university are interested in taking a certain advanced course the next semester, it would be very difficult to ask everyone this question. Even if I could locate all of them, it might be hard to get all of them to reply to a questionnaire. If we wanted to know how many third-grade children throughout America can add two-digit numbers, we would find it a lot more convenient to administer our test to some smaller sample than to every third-grade child in the entire country.

The following are a few examples of questions related to education where sampling would be helpful in finding the answers:

- In a school with 500 children, how many parents would come to PTA meetings each month if a baby-sitting and child-care service were initiated?
- What percentage of the 200 freshmen in the high school would be considered formal operational according to the standards accompanying an interview format that takes an hour to administer to each student?
- How many of the English teachers in the State of Pennsylvania approve of a set of recommended changes in the English curriculum?

- What percentage of Smith's *5000 Books for High School Libraries* does our high school have in the library? What percentage of these have been borrowed in the last year?
- Would the alumni support our athletic program more enthusiastically if we would build a new stadium? Would this additional support offset the cost of construction?
- How would the teachers in our school system react to a system of teacher incentives based on student performance?
- What percentage of the elementary teachers in our school system are willing to have learning disabled children mainstreamed in their classrooms? Do these attitudes differ at different grade levels? Do these attitudes depend on previous experience with such children? Do teachers who attended an intensive training program regarding such children have attitudes which are different from the other teachers?

In many of the above cases, sampling would be helpful simply because there is a very large number of persons in the target population. In other cases, the number of respondents would be small enough to handle if the instrument to be administered were brief, but the length of time necessary for measurement makes it desirable to deal with a small group of respondents. By dealing with a smaller number of freshman students, for example, a teacher would have time to administer the hour-long interview necessary to find out if a child is formal operational in the second example. Likewise, by dealing with a smaller number of teachers in the sixth example, the researcher could spend time with all the teachers to make sure they clearly understood the incentive system before expressing an opinion about it.

There are many different ways to draw a sample from a population. For instance, the PTA survey in the first example given above could be based on any of the following samples:

- The president could ask for a show of hands at a meeting to see how many would come if a baby-sitting and child-care service would be started.
- The president and other officers could each call ten persons and find out the opinions of the people they talked to.
- A note could be sent home with the 500 children asking the parents to give their opinions. (Then the responses of the four persons who replied could be tabulated.)

Each of the above approaches has some fundamental weakness. As you read the rest of this chapter, you will develop guidelines for evaluating each of these sampling strategies. As you will see, the quality of sampling strategy depends on (1) how the sample is drawn, and (2) how many persons are in the sample. These factors will be discussed in the following sections.

THE BASIC SAMPLING STRATEGIES

The manner in which a sample is drawn is an extremely important factor in determining how useful the sample is for making judgments about the population from which it is drawn. It is quite possible to have a very large sample upon which no sound decision can be based. This occurs because the respondents in the sample are not really very similar to the population about which we want to make generalizations. For example, it is not at all uncommon for magazines to report the results of surveys based on a survey of thousands of readers. A close examination of such surveys often reveals that the results are less useful than if they would have been based on 20 to 25 representative respondents rather than five thousand. To be useful, *the sample has to be representative of the population about which we wish to generalize.* To provide useful information, these magazines should let the readers know what the population is about which the survey results can be generalized, but few of the magazines do this. Their reluctance to do so is probably based on their awareness of how bad the surveys really are.

Random sampling is generally the best way to draw a sample from a population. With random sampling, every member of the population has an equal opportunity to be in the sample, and pure chance is the only factor that determines who actually goes into the sample. Keeping this definition in mind, which of the following is an example of random selection?

- Going to a shopping center mall and asking every fifth person for his or her opinion about presidential candidates.
- Calling the third name from the top on each page of the telephone directory and asking the first adult to come to the phone for his or her opinion about presidential candidates.
- Going to a football game and asking an equal number of Democrats and Republicans for their opinions about presidential candidates.

The answer is that none of the above is an example of random selection, because in each case some factor in addition to chance includes or excludes respondents from the sample. If the population about which we want to generalize is all adult citizens who are eligible to vote in this city, then we cannot use any of the above to make a valid generalization about this population. Both of the following examples *would* be examples of random selection:

- Get a list of all the adult citizens who are eligible to vote in the city, put each name on a card, and select the cards through a process of pure chance selection.
- Get a list of all the adult citizens who are eligible to vote in the city, assign a number to each person, and then use a table of random numbers to select names off this list. (The use of the table of random numbers is described in Chapter 9.)

In both of these cases, chance is the *only* factor which determines who will be in the sample.

To select a strictly random sample, it is essential to have a complete list of all the members of the population. This is often very difficult to accomplish. For instance, in the example under consideration, if the target population about which we want to generalize includes both registered and unregistered voters, such a total list would be very hard to compile. On the other hand, if we decided to limit our generalizations to registered voters, then a list would be more readily accessible.

When we deal with smaller, more clearly defined populations, the process of devising a comprehensive list is much simpler. For example, for each of the hypothetical situations described on this page, a list would already be available or could easily be compiled. To draw a random sample, it would be necessary merely to draw a sample of names from these lists at random. Random sampling has such a clear advantage over the other methods with regard to the generalizations which we can base on the results that it should be used as often as possible. This means, for example, that if we have a choice of collecting responses from 50 respondents through a random sampling process or from 300 respondents through a nonrandom process, the small but random sample is almost always to be preferred.

Biased sampling is the worst way to draw a sample. With this "method," we put together our sample by using naturally occurring or artificially constructed groups of subjects without the benefit of random selection. For example, if a professor wants to determine how many students would enroll in an experimental course, she could ask the 30 students taking her Introductory Educational Research course this question. This would be a biased sample. There's really no good reason to believe that these 30 students would be typical of the other 970 graduate students in the university. Likewise, if a researcher would stand in the mall of a shopping center and question whoever walked past, she would be getting a biased sample. What makes her think that the people in the shopping center are representative of any population about which she wants to generalize? And furthermore, what makes her think that the person who walks up and talks to her is similar to the person who looks down and dodges her or actually slithers along the wall to avoid talking to her?

The magazine surveys cited earlier were examples of biased sampling, and it is this biased sampling that renders such surveys so useless for making generalizations. I once heard of a now defunct (then moribund) magazine which each month published the results of a reader survey. The editors decided they wanted a representative sample, and so they decided to do something random. They decided that expiration dates on subscriptions occurred in a near random manner, and so with each renewal notice they sent out a survey form. This way they were able to get what they presented as a random sample of readers' views on a new issue (which they duly published as such) each month. The respondent simply enclosed the completed questionnaire when sending in payment for the next year's subscription! The problem, of course, is that this is a biased sample, not a random sample. Neither the readers who are new subscribers nor those who decided not to renew were included in the sample. This may be an interesting sales gimmick, but it is a poor technique to get a representative sample of opinions.

On the other hand, many reputable organizations are forced to rely on nonrandom sampling. This is the case because for very large-scale surveys, random sampling is very difficult. If we want to find out how American teenagers, for example, feel about sex or drugs, it's impossible to take a random sample of all the teenagers in the country—and it would be very expensive even to come close. It is possible to take a random sample of all the students in a given city, perhaps; but once we try to use the results of a few such small-scale studies to generalize to the adolescents of the whole country, we're really using a biased sample. Such nonrandom sampling is most justifiable in cases where it is actually impossible to derive a true random sample. In such cases, reputable organizations upgrade their nonrandom sample by making it a quota or stratified sample (discussed next in this section) and by carefully delineating the precise nature of the sample and the limitations in generalizing to specific populations. These limitations should be kept in mind when we interpret such surveys.

In most cases when educators need to use a sampling strategy, they can do better than using a biased technique. In spite of this, various forms of biased sampling seem to be the most widely prevalent sampling techniques in educational settings. Unfortunately, most of the persons who use biased techniques are not aware of what they are doing wrong. For example, many actually believe that talking to every fifth person who walks through the door or talking to whoever happens to be in the lounge are good ways to get representative opinions. Such methods are examples of biased sampling, and they often result in nonrepresentative results.

It is important to cite one more example before moving beyond biased samples. What happens if you have a population of 1000 people and take a genuine random sample of 200, then send out a survey to which only 25% respond? Are these 50 respondents a random sample or not? The answer is no! They typically represent a biased sample. The obvious bias is that only those who volunteered to respond are part of the actual sample available for analysis. A much better strategy would have been to select a smaller sample and to attempt to get 100% responses. In this case, responses from 50 out of 50 would have been vastly superior to 50 responses out of 200.

To summarize, random sampling is the best technique; biased sampling is the worst. The next strategies to be discussed are those which make a nonrandom sample come as close as possible to possessing the characteristics of a random sample.

Quota sampling provides an attempt to give respectability to a nonrandom sample. When using this strategy, the researcher identifies important characteristics which he knows the target population possesses and selects the sample in such a way as to make it correspond to the population with regard to these characteristics. We might get a quota sample of American teenagers in a city by consulting census information and discovering what percentage of teenagers in that city are of each sex, what percentage belong to each of the various races, and what percentage live in each of several different socioeconomic neighborhoods. Based on this information, we would set quotas before we even set out to do our survey, determining that we would get a certain number of males, a certain number of females, a certain number of whites, of blacks, and so on. When conducting the survey, we would use these quotas to set the limit on how many persons possessing each characteristic we would include in our survey.

Cluster sampling occurs when we select the members of our sample in clusters, rather than as separate individuals. For example, if I want a sample of 100 of the 1000 graduate education students at my university, I might pick this sample by selecting at random four classes with twenty-five students in each class. However, the resulting sample of 100 would not be a random sample. Classes of graduate students are likely to contain students with greater similarities to one another than would appear in a similar number of separately selected students.[1] If we use cluster sampling in situations where there is a very large number of clusters, then the difficulties mentioned here become less serious. We can further reduce the difficulties by combining the cluster sampling technique with the quota and stratified techniques discussed in this chapter.

Systematic sampling is a strategy where only two factors determine membership in the sample—chance and the system. The system is simply a way of speeding up the randomization process. For example, instead of using a table of random numbers to

---

[1] Technically, the problem is that the standard deviation of the group is likely to be different from the standard deviation of the separately selected individuals. Refer to the chapter by Asher in the list of references for further details.

select a sample of 100 from a numbered list of 1000 names, a researcher might randomly select a number between 1 and 10, start with that name, and then take every tenth name on the list after that. The resulting sample would be almost as good as a random sample, since the stipulation to take every tenth name is probably unrelated to any systematic bias. If the system employed were related to some sort of bias, however, this could be a very bad technique. For example, if a classroom of children were arranged so that boys and girls alternated throughout the room, then if the researcher took every tenth one, she would get either all boys or all girls from that class. Likewise, if she had a list of 2000 names and obtained a sample of 100 by starting with a random number between 1 and 10 and taking every tenth name, this would exclude the whole second half of the list, which would be a serious bias. (This problem could be overcome by taking every twentieth name instead of every tenth name.) It is usually relatively easy to identify and eliminate such biases in the system.

Stratified sampling is a strategy whereby members of the sample are selected in such a way as to guarantee appropriate numbers of respondents for future subdivision during the analysis of the data. For stratified sampling to be most effective, the respondents within each of the strata should be selected at random. Such random stratified sampling is mistakenly thought by many novice researchers to be the ideal sampling technique. This is not quite the case. In general, simple random sampling is the most desirable procedure. Stratified sampling is useful only when (1) you plan to subdivide the subjects for subsequent analysis or (2) you have too large a population to be able to assign each subject a number in advance. Readers of this book are most likely to use stratified sampling for only the first reason. National marketing and political polling organizations often use it for both reasons.

The use of stratified sampling can be illustrated by using an example from a political survey. Let us say we are going to conduct a survey during which we will ask respondents to indicate (a) their race, (b) the candidate for whom they plan to vote, and (c) their attitude toward environmental issues. A random sample of 200 people from a town of 50,000 would generally give us a good estimate of (a) how many persons of each race there were in the town, (b) how many persons planned to vote for each candidate, and (c) the percentage of persons for and against the environmental issue. However, what if we wanted to know whether black Republicans differed from black Democrats in their attitudes toward the environmental issue, or whether within the Democratic party blacks and whites differed on the environmental issue? Assuming that there were only 10% blacks in the town, this would give us 20 in the random sample. Assuming they are equally divided among Republicans and Democrats, this gives us 10 of each. As we will discover in the next section, the validity of judgments based on 10 respondents is not nearly as strong as the validity of judgments based on 200 respondents. If we wanted to make such a subanalysis, we should stack the sample by putting in more blacks, so that we could have more of them for the eventual subanalysis. Such a move, of course, would bias the overall sample by giving blacks a disproportionate representation. The over-representation would have to be countered by a strategy to be discussed later in this chapter. Stratified sampling would be used in this case specifically to provide ample numbers of subjects for subdivision and subanalysis.

Stratified sampling and quota sampling, you may have noticed, are similar in that they both set limits on the number of members of the sample with specific characteristics. You should also notice, however, that the two are completely different strategies whose purposes are entirely different. The purpose of quota sampling is to make the sample as closely representative as possible of the larger population with regard to important characteristics. This is done by assuring proportional numbers of subjects with specific characteristics. To pursue the example from the previous paragraph, if the original population had 10% blacks, then the quota sample should have 10% blacks. On the other hand, a researcher might want a stratified sampling to provide for subsequent subanalysis. To do this the researcher would deliberately select subjects in such a way as to make the sample dissimilar to the larger population. For example, the researcher might select 30% blacks so that there will be enough black respondents to provide for a meaningful subanalysis based on the race of the respondent.

Essentially random is a term which is often applied to samples which were not randomly selected but which the researcher thinks are unbiased anyway. For example, there might be 300 students in the freshman class at your high school and you might want to find out what percentage of them can read with at least sixth-grade ability. Testing all 300 would be expensive and time-consuming, but you could easily test 30 of them. Pursuing the matter, assume that you discover that the English classes are heterogeneously grouped. The only factor in determining who goes to what English class appears to be when they eat lunch. This, in turn, depends on a combination of alphabetical order and what electives they are taking. At this point, you might argue that such classes are essentially randomly selected. However, you

TABLE **7–1.** The Relative Advantages and Disadvantages of the Five Basic Sampling Techniques.

Technique	Advantages	Disadvantages
Random sampling	Theoretically most accurate. Influenced only by chance.	Sometimes a list of the entire population is unavailable or practical considerations prevent random sampling.
Systematic sampling	Similar to random sampling. Often easier than random.	The system can sometimes be biases.
Cluster sampling	It's easy to collect data on the subject.	May be biases when number of clusters is small.
Quota sampling	Can be used when random sampling is impossible. Quick to do.	There may still be biases not controlled by the quota system.
Stratified sampling	Assures large enough sample to subdivide on important variables. Needed when population is too large to list. Can be combined with other techniques.	Can be biased if strata are given false weights, unless weighting procedure is used for overall analysis.

could improve your logic further by using quota-sampling strategies. You might discover that there are about the expected number of males and females, the expected number of blacks, whites, hispanics, and other racial groups, the expected number of students from each track, and so on. This would further strengthen my case that the sample is essentially random. To top it off, you might look at their standardized test scores and discover that these are very close to the mean for the entire class. Having done all this, then your conclusion that only 35% of the freshmen can read at the level of a sixth-grader or better would have a great deal more weight than if your sample were not essentially random.

The comparative advantages and disadvantages of the five major sampling strategies are summarized in Table 7–1. Table 7–1 summarizes the following points: (1) random sampling is the simplest and best if there is a list of the population, (2) systematic sampling is almost as good as random sampling, (3) cluster sampling has major problems when the number of clusters is not large and should be avoided, (4) quota sampling gives respectability to nonrandom samples, and (5) stratified sampling is useful in those situations in which no list of the population is available or when subdivision of the sample is intended and adequate numbers are not likely to be present in the subunits through regular random sampling.

Review Quiz

1. Categorize each of the following as one of these types of sampling:

Badly biased sampling.
Random sampling.
Systematic sampling.
Cluster sampling.
Quota sampling.
Stratified sampling.

A. Miss Gilligan is surveying attitudes toward intercollegiate football. She gets her sample by interviewing people standing in line at the hot-dog stand.

B. Mr. Quinn surveys attitudes toward evening television programs by phoning the tenth person in the second column on every page of the phone book. If this is a business phone, he goes to the next number in that column.

C. Ms. Billings selects her sample of college students by obtaining a computer printout of all the students and then selects students for her sample by using a table of random numbers.

D. Mr. Vockell wanted to analyze the quality of ERIC's *Research in Education* (RIE) microfiche research for his doctoral dissertation. He obtained a list of all documents published in 1971, and then starting with the 64th document, he selected every fiftieth document on the list for his sample.

E. Mrs. Jacobs wanted a sample of students from her Educational Psychology course. She put all their names on cards, shuffled the cards, and then dealt the cards into two stacks. The cards in the left-hand stack were included in her sample.

F. Mrs. Rahner wanted to analyze the attitudes of Milwaukee school children toward busing. She selected three schools in Milwaukee and tested all third, fifth, and seventh graders. She selected these schools because the children were similar to the average for the rest of the city in intellectual ability, in ratio of whites to nonwhites, and in the percentage of students who rode buses.

G. Rev. Wachel wanted to find out how people reacted to his sermons. He specifically wanted to know if there were differences in reactions related to age level; and so he randomly selected 100 young adults, 100 middle-aged adults, and 100 elderly adults from lists of his congregation.

Answers:
A. Badly biased.
B. Systematic sampling of listed phone owners. (Biased sample of whole population.)
C. Random sampling.
D. The selection of 1971 was itself a cluster sample. However, the selection within 1971 was systematic.
E. Random sampling.
F. Quota sampling.
G. Stratified sampling.

2. Evaluate the quality of each of the above sampling techniques. How good would the sample be if the strategy were carried out.

Answers:
A. This is similar to the man-on-the-street interviews and is likely to be extremely biased. There is no reason to assume that the subjects are typical of any known population.
B. This would be a valid technique so long as there is no bias related to phone ownership or unlisted numbers. If the researcher tries to generalize his results to TV viewers instead of to telephone owners, he is actually using a biased sample.
C. Perfectly valid.
D. So long as he limits his generalizations to the *RIE* research published in 1971, he seems to have a valid sample.
E. Perfectly valid.
F. This is a cluster sample, but there are still biasing factors. Mrs. Rahner might do better to select random *classes* from the entire school system and use these as her sampling unit.
G. Perfectly valid for the subanalyses. He should use a weighting procedure if he intends to make any generalizations about the overall attitudes of his congregation.

HOW LARGE SHOULD THE SAMPLE BE?

In addition to depending on the procedure by which it was selected, the quality of a sample depends largely upon its size. In general, if a sample is scientifically selected, we can place more confidence in the results of a larger sample than we can in the results of a smaller sample. This is because the likelihood that the characteristics of a discrepant minority will improperly influence our perceptions of the whole population decreases as the sample grows larger. (Note, however, that adding 25 people to a sample of 5 will result in a much greater increase in accuracy than adding 25 people to a sample of 100.) At a certain point, the benefits from increasing the size of a sample may be outweighed by negative factors, such as the overburdening cost of sampling more respondents.

How large should a sample be? To answer this question, we need to undertake a brief exploration of confidence intervals. A confidence interval states a range of numbers, such as ±5% or ±10%. When we use a sample to estimate a population characteristic, we are aware that our sample estimate is just an estimate. The confidence interval states how accurate we think this estimate is. The confidence interval can be applied to the sample estimate to indicate the range within which the population characteristic almost certainly falls.

This can best be understood by examining an example. If a PTA president found that 37% of the parents sampled said they would come to a meeting on Thursday night if child-care service were provided, she would be aware that her estimate of 37% was not a precise measurement. If she had a confidence interval of ±15% for this estimate, this would mean that the true percentage of persons who would have said they could come to the meeting is likely to range somewhere between 52% and 22%. This is a rather wide range.[2] (The true percentage could be ascertained, of course, by asking the question to everyone in the population.) If the confidence interval would have been smaller, the range within which the true percentage would be most likely to fall would have been smaller. For example, if her confidence interval were ±5%, then it would be expected that the actual number of persons willing to come to the meeting would be somewhere between 42% and 32%. If the confidence interval were ±1%, then she would expect the actual number to be somewhere between 38% and 36%.

As you can see, by keeping the confidence intervals narrow we increase the likelihood that we are making an accurate estimate. These confidence intervals are based on sound mathematical theory, which will not be explored here. The important point is that the critical factor in determining confidence intervals is the number of members who comprise a sample. As the size of the sample increases, the confidence intervals become smaller, and our estimates are likely to be more accurate. By applying some simple mathematical procedures before we undertake a survey, we can estimate ahead of time how large a sample we will need in order to provide us with confidence intervals which will give us a satisfactory amount of confidence in the accuracy of the results we expect to receive from a sample.

Confidence intervals can be estimated through the use of mathematical formulas. However, this text recommends using tables which are based on such formulas. By using these tables, you can avoid the more complex computations and obtain accurate confidence intervals by performing only a few simple computations. In many cases, the confidence intervals for a sample can be obtained directly from Table 7–2. In other cases, however, the initial estimate from Table 7–2 can be made more precise by referring to Tables 7–3 and 7–4. An example will help you understand how to use these tables.

Let us take our PTA president who wants to find out how many families would be able to have at least one parent present at the monthly meeting if child-care services were provided. There are 300 families in her school, and she has a complete list of these families. She decides that she wants a very accurate estimate, and so she decides to try for ±5% confidence intervals. Looking at Table 7–2, she finds that if she samples 150 families she will have an initial confidence interval of ±8%. Going on to Table 7–3, she ignores this table because she has no idea how common the answer "Yes" will be. Going on to Table 7–4, she finds a correction factor of .71 for samples which are 50% of the population. (She got 50% by dividing 300 into 150. Multiplying this correction factor times her initial confidence interval, she gets ±5.68%. This is slightly higher than the confidence intervals she had hoped to attain. If she used 175

---

[2] Actually, a confidence interval of ±15% typically means that there's a 95% probability that the true percentage falls between 52% and 22%. The tables in this book are based on 95% confidence intervals. Other possibilities (such as 99% confidence intervals) could be used as well. Technical language has been avoided in this discussion.

TABLE **7–2.** Initial Estimates of Confidence Intervals Based on Simple Size.*

Sample Size	Plus and Minus Confidence Interval Limit
5	±44%
10	±31%
20	±22%
30	±18%
40	±16%
50	±14%
60	±13%
70	±12%
80	±11%
90	±10.3%
100	± 9.8%
125	± 8.8%
150	± 8.0%
175	± 7.4%
200	± 6.9%
225	± 6.5%
250	± 6.2%
275	± 5.9%
300	± 5.6%
400	± 4.9%
500	± 4.4%
750	± 3.6%
1000	± 3.1%
2000	± 2.2%
5000	± 1.4%

*Refer to Tables 7–3 and 7–4 for correction factors.

Technical note: These are 95% confidence intervals, based on the formula

$$\frac{1.96 \sqrt{2500}}{\sqrt{n}}$$

families, she would have an initial confidence interval of ±7.4% (Table 7–2) and a correction factor of .63 (Table 7–4); and this would give her a confidence interval of ±4.7%. If she wants this high degree of accuracy, the PTA president should arrange to randomly sample 175 families.

Note that if the PTA president would have been willing to settle for ±10% accuracy, she could have accomplished this with a much smaller sample. In this case, a sample of 80 would have given her an initial confidence interval of ±11% (Table 7–2) and a correction factor of .87 (Table 7–4); and this would have given her a confidence interval of ±9.6%. By cutting her sample size in half, she would still retain a reasonable degree of accuracy.

How many families should the PTA president actually sample? Her decision would depend on (1) the cost (in terms of time and money) incurred in sampling each family, and (2) the benefits arising from the gain in accuracy. Contacting 175 families by herself would be an arduous task. On the other hand, if ten members would help, this

TABLE 7–3. Correction Factors for Instances When the Characteristic Being Measured Is Either Very Common or Very Rare.*

Frequency with Which Character-istic Occurs in Population	Correction Factor
50%	none
40%, 60%	.98
35%, 65%	.95
30%, 70%	.92
25%, 75%	.87
20%, 80%	.80
15%, 85%	.71
10%, 90%	.60
5%, 95%	.44
2.5%, 97.5%	.31

*Use this table only if you have a specific reason to believe the characteristic will occur either below or above a certain percentage of the respondents.

Technical note: This correction factor is based on the formula

$$\sqrt{\frac{(P)\,(1-P)}{2500}} \quad \text{where } P = \text{estimated percentage of incidence}$$

would necessitate only 17 or 18 contacts apiece. Likewise, what would happen if her estimate was wrong? If the organization would be subject to lawsuit for underestimating the number of children present for the child-care service, then a more precise estimate would be needed. On the other hand, if the consequences of an inaccurate estimate were less formidable, then the broader confidence interval from the smaller sample would be satisfactory.

TABLE 7–4. Correction Factor for Instances When Sample Size Is an Important Part of the Population.*

Percent Sample/Population	Correction Factor
5%	.98
10%	.95
15%	.92
20%	.89
25%	.87
30%	.84
40%	.78
50%	.71
60%	.63
70%	.55

*Use this table only if the sample size divided by the population size is greater than .05.

Technical note: This correction factor is based on the formula

$$\sqrt{\frac{N-n}{N-1}} \quad N = \text{population size and } n = \text{sample size}$$

Notice that in either case, the president would select a random sample of a designated size and then attempt to contact all members of that sample. Once she would depart from random sampling, the numbers in the confidence intervals would lose their meaning. Additional examples of the use of these tables to estimate confidence intervals are provided in the boxes below.

Ms. Smith wants to find out how many of the freshman students in her high school have reached the highest level of thinking according to the theory of Jean Piaget. She has read the literature on this theory carefully, and she knows that very few (less than 10%) of the freshmen will have reached this level. She has a valid test, but it takes an hour to administer. She wants confidence intervals of ± 10%. There are 200 freshmen in her school. How large a sample does she need?

Starting with Table 7–2, we find that 30 students would give an initial confidence interval of ±18%.

Going to Table 7–3, we see that a characteristic which occurs 10% of the time has a correction factor of .60.

$$18\% \times .60 = 10.8\%$$

Going to Table 7–4, we note that 30 students represent 15% of the population. The correction factor for 15% of the students is .92.

$$10.8\% \times .92 = \pm 9.93\%$$

This corrected confidence interval rounds off to 9.9%. The reason she can get by with such a small sample is that the characteristic (being at the highest level of Piagetian thinking) is a relatively rare characteristic among her population.

Mr. Parker wants to find out what percentage of the citizens of his city plan to support the school tax levy. He wants to have an estimate with a confidence interval of ± 10% to present to his school board meeting. There are 100,000 citizens in the city who are eligible to vote. How large a sample does Mr. Parker need?

Let us start with a sample of 90. This gives us an initial confidence interval of ± 10.3% from Table 7–2.

Going to Table 7–3, we find that this table is irrelevant to this problem. We have no idea how common this characteristic will be, and therefore we assume it must be around 50%. There is, therefore, no correction factor from Table 7–3.

A sample of 90 subjects is not even 1% of 100,000 citizens. Therefore, there is no correction factor from Table 7–4.

The initial confidence interval of ± 10.3% has not been altered by any of the correction factors. This interval is too large, and so we must try a larger number of subjects.

A sample of 100 respondents would give us a confidence interval of ± 9.8%. Tables 7–3 and 7–4 are still irrelevant. Therefore, the interval of ± 9.8% would be the confidence interval if a sample of 100 were selected.

A valuable use which can be made of survey results is to perform various subanalyses. For example, our PTA president might want to know whether the responses of persons who attended meetings the previous year differed from those who had never previously come to a meeting. She might also want to know whether parents with more than one child in the school gave different responses than parents with only one child in attendance. Likewise, she might be interested in knowing if the answers from one-parent families are different from those from two-parent families. Such information can be very useful in helping us make decisions.

It is important to remember that whenever we subdivide the original sample for such subanalyses, we reduce the size of our sample—and therefore increase the size of our confidence intervals. The result is a lessening in accuracy. For example, assume that our PTA president decided to sample 80 familes. This gave her a confidence interval of ±9.7% for her whole sample. What if she wanted to compare the responses of families who had attended meetings the previous year with those who had not attended previously? Let's assume that in the original population of 300 families 75 had attended in the past and 225 had not attended. This would mean that her sample of 80 would be likely to consist of 60 nonattenders and 20 attenders. What kind of confidence intervals would she have for the responses of the attenders? A glance at Table 7–2 gives us an initial confidence interval of ±22%, and when we correct this by a correction factor of .87 from Table 7–4, this leaves us with a confidence interval of ±19%. On the other hand, the 60 nonattenders wold have a confidence interval of ±11.3% (13% × .87 = 11.3%).

Faced with such difficulties, our president would be left with two alternatives: (1) keep the same sample and merely acknowledge the weaknesses of the confidence intervals in the subanalyses, or (2) draw the sample in such a way as to insure a sufficiently large sample for the subanalyses. Accepting the first alternative would be a reasonable decision in many circumstances; it would merely be necessary to keep in mind that judgments based on the subanalyses would not be on as firm a footing as those derived from the overall sample. The second alternative requires stratified sampling.

To use stratified sampling, we would select our sample in such a way that each subsample (stratum) for subanalysis will have enough members to provide the desired confidence interval. Thus, if our PTA president wanted to do the subanalysis comparing attenders to nonattenders, she would have to select enough families to provide 10% confidence intervals for each of these subgroups. The procedure would be as follows:

Attenders (population = 75 families)
   50 families give an initial confidence interval (Table 7–2) of ±14%.
   Correction factor for 60% of the population is .63.
   Corrected confidence interval = ±8.82%.
Nonattenders (population = 225 families)
   70 families gives an initial confidence interval (7–2) of ±12%.
   Correction factor for 30% of the population is .84.
   Corrected confidence interval = ±10.0%.

The president would therefore sample 50 attending families and 70 nonattending families—a total sample of 120 families. This is good for the subanalysis, but notice what has happened to the overall analysis. In the original population, there were 75%

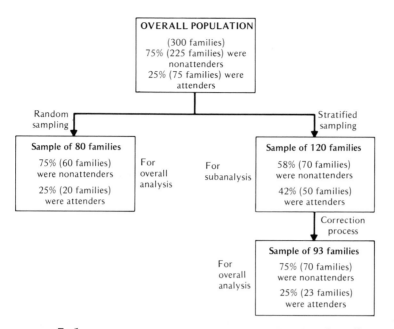

FIGURE **7–1.** Stratified Sampling Compared to Random Sampling.

nonattenders and 25% attenders. In the sample, however, there are now 58% nonattenders and 42% attenders. Thus, the adjustment to improve the confidence intervals has resulted in a bias in the overall sample. This could be corrected, of course, by increasing the size of the sample beyond 120 and including proportionately more nonattenders. Or it could be corrected by keeping the sample size at 120 and excluding 27 of the attenders from the overall analysis. This exclusion would reduce their number in the overall sample to 25%, which was their representation in the original population. This stratified sampling and correction procedure is diagrammed in Figure 7–1.

Review Quiz

1. Mr. Fenwick, the school librarian, wants to find out what proportion of the books listed in Smith's *5000 Books for School Libraries* are in his library. He wants to be within ± 5% in his estimate. He wants to take a random sample from Smith's book and check to see if each book sampled is in the library. How many entries would Mr. Fenwick have to sample to be within ± 5%?

Answer:
400 books. His actual confidence interval would be ± 4.9% (Table 7–2) times a correction factor of .98 (Table 7–4): and this gives an answer of ± 4.8.

2. Mrs. Peters, a probation officer, wants to find out what proportion of the adolescents in her caseload would be willing to take a day off from school (with their parents' permission) to go on a field trip to a penal institution. She knows another probation officer who gained 90% participation for a similar project, and she expects that her group would be equally

interested. She has 250 young men and women in her caseload. How many would she have to sample to have a confidence interval of ±10%?

Answer:
40 persons. (Actually, a number between 30 and 40 would be an acceptable answer.)
Table 7–2 gives an interval of ±16% for a sample size of 40. The correction factor for a 90% characteristic (Table 7–3) is .60. The correction factor for 15% of the total population is .92.

$$16 \times .60 \times .93 = 8.8\%$$

This is actually too narrow. However, a sample size of 30 gives a confidence interval of 18% × .60 × .95 = 10.2%. This is too broad an interval. Mrs. Peters should probably use 35 respondents.

---

3. There are 500 teachers in the Nice City School System. Miss Good, the superintendent, wants to find out how many of them would be willing to accept a system of incentive pay based on student performance. She knows that this is a volatile issue, and she fears that if a questionnaire is mailed out, people will react without thinking. She feels that it is necessary for an interviewer to explain to each respondent individually what is meant by the incentive plan before answering. Since this will take time, she wants to keep the sample as small as possible. She also wants to know if secondary teachers react differently to the survey than elementary teachers. There are 300 elementary teachers and 200 secondary teachers in the Nice City School System. How many does Miss Good have to include in her sample in order to be within ±10% on all her analyses?

Answer:
150 teachers (80 elementary and 70 secondary). Table 7–3 is irrelevant to both samples. Based on Tables 7–2 and 7–4, we get the following:

$$12\% \times .84 = \pm 10.0\% \text{ for secondary teachers}$$
$$11\% \times .87 = \pm 9.6\% \text{ for elementary teachers}$$

This would give a biased over-representation of secondary teachers in the sample of 150. Thirty of them should be randomly eliminated from the overall analysis to give a true picture of how all teachers feel about this issue.

PUTTING IT ALL TOGETHER

In order to collect background data for his research, Eugene Anderson decided to find out how many people within his city owned pets, what percentage of the pet owners had their pets altered to prevent unwanted pregnancies, and how various people felt about increasing licensing fees for pets. There were 750,000 people living in his city. He wanted to sample 500 respondents, but the task of locating 500 randomly selected people seemed overwhelming, even if he could handle most of the work by telephone. They would be too spread out and many would be hard to reach. Therefore, he contacted a friend at a local marketing research firm, and he discovered that there was a shopping center at which the marketing firm conducted much of its research. The marketing firm had discovered that samples drawn from this shopping center were usually very similar to the rest of the city with regard to most characteristics. Indeed, the conclusions of the research which the firm conducted on this one location were usually representative of what would have been concluded if the whole city were surveyed.

This was a valuable discovery. By drawing his sample from this shopping center, Mr. Anderson would have a very high quality quota sample. He followed the same procedure his friend from the marketing firm followed. He stood near the fountain in the mall and asked his questions to the first person to approach from the west at the end of each two-minute interval. In this way, he easily got his sample of 500 within two weeks. He found that 62% of those sampled owned pets, that 36% did not, and that 2% refused to talk to him. (For purposes of his research, he restricted pets to dogs and cats.) Of those who owned pets, 20% had their pets spayed or neutered, whereas the other 80% had not done so. Of those who had their pets altered, 45% favored raising the licensing fee. Of those who had not had their pets altered, only 40% favored raising the licensing fee.

Mr. Anderson started to conclude that pet owners who had their pets spayed or neutered were slightly more likely to favor raising the fees. However, first he checked his confidence intervals. The confidence intervals for a sample of 500 were ±4.4%, and therefore his estimate that 62% owned pets and 36% did not was probably pretty accurate. Since there were 300 pet owners responding to his question about altering the pets, this gave him an initial confidence interval of ±5.6%. Since this turned out to be a rare characteristic, the correction factor from Table 7–3 reduced these intervals to ±4.5%. Therefore, this estimate was just about as accurate as his first. However, when he went to his next question, he discovered that his estimates were not nearly so precise. He had 240 respondents who had not had their pets altered, and only 60 who had. This meant that his estimate for the first group (alterers) was within a satisfactory ±6.2%, but his confidence interval for the second group (nonalterers) was ±14%. This estimate was too imprecise. Therefore, he decided that it would be rash to base any judgments on the relatively small discrepancy in opinions which he had discovered.

SUMMARY

Sampling makes it possible to estimate the characteristics of a larger group by examining the characteristics of a smaller group drawn from this larger group. The larger group is referred to as a *population*. The smaller group drawn from the population is called a *sample*. To provide an accurate estimate of the characteristics of a population, a sampling procedure should provide a sample which resembles the population as closely as possible. Random sampling is the best procedure for drawing a sample from a population, since it maximizes the likelihood that the sample will be like the population. Biased sampling is the worst sampling technique. Since it allows uncontrolled biases into the sample, we no longer know how closely the biased sample resembles the overall population. Quota sampling attempts to upgrade nonrandom sampling by removing some of the most obvious biases. Systematic sampling is very similar to random sampling; it starts at a random point in a population list and then systematically selects members for the sample. Stratified sampling is useful when we have no list of the population or when we want to guarantee ourselves that we shall have enough members of subgroups within our sample to allow us to do further subanalyses of the data.

Larger samples are more likely to provide accurate representations of their populations than are smaller samples. It is possible to estimate how accurately a sample of a given size from a designated population will represent the characteristics of that population. This information can be used to determine ahead of time how large a sample we would have to draw to be within a designated degree of accuracy in estimating the characteristics of a target population.

Annotated Bibliography

ASHER, J.W. *Educational Research and Evaluation Methods* (Boston: Little, Brown and Company, 1976). Chapter 7 provides a thorough discussion of the rationale behind the determination of sample size and sampling methodologies.

FREEDMAN, D., PISANI, R. and PURVES, R. *Statistics* (New York: W.W. Norton, 1978). Chapters 19 to 23 provide a clear and comprehensive treatment of sampling theory. The treatment is replete with useful examples. Of all the citations listed here, this is by far the most thorough. The presentation is advanced, yet quite comprehensible to the serious reader who wants to learn more about sampling than is contained in the present textbook.

Professional Journals

The following articles provide good examples of sampling strategies.

CICHON, D.J., and KOFF, R.H. "Stress and teaching," *NASSP Bulletin* 64 (1980): 91–104. The authors use an admittedly nonrandom sampling technique, but then they use quota-like strategies to show that the resulting sample is in most demographic respects similar to the overall population. They suggest that the nonrandomness has probably not introduced systematic bias into their results. They carefully confine their conclusions regarding stress to the large school system from which they drew the sample.

DROTT, M.C. and MANCALL, J. "Magazines as information sources: Patterns of student use," *School Media Quarterly* 8 (1980: 240–250. The authors use a high quality cluster example to examine the habits of high school students who cite magazines in their term papers.

WILLOWER, D.J., and FRASER, H.W. "School superintendents on their work," *Administrator's Notebook* 28 (1980): (5). These authors obtained 100% participation in a random sampling of school superintendents to whom they administered a telephone interview.

Postscript to Chapter 7

We have now covered the basics of Level I research. This level deals with the accurate assessment of the outcomes occurring in a classroom or other educational setting. This is the sort of research that all teachers should do every day. A very large number of the most serious problems we encounter as we attempt to educate our students occur because we fail to collect outcome data or because we collect invalid data. A careful understanding and application of the principles discussed in Chapters 2 through 7 will help you overcome such problems.

Chapter 8 begins the discussion of Level II research. This second level deals with identifying cause-and-effect relationships in the educational process. The reason teachers spend less time engaging in Level II than in Level I research is that they feel that conducting such higher level research is more likely to disrupt their teaching efforts. You can go on with your daily routine while doing Level I research, but it is much more difficult to proceed without interruption while doing Level II research. Many teachers say they are not concerned about their inability to find time to do Level II research. They say they are concerned about *what* is happening in their classroom, not *why* it is happening. To a very great extent, these teachers are right.

Nevertheless, there are times when it is important to establish cause-and-effect relationships. For example, if you have only 15 minutes a day for the next 8 weeks to work with a child on a reading problem, you'd probably prefer to know whether the first method you tried has *caused* improvements. Likewise, if you put an extraordinary amount of effort into preparing a lesson, you may be interested in knowing more than whether or not the students can master the outcomes; you would like to know if your efforts *caused* the improvements. If they did, you will repeat your efforts; otherwise, you can find a better way to spend your time. The same thing holds true when you are spending a great deal of money on a program. If it caused improvements, you will want to keep it; otherwise you might as well try a less expensive program.

In reading the next few chapters of this book, you will see that while Level II research is somewhat more time consuming and interruptive than Level I research, it is still possible for the ordinary classroom teacher to do such research to her own satisfaction and to the advantage of her students. By careful planning, the cause and effect research can be done without disturbing the instructional processes. The major portion of the additional effort can be done at the planning stage and at the analysis stage. The teacher is able to carry out her instructional obligations as effectively as usual; and in addition, she will have useful information about what to do on similar occasions in the future.

Level II research is often no more difficult than Level I research, and in many ways it's more exciting. Level II research may sometimes be more difficult to perform than Level I research, but it is not more difficult to understand. As a matter of fact, if you understand the essentials of Level I research, you already understand a large amount of what goes on at Level II. This is because when you do Level II research, you first do Level I and then add something to it to make it Level II. In other words, to establish a cause and effect relationship, you first have to identify what outcomes are occurring (Level I), and then you have to establish the causality for these outcomes (Level II). A very large number of the mistakes that occur in Level II research occur because the researcher has measured the outcomes improperly.

In reading the next chapters, look for ways to implement the strategies discussed there in such a manner as to get their advantages without disrupting what you are trying to do in your classroom. If you can do this, you will be able to develop a storehouse of effective strategies which you know are effective. Your confidence will be based on formal and informal Level II research which will have enabled you to examine cause and effect relationships.

8 Internal Validity

Chapter Preview

Internal validity deals with the authenticity of cause and effect relationships. It asks the question, "Did the treatment really cause the observed outcome, or are there some other factors at work?" The way to establish internal validity is by ruling out the threats to internal validity. These threats are other factors—variables other than the treatment—which could produce an impact on the outcome variable. It is true that teachers do not always have the time or money necessary to conduct scientific experiments in their classrooms. Nevertheless, it is also true that the ability to rule out threats to internal validity will help you draw correct conclusions about the cause and effect relationships you observe in educational settings. In addition, the ability to identify these threats will help you avoid drawing false conclusions when you are confronted with faulty research in the professional literature and in other sources.

After completing this chapter, you should be able to

- Define internal validity.
- Define and give examples of each of the major threats to internal validity.
- Describe how each of these threats operates to weaken the internal validity of a conclusion about a treatment.

INTRODUCTION

Mrs. Johnson is a science teacher at a large metropolitan high school. She has taken a course at a nearby university and has learned how to design and use computer simulations in her classroom. She has discovered that by interacting with the computer, her students can experience many realistic situations which would otherwise be too expensive, physically impossible, or too dangerous to undertake in a normal science lab. She believes that such interacting with the computer would provide her students with the motivations and insights necessary to understand science. She feels that such computer simulations should be introduced in science courses throughout the high school curriculum.

It would cost $20,000 to purchase the necessary hardware (computer terminals) to implement Mrs. Johnson's idea. Software (programs) and expert consultation to get the programs running correctly would cost another $10,000. However, these large expenditures would occur only during the first year; thereafter, a budget of less than $2000 a year would quite easily keep the project running and updated.

Mrs. Johnson brings her idea to the principal and he replies that this sounds very interesting, but he does not have $30,000 to budget for this purpose. Mrs. Johnson persists, however and finally the principal agrees that if she can actually provide evidence that the computer programs *cause* improvements in scientific skills and attitudes, they would be worth the expenditure. He even grants her a small budget, which combined with her own ingenuity and some generosity from the university enables her to run a pilot project in one of her classes.

Mrs. Johnson has read this textbook up to this point, and so she knows that she needs some way to find out what outcomes are actually occurring in her science class. She carefully selects a standardized science test which measures *both* knowledge of facts and scientific problem solving ability. She feels this test validly measures what she wants to teach. She is satisfied that if the students score high on the test they will be showing an understanding of science.

She pretests her third-period students and finds that at the beginning of the year they averaged in the 34th percentile on the test. She then integrates the computer into the curriculum for this class. At the end of the year, she retests and finds that the students are now in the 57th percentile. Moreover, attitudes which were negative at the beginning of the year became positive at the end of the year. She concludes that the computers did in fact *cause* an improvement both in scientific problem solving ability and in attitudes toward science.

Is Mrs. Johnson right? Did working with the computers cause the observed improvements? The answer is that she would need better evidence before any sensible person would give her $30,000.

Mrs. Johnson is assuming that the process diagrammed in Figure 8–1 is occurring among her students. The computers, she feels, are producing favorable motivation and new insights, and these lead to improved test performance. To the extent that she can demonstrate that this process is actually occurring, Mrs. Johnson has shown that her computers are effective. However, Mrs. Johnson has to rule out the likelihood that the process diagrammed in Figure 8–2 could explain the observed improvements in test scores. This diagram suggests that a combination of a nice social studies teacher who is enthusiastic about science, a good TV show dealing with science, and the other information about science presented in her ordinary curriculum led to appropriate motivations and insights which in turn led to higher test scores. In order

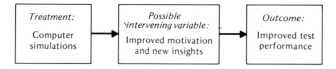

FIGURE 8–1. The Cause and Effect Relationship Which Mrs. Johnson *Assumes* Has Produced the Observed Outcome.

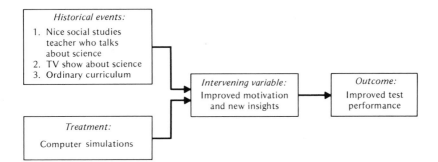

FIGURE 8–2.   An Alternate Explanation of the Outcome Which Mrs. Johnson Observed. (Now it is impossible to know for sure what actually caused the observed outcome.)

to build a really convincing argument that the computer programs actually *caused* the change, Mrs. Johnson has to rule out this and many similar alternate explanations for the improvement.

Mrs. Johnson needs to know more than *what* is happening. She needs to know *why* it is happening.

INTERNAL VALIDITY

Internal validity deals with the question of whether or not the treatment actually caused the observed outcomes in an experiment. In other words, it deals with the authenticity of a purported cause and effect relationship. The appropriate way to establish internal validity is to rule out all the threats to internal validity. These threats are other factors—variables other than the treatment— which could have an impact on the outcome variable. By showing that these other factors did not produce the effect observed in your experiment, you increase the strength of your argument that the treatment is indeed the factor that produced the observed outcome.

Establishing internal validity is very much like a detective game. I often play Clue with my son and his friends. In this game a highly effective way to find out who did it is to rule out suspects who didn't do it. For instance, if I know that everyone except Colonel Mustard is innocent, then I know Colonel Mustard is guilty. The same logic can be applied to establishing internal validity. If you can rule out all the threats to internal validity as causes of an outcome, then you know that the treatment (and not any of the irrelevant, extraneous factors) caused the observed impact.

In the example discussed at the beginning of this chapter, Mrs. Johnson and her principal should be concerned about the internal validity of the cause and effect relationship she claims to have established. Did the treatment (computers) cause the observed improvement, or was some other factor (such as the nice social studies teacher or good TV show from Figure 8–2) actually responsible for the improvement? Would the improvement have occurred even if there would have been no computer simulations? To the extent that it's likely that one of these factors besides her simulations caused the improvement, Mrs. Johnson has weak internal validity. On the other hand, to the extent that she can rule out these and other irrelevant explanations, Mrs. Johnson is strengthening her internal validity.

The present chapter will provide a thorough discussion of the major threats to internal validity.[1] Chapters 9 and 10 will provide a discussion of the most popular strategies for overcoming these threats. Even as you read the present chapter, however, it should become obvious to you that these threats are not insurmountable. With reasonable care, a teacher can rule out most of these threats and thereby increase the soundness of decisions based on the observation of apparent cause and effect relationships in the classroom.

Review Quiz

Write *Yes* before each of the following statements where the question is one of internal validity. Write *No* if it is not a question of internal validity.

1. _____ Joey Schneider was extremely shy around girls when he was in the seventh grade. Mr. Schneider bought Joey a sex book to read during the summer. During the eighth grade, Joey got along quite well with girls. Mr. Schneider wonders whether the book really caused the difference in Joey.

2. _____ The superintendent of police wonders about the location of the nearest center at which he can train new police officers.

3. _____ The teacher wants to know how her fifth graders compare to the national norms in reading and in math.

4. _____ The school board abolished corporal punishment one year. The next year there was much more vandalism than there had been the previous year. The superintendent wanted to know whether the change in policy regarding corporal punishment caused this difference or whether some other factor was responsible.

5. _____ The teacher wanted to know whether a film he wanted to show met the guidelines of the local PTA.

6. _____ After Mr. Johnson showed his fourth graders his slides about his trip to Russia, the pupils seemed to be much more interested in world affairs. He wondered whether or not his slide show had actually caused this change in behavior.

7. _____ Mr. Campbell is a probation officer. Thirty percent of his charges were arrested for criminal offenses last year. He tried a new method of working with his charges, but still thirty percent were arrested. He looked at the statistics for other probation officers in the same area, and he discovered that their rates had jumped to fifty percent. He wanted to know whether his new method had actually acted as a deterrent to prevent an increase among his own group.

---

[1] In order to make this chapter as straightforward and unconfusing as possible, I have written it as if internal validity referred simply to whether or not an observed effect is a real effect of an experimental treatment. This is just slightly inaccurate—or at least incomplete. My approach is an oversimplification because it ignores the fact that internal validity would also be involved if a researcher wanted to know whether or not the absence of any effect was truly an absence of that effect. For example, if a researcher gave a reading program to a group of students, they might actually improve, but problems with internal validity might might make it look as if there had been no improvement. The question of whether or not a non-effect is really a non-effect, therefore, is a valid concern of internal validity. It's actually not a very complicated concept, and the reader who understands this chapter will almost automatically apply the principles correctly to both effects and non-effects. The only problem is that if I try to include both concepts while I'm writing this chapter, I wind up with hopelessly tangled, complex sentences. My solution has been to allow this slight inaccuracy in this chapter and to rectify the situation by informing you in this footnote of my deliberate error.

8. _____ Mrs. Smith tried a new reading program. The children did no better after the program than before it. However, she realized that there had been extreme unrest in her school that year because of racial busing problems. She wondered whether or not the program might have actually been effective, but the unrelated problem lowered the scores.

Answers:
1. Yes
2. No
3. No
4. Yes
5. No
6. Yes
7. Yes
8. Yes

HISTORY

One of the major threats to internal validity is history. The term history refers to *any extraneous events occurring in the environment at the same time the experimental variable (the treatment) is being tested.* It is not past history with which we are concerned, but rather current history—the events which occur *while* the treatment is being administered. (See Figure 8–3) For example, if a science teacher would try a new science curriculum for adolescents during the same year that a brilliant new science related show appeared on television, it is possible that improvements in science performance might be more the result of the new TV show than of the science curriculum. In this example, the new TV show is an historical event which poses a threat to the internal validity of the conclusion that the new science curriculum actually caused improved performance in science.

History is a serious and obvious threat to internal validity whenever we compare two different periods of time and try to demonstrate that the different outcomes which are occurring are the result of some single factor that has changed. For example, many schools which now ban corporal punishment have more disruptions than before the ban. Does this prove that banning corporal punishment *caused* the increase in

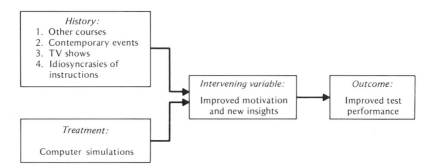

FIGURE 8–3. History as a Threat to Internal Validity. There has been an actual change in motivation and insights, but it is impossible to tell whether this change has occurred as a result of history or the treatment or some combination of the two. (The variables are taken from the Mrs. Johnson example in the "Introduction" section of this chapter.)

disruptions and that reintroducing spankings would reduce disruptions? Without further evidence we cannot draw this conclusion, for it is possible that some other extraneous factor (such as new patterns of childrearing) has caused the increase in disruptions. In this example, there would be a very large number of historical events which could pose a threat to internal validity. Additional examples of such threats would include teacher morale, social climate, curriculum content, and peer pressures. When we refer to these as threats to internal validity, we mean that before we can conclude that banning corporal punishment has led to increased disruptions, we have to rule out all these other factors as causes of the same phenomenon.

Note that we are not saying that in the first example the new television show actually did cause the improved performance in science. Nor are we saying that patterns of child rearing (rather than the ban on corporal punishment) actually did cause the increase in disruptions. All we are saying is that because the extraneous historical events were not comparable in each instance, we cannot make a sound comparison. Things are so confused that we simply do not know why the differences were observed.

When we speak of history as a threat to internal validity, we are referring to any extraneous event—not just to those which might show up in history books. For example, an experimenter might find two groups of people who are exactly the same. He might give one group a special reading treatment which he would withhold from the other and then use a standardized test to measure reading comprehension. If a leading student in one of the classes would announce to his peers that reading is sissy stuff, this would be an historical event that would make history different for the two groups of pupils.

As part of establishing the internal validity of a cause and effect relationship, therefore, it is important to ascertain that there are no extraneous events occurring in the environment at the same time as the experimental variable which could plausibly explain the observed results. We may not be able to stop history from occurring, but we can arrange events so that history does not interfere with our inferences. To the extent that we can reduce the plausibility of such extraneous explanations, we have increased the internal validity of our conclusion.

Review Quiz

Threats to Internal Validity—History

Put an X before the description which contains an example of history as a threat to internal validity.

1. _____ The students were not doing as well as the math teacher had hoped in learning long division. She purchased a series of filmstrips in which a small rodent talked to a chirping insect of the family gryllidae about the merits of long division. After the third of the eight filmstrips, unknown to the math teacher, the gym coach announced that there would be a contest. The ten children with the highest baseball batting averages would receive trophies. A very large number of children started computing their own batting averages and checking one another's every day. At the end of the year, the teacher was impressed to see the long division performance improved greatly. She was heard commenting to one of her friends, "The kids sure seemed bored during those filmstrips, but at least they learned from them. I think I'll use them every year."

2. _____ The students were not doing as well as their teacher had hoped in spelling. She decided to hold weekly spelling bees. After the third of the eight spelling bees, the gym teacher announced a contest. He would give trophies to the ten players with the highest baseball batting averages. A very large number of children started computing their averages every day and checking one another's averages. At the end of the year, the teacher was impressed at how much more accurately the children spelled common words. He commented, "They didn't seem very excited about the spelling bees; but they sure did learn to spell. I'm going to have regular spelling bees every year."

Answers:

1. There is a threat here. It is quite obvious that computing batting averages (a historical event) is likely to have caused improved ability in long division. Concluding that the filmstrips caused the improvement is therefore untenable.
2. There is no apparent threat here. There is no apparent logic behind the belief that the historical event (computing batting averages) caused children to spell common words more accurately. The historical event appears to be irrelevant and does not jeopardize the conclusion that the spelling bees paid off.

SELECTION

A second threat to internal validity is selection. With regard to internal validity, the term *selection* refers to the fact that *a group's performance on an outcome variable may arise from the composition of the group itself (as compared to other groups) rather than from the treatment which is supposed to have produced the outcome.* (See Figure 8–4) For example, if a certain baseball team adapts an innovative training procedure and then wins the championship, this could mean either that the innovative technique was effective or that they were good players who could benefit from any training procedure.

Selection is most commonly a threat to internal validity when the teacher/researcher deals with intact groups or with volunteers. An intact group is one which

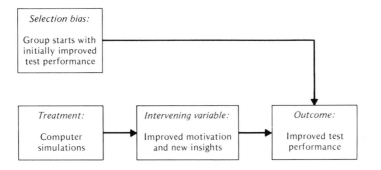

FIGURE 8–4. Selection as a Threat to Internal Validity. (There may have actually been no change at all in motivation and insights. It might merely *look* as if a change has come about, because previously existing abilities are revealed when the outcome variable is measured. It is impossible to tell whether the improved test performance has occurred because of the treatment or selection bias or some combination of the two.) (The variables are taken from the Mrs. Johnson example in the "Introduction" section of this chapter.)

already exists or was formed independently of the decision to administer the treatment. For example, if a criminal court system decided to try a new probation method in a midwestern city and to compare the results to the outcomes in a comparable southern city, it is possible that the differences might occur because of the nature of the people in the different groups rather than because of the nature of the treatment. The same confusion would occur if a teacher tried one method with his first-period English class and another with his seventh-period class. How would he know whether the differences were because of the treatment or because the subjects were different to begin with?

When a researcher asks for volunteers, it is always possible (and sometimes likely) that the persons who volunteer will, in important respects, be different from the non-volunteers. If the researcher then tries to compare volunteers with non-volunteers after some kind of treatment, it is hard to determine whether the differences arose out of the treatment or out of existing differences between the two groups. For example, if you asked for volunteers to go on a specific weight control diet, would you really be surprised to see the volunteers lose more weight than the non-volunteers? Probably not. A person who would volunteer for such an experiment is probably more interested than others in losing weight to begin with. In addition, a person who volunteers is already making a commitment and might therefore have a vested interest in adhering to the rules of the diet. Likewise, if there are two adjacent school systems, and one of them volunteers for a federally funded busing program and the other does not, could you really say that the busing *caused* the one school to have less racial strife than the other?

The examples of selection as a threat to internal validity are not always as obvious as those presented here. The important point to keep in mind is that you have to rule out the plausibility that observed outcomes might arise from the composition of the group to which the treatment is given rather than from the treatment itself. This threat to internal validity is especially likely to occur when you are dealing with either intact groups or volunteers. To the extent that you can rule out the likelihood that the composition of the group has had an impact on the outcome variable, you are increasing the internal validity of your conclusions.

Review Quiz

Threats to Internal Validity—Selection Bias

Place an X next to the descriptions that contain an example of selection bias as a threat to internal validity.

1. _____ The coach wanted to find out if Mental Practice Exercises would help her players shoot foul shots more accurately. She had 16 players on her team. She asked for 8 volunteers. These 8 spent only 10 minutes a day practicing foul shots. They spent an additional 20 minutes a day sitting in a relaxed position in a quiet room merely imagining they were shooting foul shots. The other 8 players spent 30 minutes a day shooting foul shots. After two weeks she tested the players. Those using Mental Practice Exercises made an average of 8.9 out of 10 shots, whereas those who practiced normally made only 6.7 out of 10 shots. She concluded that mental practice worked effectively.

2. _____ The other coach felt that Collective Pressure Exercises would help her players shoot foul shots. She had 16 players on her team. She randomly picked 8 of them. These 8

were sent to one end of the court and practiced their foul shots. They were not allowed to shower and go home until all 8 of them made 10 shots in a row. The others could leave separately as soon as each individual made 10 in a row. After two weeks she tested the players. Those using Collective Pressure Exercises made an average of 8.9 out of 10 shots, whereas the others made only 6.7 out of 10 shots. The coach concluded that Collective Pressure Exercises worked effectively.

3. _____ The third coach felt that Progressive Distance Training was the best way to teach foul shooting. She took all 16 players and had them start 5 feet from the basket. They would shoot from that distance until they made 5 shots in a row. Then they moved back 2 feet and repeated the process. They kept retreating until they reached a distance of 15 feet or until they had done this for an hour. After two weeks of this program, she tested her players. They made an average of 8.9 out of 10 shots, whereas her teams in the past three years had averaged only 6.7 out of 10. She concluded that Progressive Distance Training was an extremely effective technique.

4. _____ The last coach believed in Theoretical Knowledge. She, like so many other coaches, had 16 players on her team. She asked for volunteers, and 8 came forward. She randomly selected 4 of these 8 and had these 4 volunteers read The Golden Book of Basketball, while everyone else on the team (including the other 4 volunteers) merely continued their regular program. Two weeks later she tested her players. The Golden girls averaged 8.9 out of 10 shots, the other volunteers 7.1 out of 10, and the rest of the team 6.7 out of 10. She concluded that Theoretical Knowledge worked effectively as a technique to improve foul shooting.

Answers

1. There is a problem here. It is quite possible that the players with the inclination to volunteer would also have the incentive to work harder. They might have volunteered precisely because they wanted to become better. This is a serious threat to the conclusion that the Mental Practice Exercises actually accomplished anything.
2. There is no apparent threat here. There is no obvious reason why one group would have a pre-existing advantage over the other. Random assignment to comparison groups is an excellent way to rule out selection biases. This method will be discussed in Chapter 9.
3. There is a problem here. The coach is comparing this year's group to the other teams, and it is not at all obvious that the groups are similar. She might just have a highly motivated group this year. Her conclusion would be strengthened if she had evidence to show that the group was, in fact, quite similar to the other groups. (Note that a sensible coach might still use the new method. She would merely be a bit wary. She has not yet proven anything, and she would look for further evidence to support her conclusion.)
4. There is no problem of selection bias here. The important comparison is between the 4 Golden Book volunteers and the 4 volunteers who did not get the book. All 8 of these were volunteers and likely to have similar characteristics. Random assignment to groups (as in example 2) solved the problem. (If you were upset that there were only 4 in each group, your concern was well founded. Random assignment works better with larger groups. However, this is technically a problem not of selection bias but of instability which will be discussed later.)

MATURATION

As a threat to internal validity, *maturation* refers to *the fact that changes in an outcome variable may occur routinely as a result of the passage of time rather than as a result of the treatment which occurred while this time was passing* (see Figure 8–5). For example, a

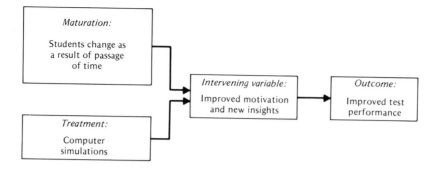

FIGURE 8–5. Maturation as a Threat to Internal Validity. (There has actually been a change in motivation and insights, but it is impossible to tell whether this change has occurred as a result of maturation or history or some combination of the two.) (The variables are taken from the Mrs. Johnson example in the "Introduction" section of this chapter.)

certain amount of biological maturity is necessary for a child to pay attention to a teacher for a prolonged period of time. If a psychiatrist treats a hyperactive child and demonstrates his success by pointing out that the child is much more attentive at the beginning of the second grade than he was at the beginning of the first grade, the internal validity of this conclusion would be vulnerable to the threat of maturation. In other words, the psychiatrist would have to rule out the likelihood that the mere passage of time and the accompanying biological maturation (without any psychiatric intervention) would have led to the same improvement.

Maturation is a serious problem only when some sort of change is likely to occur as time passes. For example, although it was a plausible problem in the example of the hyperactive first grader cited in the above paragraph, maturation would not be a plausible threat at all to the internal validity of the conclusion that a fifty-year-old adult underwent a similar reduction in hyperactivity within the same period of time. If a person has been hyperactive for fifty years and suddenly calms down after psychiatric treatment, there is no logical reason to attribute this change to maturation.

It is important to note, however, that maturation does not refer solely to those biological and psychological phenomena usually treated as maturation in human development textbooks. The term encompasses any factors that produce change as time passes. Thus the term is used in research to include the possibility that a person might change because he gets tired of or gets acclimated to someone or something as time passes. Imagine that a baby who has been crying for an hour has persisted even when her mother has picked her up stops crying when her father picks her up. This change could have been caused by maturation (getting tired of crying as time passed) rather than by the treatment (the father rather than the mother picking her up).

Maturation often creeps in as a problem in research where two groups being compared over a period of time are likely to mature at different rates. If you have a group of slow learning fourth graders who read poorly, you might use the same instructional materials with this group as you would with some second graders. You might find that the second graders are learning more quickly than the fourth graders and conclude that the materials are ineffective for the fourth graders. In fact, it might be possible that the fourth graders are benefiting more than the others from the materials, whereas the younger children are benefiting largely from maturation.

It is important, therefore, to keep in mind that changes can occur as time passes. If you can rule out the plausibility that it is these maturational changes rather than the treatment with which you are concerned that has caused the observed outcome, you will take another step toward strengthening the internal validity of your conclusions.

Review Quiz

Threats to Internal Validity—Maturation

Place an X next to the description that contains an example of maturation as a threat to internal validity.

1. _____ The fourth-grade students were reading at only the 3.1 grade level. The teacher used the FANTASTIC Reading Program. The scores went up to 4.1 after six months.

2. _____ The slow-learning twelfth graders were reading at only the 3.1 grade level. The teacher used the FANTASTIC Reading Program. The scores went up to 4.1 after six months.

Answers:
1. There is an obvious problem here. It is perfectly normal for fourth graders to mature as the year goes on, and at least part of their improvement would be due to maturation rather than to the FANTASTIC Program.
2. There is no apparent problem from maturation here. If twelfth graders have progressed only to the third-grade reading level in twelve years of schooling, it would be illogical to expect them to mature a full year in only six months. They have progressed further than would be expected by maturation alone.

INSTRUMENTATION

The only way we can measure the impact of a treatment upon an outcome variable is with a measuring instrument or observation of some kind. Instrumentation as a threat to internal validity refers to the fact that *observed differences in an outcome variable could be the result of changes in an instrument rather than the result of the treatment itself* (see Figure 8–6). *Changes in an instrument* include not only alterations in the items, but also changes in the way the instrument is administered, differences in observers, and any other variations which may influence the way performance of the outcome variable is recorded.

Although changes in the instrument itself are rare in the published literature, such changes often occur in informal classroom research. For example, after giving a pretest, a teacher might discover that some of the students missed items because the questions were ambiguous. Therefore, she might (quite logically) try hard to write better items for the posttest. If she does this, and if the scores of the students improve, how can she tell whether the improvements she observes are the result of her treatment (good instruction) or the result of changes in the test (instrumentation)?

A more frequent difficulty with regard to instrumentation is to make subtle, accidental changes in the way in which the instrument is administered. This often occurs in interviewing and personality testing. For example, changed performance of respondents to an interview between pretest and posttest might occur not because the

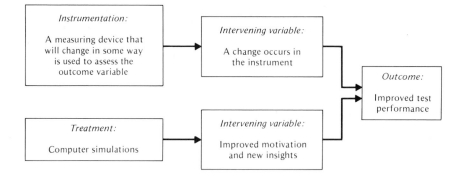

FIGURE 8–6. Instrumentation as a Threat to Internal Validity. (There may actually have been no change at all in motivation and insights. The improved test performance might have occurred merely as a result of the change in the instrument. It is impossible to tell whether this change has occurred as a result of the treatment, the change in the instrument, or some combination of the two.) (The variables are taken from the Mrs. Johnson example in the "Introduction" section of this chapter.)

respondents actually changed, but rather because the interviewer has gotten better at interviewing as he gained more practice. Similarly, if a white female administers a racial attitudes pretest and a black male administers the same questionnaire as a posttest, have the respondents really responded to the same instrument?

A related problem occurs even if you are using impartial interviewers, observers, or scorers. If these assistants become aware of the purpose of the study as it progresses, it is possible that they may (even unconsciously) attempt to make the results come out the way "they're supposed to."

A similar problem occurs when the grade point average (GPA) is used as a measure of student performance. If a student goes to a new school (or enters a new program) and her GPA increases, this increase could occur because of changes in grading policies rather than because of accelerated achievement. Differences in competition or differences in the attitudes of school personnel toward grades could make high grades easier to obtain at one school than at the other. If the two GPAs are interpreted as having the same general meaning, this would be an example of instrumentation as a threat to internal validity.

It is important, therefore, to be sure that the changes you observe are actually in the outcome variable itself, not merely in the instrument you are using to assess that outcome. The techniques discussed in the earlier chapters of this book (Level I research) will help you devise and use your instruments as effectively as possible. To the extent that you can say that the observed differences are really the result of the treatment and not the result of changes in instrumentation, you will increase the internal validity of your conclusions.

Review Quiz

Threats to Internal Validity—Instrumentation

Place an X next to the description which contains an example of instrumentation as a threat to internal validity.

1. _____ Mr. Schultz designed two versions of his test on basic facts. He accomplished this by writing 100 items, matching them in pairs, and then randomly putting one item from each pair on the first version and the other on the second version. He gave one version to his students as a pretest. The students did poorly averaging just 21.9 out of 50. He felt they should have averaged at least 45 out of 50. The students complained about what they considered to be poor items on the test, but Mr. Schultz considered this to be a mere excuse to rationalize poor performance. The next day Mr. Schultz sent a letter home to each of the parents, stressing that the students should know these basic facts before taking his course and urging the parents to see to it that their children reviewed them. He also announced that there would be another test the next Friday. When that Friday came, he administered the second form of his test to the students. They averaged 47.3 out of 50. Mr. Schultz considered his letter to the parents quite successful.

2. _____ Mrs. Snyder gave her students a pretest which she had devised on basic facts that were prerequisite to the course she was teaching. The students did poorly averaging just 21.9 out of 50. She felt they should have averaged at least 45 out of 50. The students complained about what they considered to be poor items on the test, but Mrs. Snyder considered this to be a mere excuse to rationalize poor performance. The next day she used some group dynamics techniques to instill a greater sense of responsibility among the students. She then told them they would have another test the next Friday. She devised a new 50-item test. She constructed the items very carefully, in order to rule out any excuses the students might try to base on the quality of the items. When they took the retest, the students averaged 47.3 out of 50. Mrs. Snyder considered her attempt to instill responsibility to be quite successful.

Answers:
1. There is no apparent threat of instrumentation. The tests were apparently equivalent and administered in the same manner.
2. There is a problem here with regard to instrumentation. The test the students took after the group dynamics treatment was different from the one they took before the treatment. It is quite possible that the improved performance on the posttest occurred becaused it was a better or easier test rather than because the students knew more.

STATISTICAL REGRESSION

Statistical regression occurs when a subgroup is selected from a larger group based on the extreme scores (high or low) of the subgroup. The term refers to the *tendency of the subgroup, when retested on the same or related variables, to have a mean score closer to the mean of the original group* (see Figure 8–7). Subgroups selected because they originally had extremely high scores, therefore, will score lower, but still above the mean. Subgroups selected because they originally scored low, on the other hand, will score higher, but still below the mean. This regression toward the mean occurs because of statistical unreliability in the measuring instrument. If a test is perfectly reliable (and none is), there would be no regression. If it is extremely unreliable, there will be a large amount of regression.

This concept sounds complicated and mysterious. Simply stated, however, the reason such regression occurs is that the chance factors in unreliable tests (discussed in Chapter 3) are most likely to occur in extreme scores within a group. Such chance

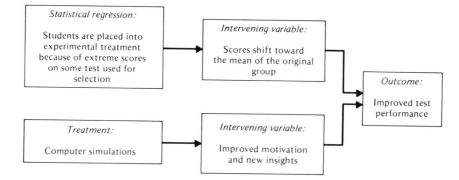

FIGURE 8–7. Statistical Regression as a Threat to Internal Validity. (There may actually have been no change at all in motivation and insights. It may merely *look* like a change has occurred because the scores have shifted towards the mean of the original group. It's impossible to tell whether this change has occurred because of the treatment, the statistical regression, or some combination of the two.) (The variables are taken from the Mrs. Johnson example in the "Introduction" section of this chapter.)

factors are unlikely to reoccur for the same individuals on subsequent testing occasions. For example, headaches and guessing are most likely to influence the scores of people at the extreme top or extreme bottom on a test. It is unlikely that the same persons will have unbearable headaches or fantastic guessing streaks on each testing occasion. Even if you find the mathematics behind this concept hard to understand, statistical regression is relatively easy to watch out for.

One place where statistical regression can easily occur is in remedial reading programs. Assume that a school has a hundred third graders who take a reading screening test at the beginning of the year. The ten who score the lowest are considered slow readers and get the special attention of the reading specialist for a half hour a day for the rest of the year. When they are retested, they score considerably higher. At least part of this improvement has to be attributed to regression toward the mean. Even if they would have done nothing all year, it is likely that this low-scoring group would have moved up, in the direction of the class mean, on the second testing occasion.

The same phenomenon will occur with groups selected on the basis of extremely high scores. If you retest them a year later, statistical regression is likely to pull their scores down toward the mean. This means that if the school in the above example took its ten best readers (based on the screening test) and gave them accelerated treatment, the program's gains would be clouded by regression toward the mean. In other words, the program might result in large improvements, but these improvements might show up as slight or nonexistent because statistical regression pulled the scores toward the mean of the original group.[2] What happened here is that some pupils got lucky on the screening test and therefore looked better than they really were. When they retook the test, the luck balanced out. The second test may have been a more realistic appraisal of their ability. In fact, they had improved, but the comparison to the unreliable screening test made it look as if they had done somewhat worse.

Note that regression to the mean occurs only when the group being measured was

---

[2] This is a good example of the phenomenon cited in footnote 1 in this chapter.

selected on the basis of extreme scores. If the principal of Public School 101 discovers that the students in the third grade scored at the 2.1 grade level on their reading test and that this was the worst in the city, statistical regression is irrelevant here. It is irrelevant because the third grade was not selected on the basis of extreme scores. Within the third grade, there were both lucky kids and unlucky kids, and their luck probably evened out, giving them a score of 2.1. However, if the superintendent would have given the test to everyone in the city and then assigned the 25 slowest third graders to the school in question, then regression would have been a factor. This is because they were selected on the basis of their low scores. With this grouping, there would be a disproportionate share of unlucky pupils in the third grade, and chances are that their bad luck would not be present again the next time they were tested.

In summary, statistical regression occurs when subgroups are selected from some larger group based on their extreme scores. The more extreme the subgroup, the more likely it is that regression will occur. Likewise, the more unreliable the test and/or the longer it is between testing occasions, the greater the regression is likely to be. The extreme subgroup will regress in the direction of the mean. Extreme groups with high scores will artificially drop and extreme groups with low scores will move up. If a group progresses in the direction you would expect based on regression, view this progress with skepticism. If you can rule out the likelihood that your results are artificially influenced by statistical regression, you will strengthen the internal validity of your conclusions.

Review Quiz

Threats to Internal Validity—Regression Toward the Mean

Place an X next to any description which contains an example of regression as a threat to internal validity.

1. _____ The 300 freshmen at Gotham City High School averaged 65.7 on the English admissions test. The lowest scoring 30 (who had an average of 39.6 on the admissions test) were put in the Remedial Class. At the end of just one semester in the Remedial Class, their scores went up to 52.8. The Remedial Class was considered to be a success.

2. _____ The 300 freshmen at Gotham City High School averaged 65.7 on the English admissions test. The highest scoring 30 (who had averaged 90.4 on the admissions test) were put in the Smart Class. At the end of the semester their scores actually went down slightly to 90.3. The Smart Class was considered to be a failure.

3. _____ The 300 freshmen students at Central High School averaged 50.3 on the English admissions test. This was lower than expected. A random group of 30 (who averaged 50.5) were put into the Remedial Class. At the end of the semester their scores went up to 65.6. The Remedial class was considered to be a success.

4. _____ The 300 freshmen at Gotham City High School averaged 65.7 on the English admissions test. The lowest scoring 30 (who had averaged 39.6 on the admissions test) were randomly divided in half. Fifteen were put in the Remedial Class and 15 in the regular program. At the end of the semester the Remedial students brought their scores up to 52.8, while those in the regular program scored only 43.2. The Remedial Class was considered to be a success.

5. _____ The 300 freshmen at Gotham City High School averaged 65.7 on the English admissions test. The highest scoring 30 (who had averaged 90.4 on the test) were randomly divided in half. Fifteen were put in the Smart Class and 15 stayed in the regular program. At the end of the semester the Smart students scored 90.3, whereas the 15 who had stayed in the regular program averaged 81.4. The Smart Class was considered to be a success.

Answers:

1. There is a problem of statistical regression here. The 30 students in the Remedial Class were selected because they had the extremely lowest scores on the admissions test. On the retest, therefore, their scores would be likely to move toward the mean of the original group of 300 students.

2. There is a problem of statistical regression here. The 30 students in the smart class were selected because they had the extremely highest scores on the admissions test. When retested, therefore, their scores would be likely to move down toward the mean of the original group of 300 students.

DEAR RESEARCHER: I'm the principal of a junior high school. We have 300 students at each grade level, sixth through eighth. Mrs. Smith (not her real name) had always been a rather mediocre teacher until one summer when she took a course on educational research. That year when she came back to school, she made a deal with me. She would take the 25 slowest seventh graders (based on standardized tests) and teach them for one year. Mr. Jones (not his real name) would teach the 25 brightest seventh graders during the same time period. If her students improved more than Mr. Jones's, she'd get double pay. If hers did worse, she'd resign. This sounded like a good way to ease a weak but tenured teacher out of the system. I'm sure Mr. Jones is the better teacher, but Mrs. Smith has taken me to the cleaners eight years in a row now. What's wrong? (signed) DISMAYED PRINCIPAL.

DEAR DISMAYED: You've been the victim of the old Regression-toward-the-mean Scam. It's the oldest trick in the book. If you select a group based on the extreme scores from a larger group, the extreme scores will "regress" toward the mean on subsequent tests simply because of the unreliability of the tests. If you want to solve your problem, give Mrs. Smith a "break" and insist that she take the 25 brightest students next year and give Jones the 25 weakest. I'm sure the pattern will reverse itself. If it's any consolation to you, this scam goes on all over the world. In major league baseball, for example, when a team comes in last at the end of a season, the owners go through the ritual of firing the manager and hiring a new one. The new manager is inevitably some guy who has coached other losing teams before, and nobody seriously believes he's actually any better than the one who was fired. Almost always the team improves under the new leadership. Why? Regression-toward-the-mean. There was also an obscure millionaire named Harold Ewes who got rich by applying regression-to-the-mean to the stock market. I'm not at liberty to disclose how Mr. Ewes did it, however. It was a condition of his will. (signed) THE LONELY RESEARCHER.

3. There is no problem of statistical regression here. The 30 students in the Remedial Class were not selected for that class because of their extreme scores. Rather, their mean was about equal to the mean of the original group.
4. There is no problem of statistical regression. Both the experimental and control groups were selected because of their extreme scores. But since both were equally likely to regress toward the mean, this statistical regression cannot account for the difference in scores between the two groups. Therefore, although regression toward the mean did occur, it was not a threat to the internal validity of the study.
5. There is no problem here. The reasoning is the same as in Number 4. Regression occurred, but it did not threaten the internal validity of the study.

EXPERIMENTAL MORTALITY

From time to time, subjects drop out of an experimental treatment, and the absence of these dropouts influences the computed average performance of the group. *Experimental mortality* refers to *the fact that differences in the outcome variable might occur because of changes in group composition rather than as a result of the treatment the group experienced* (see Figure 8–8). To put it another way, I can get the average score of 25 pupils to go up by simply eliminating the 5 slowest pupils from the group. The 20 who are left might not be any brighter than they were before, but their average would be higher, since the lower scores would no longer be used in computing the mean.

Imagine a high school situation in which students have previously been offered only academic courses. One year the principal announces that an experimental business office education program will be offered to juniors. Fifty students sign up for the program, but it can handle only 25. To be fair, the administrators select 25 at random, and use the other 25 as a control group for comparison purposes. (As you will see in the next chapter, so far this is a pretty good procedure.) The students are pretested in some way, and the two groups are about even. On the posttest, they are

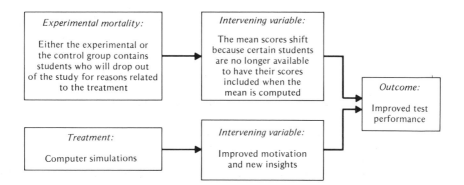

FIGURE 8–8. Experimental Mortality as a Threat to Internal Validity. (There may have actually been no change at all in motivation or insights. It may merely *look* as if a change has occurred because the means have shifted due to the absence of certain students on the posttest. It is impossible to tell whether the observed difference has occurred because of the treatment, because of this experimental mortality, or because of some combination of the two.) (The variables are taken from the Mrs. Johnson example in the "Introduction" section of this chapter.)

still about even. Has the program been ineffective? The administrators look at the results more closely and discover that all 25 are still in the experimental group; but only 20 are left in the control group while 5 controls are no longer in school. The comparison has become clouded because of experimental mortality. It is likely that the average performance of the experimental group improved because the students learned something, whereas the improvement of the control group probably occurred because the slower students were the ones most likely to drop out of the school.

To be a threat to internal validity, such mortality has to be selective. The situation described in the previous paragraph provides an example of a threat to internal validity because the students who dropped out did so for reasons related to the treatment. If 5 students had dropped out of each group, and if it could be shown that all 5 dropouts occurred because of routine relocations arising from employment of the parents, then such mortality would not be a threat to internal validity.

Experimental mortality, then, is a problem when a group that finishes an experiment (completes a treatment or control condition) is not the same group that started it. When such mortality occurs, it is important to check to see if it is related to the treatment in any way. If you can rule out such experimental mortality as an explanation of the differences you observe in your experiment, you will strengthen the internal validity of your conclusions.

Review Quiz

Threats to Internal Validity—Experimental Mortality

Place an X next to the description which contains an example of experimental mortality as a threat to internal validity.

1. _____ Gotham State University has a rugged chemistry program. Over half the students who take chemistry courses flunk out. Those who remain, however, receive Quality Education. In fact, Gotham graduates average 87.4 (78th percentile) on the National Chemistry Exam. This can be compared to nearby Mickey Mouse University, where the students are very similar, but where very few flunk out of chemistry. MMU graduates average 63.8 (61st percentile) on the National Chemistry Exam. Gotham alumni are quite proud of their chemistry program.

2. _____ Students at Public School 101 and at Public School 202 are from about the same neighborhoods and about the same ability. At PS 101 the school board has asked the faculty to introduce the Mastery approach to teaching biology. At PS 202 the faculty continues with the old approach. At PS 101 84% of the Mastery students finish the year, and these average 77.6 (80th percentile) on the Biological Knowledge Test. At PS 202, however, 90% finish the year and average 62.8 (47th percentile) on the same test. These dropout rates are about what they have always been and appear to be related to family mobility rather than to anything relating to the school. The school board concludes that the Mastery approach is superior and recommends that it be implemented throughout the entire system.

Answers:
1. There is a problem of experimental mortality here. The average of GSU students is probably high on the National Chemistry Exam because the students who would have lowered the average were eliminated before taking the exam. This would lead to an artificial inflation of the GSU average.

2. There is no apparent threat from experimental mortality here. The higher dropout rate at PS 101 is about the same as it has been even before the experimental treatment. It appears to be unrelated to the treatment (that is, it is not apparent that anyone is either staying at or leaving either school in order to either obtain or avoid the Mastery approach in biology). Therefore, although the dropout rates were different, this does not constitute a threat to internal validity.

PRETESTING

With regard to internal validity, the threat of pretesting refers to *the fact that it might be the benefits derived from the pretest rather than the impact of the treatment that resulted in the changes observed in the outcome variable* (see Figure 8–9). For example, a person running an antismoking program might have participants write down the number of cigarettes they smoked each day for a week. Then he might show them a film about the evils of smoking. Finally, he might have them write down again how many cigarettes they smoked each day during the next week. If the number of cigarettes is lower after the film, the threat to internal validity is that it is possible that this reduction might be a result of the attention focused on smoking during the previous week (the pretest) rather than a result of the treatment itself.

Pretesting is a problem with achievement tests to the extent that they familiarize the students with the type of test questions they will have to deal with later and therefore artificially inflate their scores. In cases where the pretest is identical with the posttest, such familiarity with the pretest can sometimes be more useful to uninformed students than the lesson itself. For example, if you give students a set of 20 spelling words as a pretest, then teach them a list of 200 words for the next two weeks, and finally retest them with the same list of 20 words, it is obvious that the improvement on the posttest might have arisen from the previous test experience. The threat to internal validity would be greatly reduced by using one random set of 20 words on the pretest and another set on the posttest.

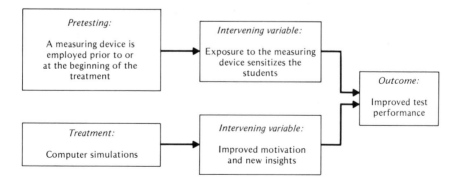

FIGURE 8–9. Pretesting as a Threat to Internal Validity. (There may actually have been no change at all in motivation or insights. It might merely appear that there has been a change, because exposure to the pretest has led the students to react differently to the posttest. Even if there has been a change in motivation and insights, it is possible that this change occurred as a reaction to the sensitization arising from the pretest rather than from the treatment.) (The variables are taken from the Mrs. Johnson example in the "Introduction" section of this chapter.)

The problem is somewhat different with regard to attitude and personality testing. In these cases, the pretest serves to sensitize the person, and this sensitization actually serves as a second treatment. If I give a person a questionnaire regarding attitudes toward various ethnic groups, for example, and then follow this up with some kind of program to enhance ethnic awareness, it is possible that the person might do a great deal of thinking while sorting out his feelings on the questionnaire. It might be this thinking at the time of the pretesting and during the interval before the posttest (rather than the ethnic awareness program) that caused an improved attitude.

In many cases in education, pretesting probably does not have the effect described in the above paragraph. Nevertheless the possibility exists, and the teacher/researcher should take precautions to reduce the chances that pretesting will provide artificial results. By using unobtrusive measurement techniques (discussed in Chapter 6) and by using several measurement strategies to crosscheck one another, this threat can be reduced. If you can reduce the likelihood that the observed results have arisen from experiencing the pretest rather than from experiencing the treatment, you will increase the internal validity of your conclusions.

Review Quiz

Threats to Internal Validity—Pretesting

Put an X before the description which contains an example of pretesting as a threat to internal validity.

1. _____ The students averaged 60 on the punctuation exam at the end of the first semester. The English teacher was upset by the low scores and gave the students detailed programmed materials to help them learn how to punctuate more effectively. The students used the materials, and then scored 84 when the same test was administered at the end of the second semester. The English teacher concluded that the programmed materials had caused the improvement and recommended spending 40% of the English department budget to purchase these materials.

2. _____ The students scored 60 on the punctuation exam at the end of the first semester. The English teacher was upset over how low this score was. He taught four sections of composition. To two of these sections he gave detailed, programmed materials to help the students learn how to punctuate more effectively. To the other two sections he gave no new materials, but rather continued with the usual method of instruction. At the end of the second semester, he gave the same punctuation test. The students with the new materials scored 84; but those with the old materials scored 63. The English teacher concluded that the programmed materials had caused the improvement and recommended that the department spend 40% of its budget to purchase these materials.

3. _____ The students in the English class turned in essays which were to be graded on content rather than on mechanics. As the teacher looked over the papers he was concerned about the poor quality of the punctuation. Without making any marks on the papers he recorded a separate score for mechanics. He did not convey this mechanics grade to the students, nor did he let it influence their grades. The students did not even know that they had been tested on mechanics. He then gave them detailed programmed materials to teach them to punctuate effectively. Three

months later he examined a similar assignment for mechanics. Whereas the students had made an average of 11.4 errors per essay on the pretest, he found that on the posttest they made only 2.1 errors. He concluded that the programmed materials had caused the improvement and recommended that they be incorporated into the regular English curriculum.

Answers:

1. Since the same test was used on the pretest and on the posttest, there is a serious problem here. For example, it is possible that the students who got items wrong might have asked their friends for the correct answers and remembered this information at the time of the posttest. Without further evidence, it would be rash to conclude that the programmed materials had caused a significant improvement.

2. Pretesting is not a problem here. If pretesting were causing the improvement, this effect would occur in all four sections, not just in the sections receiving the treatment. There may be other problems here (such as biased selection), but pretesting is not a threat to the internal validity of this study.

3. There is no apparent problem with pretesting here. The students took an unobtrusive pretest, and the posttest was based on different material. It seems unlikely that this pretest alone would produce the posttest results.

INSTABILITY

Instability is a threat to the internal validity of an experiment to the extent that *chance fluctuations in the test scores rather than the actual treatment can account for observed differences between groups* (see Figure 8–10). Such instability can be reduced by designing more reliable measurement devices and by using larger groups. In addition, the likelihood that a result will occur by chance can be estimated statistically, and such information can be useful to you in drawing conclusions from an experiment. Such statistical procedures will be discussed in Chapter 12.

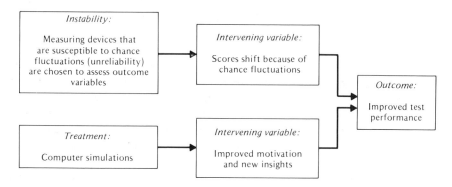

FIGURE 8–10. Instability as a Threat to Internal Validity. (There may actually have been no change at all in motivation or insights. It may merely look as if there has been a change because of the instability in the test scores. It is impossible to tell whether the improved test performance is a result of the treatment, of the instability, or of some combination of the two.) (The variables are taken from the Mrs. Johnson example in the "Introduction" section of this chapter.)

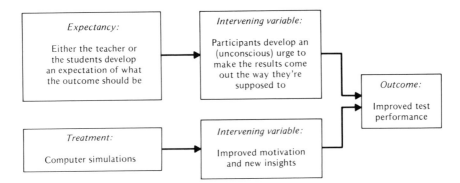

FIGURE **8–11.** Expectancy as a Threat to Internal Validity. (There may have been an actual change in motivation or insights, but it is impossible to tell whether this change occurred as a result of the treatment or as a result of an urge to make the experiment come out "right" or as a result of some combination of the two. It is also possible that motivation and insights did not change at all. It might merely appear that a change has occurred, because the participants' urge to make the results come out "right" led them to react differently to the posttest.)

EXPECTANCY EFFECTS

If either the experimenter or the subjects expect a certain outcome in an experiment, it is possible that their behavior will be (perhaps unconsciously) influenced by such expectations. *The fact that it could be these expectations rather than the actual treatment that produce the observed outcomes* is referred to as an expectancy effect (see Figure 8–11). It has been shown that researchers sometimes cheat in unconscious, subtle ways to get the results they expect. "Smart" rats which were genetically identical to "dumb" ones have been known to run mazes better simply because the students handling them were convinced by the false labeling. In addition, people who take part in experiments often try to figure out what the experiment is about, and act the way they feel they're supposed to act. In addition, sometimes the opposite occurs; a participant tries to figure out what the result is supposed to be and does the opposite, in order to thwart the experimenter.

In all these cases, it could be the artificial expectations aroused by the experiment rather than the actual treatment which accounts for the outcome. If you can rule out such artificial expectations, you can increase the internal validity of your conclusions.

(Expectancy effects are also an important consideration in external validity. Because they will be discussed more fully in Chapter 13, no more detailed treatment will be given to them at this time. Many students find it difficult to distinguish between expectancy as a threat to internal validity and as a threat to external validity. There is a distinction, but it is not particularly important to isolate what aspects of expectancy influence internal validity and what aspects influence external validity. The important thing is to reduce such artificial influences so that you can draw valid conclusions.)

INTERACTION OF SEVERAL FACTORS

The examples given so far in this chapter have focused on one effect at a time. It should be obvious that many of these threats could simultaneously threaten the

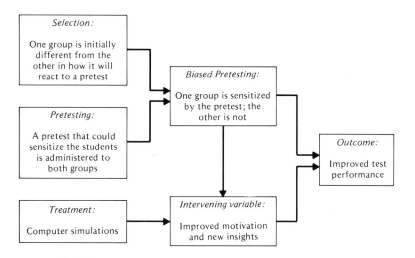

FIGURE **8–12.**   The Interaction of Several Factors as a Threat to Internal Validity. (It is possible that there has been a change in motivation and insights, but this change may have occurred because of differences in the way the separate groups reacted to the pretest. Or it is possible that it merely appears that there has been a change, because one of the groups (but not the other) was sensitized by the pretest to do better on the posttest.) (The variables are taken from the Mrs. Johnson example in the "Introduction" section of this chapter.)

internal validity of the same experiment. What may not be so obvious is that these factors not only accumulate, *they also interact*. In other words, *the different factors mix together in such a way as to provide unique factors in their own rights* (Figure 8–12).

To take an example, history and selection often interact in experiments when volunteers are used. This occurs because it is often true that a person who would volunteer to be part of an experiment is also a person who is more attuned to what is going on around him. For this reason, the volunteer is likely to react to history differently than a person who is a non-volunteer. In a very real sense, therefore, history is different for the volunteer. In a sense, a new variable (called biased history, perhaps) has been created. In this way, history and selection can interact to threaten the internal validity of a study.

When you are examining an experiment to rule out each of the threats to internal validity, therefore, it is important to look for them in interaction with one another, as well as operating separately. For example, although the volunteers receiving a treatment might be quite similar in all other apparent respects to the non-volunteers who are not receiving it, it is still possible that the subtle interaction of volunteering with history or pretesting could contaminate the internal validity of the study. If you can rule out such interactions, you can strengthen the internal validity of your conclusions.

Many readers will find it hard to distinguish between the simple impact of the threats discussed in this chapter and the interactive effects described in this section. There is a difference, and it is important to control both simple threats and interactive effects. However, the distinction appears needlessly subtle to some readers. If you examine the exercises at the end of this section and see that there are problems but have trouble explaining why these are interactive rather than simple threats, you should probably not be concerned. The important thing is to recognize and control the threats, not to define and classify them.

Review Quiz

Threats to Internal Validity—Interaction of Several Factors

Put an X next to any description which contains an example of two or more factors interacting to pose a threat to internal validity.

1. _____ Mr. Sander's first-grade pupils were doing poorly on their basic math facts. He had given them a test on which their average should have been 50, but they had averaged only 25. He knew of a technique which might help them, but it would be very time consuming. Therefore, he decided to do an experiment; because unless the new technique really worked, he did not want to bother with it again the next year. Since there were no other first graders in his school building, he asked the second-grade teacher, Ms. Adams, if he could use some of her children as a control group. He found 10 of her slower children, who also averaged 25 on the same test. He then used his new technique with his first graders, while the control group used normal methods. He tested them at the end of the year with an alternate form of the same test. His first graders scored 37, whereas the control group of second graders scored only 27. He concluded that although he would have liked to have seen even more improvement, the new technique did seem to be having a beneficial effect. And so he decided to use the technique regularly in the future.

2. _____ Miss Dawson wanted to find out if the use of computer simulations would help her science students learn the skills of scientific problem solving. She had 24 students in her class. She asked for 12 volunteers to use the computer simulations. The other 12 served as a control group. She gave them a pretest, on which both groups scored about 35. Four months later, she gave them a posttest. This time the control group scored around 55, whereas the students who had used the computer simulations scored nearly 65. Miss Dawson concluded that the computer simulations were more effective than the ordinary instruction in teaching scientific problem solving skills.

3. _____ Mr. Bellow wanted to find out if a physical fitness program would promote an improved self-concept among adults. He posted a notice on a college bulletin board that stated that he needed volunteers for a project involving physical exercise. A hundred volunteers signed up. From these 100 volunteers, he randomly selected 25 to serve as an experimental group (who got the exercise) and 25 to serve as a control group (who were tested but did not get the exercise program). He told the other 50 that he appreciated their interest, but he could not use them this time. After three months in his program, the people undergoing the physical fitness program had significantly better self-concepts than those who were in the control group. Mr. Bellow concluded that the physical fitness program had caused an improved self-concept among these people.

Answers:
1. There is a problem here, consisting of an interaction of selection and maturation. The subjects who were selected for one group (second graders) responded differently to maturation than did those selected for the other group (first graders).
2. There is a problem here. This is an example of the interaction of selection and pretesting. The subjects in one group (volunteers) were likely to react differently to pretesting than the subjects in the other group (non-volunteers).
3. There are no uncontrolled threats to internal validity in this study. This is an excellent study. Such randomized assignment to experimental and control groups will be described in the next chapter as an excellent way to control many of the threats to internal validity.

PUTTING IT ALL TOGETHER

Eugene Anderson, our humane educator, developed an Animal Life Package (ALP) which he believed would help children develop favorable attitudes toward animal life. He wanted to test it, to make sure it worked, and then he wanted to promote its use throughout the country.

He got out his Fireman Tests (Chapters 3 to 7), which existed in two forms. He went to Mortimer Peterson Elementary School. He gave one form of the test as a pretest to all fourth through sixth graders. Two weeks later he presented the ALP to the same classes. He returned in another two weeks and administered the posttest. He found that on the pretest the children chose an average of only 1.34 animals each, but after the treatment they chose 2.21 animals each. He was impressed with his findings.

However, as fate would have it, that evening Mr. Anderson chanced upon this very textbook. He found it on the table in the principal's office. He perused the chapter on internal validity. Was it possible that his study had threats to its internal validity? Was it possible that something other than the ALP had caused the enhanced performance on the posttest.

After a sleepless night Mr. Anderson spent the next day desperately evaluating the threats to the internal validity of his study. He found good news and bad news. The good news was that he had no serious threats from selection, history, maturation, instrumentation, instability, statistical regression, experimental mortality, or the interactive effects of any of these.

He ruled out selection, because if the children had already possessed good attitudes this would have shown up on the pretest. He eliminated history because after making a careful examination of everything that had happened at school, on TV, and around the neighborhood, he discovered nothing that would have logically caused them to change attitudes. Maturation was no problem, because there was no logical reason why the passage of four weeks should suddenly lead to improved attitudes toward animals. He ruled out both instrumentation and stability because he had already established that the tests possessed both test-retest and alternate-form reliability. Statistical regression was no problem, because there had been no selection resulting in extreme groups. Finally, experimental mortality was no problem, since all the children had been present for both the pretest and the posttest.

The bad news was that he had serious problems with expectancy and pretesting. Expectancy had been a problem because the principal had announced to the teachers and children that Mr. Anderson was going to present an interesting new program about animals and she hoped they would do well. Even worse, Mr. Anderson discovered that after the children had taken the pretest, several of them had been heard talking about it and commenting that they thought it was about how much we like animals. Mr. Anderson had to admit that he could not tell whether it had been the ALP, the exhortation from the principal, or the reaction of the children to the pretest that had led to the improved posttest scores.

Mr. Anderson realized the error of his ways and eagerly read the next chapter of this book to discover effective strategies to control these threats to internal validity.

SUMMARY OF THE THREATS TO INTERNAL VALIDITY

Each of the threats described in this chapter creates problems for either of two reasons. First, they may bring about a change in the desired outcome which may mistakenly be attributed to the treatment. Second, they may influence the measurement of the outcome variable in such a way as to make it appear that an outcome has occurred when, in fact, no such outcome has occurred. To the extent that we can rule out these threats, therefore, we strengthen the logic of our conclusion that it is the treatment which is responsible for the observed effects.

As you read the following summaries of each of the major threats to internal validity, determine whether or not you understand the principles involved. If you do not you should reexamine the relevant sections before proceeding to Chapter 9.

History refers to the threat that some extraneous event (or combination of events) other than the treatment is responsible for the observed outcome.

Selection is concerned with the problem that a group's performance on an outcome variable may arise from the composition of the group itself rather than from the treatment.

Maturation refers to the fact that changes in an outcome variable may occur as a routine result of the passage of time rather than because of the treatment.

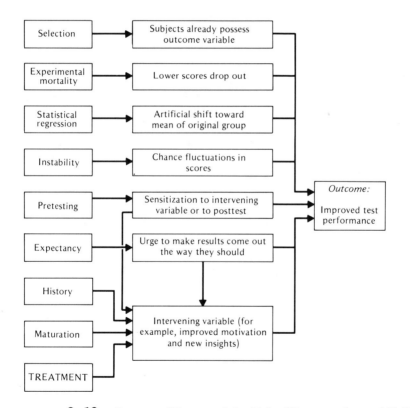

FIGURE 8–13. Summary Diagram of the Major Threats to Internal Validity. (Interactions are not included in this diagram as a separate threat.) The role of the teacher/researcher is to rule out each of these threats and therefore make it possible to conclude that the treatment (and not one of these irrelevant threats) actually caused the observed outcome. It is not always possible to control all these threats, but to the extent that they can be controlled the validity of your conclusions will be strengthened.) (The variables are taken from the Mrs. Johnson example in the "Introduction" section of this chapter.)

Instrumentation can be a problem because changes in the instrument or in the way it is administered may make it look as though a change has occurred when in fact nothing has happened.

Statistical regression is a threat because subgroups selected on the basis of their extreme scores tend to give a false impression of change by shifting toward the mean on subsequent tests.

Experimental mortality is a threat when the composition of the group changes because of dropouts and this change gives the false impression that the performance of the members of the group has changed.

Pretesting refers to the fact that it might be the benefits derived from the pretest rather than from the treatment which have resulted in the differences observed in the outcome variable.

Instability consists of chance fluctuations in the test scores, which can give a false impression that differences have been found where there are none.

Expectancy refers to the fact that artificial expectations arising from the experimental situation can give the false impression that the treatment has had an impact.

The interaction of several factors refers to the possibility that these factors can act in combination as well as alone to achieve their impact on the internal validity of a study.

These threats are summarized in Figure 8–13. The job of the teacher/researcher/decision-maker is to rule out or account for each of these threats. The next chapter will begin with a discussion of how to control these threats and thereby increase the internal validity of your cause and effect conclusions.

Annotated Bibliography

CAMPBELL, D.T. and STANLEY, J.C. *Experimental and Quasi-Experimental Designs for Research* (Chicago: Rand McNally, 1966). Until it is eventually supplanted by Cook and Campbell (1979), this will continue to be the most widely cited work on the threats to internal validity.

COOK, T.D. and CAMPBELL, D.T. *Quasi-Experimentation: Design and Analysis Issues for Field Settings* (Chicago: Rand McNally, 1979). Chapter 2 contains the most complete treatment available of the concept of internal validity. Although a few chapters in this book are extremely complex, Chapter 2 is easily understandable and useful to teachers and others interested in doing serious applied research.

Professional Journals

The following article deals with a major threat to the internal validity of a study. In addition, most of the articles cited at the end of chapters 9 through 11 (as well as many of those cited in chapters 14 and 15) deal with ways to overcome threats to internal validity, and therefore specific threats are discussed in many of these articles.

EVERTSON, C.M., EMMER, E.T., and BROPHY, J.E. "Predictors of effective teaching in junior high mathematics classrooms," *Journal for Research in Mathematics Education* 11 (1980): 167–178. The authors identify the factors that differentiate effective teachers from less effective teachers. They realize that selection bias could be a threat to the internal validity of their conclusions, and they state evidence that can be brought to bear on the severity of this threat.

9 Research Design: Controlling the Threats to Internal Validity

Chapter Preview

Chapter 8 introduced the concept of internal validity and identified the major threats to internal validity. The present chapter introduces the basic strategies for minimizing these threats through the careful scheduling of treatments and observations of the persons to whom the treatments are administered.

This chapter introduces the ideal strategies for dealing with the threats and identifies ways to put the ideal strategies into practice. Chapter 10 will introduce ways to modify the ideal strategies to provide as much control of the threats as possible in situations where the high degree of control described in the present chapter is impossible.

After reading this chapter you should be able to

- Define research design and identify its purpose.
- Define and give examples of the important terms used in discussing research design.
- Describe the Basic Strategy of Research Design and apply this basic strategy to concrete situations.
- Define and give examples of random assignment of subjects to experimental treatments.
- Describe how to apply random assignment to a concrete situation.
- Describe the underlying theory regarding how random assignment overcomes the major threats to internal validity.
- Describe the use of matching and its relationship to random assignment.
- Describe strategies for controlling those threats to internal validity which are not controlled by random assignment of subjects to groups.
- Describe the strategy of the two true experimental designs and apply these designs to concrete research settings.

RESEARCH DESIGN

Research design refers to the systematic scheduling of the times at which treatments are administered to subjects and at which observations are made of the performance of the subjects. This careful scheduling of the treatments and observations can be very helpful in reducing the threats to internal validity which were discussed in the previous chapter. Research design is not a replacement for careful measurement, careful analysis, and careful reasoning. It is rather an important component of the research process—of the process of establishing cause and effect relationships. By combining careful research design with appropriate measurement, analysis, and reasoning, we can strengthen the validity of the conclusions we can draw from our research efforts.

In solving the threats to internal validity, we can either (1) reason carefully about what happened in our experiment or (2) use a well-planned research design. The two strategies are not really separate. A good research design merely makes reasoning easier. Many educators by necessity have to reason with the data that they can get—and a good research design is not always available. Under such circumstances, thinking carefully about the threats to internal validity and carefully weighing their impact upon the conclusions under consideration is a valid and important endeavor. Teachers and other professionals may have to do much of their thinking and decision making without benefit of a good research design.

Nevertheless, in this and the next chapter, priority will be given to research design. This order of priority has been chosen because (1) correct research design is by far the best course of action and you should always come as close as possible to using a good research design to support your conclusions, and (2) the alternate routes are often really patched-up techniques to improvise a research design when no good one exists. An understanding of the principles of research design will sharpen your ability to deal with the threats to internal validity in order to strengthen your conclusions.

Important Terms Used in Discussing Research Design

In discussing research design it will be useful to understand some basic terms. The definition of many of these terms would probably be self-evident to many readers reading this chapter, but it seems appropriate to state these definitions at this time.

An *experiment* refers to any attempt to establish a cause and effect relationship by administering a treatment to one group and withholding it from another group. In a very strict sense, the term is used only when there is an actual *manipulation* of the subjects—that is, when one set of subjects receives a treatment and a different set of subjects receives no treatment. In a looser, but still adequate, sense, the term refers to those situations where there is an attempt to establish cause and effect relationships even when there is no manipulation. For example, it might be suggested that the sex of the subject causes certain attitudes, even if boys and girls cannot be assigned to the boy and girl treatments.

A *subject* is a person who takes part in an experiment. The subject receives the treatment. (Subjects in the control group have the treatment withheld.) In some cases, something other than a person (school buildings, for instance) can be the subject of an experiment.

A *treatment* is an event or activity which is expected to produce an outcome. Reading programs, grades, decisions to keep children after school for detention, and similar events and activities are examples of treatments. In a later chapter, the treatment will be referred to as the *"independent variable."*

Observation refers to the act of collecting data about the performance of a subject. The term covers all types of measurement, not just those accomplished through visual observation. An observation conducted prior to a treatment is referred to as a *pretest.* An observation conducted after the treatment has been administered is referred to as a *posttest.*

The *experimental group* is the group of subjects which receives the treatment.

The *control group* is the group of subjects from which the treatment is withheld. A related term is *comparison group*. The two terms are often used interchangeably. The actual distinction, when there is one, is that the control group receives no treatment, whereas a comparison group receives an alternate treatment.

Let us summarize with an example. If a teacher wants to find out whether a new reading program works, she can do this by setting up an *experiment*. She *manipulates* the *subjects* by randomly assigning half to the *experimental group* and half to the *control group*. She conducts *pretest* and *posttest observations* and makes comparisons afterwards to see if the treatment caused improvements among those who received it.

Additional terms (such as *random assignment* and *quasi-experiment*) will be defined in specific detail as the need for them arises.

THE BASIC STRATEGY OF RESEARCH DESIGN

In theory, the most straightforward strategy for ascertaining cause and effect relationships is extremely simple. This Basic Strategy of Research Design can be summarized as follows:

- Compare the performance of the group receiving the treatment to the performance of another group which is exactly the same in all respects except that this second group has not received the treatment.
- If the group that received the treatment subsequently performs differently with regard to a specified outcome than the group that received no treatment, then the treatment caused this effect.
  Otherwise, the treatment made no difference.

This Basic Strategy of Research Design is diagrammed in Figure 9–1. The catch is that it is actually very difficult to put this "simple" theory into practice. This difficulty arises from the two great problems in educational experiments:

- It is almost impossible to find two groups that are exactly identical in all respects except with regard to the experimental treatment; and
- Because educational measurement is not perfectly reliable or perfectly valid, it is often difficult to tell whether two groups actually differ after a treatment.

In many of the sciences outside education, the above problems do not seriously interfere with drawing cause and effect inferences. This is because it is actually possible to find nearly perfectly matched groups and perfectly standardized materials and to make extremely precise measurements. This is not the case in education. The first of the above problems will be dealt with in this Chapter and in Chapter 10. The second problem has already be discussed briefly in Chapter 3 and will be discussed further in Chapter 12.

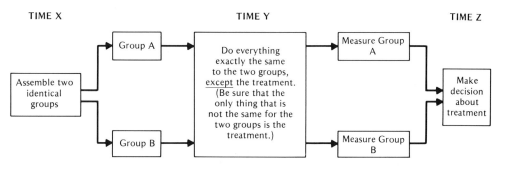

FIGURE 9–1. The Basic Strategy of Research Design.

HOW TO FIND EQUAL GROUPS

Assume that you want to know whether or not a new method of teaching reading to fifth graders is really better than your traditional method. According to the Basic Strategy of Research Design, you should give the new method to one group while you simultaneously give the traditional method to another group which is initially identical to this experimental group. How would you go about finding two groups that are exactly identical? Admitting that this is impossible, how would you go about finding two groups that are as nearly identical as possible? Which of the following strategies would be best to follow?

- Examine all 45 fifth-grade classes in the school system and find the two that are closest to each other in average (mean) age and I.Q. Then give the reading treatment to one class and the traditional method to the other.
- Find two fifth grades within one school with 30 students in each. Compute the average IQ and age. Then eliminate 5 students from each grade in such a way as to make the two grades as nearly equal as possible with regard to age and IQ.
- Find a school with two fifth grades within the same building. Simply give one of the classes the new program and the other the old program.
- Find a school which is going to have to assign its fifth graders to two separate classes. Have these classes assigned completely at random (without reference to age, IQ, or any other factor). Then choose one of these groups at random and give it the new program. Give the other group the traditional program.

Which of the above would be the best strategy? The answer is number 4, because this strategy relies completely upon randomization. Nothing other than chance influences the formation of the groups. In all the other cases, some factor(s) other than chance went into the formation of the groups, and therefore the groups are likely to be biased in ways related to their ability to profit from the program.

One of the most important realizations in the history of social science research has been that random assignment is the most powerful way to make it likely that two or more groups are intially equivalent. Therefore, comparisons which are based on random assignment are the most powerful comparisons, and random assignment is the preferred strategy for examining cause and effect relationships.

HOW RANDOM ASSIGNMENT WORKS

If I wanted to divide a classroom of 50 graduate students randomly into two groups, how could I accomplish this?

- Should I get to the classroom before anyone arrived, and then count the first 25 who came into the room, placing them in one group, and then place the remaining 25 in another group?
- Should I wait until all 50 were in the room and then count off 25 from the front of the room, putting these in one group and the other 25 in the second group?
- Should I take the class list and put the first 25 in alphabetical order into one group and the last 25 in the other group?

The answer is that none of the above is an example of random assignment to groups. In the first case, it seems obvious that those who arrive early for a class probably possess certain characteristics that make them different from those who arrive later. Even if I wait until everyone gets into the room (the second case), there is a reasonable chance that friends will sit together, that everyone who came early went to the back of the room, or that some similar factor will cause the groups to be different. In the case of using the alphabetical list, the biasing factors are perhaps more subtle; but is it not possible that persons close together in the alphabet might become friends and that friends might become more alike? Indeed, names which are adjacent in the alphabet are more likely to belong to husbands and wives or mothers and daughters than are names separated in the alphabet.

Random assignment minimizes the chance that biases will occur. The only factor that determines placement in a group is chance alone. In the class of graduate students, random assignment could be accomplished in several ways.

- Take the list of 50 students and assign each student a number between 1 and 50. Then go to a list of random numbers and select 25 numbers at random between 1 and 50. Put the students whose names correspond to these numbers into one group and the others into the second group. Then flip a coin to determine which one is the experimental group.
- Take the list of 50 students and put the names on cards. Shuffle the cards thoroughly, and then deal them into two stacks. Make the cards on the left the members of your control group and those on the right your experimental group.
- Match the students into pairs, based on important characteristics such as age or previous course grades. Obtain 25 pairs in this way. Then flip a coin for each pair and assign the person who gets heads to the control group and the one who gets tails to the experimental group.

All three of these strategies would provide randomly assigned groups. The third strategy is an example of random assignment with matching. This strategy will be discussed later in this chapter, but it should be pointed out here that either of the first two is almost always just as effective and quite a bit simpler.

HOW TO USE A TABLE OF RANDOM NUMBERS

A table of random numbers (Appendix B, Table 2,) is a list of numbers arranged in random order. By using this list of numbers to select a sample for a survey (see Chapter 7) or to assign members to experimental and control groups, we can be sure we are doing so with no bias affecting our selection or assignment.

There are actually many ways we could use such a list. All we have to do is be sure we do not accidentally introduce some sort of bias into our selection of subjects. The following paragraph will describe one of the methods for using random numbers to assign subjects to experimental and control groups.

Assume that we have 60 subjects whom we wish to assign to two groups, an experimental and a control group. First we would list all 60 names and assign numbers 1 through 60 to each name. (At this point, it does not matter how systematically or unsystematically the names are arranged.) Next, we would turn to the table of random numbers and choose a number from that table at a point determined by chance. (A blind pointing will do). For example, such a chance entry into the table of random numbers might give us a starting point at the thirty-first number down in the third row. In our table, this is a 72. Since 72 is greater than 60, we ignore it. Next we might go across the page, selecting any number that falls between 1 and 60. The next number on our table would be 85, which is still too high. Next comes 22. This falls within our range of 1 to 60. Therefore we would put the subject numbered 22 in one group. We would continue across the page, putting subjects 38, 56, 01, and 30 into the same group as our first subject. At the end of that line, we would continue to the next line down on the page. If we came to a number that we had already used, we would skip that number. Eventually, we would get 30 subjects on our list for one group. We would then put the remaining 30 subjects in the other group. Finally, we would flip a coin to decide which group would be the experimental and which would be the control group.

The above method would result in a random assignment of subjects to groups. Of course, if we wanted three groups instead of two, or if we had 150 subjects to put into two groups, we would have to vary the process somewhat. The important thing is to let no biasing factor enter our assignment process. An example of biased use of the table would be to have the subjects sign a list as they arrive for the experiment, then assign numbers according to order of arrival, and finally select a single number from the random tables, putting the first 30 names after that number in the experimental group and the rest in the control group. This would be a biased method, because subjects would be clustered together in a nonrandom fashion. Friends would be likely to be in the same group, people of similar backgrounds and intelligence might be clustered together, and so on.

WHY RANDOM ASSIGNMENT WORKS

Random assignment is based on some simple principles of mathematical probability. Simply summarized, these principles state that when subjects have been assigned to groups at random, *these groups are likely to differ with regard to any characteristic only to the extent that they would be expected to differ by chance.* This is slightly different from saying that they are likely to be equal. The groups will, in fact, be slightly different from sample to sample. However, when chance is the only factor operating, then it is possible to state mathematically the degree of confidence that these differences will fall within a certain range. Once we know this range of probability, then we can examine data after a treatment and see whether or not our results fall inside or outside this range. By doing this, we can make a conclusion about how likely it is that our treatment caused this effect to come about.

The above paragraph is a brief but precise statement of the theory behind randomization. Since it involves mathematical assumptions and implies statistical analysis, it may seem incomprehensible to many readers at this point. This is not because educators are unintelligent, but rather because many of us have developed conditioned reflexes which cause us to turn off any ideas involving mathematics or statistics. With this in mind, I would recommend that you reexamine the above paragraph if either now or later you have a further desire to understand the underlying logic of random assignment. If you do not have such an urge, read on.

To take a concrete example, assume that I have two really bright students among my 50 graduate students about to be assigned to two groups. If I use any of the three methods described on page 154 to assign these students to experimental and control groups, there is a pretty good chance that they will both wind up in the same group. This is because of such biases as those mentioned on page 1000. On the other hand, if I assign them at random (through one of the strategies described on page 155), there is a 50–50 chance for each one that he will be in the experimental group and a 50–50 chance that he will be in the control group. There's still a reasonable (50–50) chance that they will both wind up in the same group, but *we know what this probability is.* (It's a 50 percent probability.)

The larger the group becomes, the more likely it is that random assignment will reduce chance biases with regard to any characteristic. For example, assume that I have six exceptionally able mathematics students among my 50 graduate students. If I used any of the biased (nonrandom) strategies mentioned on page 154 to put them in experimental and control groups, there is still a good chance that the subtle biases will result in most or all of them being in one group. On the other hand, the odds are more remote that all six of them would be in the same group if I used random assignment.

Random assignment has the advantage of mathematically equating all characteristics of people, even if I do not know what these characteristics are and even if I have been unable to measure them. For example, it might not even occur to me that there could be six graduate students in my class who are excessively shy and prone to avoid novel teaching techniques and who sit together near the back of the room. If I use one of the biased methods on page 154, I might inadvertently put all six of these in one group. I might then look at my group and notice that both groups had students of about the same age and ability level, and this might convince me that my groups were equal. Unknown to me, the groups would differ on a very important variable closely related to the outcome of my experiment. On the other hand, if I used random assignment, these six shy students would have a good chance of being evenly distributed—even though I would not be aware of this characteristic at the time of random assignment (or at any other time, for that matter).

The larger the group becomes, the less likely it is that discrepant characteristics (unusually different scores) will arise in the several groups. The logic is precisely the same as in coin tossing. If a friend tosses a coin twice and gets both heads or both tails, I am not going to accuse him of cheating. But if he tosses the coin 15 times and gets all 15 heads, then I am going to become suspicious. This is because there is an exact statement of the probability of getting the same result 15 times in a row (odds are 16,383 to 1 against it), and I would recognize that the result departs from this probability. Likewise, as samples become larger, we can make more precise statements about how likely it is that the two groups will be about the same. The larger the groups become, the less likely it is that randomly assigned groups will differ with regard to any specified characteristic.

Random assignment sounds mysterious—even eerie—to some readers. But it works. It is based on perfectly sound mathematical theory. A study based on random assignment gives much more valid results than much larger studies based on biased assignment to treatments. Through careful planning, it is often possible to use random assignment. This often requires the foresight to seek cooperation from the person who assigns students to classes. Whenever possible, use random assignment.

THE PURPOSE OF RANDOM ASSIGNMENT

The purpose of random assignment is to make the groups initially as equal as possible on all variables. As Figure 9–1 has indicated, if a treatment is administered to one randomly assigned group while a second randomly assigned group receives no treatment, then any differences in the two groups which appear on subsequent measurements are the result of either (a) chance or (b) the treatment. The probable impact of chance can be estimated through statistical procedures and can often be ruled out as a plausible explanation. (Ways to do this are discussed in Chapter 12.)

This leaves the treatment as the only reasonably plausible explanation of the observed differences.

Essential to integrating the previous chapter with the present chapter is the idea that random assignment makes the groups initially as equal as possible with regard to each of the threats to internal validity. Selection bias is obviously removed. In addition, subjects in one group are likely to be initially comparable to those in the other in their past histories, in their tendencies to mature during the duration of the experiment, and in their reactions to the measurement instruments. Both groups are equally likely to regress toward the mean, if this is a possiblity. The *initial proclivities* of the subjects in the two groups to drop out of the experiment, to display unstable test results, or to develop attitudes of expectancy are likely to be quite similar.

Although random assignment thus minimizes most of the threats to internal validity, some threats still remain. Experimental mortality, instability, and expectancy are problems which develop after the start of the treatment, and therefore they are not controlled simply by making the groups initially equivalent. These three problems are discussed later in this chapter. Furthermore, even though randomization makes it likely that the subjects in both groups will be quite similar with regard to past, present, and future history *outside* the experimental setting, this does not rule out the possibility that history could differ *within* the experimental setting. For example, if one experimental group would meet before lunch and the other experimental group after lunch, this could introduce aspects of history not affected by random assignment.

By making the groups as equal as possible in their susceptibility to the threats to internal validity, therefore, random assignment emerges as a highly effective tool for strengthening the internal validity of our cause and effect inferences. Although randomization is not perfect in its control of these extraneous factors, it is by far the best single strategy available for group research. Supplemented by additional careful procedures, random assignment lends strength to our ability to draw cause and effect inferences from experimental research.

MATCHING AND RANDOM ASSIGNMENT

Sometimes you may have to deal with intact groups—groups where you have no control over who goes into the group, but which come as already formed groups at the beginning of an experiment. Under such circumstances, many novice researchers resort to a process called matching in order to artifically construct two groups to use in the experiment. This is an absolutely wrong way to proceed. This erroneous process is described here only to help you avoid it. See if you can understand the reasons why this is an improper method for assembling experimental and control groups.

Assume that a high school basketball coach wants to try a new method to teach his players how to shoot freethrows. He decides to use his varsity players for the experimental group and his junior varsity players for the control group. He checks out his statistics and discovers that his twelve varsity players have averaged 80% from the foul line this year, whereas the twelve junior varsity players have averaged only 60%. The groups are not equal. So he decides to create two equal groups by taking five of the varsity players and matching them up with junior varsity players with identical freethrow percentages. He therefore has an experimental group of five varsity players with a freethrow average of 70% and a control group of five junior varsity players with a freethrow percentage of 70% (see Figure 9–2). The groups are exactly equal—or are they?

The problem which the coach has ignored is that of statistical regression. As you may recall from Chapter 8, statistical regression refers to the tendency of the scores of extreme subgroups to regress on subsequent testing occasions toward the mean of the group from which they were taken. In this case, the coach has two extreme subgroups, and both of them are likely to regress toward the mean of their original group, as shown in Figure 9–2. To get his group of 70%-shooters from the varsity, he had to select the players with the lowest shooting averages on that squad. When retested, (that is, when they shoot some more freethrows) these extreme low scorers are likely to score closer to the mean of their group—closer to 80%. Likewise, to get his group of 70%-shooters from the junior varsity, the coach had to select the best shooters on the squad. When retested, these extreme high scorers will score closer to the mean of their group—closer to 60%. In his attempt to obtain two identical groups, the coach has in fact taken steps to guarantee that the groups are actually unequal!

The only time matching is a valid strategy is when you are able to follow it with random assignment to groups. For example, if the coach in the previous example would have taken his twelve varsity players and matched them in pairs based on nearly equal scores, he could have then assigned one player from each of these six pairs to the experimental and the other to the control treatment. Such matching accompanied by random assignment is a perfectly valid research strategy, since it involves no biases or regression problems. It is not an especially useful strategy, however, since the resulting groups are seldom superior for research purposes to groups assembled with simple random assignment without matching. There are only a few instances when the matching plus random assignment procedure is preferred. For example, if you expect experimental mortality during your experiment, then matching plus random assignment can help you know what subjects to delete from posttest analysis as a possible help to overcome that threat to internal validity. (This problem is discussed in the next section of this chapter.) In addition, if you have subjects with widely varying scores in a situation where it would be obviously undesirable to have a disproportionate number of these discrepant scorers in a single

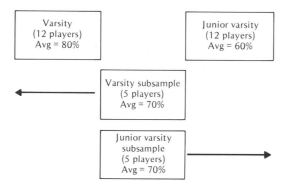

FIGURE 9–2. An Example of Regression Toward the Mean Resulting from Matching. (Each of the subsamples will regress toward the mean of the group from which it was originally selected. The arrows in the above diagram indicate the direction of this statistical regression.)

group, then matching plus random assignment would be preferable to simple random assignment. This will most often be the case when only a very small number of subjects are available for a study and some of them have unusual scores.

The above discussion may be viewed as unnecessarily technical by some readers. If this is the case, then just remember the following simple rule. Never match from intact groups. If you do match, always follow the matching with random assignment to groups. Or, as the Bard says:

> Don't tug on Superman's cape.
> Don't spit into the wind.
> And never match from intact groups without subsequent random assignment to treatment groups.

SOME THREATS UNTOUCHED BY RANDOM ASSIGNMENT

The previous section indicated that random assignment assembles two groups which are likely to be as equal as possible with regard to the following threats to internal validity: selection, maturation, history, pretesting, statistical regression, instrumentation, and the interactions of any of these variables. Even with random assignment, however the following threats to internal validity are left uncontrolled: experimental mortality, instability, and expectancy effects. Random assignment will provide groups which are likely to be equal in their susceptibility to these three threats, but the events which comprise these threats occur after the assignment of treatments, and consequently these threats can be uncontrolled even in a properly randomized experiment.

None of the designs discussed in this chapter or the next controls these three threats to internal validity. These threats have to be controlled through methods other than experimental design. The following paragraphs will briefly describe methods for controlling them. In discussing the research designs throughout the rest of this chapter, I am assuming that appropriate steps were undertaken to control these three threats.

Experimental mortality refers to the fact that measures of group performance might change because self-selected subjects drop out of the group rather than because the members of the group have actually improved their performance. The only sure way to rule out the threat of experimental mortality is to have no dropouts. If the subjects in both the experimental group and the control group who finish an experiment are the same ones who started it, then experimental mortality is no problem at all. Such complete participation is often quite possible. If there is likely to be a problem in this regard, it is often a good idea to try for 100% posttest performance from a small group of subjects rather than a lower percentage of posttest participation from a initially larger group of subjects.

If subjects do drop out of your experiment (and sometimes this is unavoidable), there are a few steps you can take. First, you can compare the pretest scores (if you have them) of the subjects who dropped out to the pretest scores of those who remained in the experiment. If the scores are approximately the same, then it is likely that the dropouts have not biased your study. (However, this is a likelihood, not a certainty. Since the dropping out is a nonrandom process, you will run into subtle problems that are very similar to the interactions of selection with other factors, discussed in Chapters 8 and 10. This is a complex issue which will not be discussed further in this book.) Second, you can examine the reasons why subjects dropped out. If they dropped out because of reasons completely unrelated to the treatment, then your problems are minimized. On the other hand, if there appears to be a connection between the decision to drop out and your experimental treatment, this is a threat to your internal validity. Finally, if you assigned subjects by random assignment after matching into pairs, you can exclude the matched pair for each dropout from the other group from the posttest analysis. This is an imperfect but partial solution.

The strategies discussed above provide a useful control for experimental mortality. The only perfect way to control this threat, however, is to have no dropouts.

Instability refers to the tendency of a result to show up on one experimental occasion but not on others. It is a result of unreliability. This threat is controlled by stating the probability of instability in statistical terms. The use and interpretation of these statistical strategies will be discussed in Chapter 12.

Expectancy effects arise when subtle expectations of the experimenter or of the subjects influence the outcome of an experiment. Such effects occur most often when the experiment is an obviously artifical situation or when someone (such as the experimenter) has a vested interest in seeing the results turn out a certain way. Expectancy effects influence external as well as internal validity, and therefore a detailed discussion of how to deal with them will be delayed until Chapter 13. At this time, only the following important point will be made. As you read the rest of this and the following chapter, it will be obvious that in most cases a true experimental design will be preferable to a quasi-experimental design for controlling the threats to internal validity. The threat of invalidity from expectancy effects can provide an exception to this rule. If the activity involved in randomization results in an artificial situation which is likely to arouse expectancy effects, then the true experiment is actually more likely to lead to this source of invalidity than a less obtrusive quasi-experimental design. In such a case the quasi-experimental design (which is less rigorous in other respects) may be preferable. Such artificiality, however, is not an essential component of randomization, and it is possible in many cases to use true experimental designs which do not produce expectancy threats to internal validity.

Terminology and Symbols Used in Describing Research Designs

For the sake of clarity and simplicity, each of the various designs discussed in this chapter will be accompanied by a diagram. Such diagrams show the basic components of each experimental design. In order to understand these diagrams it is necessary to become familar with the symbols used in them. The basic symbols are described below:

R stands for *random assignment to groups*. This symbol is placed at the beginning of a line if the group described on that line is randomly assigned.

O stands for an *observation* or measurement. Subscripts accompanying this symbol (O_1, O_2, etc.) are merely labels to identify specific instances of measurement so that these can be discussed in the text. There is no assumption, therefore, that O_1 precedes O_2.

X stands for a *treatment*. The absence of X stands for the absence of treatment.

A row of dashes (-----) between two lines in the diagram indicates that the groups described on the two lines were *intact groups* (not randomly assigned).

Additional symbols will be described as the need arises in this chapter. The following is an example of the use of these symbols:

$$
\begin{array}{ccc}
\hline
R & X & O_1 \\
R & & O_2 \\
\hline
\end{array}
$$

The above diagram shows an experimental design in which one large group was divided into two smaller groups at random (R). Neither was pretested. One received the treatment (X), while the other received either nothing or an alternate treatment of some sort. Then they were both tested (O_1 and O_2).

Here is a second example of the use of these symbols:

$$
\begin{array}{ccc}
\hline
O_1 & X & O_2 \\
\text{-----------} \\
O_3 & & O_4 \\
\hline
\end{array}
$$

This diagram shows an experimental design in which the two groups were initially intact (symbolized by the line of dashes). There was no random assignment. Both groups were pretested (O_1 and O_3). Next one group received the treatment (X), while the other received nothing. Finally, both groups were posttested (O_2 and O_4).

THE TRUE EXPERIMENTS

A true experiment is one in which a clear-cut comparison is possible between an experimental group and a control group, which were intially considered to be equal because of random assignment to treatments. The term *true experiment* is used to distinguish such strategies from *quasi-experiments*, which do not have randomly assigned groups but compensate for this weakness through various strategies to be discussed in the next chapter.

The *posttest-only control group design* is a true experimental design. It can be diagrammed as follows:

$$
\begin{array}{ccc}
\hline
R & X & O_1 \\
R & & O_2 \\
\hline
\end{array}
$$

In this design, the subjects from one pool of subjects are assigned to the two groups at random. This random assignment is accomplished according to the guidelines discussed previously in this chapter. The considerable strengths and the few weaknesses discussed in the section of this chapter entitled "The Purpose of Random Assignment" accompany this design.

A very similar design is the *pretest-posttest control group design* which is diagrammed as follows:

$$
\begin{array}{c c c c}
\text{R} & \text{O}_1 & \text{X} & \text{O}_2 \\
\text{R} & \text{O}_3 & \text{X} & \text{O}_4
\end{array}
$$

The only difference between this and the previous design is that this one includes a pretest for both groups. The presence of the pretest makes this design differ from the previous design in the following ways: (1) pretesting consumes additional time and effort on the part of the experimenter; (2) it might make the experimental situation more obtrusive and thus arouse expectancy effects; (3) it can provide a check to see whether or not randomization really equated the groups on the outcome variable—a check which is usually unnecessary, except in the case of small numbers of subjects; (4) it makes it possible that the observed gains could be the result of a combination (interaction) of the treatment and the pretest—in other words, the treatment might work only when it occurs after a pretest; (5) it enables the researcher to measure *gains* rather than merely posttest scores; and (6) if subjects drop out of the experiment, it enables the researcher to ascertain whether the dropouts were initally similar to those who remained in the experiment.

None of these factors is strong enough to warrant a blanket recommendation that one strategy be preferred to the other. Many novice researchers have a tendency to use pretests unnecessarily in randomized designs, simply because they do not believe that randomization really works. This is not a very good reason to use the latter design. On the other hand, the major weaknesses of the second design occur because pretests take time and are obtrusive. If measurement can be efficiently and unobtrusively done (See Chapter 6), then these disadvantages vanish. Of course, if pretest data already exist (as in the case of yearly school-wide testing), it should be incorporated into the experimental design.

A major advantage of the true experimental designs is that the results are extremely easy to interpret. In Figure 9.3, diagrams A and B present the results for an experimental and a control group who have received a treatment and then had their performances measured in some way after the treatment (posttest-only control group design). The results presented in Diagram A indicate that the treatment did, in fact, make a difference, since the experimental group has scored higher than the control group.[1] On the other hand, the results in Diagram B indicate that the treatment did not cause an observable difference, since the scores are approximately equal.

Likewise, the results for the randomized pretest-posttest control group design (Diagrams C through E) are easy to interpret. Diagram C indicates that the treatment probably caused a difference, since the two groups started out the same and became different. Diagrams D and E, on the other hand, indicate no causal effect, since the two groups were approximately the same at both the beginning and the end of the experimental treatment. Because of the random assignment to treatments, these results are straightforward and easy to interpret. In the next chapter, you will discover that some of the other designs present considerably more ambiguous results for interpretation.

[1] The problem of whether such differences are big enough to be significant will be discussed in Chapter 12.

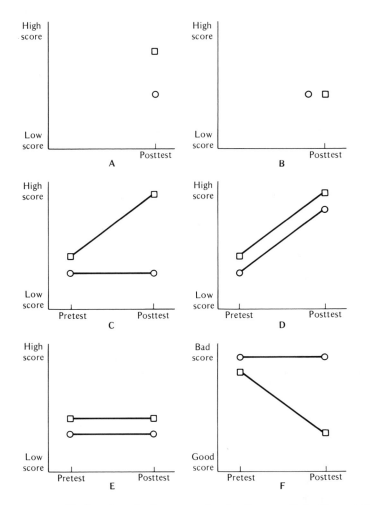

FIGURE 9–3. Sample Outcomes for the Posttest-Only Control Group Design and for the Pretest-Posttest Control Group Design. (In such diagrams, the control group will be symbolized by a circle and the experimental group by a square.)

Diagram F is included in Figure 9–3 to clarify a point which often confuses readers who are looking at this sort of diagram for the first time. Many novice readers think that Diagram F indicates that the treatment has failed, since the experimental group finishes below the control group. This is not the case, for in this diagram being low is considered good, and therefore an indication of success. For example, if a treatment were undertaken to reduce rude behavior among high school freshmen, the results in Diagram F would indicate that the treatment had been successful, since rude behavior went down after the treatment. It is important, therefore, to understand what such diagrams mean before attempting to interpret them.

True experiments present powerful designs. Carefully applied in conjunction with other appropriate experimental procedures, they can control all the major threats to internal validity. Whenever they are logistically possible, they are simple to initiate. In addition, they are easy to interpret. They should be used whenever appropriate and possible.

WHEN NOT TO USE TRUE EXPERIMENTS

Even though random assignment is highly desirable, there are four good reasons which often make random assignment to groups an undesirable alternative:

- The resulting groups may be absurdly small (e.g., one or two persons to a group), or impossibly small (e.g., one half person to a group).
- The logistics of the situation may prohibit altering the existing groups in a way that would permit random assignment.
- Your goal may be to examine an individual, not a group.
- Random assignment may produce a highly artificial situation which would produce expectancy effects or lessen the generalizability of the research. (This refers to external validity, which is discussed in Chapter 13.)

In such cases, your goal is to accomplish the same thing that random assignment accomplishes by using other strategies. Since these other strategies are almost always less effective than random assignment, this usually means that you will have to do the best you can, be aware of your weaknesses, and interpret your results in terms of these weaknesses.

REVIEW QUESTIONS

Throughout most of the chapters in this book, there have been review questions after short segments of theoretical presentation. The idea has been to let you read a segment and then test yourself to make sure you understand a given portion before proceeding to the next section. These questions have been omitted from the present and the following chapters. The reason for this omission is not that such self-review is unnecessary, but rather that the type of questions needed to review the material in this chapter requires a considerable amount of stage setting. Thus, they would become very long questions, and this would result in a highly disjointed presentation. Therefore these questions have been omitted in this textbook. However, such questions are available in the workbook accompanying this text, and it would be to your advantage to examine those questions before proceeding to the next chapter.

PUTTING IT ALL TOGETHER

Mr. Anderson had been seriously disheartened to discover that his first attempt at researching the effectiveness of the Animal Life Package (ALP) had been seriously weakened by major threats to internal validity (see Chapter 8.) He resolved to try again, and to do his research right the next time.

As chance would have it, he came across another copy of this textbook. He was at a professional basketball game, and he noticed that an elderly lady sitting next to him was reading the book during lulls in the action. He asked to borrow the book, and during the first and second overtimes he eagerly devoured the chapter "Research Design: Controlling the Threats to Internal Validity."

Armed with the information from this chapter, he set forth to apply the Basic Strategy of Research Design. His determination withered into discouragement, however, as colleague after colleague informed him that the classes in their schools were not established through pure random assignment. A well-meaning principal said that there were two fifth grades in her school, and it would probably meet with the board's approval if Mr. Anderson would select a matched group from each class and use one for the experimental and one for the control group. Mr. Anderson explained to this principal the problems of statistical regression which were likely to accompany such matching without subsequent random assignment to groups. The principal replied that she had known that all along and had merely been testing him. Mr. Anderson was not sure he believed that.

On several occasions, teachers and principals had offered to take intact classes and split the students into two groups at random. Then Mr. Anderson could take half of the students to a different room for the ALP and use the others for the control group. It would even be possible to give the control group some sort of placebo treatment. Mr. Anderson thought these offers over carefully; but in the end, he decided not to accept them, because the resulting experimental situations would be too artificial. The ALP was designed to work in a regular classroom as a normal part of the classroom routine. To demonstrate that it caused improved attitudes in a highly artificial setting would be of no great benefit.

Although Mr. Anderson was saddened at his repeated failure to find a setting in which he could run a true experiment, at the same time he felt glad that he at least knew his limitations and had refrained from jumping to false conclusions. Indeed, he knew there were ways around his obstacles. For, at that fateful basketball game, just before the elderly lady had smiled and snatched her book out of his hands as the winning basket had swished through the hoop at the final buzzer, he had glanced at the title of the next chapter, "Research Design: What to Do When True Experiments Are Impossible." He knew that some day, somewhere, fate would lead him again to that priceless volume. How he envied those readers who could turn immediately to the next chapter and find out how to control the threats to internal validity when true experiments were impossible!

SUMMARY

The Basic Strategy of Research Design suggests that if we could find two groups which were exactly the same, then we could give one of them an experimental treatment while we withheld this treatment from the other. If the groups were then treated exactly the same in all respects except for the treatment, any differences on a posttest would have to be attributed to the experimental treatment. Therefore, if the experimental group differed after the treatment, this would be strong evidence that the treatment had caused the impact.

The problem is that it is impossible to find groups which are identical. The closest approximation to this ideal situation is brought about by random assignment. With random assignment, the two groups are likely to be initially equal on all characteristics except as they happen to differ by chance. The larger the groups become, the less likely it is that chance will result in major differences with regard to any characteristics. In addition, there are statistical methods for estimating the likelihood that chance is a major factor in an experiment. Therefore, experiments based on random assignment of subjects to treatment and control groups are the most effective method for controlling the major threats to internal validity. When such true experiments are carried out with proper control for experimental mortality, instability, and expectancy effects, all the major threats to internal validity can be controlled.

Matching subjects to obtain equivalent experimental and control groups is a proper strategy only if the matching is followed by subsequent random assignment to treatment conditions. Otherwise, matching will lead to problems of statistical regression, which will pose a serious threat to internal validity.

True experiments should be used whenever they are appropriate; but in those situations where they are inappropriate, other designs are possible. These other designs are the subject of the next chapter.

Annotated Bibliography

AGNEW, N.M. and PYKE, S.W. *The Science Game: An Introduction to Research in the Behavioral Sciences* (2nd ed.) (Englewood Cliffs, N.J.: Prentice-Hall, 1978). Chapter 6 provides a different approach to the problems of experimental control.

ANDERSON, B.F. *The Psychology Experiment* (2nd ed.) (Belmont, Cal.: Brooks/Cole, 1971). The third and fourth chapters give a simple and straightforward description of how to conduct a psychological experiment.

ASHER, J.W. *Educational Research and Evaluation Methods* (Boston: Little, Brown, 1976). Chapter 2 provides a good discussion of the underlying rationale behind experimental research in education.

COOK, T.D. and CAMPBELL, D.T. *Quasi-Experimentation: Design and Analysis Issues for Field Settings* (Chicago: Rand McNally, 1979). The final chapter in this book provides a thorough discussion of the rationale behind true-experimental research as well as useful strategies for actually carrying out randomized experiments in real life settings.

Professional Journals

The following articles contain reports on studies using true experimental designs. Many of the studies are easy to emulate, and each provides compelling evidence to support a causal inference.

GERLER, E.R. "A longitudinal study of multimodal approaches to small group psychological education," *The School Counselor* 27 (1980): 184–190. This is a simple study using random assignment, two experimental groups, a placebo group, and a control group to examine the impact of psychological education programs on elementary school students. It examines the HDP and DUSO programs.

JOSEPHSON, S.C., and ROSEN, R.C. "The experimental modification of sonorous breathing," *Journal of Applied Behavior Analysis* 13 (1980): 373–378. The authors use a true-experimental design to examine the effectiveness of strategies to control sonorous breathing (snoring).

RICHTER, F.D., and TJOSVOLD, D. "Effects of student participation in classroom decision making on attitudes, peer interaction, motivation, and learning," *Journal of Applied Psychology* 65 (1980): 74–80. These authors assigned subjects to groups in a manner which approached random assignment. Within each grade, subjects were ranked according to achievement levels, and then every other student was assigned either to an experimental or to a control class. Modifications were made to balance behavior problems and sex. Because of this variation from pure random assignment, the authors used a pretest-posttest design to interpret the results.

Santopietro, M.C.S. "Effectiveness of a self-instructional module in human sexuality counseling," *Nursing Research* 29 (1980): 14–19. This study uses a pretest-posttest control group design to evaluate the effectiveness of a self-instructional module in a nursing education program.

Trovato, J., and Bucher, B. "Peer tutoring with or without home-based reinforcement for reading remediation," *Journal of Applied Behavior Analysis* 13 (1980): 129–141. This study uses matching correctly to examine the effects of a peer tutoring program on reading abilities. Children were first matched into groups of three, and then each member of the group was assigned at random to one of three levels of the treatment.

10 Research Design: What to Do When True Experiments Are Impossible

Chapter Preview

The preceding chapter described useful procedures for controlling the major threats to internal validity as effectively as possible through a combination of random assignment and the appropriate scheduling of treatments and observations. Sometimes, however, such careful control of these threats is not possible. The present chapter deals with quasi-experimental procedures—research designs which do not use random assignment, but attempt to compensate for this weakness through additional attention to the careful scheduling of observations and treatments in such a way as to rule out many of the threats to internal validity.

After completing this chapter you should be able to

- Identify the major weaknesses of the non-designs.
- Define and give examples of quasi-experiments.
- Describe the logic behind each of the following quasi-experimental designs:
  –Untreated control group design with pretest and posttest.
  –Nonequivalent dependent variables design.
  –Repeated treatment design.
  –Interrupted time series design.
  –Cohort designs.
- Identify the major strengths and weaknesses of each of the above quasi-experimental designs.
- Apply the above quasi-experimental designs to real life settings.
- Describe the differences among true-experimental, quasi-experimental, and non-designs with regard to their ability to control the threats to internal validity.
- Describe strategies for combining several quasi-experimental designs to evaluate a single treatment.

THE NON-DESIGNS

The true experiments described in the previous chapter represent the strongest contribution that research design can make to the process of ascertaining cause and effect relationships. The designs discussed in this non-design section of the present chapter, on the other hand, are the *weakest* designs. They are so weak, in fact, that they are often ignominiously referred to as *non-designs*. True experiments require careful planning and occur relatively rarely in classroom research. Non-designs, on the other hand, require little planning. Almost anyone can carry out a non-design.

There are two reasons for discussing non-designs at this point in the text. First, even though they have severe weaknesses, the non-designs are not totally without merit. It is possible (but difficult) to draw valid inferences from some experiments in which these non-designs are employed. Second, they provide a good basis for approaching the quasi-experimental designs discussed in the next section. In a very true sense, quasi-experiments modify and improve the non-designs in such a way as to make them come as close as possible to providing the impact of true experiments. Therefore, by understanding the logic of true experiments and the weaknesses of the non-designs, it is possible to derive a good understanding of how to proceed in those many instances when it is desirable to do cause and effect research but impossible to perform a true experiment.

The one-group pretest-posttest design is one of the most frequently used designs in education. It can be diagrammed as follows:

$$\overline{O_1 \quad X \quad O_2}$$

A pretest is given to a group of subjects. Then the experimental treatment is administered to that group, and finally a posttest is administered. Although this design is far from useless, it is obviously the weakest design discussed so far. The reason for its weakness is that this design controls almost none of the major threats to internal validity. Simple selection bias can be ruled out, since the subjects who are posttested are the same as those pretested. However, none of the other threats is controlled by this design. If there is an improvement on O_2 compared to O_1, such a gain can quite plausibly be attributed to an irrelevant historical event, to maturation, to the pretest, to changes in instrumentation, to statistical regression, or to some combination of these. The design makes no provision to control any of these major threats to internal validity.

Why do I say, then, that the design is far from useless? The design does have some redeeming value because it does control at least selection bias and because it does at least provide data (pre- and post-measurements) on the performance of the subjects. *It is simply necessary to rule out the uncontrolled threats through some procedure other than the research design.* The word *simply* in this sentence is an understatement; ruling out these threats through processes other than research design is often a formidable task.

The task is much easier for the physical scientist than for the educational researcher. For example, if a certain chemical in a carefully controlled environment has always reacted to another chemical in a certain way but reacts differently when a third chemical is simultaneously introduced, the physical scientist can usually conclude that this third chemical actually caused the change. There is no reason to worry about history, maturation, statistical regression, or the other threats which beset the educational researcher.

In the absence of controlled research designs, however, the educational researcher has to look for other information to rule out each of these threats to internal validity. For example, if she is dealing with 18-year-old non-readers, it is unlikely that maturation caused the observed improvement in reading ability after a new reading program; and therefore she can rule out this threat, even though it was not controlled by her research design. Likewise, if it can be carefully demonstrated that the students were not selected for treatment based on extreme scores, then it is safe to conclude that statistical regression was not the cause of the change. In the same way, if the teacher can demonstrate that the pretest was so unobtrusive as to be almost certain not to stimulate altered performance, then pretesting can be ruled out as a plausible threat to internal validity. In addition, if she can demonstrate that her measuring device did not change either in its structure or in the way it was administered or received, then she can rule out instrumentation as a threat to internal validity.

History is one of the hardest threats to control without help from the research design. It is very difficult to demonstrate that there were no extraneous historical events occurring at the same time as the treatment which could explain the observed differences. However, if our researcher can succeed in demonstrating that the time during which this event occurred was typical in all respects, then she can rule out history as a threat to internal validity.

Replication of the study under different circumstances is an excellent idea when a researcher is forced to use this weak design. Indeed, replication is probably the best way to control the threat of history without the help of a good design. If the results consistently come out the same under several different historical circumstances, then it is unlikely that some unique historical event is responsible for the results. In addition, replicating a study a second or third time helps control the other threats to internal validity which might be difficult to observe and which might creep in by accident on a single occasion but not on repeated occasions. (As will be seen in a later chapter, replication is also very helpful with regard to external validity.)

The one-group posttest-only design is the weakest design discussed in this book. It is diagrammed as follows:

$$\overline{ \text{X} \quad \text{O} }$$

A treatment is given, and then a measurement is taken. That is all. This design controls none of the threats to internal validity. If you use this design, then you have to find other ways to rule out each of the threats to internal validity. The design provides you with no help whatsoever in this regard.

As weak as it is, however, this design does have some merit. It does include an observation after the treatment, and such an observation is an improvement over merely giving the treatment and hoping that something happened. To take an extreme example, if a distraught student comes into my fifth-floor office, steps onto the windowsill and prepares to commit suicide, I might engage in some sort of crisis intervention. If I talk him off the windowsill and have him imbued with a love of life before he leaves me, I might seriously want to know whether or not it was my treatment that helped him. If my efforts caused the improvement, I would want to try them again, if the occasion should arise. I could give him a posttest to establish his post-treatment sanity, but the fact that the fellow was not courteous enough to come in for a pretest relegates me to this very weak, one-group posttest-only design. If I examine all the circumstances carefully and rule out all the threats to internal validity, then I can say that my treatment actually caused the change. If you are a careful reader, you are perhaps muttering at this point, "Fat chance!" And you would be right. This is such a weak design, that it is very difficult to rule out the various threats to internal validity.

Remember how easy it was to interpret the results of the true experimental designs in Figure 9–1? The situation is drastically different with the non-designs. Diagram A in Figure 10–1 presents the results of a one-group posttest only design. A treatment was administered to a group of subjects, and then a posttest was administered, and the group's average performance is indicated in the diagram. For use in making causal inferences, this result is absolutely devoid of meaning. Similarly, in Diagram B, although we at least know that the group scored higher after the treatment than before it, it is still quite possible that the group might have followed this pattern even in the absence of a treatment. Likewise, Diagram C seems to indicate that the treatment was unsuccessful, but how do we know what the performance of this group would have been in the absence of a treatment? For all we know, the group might have scored even lower on the posttest if it were not exposed to the treatment, and arresting such a downward trend is surely a sign of a successful treatment.

The basic problem with the results presented in Figure 10–1 is that we have no basis for comparison, and therefore interpreting the results *on the basis of the design alone* is simply impossible. Recall, however, that it is possible (but difficult) to use strategies other than research design to interpret these results. For example, if a researcher knows for some good reason that the group in Diagram B would have

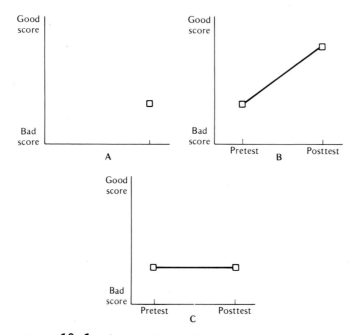

FIGURE 10–1. Sample Results from the Non-designs.

stayed low without the treatment, then she can conclude that the treatment caused an improvement. Also note that even though I have said that the non-designs provide no direct basis for causal inference, this does not render the researcher's efforts completely useless for experimental purposes. For one thing, the results of such designs can provide useful hypotheses for better designs. In addition, the data already collected can sometimes be patched up and incorporated into a more useful quasi-experimental design, to be discussed in the following sections of this chapter.

In spite of the weaknesses of these two non-designs, they are probably the most widely used designs in education. By this I do not mean that they are widely used in reputable research journals (although they show up there too!), but rather that when teachers in their classrooms draw cause and effect conclusions, they often base such conclusions on these designs. My hope is that you will realize that these designs are prevalent, and profit from reading this chapter in several ways. First, you should realize that these non-designs are better than nothing. These designs at least include data and it is possible to base some conclusions on such data. Second, you should realize the weaknesses of these designs and develop the habit of automatically looking for other than research-design strategies for ruling out the threats to internal validity which are left uncontrolled by these designs. And you should realize that it is often possible (and very worthwhile) to move from one of these weak designs to a much stronger design. The difference between the weak designs and the strong designs lies in the planning of the research strategy. For a moderate amount of time invested at the planning stage, the returns can be great in terms of the strength of the inferences you can draw after the experiment.

As you can see from reading this section, it is an exceedingly difficult task to eliminate the threats to internal validity without the help of a good research design. What the researcher has to do under such circumstances is isolate each of the threats to internal validity separately and demonstrate why they are not plausible threats. In many cases this is an impossible task; evidence for such demonstrations simply does not exist. In such cases the conclusion must remain ambiguous. If it is possible to do so, it is much more effective to use a better research design. By scheduling the timing of the treatments and the observations more appropriately, a researcher can control the many extraneous factors that otherwise can be controlled only through laborious efforts at reasoning, if they can be controlled at all. In many cases, by planning more carefully it is easily possible for a researcher to move from one of these non-designs to a quasi-experimental or even a true experimental design. In terms of the control obtained over threats to internal validity, this step is always worth it.

QUASI-EXPERIMENTAL DESIGNS

Quasi-experimental designs are not based on random assignment of subjects to experimental and control groups. However, they attempt to overcome this shortcoming through the careful scheduling of observations and treatments in such a way as to eliminate many of the threats to internal validity. Since such designs do not employ random assignment, they are almost always weaker than the true experimental designs; but since they do employ careful scheduling of treatments and observations, they are almost always stronger than the non-designs. In addition, it is possible to combine several quasi-experimental designs in a single experiment. By doing so, it is possible to take advantage of the strengths of several different designs in such a way as to control the threats to internal validity almost as effectively as if a true experimental design had been employed.

There are many more quasi-experimental designs than can be discussed in this brief chapter. A sensible procedure for you to follow in reading this text is to gain an understanding of the basic principles of quasi-experimenting and then invent your own designs. If you would do this carefully, many of the designs you would invent would be those discussed in this chapter and in the references cited in the Annotated Bibliography. Only a few of the most common and most representative designs will be discussed on the following pages. In examining these designs, your task is not to memorize the labels or diagrams, but rather to understand how each design eliminates certain threats to internal validity while leaving others uncontrolled. Your eventual goal should be to learn to use these designs in your daily work in such a way as to strengthen the validity of your cause and effect inferences and thereby improve your ability to promote useful educational outcomes.

THE UNTREATED CONTROL GROUP DESIGN WITH PRETEST AND POSTTEST

This is the most common quasi-experimental design. It is diagrammed below:

$$O_1 \quad X \quad O_2$$

$$O_3 \qquad O_4$$

As you can see, this diagram is the same as that for one of the true experimental designs (p. 163), except that the R for random assignment has been removed. Thus, this design can be viewed as a weakened variation of a true experimental design. Another way to look at this diagram is to view it as similar to the diagram for one of the non-designs (p. 170), with a second line added to the diagram. This second line provides a control group for comparison, and therefore this quasi-experimental design can be viewed as a strengthened variation of this non-design.

To use this design, you would find two intact groups of subjects. (An intact group is one which is already formed or is assembled on some basis other than random assignment.) You would pretest each of the groups, then administer the treatment to one group while withholding it from the other, and finally administer the posttest to both groups.

Note that in the comparable true experimental design, the pretest was optional. When subjects are not randomly assigned to groups, however, the pretest is much more important. It is only by comparing the pretest scores of the two groups that we can rule out selection as a threat to internal validity. If the two groups perform similarly before the treatment but differently after the treatment, we can rule out selection as a threat to internal validity. If we had no pretest, we would have no way of ruling out the possibility that observed differences on the posttest were merely indications of differences which would have existed even if there would have been no treatment.

In addition to selection bias, what threats to internal validity are controlled by this design? If maturation were likely to be a problem, it would be equally likely to affect both groups; and therefore a simple comparison of the experimental to the control group rules out maturation as a threat. The same reasoning holds true for pretesting. If it were exposure to the pretest (rather than the experimental treatment) that led to improved performance, then such spurious improvements would appear in both the experimental and control groups. If the experimental group improves and the control group does not, then this is evidence that the treatment (and not the pretest) is the factor that caused this improvement. The reasoning is the same for statistical regression, instrumentation, and history. These factors are controlled in this setting by the same logic which controls in the true experimental setting.

However, there are some threats to internal validity that are not controlled by this design. All of these uncontrolled threats arise out of the interaction of selection and one of the other threats to internal validity. An example of one of these interactive threats is that of the *interaction of selection and maturation*. In the previous paragraph, I stated that maturation was not a problem, because the subjects in each group would have equal time to mature. Therefore if maturation did occur, it would happen to both groups and therefore even out on the posttest. This statement assumes that the two groups are equal in their susceptibility to maturation. But what happens if one group is likely to mature more quickly than the other? In such a case, maturation would no longer be controlled. This is what is meant by the interaction of selection and maturation. The subjects have been selected into their groups in such a way that one of the groups is more likely to benefit from maturation than the other.

A specific example of the interaction of selection and maturation will be helpful. Assume that a preschool teacher has a group of ten children who are labeled nonverbal; that is, they are six-year-olds who do not yet speak in coherent sentence structures. She has purchased a language program which is supposed to help such children develop their language skills. To find out if this program really causes improvements, she decides to use her ten children as an experimental group and another group of ten equally nonverbal children as a control group. The only comparably nonverbal children she can find are a group of three-year-olds. After using her new language program for six months, the teacher discovers that her children have gained no more than the control children. This comparison is clouded by the interaction of selection and maturation. The three-year-olds were much more likely to mature with regard to language related abilities than were the six-year-olds. In other words, the groups had been assembled for the experiment in such a way that the control subjects were much more likely to benefit from maturation than were the experimental subjects. Of course, it would be possible to do the opposite. If the teacher would have selected a control group of twelve-year-old nonverbal students for the control group, then her six-year-olds would have had the edge with regard to maturation; and in such a case the interaction of maturation and selection would have operated in favor of the experimental group.

All the interactions discussed in this section operate in exactly this same fashion. Subjects are selected in such a way that the subjects in one group are more susceptible to one of the major threats to internal validity than are the subjects in the other group.

Let us next examine the *interaction of selection and history*. Such interactions would occur, for example, if the experimental group met immediately before lunch and the control group immediately after lunch. This would provide a sort of local history for each group. Unique historical events could have an impact on either group without occurring to the other group.

Another frequent problem is the *interaction of selection and instrumentation*. It is possible to select subjects in such a way that an instrument undergoes subtle changes for one group but not for the other. For example, assume that one group averages at the 50th percentile on a pretest and the other averages at the 90th percentile on the same pretest. At the time of the posttest, the second group will be taking a test upon which it has already scored very near the ceiling; it is going to be very difficult for them to obtain higher scores on the posttest. In such cases, they might improve with regard to an outcome variable; but the test simply will not register this improvement because it is not sensitive enough to do so. On the other hand, the group that scored at the 50th percentile has plenty of room for improvement. The subjects in this group are not going to be frustrated by an artificial ceiling; if they improve, the test is going to be sensitive enough to register these improvements. In a very real sense, the two groups are no longer taking the same test, and this fact can confuse comparisons which a researcher might try to make between the two groups.

It would also be possible that subjects could be selected for the two groups in such a way that one of the groups would be much more susceptible to *regression toward the mean* than the other group. This would occur, for instance, if a group of children from a special education setting were used for the experimental group, and a group of children with similar pretest scores from an ordinary classroom for the control group. The special education children in the experimental group would be very close to their mean on the pretest, and they would not regress statistically on the posttest. In order to get children from the ordinary classroom with pretest scores comparable to those of the experimental group, however, it would have been necessary to take those with the lowest scores from the ordinary classroom. These children would have an average score far below the average of the group from which they were selected. Therefore, on the posttest, the scores of these control children would go up (toward the mean of their original class), even in the absence of any treatment. Thus, the interaction refers to the fact that the scores of one group will artificially increase between pretest and posttest, while the scores of the other group will receive no similar artificial boost. This artificial increase in one group but not in the other will cloud any comparisons made at the time of the posttest.

In summary, the untreated control group design with pretest and posttest is a quasi-experimental design which controls the same major threats to internal validity that would be controlled by a true experiment except those that arise out of interactions. The reason these interactions are controlled in the true experiments is that the subjects are assigned to groups at random, and such randomization makes it probable that the two groups are about equal on all characteristics, including their susceptibility to react to the threats to internal validity. In the absence of random assignment, this quasi-experimental design is not able to control the impact of such interactions. Therefore, the threats to internal validity from these interactions have to be controlled by either (1) reasoning carefully about the probability of such interactions occurring, or (2) adding something to the quasi-experimental design to rule out the impact of these interactions.

The results of this quasi-experimental design are relatively easy to interpret *if* the groups score about the same on the pretest and *if* there is no obvious occurrence of the interactive threats to internal validity discussed in this section. Examine Figure 10–2 and decide whether or not the treatment was successful in each diagram.

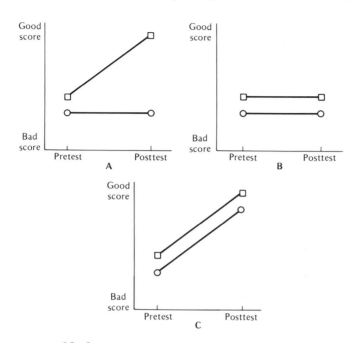

FIGURE 10–2.   Sample Results from Untreated Control Group Design with Pretest and Posttest.

Diagram A indicates that the treatment was successful (caused an improvement), whereas diagrams B and C indicate no causal impact. In Diagram B, neither group improved, and so it is apparent that the treatment did not have an effect. In Diagram C, the experimental group improved, but so did the control group. It therefore seems likely that in this case some extraneous factor (such as history, pretesting, or maturation) caused comparable improvements in the two groups.

It is when the groups are not comparable or when we cannot rule out the interactive threats that the analysis of the results of this design becomes difficult. Some of these more ambiguous possibilities are presented in Figure 10–3. In Diagram D, the experimental group improves slightly, but the control group improves even more. Is this an indication that the treatment failed to produce an effect? That could be the case, but it is also possible that the control group regressed more toward the mean or that the experimental group was subject to a ceiling (instrumentation) effect which did not influence the control group. Likewise, the same sort of interactive effects of selection with one of the other factors could account for the results presented in Diagram E. In this case, perhaps the control group was hampered by a ceiling effect which would not have impeded the progress of the experimental group. Diagram F, on the other hand, seems to present results which provide a stronger indication of a causal effect. In this diagram, the experimental group has started out below the control group and finished above the control group. It is hard to imagine an interaction of selection and one of the other factors which could account for this result.

From the preceding discussion, you can see that the results of this first quasi-experimental design are more difficult to interpret than the results of true experiments, but they are also far more useful for causal inferences than the results of

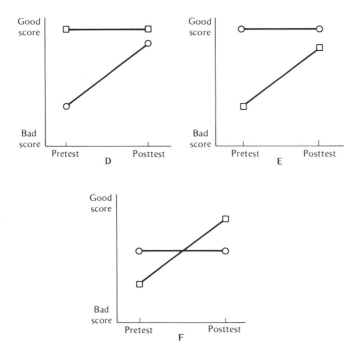

FIGURE 10–3. Some Ambiguous Results from the Untreated Control Group Design with Pretest and Posttest.

the non-designs. What can you do to improve the quality of the inferences you can draw from this design? There are two answers: First, you can reason carefully about each of the factors that could interact with selection to contaminate your results and try through such logic to rule out these interactive threats. Sometimes you will be able to rule out these threats; but in many cases you will have to admit that you cannot rule out certain threats, and in such cases you are left with a weakened inference. Second, you can improve the design by combining it with other quasi-experimental designs. For example, you can rule out the threats of statistical regression or maturation interacting with selection by using a second or third pretest (multiple baseline design) in conjunction with the design just discussed. Additional quasi-experimental strategies and ideas for combining them into a single experiment will be discussed in the rest of this chapter.

A COMPARISON OF THREE DESIGNS

Before we go on, it will be useful to make a systematic comparison of the three basic designs discussed so far. Table 10–1 lists three of the distinctly different designs that we have discussed. They are similar to the extent that they all involve a pretest-treatment-posttest format. They differ with regard to the variables that are controlled by the design and with regard to the inferences we can draw. The second column of Table 10–1 indicates what events are controlled (likely to be identical) for both the experimental and the control group. (Of course, with the non-design there is no control group.) The third column indicates what events are uncontrolled—that is, allowed to be different.

control group.) The third column indicates what events are uncontrolled—that is, allowed to be different.

The basic logic of experimental design can be stated as follows:

> If two groups start out the same at time A,
> But are different at time B,
> Then the cause of the difference has to be something
> that was different between time A and time B.

TABLE 10–1. Comparison of Three of the Possible Research Designs with Regard to Possible Explanations of Observed Differences.

Design and diagram	Events that are controlled. (They are likely to be the same for both the experimental and control groups.)	Events that are allowed to be different for the experimental and control groups.	What could possibly explain the difference between groups (if there is a difference)?	What could possibly explain the absence of a difference between groups (if there is no difference)?
Pretest-posttest control group design (true experiment) $R\ O_1\ X\ O_2$ $R\ O_3\quad O_4$	Selection Maturation History Pretesting Statistical regression Instrumentation Interactions of the above factors	Treatment	Treatment	Treatment did not make a difference.
One-group pretest-posttest design (non-design) $O_1\ X\ O_2$	Selection	Treatment Maturation History Pretesting Statistical regression Instrumentation Interactions of the above factors	Treatment Maturation History Pretesting Statistical regression Instrumentation Interaction of the above factors	Treatment did not make a difference or treatment made a difference but its impact was suppressed by the other factors.
Untreated control group design with pretest and posttest (quasi-experimental design) $O_1\ X\ O_2$ $O_3\quad O_4$	(Selection) Maturation History Pretesting Statistical regression Instrumentation	Treatment Interaction of the major threats with selection bias treatment	Treatment Interaction of the major threats with selection bias treatment	Treatment did not make a difference or treatment made a difference but its impact was suppressed by the interaction of selection and one or more of the threats.

Using this logic, the fourth column in Table 10–1 lists the possible causes of observed differences (if there were any) after an experimental treatment using each of these three designs. The fifth column reverses this logic and lists the possible explanations of a finding of no difference using each of these designs. As this table indicates, when we use a true experimental design there is only one explanation if the results show a difference and only one explanation if the results show no difference. This is why it is easy to draw valid inferences from true experiments.

On the other hand, with the non-design the treatment is only one of several possible explanations of the outcome if the experiment shows a difference; and likewise the inference that the treatment failed to make an impact is only one of a host of valid conclusions if the experiment shows no difference between pretest and posttest.

Finally, with the quasi-experimental design, if differences are observed after a treatment, the inference has to be that either the treatment or an interaction of selection and one of the other threats has caused this outcome. This list of possible causes is considerably shorter than the list for the non-design, but not as restricted as for the true experimental design. If the results of the quasi-experimental design indicate no difference after the treatment, this means either that the treatment produced no effect or that there was an effect which was suppressed by the interaction of selection and one of the other threats. Again, this finding of no difference from this design is much more subject to clear interpretation than the non-design, but not as clearly interpretable as the true experimental design.

NONEQUIVALENT DEPENDENT VARIABLES DESIGN

This is a good design to use when you have access to only one group for your experiment. This design is diagrammed below:

$$O_{A1} \quad X \quad O_{A2}$$
$$O_{B1} \qquad O_{B2}$$

In this diagram, A stands for an outcome variable which is expected to change because of the treatment, whereas B stands for an outcome variable which is not expected to change after the treatment. In using this design, you would measure the group with regard to both variables before the treatment, then you would give the treatment, then you would measure the group again after the treatment with regard to both variables. If the treatment worked, then the group's performance would improve on outcome variable A but not on outcome variable B.

In using this design, a researcher has to be very careful in selecting the two outcome variables. Variable A is easy to choose. It is the outcome you are trying to achieve with the treatment. However, variable B is much more difficult to select. This second variable has to be one which would show a gain if an irrelevant factor (such as history, maturation, or pretesting) were causing the outcome, but would *not* increase if the treatment were causing the outcome.

An example will make this clear. Suppose that a speech therapist is working with a child who is having problems articulating certain sounds. This therapist attends a convention where he hears of a new speech enhancement technique that is expected to accomplish exactly what he is trying to do with this child. He decides to apply this strategy to teaching one sound—and only to teaching that one sound. He continues to use his traditional method for all other sounds. He identifies the percentage of correct pronunciations of this target sound as Variable A. He selects another sound (for which he is still using the traditional method) as Variable B. After two weeks, he discovers that the child has made remarkable improvements in the first sound (Variable A), but has remained approximately the same with regard to the second sound (Variable B). Such data would provide a rather solid basis for the inference that the speech enhancement technique caused the improvement in correct pronunciation of the first sound. If some other factor (such as history, maturation, or pretesting) would have been responsible for the improvement in Variable A, then this same factor should have had a similar impact on Variable B. (This logic would be weakened if the child developed a new tooth, which would influence one sound but not the other.)

Note that the therapist in the above example could have strengthened his inference further by adding Variables C, D, and E to his design. If he could demonstrate that the child's performance on each variable stayed low until he started using the speech enhancement technique to develop that sound but accelerated after the new technique was directed at that sound, then his support for the inference that his new technique actually caused the improvements would be even stronger.

In the above example, if the therapist would have used performance on a speech test as Variable A and performance on a math test as Variable B, this would have provided very little (if any) support for his inference that the new treatment worked. This is because it could be argued that an irrelevant event could plausibly have had an impact on the child's speech behavior without influencing his math ability. For example, someone might plausibly argue that children of that age are more likely to automatically develop improved speech as they grow older (maturation) than they are to spontaneously acquire improved math skills. Likewise, someone could argue that the speech pretest was more likely to stimulate improvement even in the absence of a treatment than was the math pretest. This is what is meant when we say that Variable B must be one that would show an improvement if an irrelevant variable is having an impact but that would not be expected to improve if the treatment were having its impact on the targeted outcome. (Variable A).

The weakness of this design is that it relies heavily on finding and measuring variables that logically meet the criteria described for Variables A and B. Not every experimental treatment lends itself to the easy identification of variables that would register improvements if the various threats to internal validity were the critical factor but not if the treatment were the critical factor. In other cases, these additional variables can be identified, but they are expensive (in terms of either time or money) and the researcher does not have access to them. Sometimes there are indirect effects by which the treatment actually causes improvements on the unrelated variable. For example, a child might be the recipient of a new reading program that causes him to read better, which in turn causes him to have an improved self-concept, which in turn causes him to work harder and therefore to score higher on his math tests. A researcher using the nonequivalent dependent variable design might wrongly conclude that the treatment had been ineffective because the child has improved

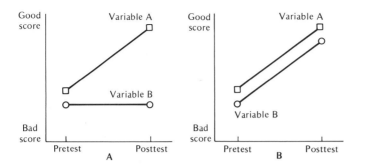

FIGURE **10–4.** Sample Results from the Nonequivalent Dependent Variables Design.

about equally on both the reading and math variable. Because the logical prerequisites for Variable B are difficult to demonstrate, this design is often recommended as a supplement to other designs (see page 175), rather than as a design to be used alone.

The results of this design are straightforward to interpret *if* the logical assumptions of the design are met. Diagram A in Figure 10–4 provides an example of an experiment where the treatment apparently caused an outcome. (In reading these diagrams, remember that the different sets of data refer to two variables–not to two groups, as they have in previous diagrams.) Diagram B, on the other hand, indicates that the treatment was not successful in producing an outcome.

It is possible, of course, to combine this quasi-experimental design with the untreated control group design discussed earlier in this chapter. By doing so, we can rule out some of the interactive threats that remained with that design. For example, when we discussed the untreated control group design, we used the example (p.000) of the teacher who used her six-year-old nonverbal children as an experimental group and some three-year-old nonverbal children as a control group. Since it was possible that the three-year-olds might mature at a different rate than the six-year-olds, this teacher had a problem of interaction of selection and maturation. However, if she would select and measure *two* verbal outcomes (Variable A and Variable B), she could rule out this interactive threat. If her results were like those shown in Figure 10–5, then she could safely conclude that maturation was not a threat—even in interaction with selection. Using this design as a supplement to other designs *is a highly recommended strategy*.

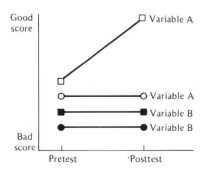

FIGURE **10–5.** Sample Results of Nonequivalent Dependent Variables Design Combined with Untreated Control Group Design.

REPEATED TREATMENT DESIGN

This is another strategy which is useful when only one group (often a very small group, such as one person) is available for the experimental treatment. This design is diagrammed below:

$$O_1 \quad X \quad O_2 \quad \bar{X} \quad O_3 \quad X \quad O_4$$

If you wanted to use this design, you would measure the performance of the group (O_1). Then you would introduce the treatment (X), and afterward measure the group's performance a second time (O_2). Next you would *remove* the treatment (symbolized by $\bar{X}$). After this removal, you would measure the group's performance a third time (O_3). Then you would reintroduce the treatment (X), and finally measure the group's performance a fourth time (O_4). The time between each of the measurement occasions should be equal. If the treatment is successful in producing the desired outcome, the groups will average high on occasions O_2 and O_4 and low on occasions O_1 and O_3.

This design is useful only when the treatment produces *transient* (nonpermanent) effects. It is useful in those situations where a treatment must be continuously provided if it is to have its impact, but not in those situations where an outcome is permanently attained once a treatment has been administered. For example, a teacher might find that a child sits in his seat when he is given points, engages in out-of-seat behavior during the period of time when points are not given, and again remains in his seat when the points are reinstated. This repeated treatment design is useful for

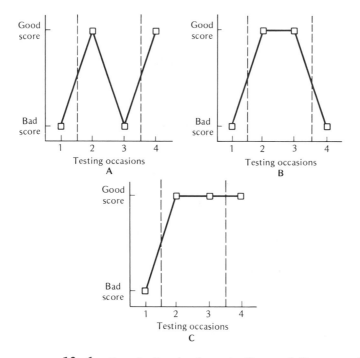

FIGURE 10–6. Sample Results from the Repeated Treatment Design.

ascertaining such impacts. However, this design would not be helpful to a teacher who wanted to teach her high school students how to apply the quadratic equation. If she would start out with her new approach, then withdraw it, and then reinstate it, what would she find? It is unlikely that the students who learned to solve such equations initially would forget when the treatment was withdrawn, and therefore this design would provide a false conclusion.

If the assumptions of this design are met (that is, if the treatment has an outcome of a transient nature on the outcome variable), then the results are often easy to interpret. For example, Diagram A in Figure 10–6 shows that the treatment appears to have been successful. Diagram B, on the other hand, suggests that some extraneous factor caused the initial improvement and the treatment did not produce the desired effect. Diagram C, however, is ambiguous. Would this pattern emerge because the treatment did not produce its desired effect, or because it did produce the effect but on a permanent rather than transient basis?

INTERRUPTED TIME SERIES DESIGNS

This design requires several repeated measurements on the same group of subjects both before and after the administration of a treatment. It can be diagrammed as follows:

$$O_1 \quad O_2 \quad O_3 \quad O_4 \quad X \quad O_5 \quad O_6 \quad O_7 \quad O_8$$

The number of diagrammed observations before and after the treatment is arbitrary. I have selected a total of eight observations; the diagram could have just as easily included six or ten observations. The guideline is that there have to be enough observations to detect any pattern that may occur. If you wanted to use this design, you measure the group of subjects on four equally spaced occasions, then administer the treatment. You would then administer the next four observations of the group's performance. The times between testing occasions (including that between O_4 and O_5, should be the same.

The purpose of the multiple measurements is to use trends in the data as a basis for evaluating threats to internal validity. For example, if maturation were causing improvements in the outcome variable, we would expect to see such improvements all along the line, not just between O_4 and O_5. Likewise statistical regression can easily be evaluated by examining the data pattern. In fact, this design provides a basis for at least partially controlling most of the same major threats to internal validity that are controlled by a true experimental design.

One threat which is not automatically controlled by this design is that of *history*. It is possible that some unique historical event occurred between O_4 and O_5 that caused an improvement. However, this design has the advantage over the non-design on p. 170 of having several sets of observations rather than merely a pretest and a posttest. By examining the data and comparing the historical events that occurred during each of the intervals, it might be possible to conclude that it is extremely unlikely that a historical event just happened to appear at the precise time that the treatment was introduced.

The same thing can be said for *selection* as a threat to the internal validity of this design. It is possible that the composition of the group might have undergone a radical change just when the treatment was introduced; but by examining the composition of the groups during the various intervals it is also possible to make an estimate of how likely it is that this explanation could account for a sudden improvement between O_4 and O_5.

Finally, it is also true that the *instrumentation* could have changed radically at the time of the treatment. This would be the case, for example, if a probation officer concluded that his new method of working with juvenile delinquents was successful, when in fact it only appeared to be successful because the court had redefined how to classify a person as delinquent. Such changes in instrumentation can be evaluated in the same manner as selection and history in the above paragraphs.

The interpretation of the results of the interrupted time series design is easy-if your results provide a simple pattern of data. For example, in Figure 10–7, Diagram A clearly suggests that the treatment caused the desired outcome—provided, of course, that the possible problems of history, selection, and instrumentation mentioned in the preceding paragraphs are taken care of. Likewise, Diagram B suggests a causal effect, since the continuous upward pattern took a dramatic upward shift after the treatment and continued to progress from this higher level. Diagram C is also easy to interpret as *no* causal effect, since it suggests that the original pattern simply continued after the introduction of the treatment. Diagram D is more ambiguous. This diagram *could* indicate a slight initial but transient increase after the treatment; but since there was no stable pattern before the treatment, it is more likely that this merely represents a chance fluctuation and no treatment effect. Diagrams E and F are also ambiguous. Diagram E could indicate a transient, nonpermanent improvement after the treatment; or it could be evidence of some temporary anomaly followed by a return to normal on testing occasions 6 through 8. To interpret Diagram E we would need further information—such as an explanation of whether the treatment is theoretically supposed to produce a transient or a permanent impact. Likewise, Diagram F *could* be evidence of a causal impact; but it could also be evidence of some other factor, since the previous pattern of continued growth did not continue after the treatment. Incidentally, you might have noticed that both Diagrams E and F could be influenced by ceiling (instrumentation) effects on the later testing occasions.

It is possible (and often very useful) to combine the interrupted time design with some of the other quasi-experimental designs. The results of some such combinations are presented in Figure 10–8. Diagrams A1 and A2 in Figure 10–8 have taken the data from Diagram A of Figure 10–7 and added a control group. The resulting hybrid design could be diagrammed as follows:

$$O_1 \quad O_2 \quad O_3 \quad O_4 \quad X \quad O_5 \quad O_6 \quad O_7 \quad O_8$$
$$\text{---}$$
$$O_1 \quad O_2 \quad O_3 \quad O_4 \qquad O_5 \quad O_6 \quad O_7 \quad O_8$$

The results presented in Diagram A1 suggest that the treatment probably did not cause its desired effect. These results support the alternative explanation that some

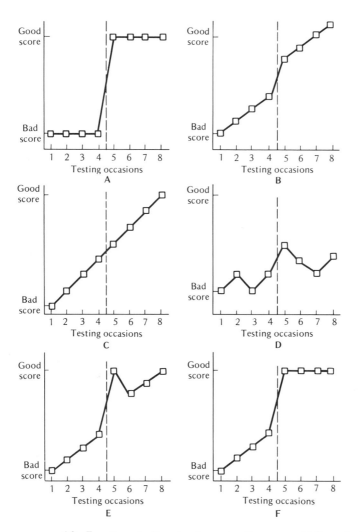

FIGURE **10–7.** Sample Results from the Interrupted Time Series Design.

external event (such as an historical event or a sudden change in instrumentation) could best explain the sudden increase in performance. On the other hand, Diagram A2 provides stronger evidence that the treatment did produce its desired impact, since the experimental group showed an improvement while the control group stayed at the lower level of performance after the introduction of the treatment

Similarly Diagram El (a modification of the data from Diagram E in Figure 10–7) suggests no causal impact; whereas the results in Diagram E2 suggest that the treatment (which was at best ambiguous in Diagram E) probably did produce the desired impact. Diagram F1 is ambiguous at best. Do we have a temporary fluctuation in the data in the experimental group, or do we have an actual improvement that is clouded by a ceiling effect? On the other hand, Diagram F2 suggests a clear causal impact—suggesting that both groups were receiving some sort of temporary stimulation that stopped just as the treatment began.

It is also possible (and useful) to combine the interrupted time series design with the nonequivalent dependent variable design. This results in a hybrid design which can be diagrammed as follows:

O_{A1}	O_{A2}	O_{A3}	O_{A4}	X	O_{A5}	O_{A6}	O_{A7}	O_{A8}
O_{B1}	O_{B2}	O_{B3}	O_{B4}		O_{B5}	O_{B6}	O_{B7}	O_{B8}

In this design, multiple baseline data is collected on two separate variables. Variable A is supposed to show an increase in response to the treatment, and Variable B only in response to such extraneous factors as maturation, history, and pretesting. An example of data from this hybrid design is shown in Diagram A of Figure 10–9. These results indicate that the treatment probably caused its desired impact. Of

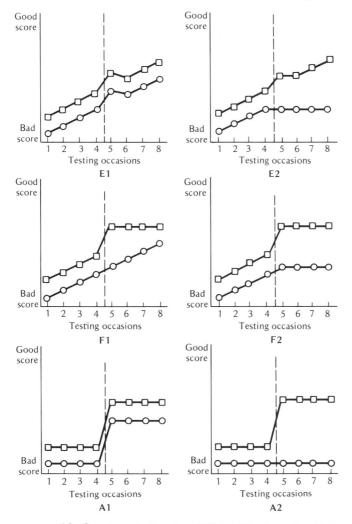

FIGURE 10–8. Sample Results of Hybrid Designs Combining the Interrupted Time Series Design with a Control Group.

course, it would also be possible to add a control group to this hybrid design, resulting in the following diagram:

O_{A1}	O_{A2}	O_{A3}	O_{A4}	X	O_{A5}	O_{A6}	O_{A7}	O_{A8}
O_{B1}	O_{B2}	O_{B3}	O_{B4}		O_{B5}	O_{B6}	O_{B7}	O_{B8}
---	---	---	---	---	---	---	---	---
O_{A1}	O_{A2}	O_{A3}	O_{A4}		O_{A5}	O_{A6}	O_{A7}	O_{A8}
O_{B1}	O_{B2}	O_{B3}	O_{B4}		O_{B5}	O_{B6}	O_{B7}	O_{B8}

Such elaborations are often sound ideas, especially if data are routinely collected anyway. If the data are hard to collect (either in terms of money needed or time involved), then we would expect to see a clear-cut advantage arising from the potential results before we would go to the trouble of undertaking such a complex design.

So far, the discussion of the interrupted time series design has presupposed a large number of observations, symmetrically arranged around a treatment. In certain cases, however, an abbreviated interrupted time series design can usefully be combined with another quasi-experimental design. For example, we can combine this design with the untreated control group design with pretest and posttest (p. 174) to get a design which can be diagrammed as follows:

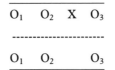

Sample results from this design are presented in Diagrams B through E of Figure 10–9. As you may recall, one of the problems with the untreated control group design was that it could not account for interactions of selection with the other threats to internal validity. The results in Diagrams B through E partially account for these interactive threats. For example, if there were an interaction of selection and maturation, we would expect the results shown in Diagram B. If instead we obtain the results shown in Diagram C, then we can rule out the likelihood of an interaction of maturation with selection. Similarly, the untreated control group design does not provide a control for the interaction of selection with statistical regression. The extra pretest shown in Diagrams D and E provides a basis for evaluating the likelihood of such interaction. The results shown in Diagram D suggest the possibility of such an interaction, whereas the results in Diagram E suggest that such an interaction probably did not occur.

The various possibilities of combining the interrupted time series design with other quasi-experimental designs have been examined at considerable length in this section. This depth of treatment has been provided because such examples are instructive. They suggest many other possibilities not listed here. Your task should not be to memorize the labels and diagrams attached to these hybrid designs, but rather to understand the fundamental idea that it is possible (and often desirable) to combine the various quasi-experimental designs. Do not combine designs just to see how complex you can make your design. Combine designs for a purpose. Find a basic design and modify or adapt it in such a way as to clarify some of the ambiguities which existed in your original design.

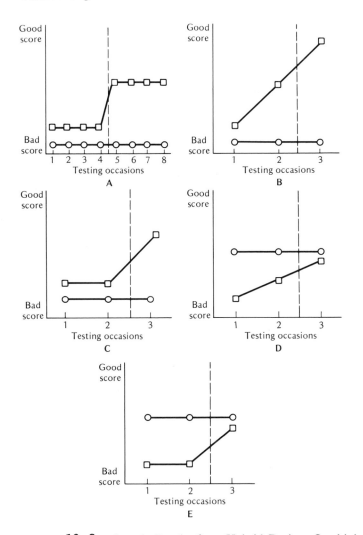

COHORT DESIGNS

The term *cohorts* refers to groups of respondents who follow each other through some institution. The simplest cohort design is described below:

$$\frac{O_1}{\overset{\displaystyle\sim\sim\sim\sim\sim}{X \quad O_1}}$$

To use this design you would test one group of subjects before the the test to this cohort. (The wavy line in the diagram indicates that the comparison is to a cohort group.) The design diagrammed above can be improved by adding observations or control groups.

Cohort designs are often good designs to use for three reasons: (1) it often happens that a cohort can receive a treatment which its predecessors did not receive; (2) although they are not randomly assigned, cohorts often differ in only minor ways from their predecessors and successors; and (3) it is often possible to use existing data to compare cohorts who have received a treatment with other cohorts in the same institution who have not received that treatment.

An example of the use of a cohort design could occur in a high school that has adopted a new English curriculum. Did the curriculum have an impact? One way to find out would be to compare the freshmen at the end of the first year after the new program to the performance of freshmen cohorts in the same school before the new curriculum. Assuming that some sort of standardized test is administered to freshmen at the end of each year, the simplest cohort design could be expanded to include several observations before the treatment and several after it. The resulting design could be diagrammed as follows:

$$
\begin{array}{cccccc}
O_1 & O_2 & O_3 & & & \\
\sim\sim\sim\sim\sim\sim\sim\sim\sim\sim\sim\sim & & & & & \\
& & & X & O_4 & O_5 & O_6
\end{array}
$$

The critical comparison, of course, is that of the cohort (or cohorts) after the treatment with those that preceded the treatment.

It is possible, of course, that the nature of the groups changed just as the treatment was introduced. This possibility can be evaluated by examining the performance of

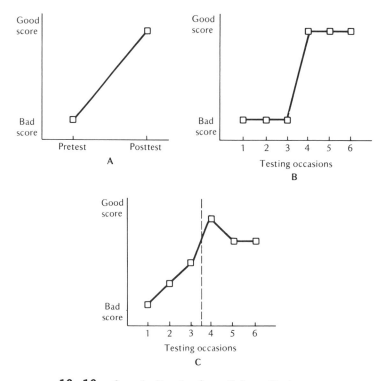

FIGURE **10–10.**   Sample Results from Cohort Designs.

both cohorts with regard to additional characteristics, such as IQ or math ability. Likewise, it is possible that some extraneous historical event could account for the improvement, and this threat has to be evaluated the same way it would be in the other quasi-experimental designs.

The results of cohort designs are interpreted in the same way as the results of other quasi-experimental designs. Sample results are presented in Figure 10–10. Diagram A suggests that an improvement occurred after the treatment. The evidence presented in Diagram B is more persuasive in this regard, since it rules out the likelihood of a chance instability at the time of the treatment. Diagram C presents results that show a temporary improvement at 0_4, followed by a return to the previous pattern. This is probably not evidence of a causal effect.

SUMMARY OF QUASI-EXPERIMENTAL DESIGNS

There are many more quasi-experimental designs which can and have been devised, but which are not discussed in the present chapter. The designs that have been included here have been selected because they are representative of what is possible through quasi-experimentation. By understanding the logic behind these designs, you should be able to devise your own designs as needed and thereby strengthen the validity of your cause and effect inferences.

Quasi-experimental designs are not as good as true experimental designs for supporting causal inferences. This is because the assumptions underlying true experimental designs are stronger. A true experiment employing a large group of subjects and careful experimental procedures controls the major threats to internal validity through mathematical probability. A quasi-experiment, on the other hand, lacks some of these controls and attempts to compensate with reasoning like this: "If this threat were a problem, it should show up at this point in my observations. But it did not show up at this point in my observations, and therefore I'm going to conclude that this threat is not a problem." Quasi-experiments, in other words, rely on a lengthy series of inferences, whereas true experiments are based on simple, straightforward mathematical probability. If you have a choice, the true experiment is usually the design you should choose.

Another difficulty with quasi-experimental designs is that the results of such experiments are not always as straightforward and easy to interpret as the results that have been used for demonstration in this chapter. These results were provided to show you how to interpret these designs, and for such purposes very nonambiguous results were often chosen. In actual practice, the results often follow a more ambiguous pattern, and in such cases it becomes more difficult to draw inferences. The results of true experiments, on the other hand, are less likely to be clouded by ambiguity. This is another reason why true experiments are preferable to quasi-experiments.

The major advantage of quasi-experiments over true experiments is that they can often be carried out with less disruption to ongoing educational programs. In many cases a teacher or researcher would be prohibited from conducting a cause and effect study if he insisted on interrupting things so that he could obtain random assignment to treatments. On the other hand, a quasi-experimental design can be carried out in almost any situation where the researcher is able to arrange for the collection of data.

Quasi-experiments are nondisruptive and nonartificial. Sometimes the artificiality of the true experiment reduces the degree to which the results can be generalized, whereas the nonartificial quasi-experimental results can be generalized much further, since the experimental situation is much more similar to real life settings. The topic of generalizing results will be explored further in Chapter 13.

The quality of the inferences that can be drawn from quasi-experimental designs can often be improved by combining several designs for use in the evaluation of a single treatment. In the present chapter, the section on the interrupted time series design was quite lengthy. This is because great attention was given in this section to combining this design with components of other designs and how such combinations rule out specific threats. Your goal as a researcher should not be to develop a design that is as complex as possible. Rather, you should select a design (or combination of designs) that will help you satisfy yourself (and others who are interested) that you have controlled as many threats to internal validity as possible and that will enable you to draw inferences that are as valid as possible.

It has been suggested earlier that all teachers should often do Level I research. At this point it should be obvious that all teachers should at least occasionally engage in Level II research. Quasi-experimental designs are effective tools which will enable you to make judgments about what is causing the various desirable and undesirable outcomes in your classroom. You should be concerned about such cause and effect relationships in your classroom. You will find that by understanding the principles discussed in this and the preceding two chapters, you will be able to make more intelligent inferences about cause and effect relationships in your classrooms, even when you are not able to undertake an actual experiment. At least occasionally, however, you will find it helpful to examine cause and effect relationships using one or more of these designs.

PUTTING IT ALL TOGETHER

In a neatly wrapped package under the Christmas tree, Eugene Anderson found the most wonderful present he had ever received in his life. It was not a piece of jewelry. It was not a necktie. Nor was it a gift certificate to a fast-food restaurant. Rather, his niece had given him a copy of the very textbook you are now reading. As others continued to open their presents, Mr. Anderson's heart leapt within him as he eagerly curled up by the fireplace and began reading the chapter he had dreamed about for the past two months, "Research Design: What to do When True Experiments Are Impossible."

There it was! He had been offered many classes for his research, but in each case he had rejected the opportunity to test his Animal Life Package (ALP) because random assignment had been impossible. But this chapter suggested that he could use intact groups in an untreated control group design with pretest and posttest. In addition, he could buttress the evidence from this design by combining it with aspects of the other designs discussed in this chapter.

Shortly after school resumed, Mr. Anderson obtained permission to evaluate the ALP in a local school system. He chose a school with two fourth grades, two fifth grades, and two sixth grades. Although the classes had not been randomly assigned, they were heterogeneously grouped, and standardized tests scores showed that the classes performed about the same within each grade level. Mr. Anderson planned to use his Fireman Tests as pretests and posttests. All students would be tested on both occasions, and between testing occasions Mr. Anderson would administer the ALP to one of the classes at each grade level.

As an additional control for threats to internal validity, Mr. Anderson cooperated with the local humane society, with the police department, and with the principal of the school to obtain a listing of animal related bad deeds and good deeds. Such a listing would not be available in all schools, but in this case it was possible to compile a list of children who had been reported to one or the other of these agencies as having performed either a good deed or a bad deed toward animals. This information was available for the past three years. He recognized that this sort of data would be somewhat unreliable and invalid, but he decided to use it as a supplementary analysis. This data would fit into an interrupted time series design which would be used to supplement the main untreated control group design.

If the ALP was successful, Mr. Anderson expected to see the following results. The experimental and control groups would score about the same on the pretest of the Fireman Test, but differently on the posttest. Likewise, although he already knew that over the past three years the number of reported good deeds and bad deeds had been about the same for the experimental and control groups, he expected the experimentals to show more good deeds and fewer bad deeds after receiving the ALP.

With these carefully laid plans and predictions, Mr. Anderson approached his experimental study with confidence and enthusiasm.

SUMMARY

Chapter 9 showed how all the major threats to internal validity can be controlled through a combination of careful experimental procedures and a research design based on random assignment. This chapter has recommended procedures for use in those many situations in which such ideal research designs are impossible. Although it is sometimes possible to draw conclusions based on the non-designs, these strategies are extremely weak and should be upgraded to a more useful design whenever possible. The quasi-experimental designs do not use random assignment, but they compensate for this shortcoming through the careful scheduling of observation and treatments in such a way as to overcome many of the threats to internal validity. This chapter has described several of the basic strategies of quasi-experimentation, with the goal of helping you understand how such strategies can overcome specific threats to internal validity. By combining several of these strategies into a single experimental design, it is possible to control most of the threats to internal validity almost as thoroughly as they would be controlled in a true experimental setting.

Annotated Bibliography

CAMPBELL, D.T. and STANLEY, J.C. *Experimental and Quasi-Experimental Designs for Research* (Chicago: Rand McNally, 1966). Also included as a chapter in N.L. Gage, ed., *Handbook of Research on Teaching*. (Chicago: Rand McNally, 1973). Everything in this resource is contained and improved upon in the Cook and Campbell resource cited below. However, when you read older research studies, this source will be cited as the bible for quasi-experimentation.

COOK, T.D. and CAMPBELL, D.T. *Quasi-Experimentation: Design and Analysis Issues for Field Settings* (Chicago: Rand McNally, 1979). This book is certain to become the bible of quasi-experimentation for years to come. It describes both how to conduct the experiments and how to analyze the results. The chapters on analysis are perhaps more complex than novice readers would care to handle. On the other hand, the chapters on how to devise quasi-experimental situations are easily comprehensible and useful to readers at any level of expertise. The terminology employed in the present text has been made compatible with that used in this more extensive resource, and therefore readers who wish to look to Cook and Campbell for further information will find the transition easy.

Professional Journals

Each of the following articles contains an example of the use of a quasi-experimental design to help control the threats to internal validity.

DENNY, M. "Reducing self-stimulatory behavior of mentally retarded persons by alternative positive practice," *American Journal of Mental Deficiency* 84 (1980): 610–615. This study employed a set of time series designs to determine the effectiveness of strategies to reduce inappropriate, stereotypic behavior of profoundly retarded children to a near zero level.

GLOVER, J.A. "A creativity-training workshop: Short-term, long-term, and transfer effects," *Journal of Genetic Psychology* 136 (1980) 3–16. The author was forced to use volunteer subjects to test the effectiveness of a creativity-training workshop. This could have been a serious threat to internal validity, but the author successfully combined several quasi-experimental designs to minimize this potential threat.

HUBER, C.H. "Research and the school counselor," *The School Counselor* 27 (1980): 210–216. The author specifies some research designs that are especially useful for counselors, who must often deal with one subject rather than with groups of subjects.

KAREGIANES, M.L., PASCARELLA, E.T., and PFLAUM, S.W. "The effects of peer editing on the writing proficiency of low-achieving tenth grade students," *Journal of Educational Research* 73 (1980): 203–207.

KIRCHNER, R.E., SCHNELLE, J.F., DOMASH, M., LARSON, L., CARR, A., and MCNEES, M. P. "The applicability of a helicopter patrol procedure to diverse areas: A cost-benefit evaluation," *Journal of Applied Behavior Analysis* 13 (1980): 143–148. The authors use a reversal design to evaluate the comparative effectiveness of police helicopter patrols to reduce burglaries in two separate types of population areas.

QUATTROCHI-TUBIN, S., and JASON, L.A. "Enhancing social interactions and activity among the elderly through a stimulus control," *Journal of Applied Behavior Analysis* 13 (1980): 159–163. These researchers used a reversal design to demonstrate the impact upon social interactions and social activity among elderly residents in a nursing home of providing free coffee and cookies in the lounge.

VAN HOUTEN, R. and NAU, P.A. "A comparison of the effects of fixed and variable ratio schedules of reinforcement on the behavior of deaf children," *Journal of Applied Behavior Analysis* 13 (1980): 13–21. This study uses a reversal design to examine the effectiveness of different reinforcement schedules in a behavior modification experiment.

ZELIE, K., STONE, C.I. and LEHR, E. "Cognitive behavioral intervention in school discipline: A preliminary study," *Personnel and Guidance Journal* 59 (1980): 80–83. This study uses groups that are essentially random to assess the effectiveness of rational behavior therapy (RBT). The authors recognize the limitations of their methods and regard this study as a useful pilot analysis.

11 Criterion Group and Correlational Research: What to Do When Experimental Research Is Impossible

Chapter Preview

The previous two chapters focused on strong and weak designs for scheduling treatments and observations in order to develop a basis for causal inference. All the designs discussed in those chapters required the manipulation of subjects—the introduction of a treatment and the evaluation of the subjects' response to this treatment. In some cases such manipulation is impossible. In such cases, however, it may still be useful to determine whether a relationship exists, even if we cannot be sure that this is a causal relationship. The present chapter will describe some useful strategies for examining such relationships.

After reading this chapter you should be able to

- Describe and give examples of the use of criterion group designs.
- Describe and give examples of the use of each of the following correlation coefficients:
  - Pearson correlation coefficient.
  - Spearman correlation coefficient.
  - Partial correlation coefficient.
  - Eta coefficient.
  - Multiple correlation coefficient.
- Given an example of each of the above correlation coefficients, you should be able to interpret it accurately.
- Given a relationship which could be examined using a correlation coefficient, you should be able to select the correct correlation coefficient for that situation.
- You should be able to evaluate the strengths and weaknesses of criterion group and correlational research strategies.

NON-EXPERIMENTAL RESEARCH

Occasionally you will speculate about a cause and effect relationship and discover that the experimental strategies described in the last two chapters simply cannot be applied to the problem at hand. This will be the case because in a given situation it may be impossible to manipulate the subjects—to assign some to a treatment and to withhold that same treatment from others. This impossibility might arise out of either practical or ethical considerations.

For example, examine the following cause and effect question: Does child abuse lead to attitudes of antagonism toward school? To settle this question through either true experimental or quasi-experimental designs, it would be necessary to have an experimental group of children who would receive child abuse and a control group from whom child abuse would be withheld. Such a research experiment is impossible for ethical reasons.

Likewise, we might want to investigate the question, "Does the sex of a child lead to (cause) stereotyped attitudes toward scientific professions?" To employ a true experimental design, we would have to find a large group of children and randomly assign some of them to the male treatment and some to the female treatment. This is not easy to do.

There are numerous cause and effect questions to which the experimental methodologies discussed in the previous two chapters cannot reasonably or easily be applied. Does a child's birth order cause him to have a certain type of self-concept? Does the environment in which a child is raised influence her attitude toward poetry? Does going to college actually cause a person to attain a higher income after graduation? Does an excessive reliance on a certain counseling methodology lead to an increase in the frequency of suicides among clients? Do pilot trainees who crash their planes do so because they were subjected to unusual anxiety during training? These are all interesting questions, and there are people who want to know the answers; but none of them can be answered by assigning one group of persons to an experimental group and another to a control group. In each case, such assignment to treatments (either randomly or otherwise) is either impossible or unethical.

In order to answer such questions, researchers have to rely on criterion group or correlational methodologies. Since these methodologies do not manipulate subjects to assign them to treatments or to withhold treatments, they do not lead to a causal inference as directly as would a true experimental or quasi-experimental methodology. Instead, these methodologies demonstrate that there is a consistent *relationship* between something which could be called a treatment, and some outcome.

For example, such methodologies might show that there is indeed a relationship between going to college and a higher income in later life. A careful examination of the data might indicate that college graduates do in fact earn more money than nongraduates. However, such a relationship is not proof (or even strong evidence) that going to college causes an increase in income. It is possible (since there was no random assignment to the college treatment) that most of the people who go to college are those who were going to make more money anyway. The researcher who wants to establish a *causal* connection between college attendance and financial income would have to think of all the plausible alternative explanations of the higher income and then rule out the likelihood that these alternative explanations (rather than college attendance) are responsible for the higher income. Ruling out these alternate explanations without the benefit of an experimental research design is a taxing (and sometimes impossible) occupation. On the other hand, if only the researcher could randomly assign 100 subjects to the college condition and 100 to the noncollege condition, then it would be quite a bit easier to rule out these threats to the internal validity of the conclusion that college attendance causes an increase in income. Such random assignment, however, is impossible, and researchers have to do the best they can with weaker methodologies.

A similar problem arises in birth order research. A consistent finding of such research is that last-borns perform more poorly (on the average) on most tests than do first-borns. The most widely held inference based on this finding is that being last born *causes* last-borns to be weaker than first-borns with regard to certain traits. This sounds like a plausible explanation, but is it not also possible that it is being weak with regard to certain traits which *causes* some children to be last born? Perhaps if a child is easy to raise, his parents feel more inclined to have another child, and therefore he will not be a last-born. However, if this would have been a very difficult child his parents might have felt less inclined to have another child, and therefore he will be a last-born. This chain of events would lead to last-borns (on the average) performing more poorly than first-borns. In the absence of random assignment (which is impossible) to the conditions of first-born, it is very difficult to establish the causal nature of the relationship.

On the other hand, if a researcher is able (even in the absence of an experimental design) to demonstrate that there is *no* relationship between some treatment and some outcome, then this *is* very strong evidence that there is no causal relationship. For example, if a researcher would demonstrate that among people coming from the same social background, college graduates earn no more than non–college graduates, then this is very compelling evidence leading to the inference that college attendance does *not* cause increased income. Likewise, if a researcher could demonstrate that among families of the same size, last-borns score about the same as first-borns on most tests, this would lead to a reasonable inference that birth order does *not* cause differences in these characteristics.

The present chapter will describe useful methodologies for ascertaining whether or not such relationships exist. Thre are other methodologies that are not discussed in the present text. The methodologies that are covered in this text are introduced because they are the most common methodologies and because they can give you a good understanding of what is possible in this regard. If you are interested in additional methodologies, you might want to refer to some of the sources cited in the Annotated Bibliography at the end of the chapter.

Post Hoc Ergo Propter Hoc (After this, therefore because of this)

The *post hoc* error refers to the tendency to assume that because there is a relationship between two events or characteristics, the first event causes the latter event. That this conclusion does not always follow can be seen from the following examples. In each case, there is an actual relationship; but the conclusion that this is a *causal* relationship is obviously absurd. See if you can identify the real causes in each case.

- As the temperature of water off the coast of California increases, the number of drownings there increases. A recent study has found the same relationship off the coast of North Carolina. The researchers recommend keeping your water at a low temperature in your swimming pool, since warmer water obviously leads to a propensity toward drowning.
- Good news for people with big feet! A recent study shows beyond any doubt that people with big feet read better than those with smaller feet. A study of 1000 randomly selected

citizens of all ages from a midwestern state showed that people with larger shoe sizes read much better than those with smaller shoe sizes.

- Research shows that there are more storks present in England during March than during any other month. Likewise, more babies are born in England during March than during any other month. The implications of this finding for sex education programs are still being discussed.*

CRITERION GROUP DESIGNS

A criterion group design is one in which groups of subjects are gathered into treatment and control groups on the basis of naturally occurring circumstances rather than on the basis of random or nonrandom assignment. For example, we might want to know how English teachers differ from math teachers, how boys compare with girls in verbal ability, or how basketball plays differ from tennis plays in muscle coordination. Although data tabulated from such designs can often look exactly like that from an experimental or quasi-experimental design, the absence of manipulation makes a crucial difference in interpretation. There are many possible formats that criterion group designs can take. The following is the simplest:

$$\begin{array}{ll} \hline C & O_1 \\ & O_2 \\ \hline \end{array}$$

The C (for *criterion*) replaces the X in this design for representing the treatment. To use this design, you would find one group of subjects which is already receiving a treatment (or which possesses a characteristic) and measure that group's performance with regard to a specified outcome variable. Then you would find another group which is similar in all other respects to the first group, but which is not receiving the treatment, and measure this second group's performance on the same outcome variable. Finally, you would compare the performance of the two groups.

This is obviously a very weak design. The most glaring difficulty is that there is no control whatsoever over the selection of subjects into the criterion group, and therefore both simple selection and the interaction of selection with other factors are extremely serious threats to the internal validity of conclusions you might want to draw from such a design. Nearly all the other threats to internal validity also pose threats with this design. The only way to control these threats is to collect additional data to try to demonstrate that the groups really are quite similar and to try to rule out other likely explanations of the observed outcomes.

Let us examine the question of whether or not child abuse leads to attitudes of antagonism toward school. The criterion group design would dictate that we operationally define child abuse and on the basis of this operational definition find a criterion group of abused children. We would then find some way to measure attitudes of antagonism toward school and use this measurement technique to assess the criterion group's attitude toward school. Next, we would find a group of children who appear to be similar in other respects to the abused children but are not

---

* Reviewer's comment: "My wife, a former nurse anesthetist whose presence was needed for births at a given hospital, is certain that the phase of the moon affects births of babies. My contention is that the relationship may be between the moon phase nine months previous, and the incidence of births."

themselves abused. Finally, we would measure this second group's antagonism toward school and compare the attitudes of the two groups. If the criterion group displays more antagonism, then this indicates that the expected relationship exists. However, because of the severe limitations of the design, we would still be far from having a sound basis for a causal inference. It is *possible* (and intuitively, even very likely) that child abuse does cause such attitudes of antagonism. But a skeptic might point out that it is also possible that some other factor (or set of factors) causes *both* child abuse and attitudes of antagonism. For example, our skeptic might argue that maybe some children are hard to get along with for some unknown reason. Being hard to get along with would tend to *cause* these children to be the subject of their parents' abuse and also tend to *cause* them to have attitudes of antagonism toward school. There are several ways that we could deal with this objection. First, we could look into the research or examine case histories of the children in our study to find out if the abused children really were likely to be viewed as hard to get along with before the onset of child abuse. Second, we could try another criterion group design, this time comparing abused children to non-abused children who are hard to get along with. The process, as you can see, would eventually become very complex—perhaps even futile.

Note, however, that if the above study would have shown that abused children did not have different attitudes than non-abused children, this would have been evidence that child abuse does *not* cause such attitudes.

In addition to using the criterion group design when other designs are impossible, some researchers select the criterion group design because it is easier (and faster) to employ than one of the stronger designs. Often such reasoning exhibits laziness or incompetence, but in certain cases there is validity behind this useage. The fact that the criterion group design is relatively easy to employ suggests that we might want to use it as a preliminary step before employing a better design. For example, we might want to know if open classrooms *cause* improved self-concepts. We are able to operationally define both open classrooms and self-concept. The best way to collect evidence for a causal inference would be with an experimental or quasi-experimental design. Such designs would be expensive in terms of time and money, however; and we might feel better about undertaking such an expense if we at least knew that a relationship actually existed. Therefore, we might find two colleagues—one of whom uses a traditional approach and the other an open classroom approach—and conduct a criterion group design in their classrooms. We might discover that the two teachers appear to be about equally competent and that the students seem to be quite similar in most respects, but that the self-concepts are superior in the open classroom. Because of this observation we might be inclined to go ahead with a quasi-experimental design. (While we are conducting this criterion group design, we could also save some time and improve efficiency by collecting baseline data for our subsequent quasi-experiment.) On the other hand, if the criterion group design shows no such relationship, then we might decide not to pursue the research any further.

CORRELATIONAL STUDIES

All the methodologies for establishing relationships which have been discussed so far in this and in previous chapters have relied on the administration of a treatment and a subsequent comparison of the average performance of groups of subjects. A group has been exposed to a treatment, and the impact of this treatment has in some way been evaluated. Correlational studies are different. These studies rely not on the evaluation of a group's reaction to a treatment, but rather on a comparison of the same people's performance with regard to two different characteristics. Correlational studies can be diagrammed as follows:

$$\overline{O_1 \quad O_2}$$

To perform a correlational study, we would identify a group of subjects and measure all the people in the group with regard to the two characteristics of interest. Then we would examine the data to see if there is a relationship between those two characteristics.

As a result of a correlational study, we might be able to conclude that two characteristics are *correlated* in that group. This means that these two characteristics occur together according to some predictable pattern. For example, we might conduct a correlational study with a group of high school students and discover that there is a correlation between sense of humor and performance in English class. This statement would mean that there is a predictable association between sense of humor and performance in English class. This might mean that persons who are in some way assessed as having a good sense of humor are also those who are assessed as doing well in English class. Likewise, students who do well in English class would also tend to have a good sense of humor. On the other hand, students with a weak sense of humor would tend to perform poorly in English class. Students with a mediocre sense of humor would perform at an in-between level in English class.

Note that in the above example, we have not demonstrated a causal relationship. We have *not* shown that a good sense of humor *causes* a person to do well in English class. It is possible that such causality is the explanation of the relationship; but it is equally possible that the causality may be reversed: a person's success in English class may cause that person to be evaluated as having a good sense of humor. In addition, it is possible that some third variable (such as intelligence) causes a person to receive high scores both in English class and on the instrument measuring sense of humor.

There are many other questions about relationships that could be investigated through correlational studies. The following are some examples:

- Are teachers who spend a great deal of time reading professional journals actually perceived as more effective by their students than those who do very little professional reading?
- Do children from large families show more respect for teachers than children from small families?
- Do students who borrow more library books spend less time than others playing intramural sports?
- Do counselors who listen more often to contemporary rock music develop better rapport with the students they counsel than those who spend less time listening to such music?

In each of the above cases we could conduct a correlational study. We would find a valid way to measure each of the two characteristics, record these measurements in a given group, and then see if there is a pattern. An important caution is in order at this point. Even though we may be interested in speculating about whether one characteristic causes the other, correlational studies tell us little about such causality. If we wanted to show that listening more frequently to rock music actually *caused* counselors to develop better rapport with students, we would have to use an experimental methodology rather than a correlational study. Simple correlational studies help us establish relationships. They seldom enable us to determine the causes of these relationships.

The results of correlational studies are often expressed in terms of correlation coefficients. There are several different types of correlation coefficients, and each type serves a specific purpose. The following sections of this chapter will describe the major types of correlation coefficients. This discussion will be nontechnical. No attempt will be made to teach you how to compute these coefficients. Your goal should be to understand the purpose of each coefficient, to know when to use each coefficient to help you solve a specific problem, and to know how to interpret each coefficient when you see a reference to it in the professional literature.

PEARSON CORRELATION COEFFICIENT

The Pearson Correlation Coefficient is the most common of the correlation coefficients. Many of the others are adaptations or modifications based on the Pearson coefficient. By understanding this coefficient, you will have a basis for undertanding any other correlation coefficient. Pearson correlation coefficients express the strength of a relationship in numbers ranging between $+1.00$ and -1.00. A high *absolute* value indicates a strong relationship, whereas a near zero value indicates a very weak relationship between the two variables being measured. (The term *absolute value* means to ignore the plus or minus sign.)

It is very useful to think of the strength of the relationship between two variables in terms of how accurately we can use our knowledge of a person's score on one characteristic to her score on the second characteristic. If there is a strong relationship, we can make a very accurate guess. If there is a weak relationship, it is very hard to make an accurate guess about the second variable. Putting this into terms of correlation coefficients, if there is a correlation of 1.00 between two characteristics, then we can make an absolutely perfect prediction of the person's performance on the second variable if we know her score on the first variable. On the other hand, if the correlation is .00, then knowing the score on the first variable provides us with no information at all about the second variable. A coefficient of .90 indicates a stronger relationship than one of .80. This means that if we make a guess about a person's second characteristic based on our knowledge of her first characteristic in a situation where the correlation is .90, we are more likely to be right than if the correlation were .80.

A correlation of either 1.00 or -1.00 indicates a perfect correlation between two variables. In either case, if we know a person's score on one of the variables, we can make a perfect guess regarding her score on the second variable. The difference between positive and negative correlations is that with a positive correlation, as a person's score on one variable increases, her score on the other variable also increases. On the other hand, a negative correlation means that as a person's score on one variable increases, her score on the other *decreases*.

To take an example, there is a high positive correlation (say, about .80) between a person's score on an IQ test and her score on a standardized reading test. This relationship is diagrammed in Figure 11–1. Students with high scores on the IQ test are also likely to have high scores on the reading test. Students with low IQ scores are likely to have low reading scores. And people in the middle range on the IQ test are likely to be in the middle range on the reading test.

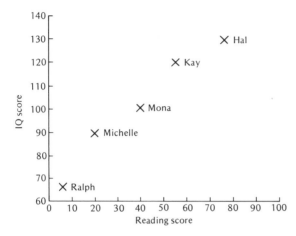

FIGURE 11–1   An Example of a Positive Correlation Between IQ Scores and Reading Scores.

On the other hand, there is a negative correlation (say, − .80) between a person's score on an IQ test and the number of days he is likely to be absent from school. This relationship is diagrammed in Figure 11–2. A person with a high IQ score is likely to be absent a very *low* number of days. A person with a low IQ is likely to be absent quite often. A person in the middle range of IQ is likely to be present a medium number of days.

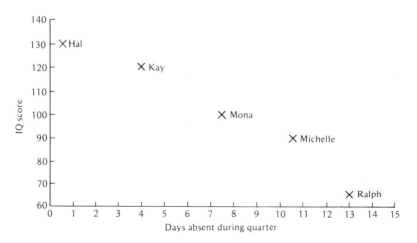

FIGURE 11–2.   An Example of a Negative Correlation Between IQ Scores and the Number of Days Absent During a Quarter.

Finally, there might be a very weak relationship (say, $-.13$) between IQ scores and the amount of time children can hold their breath under water. This relationship is diagrammed in Figure 11–3. Some persons with high IQ scores can hold their breath for a long time, others only very briefly. The same is true of low and medium IQ scorers. There is no predictable pattern. This absence of a pattern is signified by the low correlation coefficient.

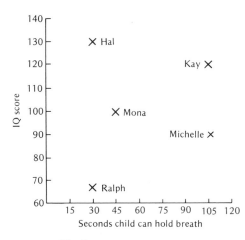

FIGURE **11–3.** An Example of a Near Zero Correlation Between IQ Scores and the Length of Time a Child Can Hold His or Her Breath Under Water.

You may have realized by now that whether a relationship will be described as positive or negative is often an arbitrary decision, based on how the researcher chooses to define the variables. For example, the negative relationship in Figure 11–2 can become the positive relationship shown in Figure 11–4 if we simply measure days present instead of days absent.

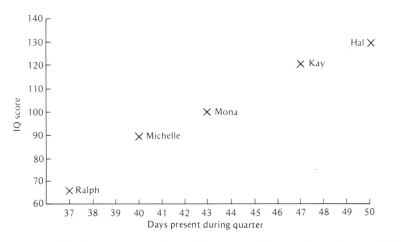

FIGURE **11–4.** The Data from Figure 11–2 Reversed to Show a Positive Rather than Negative Correlation Between IQ and Attendance in Class.

How to Read a Scattergram

If you have no trouble understanding the diagrams in Figures 11–1 to 11–4, then you should skip this section. Many readers, however, have some initial difficulty reading such diagrams (called scattergrams), and therefore a brief explanation will be provided.

In Figure 11–1, the range of IQ scores is written along the left side of the diagram, and the range of reading scores is written across the bottom of the diagram. Since each student has two scores (an IQ score and a reading score), it is possible to identify each child's performance by placing a mark at the point in the diagram that corresponds to his or her performance on the two tests. Thus, Ralph had an IQ of about 62 and a reading score of 5; and therefore in Figure 11–1 we can indicate Ralph's performance by putting a mark to the right of 62 on the IQ scale and above 5 on the reading scale. (Note that neither 62 nor 5 is actually written on the scales, but these points can be easily estimated from the numbers that are there.) Likewise, Kay had an IQ score of 123 and a reading score of 55, and therefore her performance is recorded by putting a mark to the right of 123 on the IQ scale and above 55 on the reading scale.

Let us apply the same logic to Figure 11–2. Ralph has an IQ of 62 and was absent 13 days. Therefore, his performance is indicated with a mark to the right of 62 on the IQ scale and above 13 on the days-absent scale. Kay's IQ of 123 and her 4 days of absence are recorded by a mark to the right of 123 on the IQ scale and above 4 on the days-absent scale. And so on.

After this brief introduction, test your knowledge by answering the following questions:

1. In Figure 11–1, what are Hal's scores?

2. In Figure 11–1, what are Michelle's scores?

3. In Figure 11–2, what are Mona's scores?

4. In Figure 11–3, what are Ralph's scores?

5. In Figure 11–3, what are Hal's scores?

Answers:

1. IQ about 130, reading about 80.
2. IQ about 90, reading about 20.
3. IQ about 100, days absent 7.
4. IQ about 60, about 30 seconds.
5. IQ about 130, slightly over 15 seconds.

If you got any of these wrong, and if you cannot understand the basis of your errors, you should ask someone for help. Reading these diagrams is actually not difficult, and this skill will be helpful to you in reading this text and in your professional reading. Diagrams 11–1 to 11–4 are relatively simple diagrams, since each contains data on only five subjects. Scattergrams containing much more data are interpreted in exactly the same way as these simplified examples.

How high does a correlation coefficient have to be in order to indicate a strong relationship? There is no simple answer to this question. A good way to answer this question is by asking another. Earlier we talked about correlations as indicating how accurate a guess about a second characteristic would be, based on your knowledge of a first characteristic. How accurate would such guesses have to be before you would consider it a strong relationship? A relationship of 1.00 or −1.00 indicates a perfect relationship, but such relationships never appear in educational studies. The closer you get to a value of 1.00 (or −1.00), the stronger the relationship is. A relationship of .70 is stronger than a relationship of .50. And so on. A useful interpretation of such correlation coefficients is shown in the following statements: "There's a correlation of .50 between IQ and the number of books a child reads, and a correlation of .75 between self-concept and the number of books read. This means that we can make a better estimate of how much reading children will do by measuring their self-concepts than by assessing their IQ."

To summarize, Pearson correlation coefficients range between $+1.00$ and -1.00. The strength of the relationship is indicated by the absolute value of the coefficient, disregarding the sign. A strong *positive* relationship indicates that a person with a high score on one of the variables is likely to have a high score on the other as well. A *moderate* positive relationship has the same meaning, but predictions of the second characteristic based on a knowledge of the first characteristic are not as likely to be correct. A *negative* correlation indicates that a person with a high score on one variable is likely to have a *low* score on the other variable. If this negative relationship is strong, then estimates of the second variable based on knowledge of the first are likely to be accurate. However, as the correlation coefficient approaches zero, the relationship grows weaker. When correlations are weak (near zero) there is little or no relationship between the two variables; it is impossible to make consistently good guesses about one characteristic based on a knowledge of the other.

And now a technical note. Pearson correlation coefficients can be used only when both characteristics are measured in terms of interval or ratio data (discussed in Chapter 7). In practice, this means that you have to use the special Spearman coefficient (discussed in the next section) when one or both of the characteristics are measured in terms of ordinal data. In general, a safe practice is to use the Pearson coefficient as often as possible, and use another only when the other is more appropriate.

Review Quiz

1. Which of the following coefficients states the *strongest* relationship?
   .35
   .79
   .01
  $-.85$
  $-.14$

Answer:

$-.85$ indicates the strongest relationship. If you answered .79, you forgot that it is the *absolute* value (disregarding the sign) which indicates the strength of the relationship.

---

2. Which of the following coefficients states the *weakest* relationship?
   .27
   .04
  $-.17$
  $-.86$
   .80

Answer:

.04 is the weakest relationship. If you answered $-.86$, then you are letting the sign distract you. The coefficient $-.86$ actually indicates the strongest relationship among these coefficients.

---

3. "There is a moderate positive relationship between creativity and scores on the Art Proficiency Test." This relationship would best be described by which of the following coefficients?

   .60
   .95
   .17
   $-.25$
   $-.60$

   _____

   Answer:
   .60

   _____

4. "There is a strong negative relationship between creativity and the amount of time a student can stay awake in Mr. McDonald's class." This relationship would best be described by which of the following coefficients?

   .57
   .96
   .01
   $-.63$
   $-.86$

   _____

   Answer:
   $-.86$

   _____

5. "There is almost no relationship between creativity and the number of raffle tickets a girl scout can sell." This relationship would best be described by which of the following coefficients?

   .18
   .88
   $-.79$
   $-.16$
   .51

   _____

   Answer:
   Either .18 or $-.16$ would indicate almost no relationship.

   _____

6. "There is a Pearson correlation of $-.80$ between ability in Mrs. Schmidt's French class and performance in Mr. Tut's geometry class." What does this statement mean?

   _____

   Answer:
   There is a fairly strong relationship. People who do well in Mrs. Schmidt's French class tend to do poorly in the geometry class. Likewise, the worst students in her French class are likely to be among the best in his geometry class.

   _____

7. "The correlation between amount of time spent watching television and scores on the current events exam as .17." What does this statement mean?

   _____

   Answer:
   There is practically no relationship between the two. If you know how much time a child spent watching television, you could not reasonably use this as a basis for estimating his performance on the current events exam.

Computing the Statistics

This is not a statistics book. Statistics are introduced in this text as tools to accomplish research goals. Therefore, neither the underlying mathematical theory behind procedures nor the method of computing these statistics is discussed here.

However, since some statistics are extremely easy to compute, a "cookbook" approach to computing some elementary statistics is included in Appendix D. In cases where you have a large number of subjects for whom you wish to analyze data, or if the statistic you wish to compute is more complex, you should do your analysis by computer. The use of the computer for such purposes is described in Chapter 17.

Additional skills in statistical analysis should be attained by reading further textbooks, consulting the references in the Annotated Bibliographies at the end of this and the next chapter, by taking appropriate courses, or by consulting with someone who can help you with your analysis.

SPEARMAN CORRELATION COEFFICIENT

If one or both of the characteristics in a correlational study are measured in terms of rank order data rather than in terms of precise scores, then it is not appropriate to use the Pearson correlation coefficient formulas. In such cases, the special Spearman correlation coefficient formulas can be used instead. In other words, use the Pearson

WHETHER A CORRELATION IS POSITIVE OR NEGATIVE OFTEN DEPENDS ON THE ARBITARY WAY THE VARIABLES ARE DEFINED.

coefficient if you have interval or ratio data for both variables; use the Spearman coefficient if you have merely ordinal data for one or both characteristics.

The following questions provide examples of situations in which the Spearman coefficient should be used:

- Do students who rank high in freshman English also rank high in senior English?
- Are people at the front of the line less irritable than those at the back of the line?
- Is there a strong relationship between the amount of time which parents have participated in sports themselves and the ranking which they give these sports as desirable activities for their children?
- Is there a strong relationship between a TV show's ranking in the Nielsen ratings and the amount of money budgeted for that program?

In each of the above cases, the researcher has a mere ranking (first, second, third. . .) for at least one variable, rather than a precise (interval) score; and therefore it is necessary to use the Spearman procedure. If it would be possible to collect more precise (interval) scores (for example, precise exam scores in freshman and senior English), then it would be appropriate to use the Pearson formula to compute the correlation coefficient.

Spearman coefficients are interpreted in exactly the same manner as Pearson coefficients. A high positive correlation, for example, indicates that persons who *ranked* near the top of one list also ranked near the top of another list. And so on.

Review Quiz

Only one of the following questions would be answered by computing a Spearman correlation coefficient. Choose the correct question:

a. Are boys smarter than girls?
b. Do children with high verbal ability come from families with high income?
c. Do students whom Ms. Jones ranks near the top of her Eager Beaver List get higher grades than those who are closer to the bottom of this list?
d. Is the number of victories in a chess tournament related to verbal IQ?

Answer:
(c)

PARTIAL CORRELATION

Sometimes it would be useful to know what the relationship would be between two variables if the influence of a third variable were reduced or eliminated. For example, in the box labeled "Post Hoc Ergo Propter Hoc" on p. 197, it was pointed out that there is a high positive correlation between water temperature and the number of drownings in the ocean. You might rightly have noted that this occurs because more people go swimming when it is warm; and if there are more people in the water, there is a greater likelihood that someone will drown. Let us assume that the correlation between average water temperature and number of drownings is .80. The question you might want answered is this: What would the correlation have been if the number of people in the water would have been the same all the time at each temperature? Partial correlation helps to answer this question. A partial correlation coefficient mathematically adjusts to an extent for the influence of some third factor (such as the number of people in the water) and estimates what the relationship between the other two variables would have been if the influence of this third factor were reduced. For example, even though the Pearson correlation between water temperature and number of drownings might be .80, the partial correlation would probably be closer to .00.

Partial correlations have the same range (1.00 to −1.00) as the other coefficients which have been discussed in this chapter. Partial correlation coefficients are interpreted in the same way as these other coefficients. However, the reference to the third variable makes it a bit more complicated to state this relationship in simple English prose. Here are a few hypothetical examples of partial correlations accompanied by brief paraphrases:

1. "When IQ is controlled through partial correlation, the correlation of .60 between scores on creativity tests and grades in art class drops to .20."

   If all the students would have had similar IQ's, then there would have been little or no relationship between creativity and art performance.

   (The apparent reasonably strong relationship between creativity and art performance occurred because students with higher IQ's did well both on the creativity tests and in the art class.)

2. "The Pearson correlation between mechanical aptitude and performance on the electronics exam was .75. With IQ held constant, the partial correlation was .70."

   Even when the influence of IQ is eliminated, there is still about the same relatively strong relationship between mechanical aptitude and performance on the electronics exam.

   (The relationship between mechanical aptitude and electronics performance is not caused by IQ.)

3. "The correlation between number of hours of therapy and currently rated personality adjustment after one year of therapy was −.60. However, when severity of initial prognosis was controlled, the partial correlation was .40."

   There was a strong tendency for those who received more therapy to have a lower current personality adjustment index. If everyone would have had an equally severe prognosis, however, then there would have been a moderate tendency for those who had more treatment to show more improvement.

   (The reason for the original relationship was that people who had more severe troubles took more treatment, but were less likely to have a high current rating.)

As we have noted elsewhere in this chapter, although the existence of a correlation does not demonstrate causality, the finding of no correlation is a strong step toward demonstrating that there is *no* causal relationship. If there is no relationship between two variables, then *a fortiori* one of them cannot cause the other.

Partial correlations can have an even more important bearing upon causal inferences than Pearson (or Spearman) correlations. By using partial correlations, a researcher may be able to either verify or rule out many of the alternative explanations for an observed correlation. If there is a high Pearson correlation between two variables, a researcher might run a partial correlation controlling (partialling out) the influence of some third variable. If the correlation drops dramatically when this is done, this is strong evidence that there is not a causal relationship between the original two variables. On the other hand, if the partial correlation is about as strong as the original Pearson correlation, the assumption that there *is* a causal relationship between the original two variables is strengthened because the likelihood that the relationship was caused by one specific alternative variable has been ruled out as a result of partial correlation analysis. By measuring enough variables and running enough partial correlations, the researcher can rule out many of the alternative explanations of the observed relationship. Although this procedure does not *prove* causality, it can be a significant step toward making a causal inference more likely, since it helps eliminate rival explanations. This is a useful strategy in situations where experimental research is impossible.

Review Quiz

1. Which of the following is a Pearson coefficient, which is a Spearman coefficient, and which is a partial correlation coefficient?
   $-.14$
   $.86$
   $.35$

Answer:
It is impossible to tell. All three look alike.

---

2. Which of the following would require a Pearson correlation coefficient, which a Spearman correlation coefficient, and which a partial correlation coefficient?
   a. "If we rule out the common influence of socioeconomic status on both IQ performance and appreciation of poetry, can it still be said that more intelligent students have a greater appreciation of poetry?"
   b. Did those who finished closer to first in the tennis tournament spend more time jogging than those who finished near the bottom?"
   c. "Is the amount of time a student spends in the assistant principal's office when called in for an infraction related to the severity of the punishment the child will receive?"

Answers:
a. Partial.
b. Spearman.
c. Pearson.

CURVILINEAR CORRELATIONS

Is the overall level of excitability of the human organism related to a person's ability to learn? In other words, do we become more capable of learning as our level of arousal increases? The answer seems to be that humans *do* show an increasing ability to learn more as level of arousal increases *up to a certain point of arousal*. After that point is reached, however, the process reverses itself, and thereafter the more arousal increases the less the person is able to learn. This relationship can be diagrammed in Figure 11–5. This diagram shows that a person who is either nearly asleep or near panic will learn little, whereas a person at a medium level of arousal will learn a great deal.

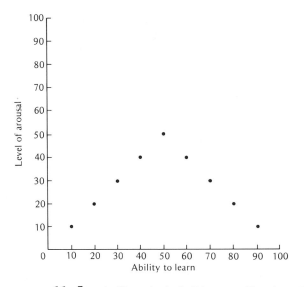

FIGURE 11–5. A Hypothetical Diagram Showing the Relationship Between Level of Arousal and the Ability to Learn. (This is a curvilinear relationship. The numbers on the side and bottom of the diagram refer to scores which could be obtained on hypothetical tests measuring level of arousal and ability to learn.)

Is there a strong relationship between level of arousal and ability to learn? Obviously, Figure 11–5 shows a very strong relationship—a very predictable pattern. However, the Pearson or Spearman coefficients would indicate a near zero correlation. This low correlation would be found because these coefficients are designed to measure linear (straight line) relationships. For example, if ability to learn would have kept increasing as level of arousal increased—so that the most aroused

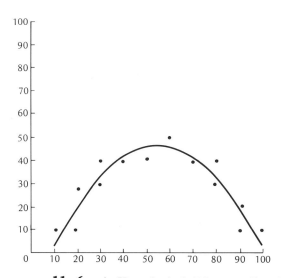

FIGURE 11–6. A Hypothetical Diagram Showing a Less than Perfect Relationship Between Level of Arousal and Ability to Learn.

person would also be the most able to learn—this would have presented a strong linear (straight line) relationship, and the Pearson correlation coefficient would have been high. Since the pattern reversed itself at midpoint, however, this drastically reduced the linear correlation coefficient.

To measure curvilinear relationships, we need a different type of correlation coefficient—one which is sensitive to nonlinear patterns. One such coefficient is the eta coefficient. Eta coefficients range from 1.00 to .00. (There are no negative curvilinear relationships.) Other than that, the interpretation of the eta coefficient is very much like that of the other correlation coefficients. A high value indicates a strong relationship, and a low value indicates a weak relationship. However, in order to interpret the eta coefficient, you need a diagram of some sort. The diagram indicates the pattern of the relationship, and the eta coefficient indicates how strongly the variables adhere to this predicted pattern. For example, Figure 11–6 shows an eta coefficient of .83 between level of arousal and ability to learn.

The diagram is absolutely essential in interpreting eta coefficients. If all we knew was that there was an eta correlation of .83 between two variables, this relationship could take a number of forms, such as those indicated in Figure 11–7. The diagram provides the pattern, and the eta coefficient indicates how strongly the data adhere to this pattern.

Those of you who are mathematically oriented might have noticed that the eta coefficient *could* be used even for linear relationships. This is because a straight

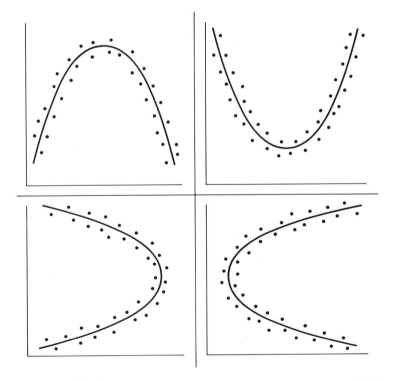

FIGURE 11–7. Four Separate Diagrams, Each Being a Possible Diagram of the Relationship Described by an Eta Coefficient of .80 Between Two Variables.

(linear) line can be viewed as a specific type of a curved line. Therefore, it would be possible to replace the Pearson coefficient with the eta coefficient. For several reasons, this has not happened. The major reasons appear to be that the Pearson correlation coefficient is more readily interpreted (no need for a diagram) than the eta coefficient and it is more easily integrated with other statistical procedures. In addition, when people speculate about relationships, they are most often interested in linear relationships. Nevertheless, the eta coefficient can be a useful tool to discover curvilinear relationships, when such relationships are thought to be important.

Review Quiz

Which of the following relationships would best be described by an eta coefficient?

a. "The hungrier children get, the less they learn. This is true both right after children have eaten and several hours later."

b. "As time passes after a meal, children learn better. This is true up to a certain point. After that point, as time passes, they learn less."

Answer:
b.

MULTIPLE CORRELATION COEFFICIENTS

It is possible that a certain ability might be caused not by a single factor, but by a combination of two or more factors. Likewise, it might be possible to make a more accurate prediction about a certain event not by using a single variable for making this prediction, but rather by combining our knowledge about several different variables to make such a prediction. This is what multiple correlation does. It enables us to state the relationship between a *combination* of several variables and some other variable. Like the other correlation coefficients, multiple correlation does not establish causality; it merely indicates that a relationship exists.

Let us examine an example of a multiple correlation coefficient. Assume that there is a multiple correlation (R) of .65 between a combination of (a) manual dexterity, (b) score on an initial interview, and (c) rating from previous employer and success as a dishwasher. This means that a weighted combination of these three factors is as strongly related to success as a dishwasher as would be a single variable (if one could be found) with a correlation of .65. Individually, manual dexterity might correlate .50 with success as a dishwasher, initial interview .35, and previous employer's rating .45; but when they are combined and used simultaneously for predictive purposes, they give us a much stronger relationship. If a prospective employer could use either IQ (which we assume correlates .60 with success as a dishwasher) or any one of the other variables to select his new dishwashers, he should use IQ, since it is more strongly related to future performance than any of the others. On the other hand, if he can combine the three into a single package to make a prediction, then this combination will give us a more accurate selection process than would the single variable of IQ.

The topic of multiple correlation is usually introduced in intermediate or advanced level statistics courses, rather than in beginning courses. This is because it requires relatively complex computational procedures and because it is possible to do some relatively complicated things with this technique. It is introduced here merely to indicate an additional direction that correlation coefficients can take. You are likely to come across multiple R's in your professional reading, and even this brief introduction can help you understand them. Likewise, in your own research it will be useful to know that there is a technique for combining several variables to ascertain their relationship to another variable, and the information given here will enable you to seek help in pursuing a multiple correlation coefficient.

Spot Quiz

Which of the following would be answered with a multiple correlation coefficient?

a. There is a correlation of .75 between a combination of IQ and creativity and performance in art class.
b. There is a correlation of .80 between creativity scores and performance in art class, and .69 between creativity scores and performance in English class.

Answer:
a. Note that the reason b is wrong is that it uses two separate Pearson correlations.

PUTTING IT ALL TOGETHER

Part of the research Mr. Anderson performed fits into the categories of the criterion group and correlational research described in this chapter. For example, he wanted to find out whether being the owner of a pet caused children to have a more favorable attitude toward animal life. The only way he could examine this question was through a criterion group design. He found several classes of children, identified the pet owners and the non-pet owners according to an appropriate criterion, and then compared the performance of these two groups on the Fireman tests. He had to use a criterion group design rather than an experimental design, because pet ownership was not a characteristic he had any control over. (True, he could have found a group of 50 non-pet owners and assigned pets to 25 and withheld pets from others. But aside from being of dubious ethical and practical merit, this experiment would not have addressed the same question as that addressed by examining the naturally occurring pattern of ownership.) Mr. Anderson administered *Johnny and the Fireman* to about 200 pet owners and 100 non-pet owners and he found that the mean number of animals chosen was 1.20 by the non-pet owners and 1.15 by the pet owners. This difference was not very substantial. (The idea of assessing the statistical significance of the results will be discussed in the next chapter.) Mr. Anderson concluded that there was no relationship between pet ownership and attitudes toward animal life.

Mr. Anderson was at first surprised to find no difference in attitudes between pet owners and nonowners, but soon he realized that this was actually quite logical. There were a lot of children who would like to own a pet, and who would be kind to a pet, but simply did not own one for reasons beyond their control. Likewise, many children who owned pets really viewed them as objects rather than as living things. He decided to pursue a new line of reasoning. He wondered if among pet owners there was a relationship between the amount of time children spent caring for their pet and their attitudes toward animal life. He broke the 200 pet owners down into three groups, based on how much time per week they spent actively caring for their pets. When he examined the scores, he found these results:

Pet owners who spent at least 30 minutes per day caring for their pets.	1.5 animals chosen
Pet owners who spent between 15 and 30 minutes a day caring for their pets	1.2 animals chosen
Pet owners who spent less than 15 minutes per day caring for their pets	0.8 animals chosen

He saw a clear pattern in these results. Pet owners who spent more time caring for their pets did, in fact, display more favorable attitudes toward animal life. (Again, the concept of statistical significance, treated in the next chapter, would be relevant here.)

Note that Mr. Anderson has examined two different questions. In one case he found no relationship, and in the other case he found a relationship. In the first case, when he found no relationship between pet ownership and attitudes toward animal life, this *can* be taken as evidence about a causal relationship. If there is no relationship between pet ownership and attitudes toward animal life, then (*a fortiori*, as the logicians say) pet ownership cannot *cause* certain types of attitudes. (If pet ownership did cause the attitudes, then there would be a relationship.) On the other hand, the finding that the amount of time spent taking care of one's pet is related to attitudes toward animal life *cannot* be taken as evidence that there is a causal relationship. It may be possible, for example, that friendly attitudes cause the children to spend more time taking care of their pets. On the other hand, it may also be possible that spending more time with one's pet causes friendlier attitudes. Without further information, all we can say is that there is a relationship, and this *may* be a causal relationship.

SUMMARY

Criterion group designs and correlational research are useful for demonstrating the existence of relationships. They do not, however, provide compelling evidence with regard to cause and effect relationships. The only strong cause and effect conclusion which can be based on these designs is that if no relationship is found using a criterion group or correlational design, then there is probably not a causal relationship. When such designs do uncover a relationship, however, further information is needed to determine the cause of this relationship. Such further information can be obtained from non-experimental reasoning, including the elimination of rival hypotheses and the examination of further criterion groups and correlations. However, the strongest evidence regarding cause and effect relationships has to be acquired from the experimental studies discussed in the previous two chapters.

The designs discussed in this chapter have two major uses. First, we can use them as a patchwork method when time is a factor or when a better design is impossible. Such designs enable us to examine on a minimally controlled basis relationships which would otherwise go unexplored if we had to wait for actual experimental evidence. It is important to note at this point that a very large amount of our daily thinking necessarily goes on without experimentation. We must constantly make decisions based on what we see in our world. In making such decisions, we necessarily invent our own criterion groups and estimate our own correlations, even if we are not specifically aware of doing so. A knowledge of the uses and limitations of non-experimental research, therefore, can help us in this routine, non-experimental decision making.

Second, these designs are often useful preliminary designs to use before undertaking more sophisticated experimental or quasi-experimental designs. If we know that a relationship exists, then we can undertake further, more scientifically controlled efforts to determine whether this is a causal relationship.

Annotated Bibliography

GUILFORD, J.P. and FRUCHTER, B. *Fundamental Statistics in Psychology and Education* (6th ed.) (New York: McGraw-Hill, 1978). This book provides a better discussion of correlation coefficients than any other textbook I have come across.

In addition to the above text, many of the sources cited in the bibliography at the end of the following chapter are closely related to the topic of this chapter as well. That list will not be repeated here.

Professional Journals

Each of the following articles uses a nonexperimental procedure to try to control the threats to internal validity.

HARBER, J.R. "Auditory perception and reading: Another look" *Learning Disabilities Quarterly* 3 (1980): (3), 19–29. This study uses partial correlation to examine the relationship between auditory perception skills and reading performance among learning disabled children. Partial correlation eliminates much of the bias introduced by differences in age and IQ.

MACMILLAN, D.L. and MORRISON, G.M. "Correlates of social status among mildly handicapped learners in self-contained special classes," *Journal of Educational Psychology* 72 (1980): 437–444. In the final paragraphs of this article the authors indicate their awareness of the limitations of their correlational methods and specify what has to be done to establish an actual cause and effect relationship. (The study bases part of its results on a statistical procedure called commonality analysis, which has not been covered in this text. However, the article explains this procedure in sufficient detail to enable novice readers to interpret it without technical expertise.)

MITCHELL, J.R. "Male adolescents' concern about a physical examination conducted by a female," *Nursing Research* 29 (1980): 165–169. This study found that younger adolescents expressed greater concern about being examined by a female during a physical examination. When age was held constant through partial correlation, stage of physiological sexual development was unrelated to any of the concerns examined in the study.

MOLDENHAUER, D.L. and MILLER, W.H. "Television and reading achievement," *Journal of Reading* 23 (1980): 615–619. What is the relationship between television viewing and reading achievement among seventh graders? This study uses the Pearson correlation coefficient to find out.

SMITH, M.D. "Prediction of self-concept among learning disabled children," *Journal of Learning Disabilities* 12 (1979): 664–669. The author finds that a combination of work knowledge, math performance, and socioeconomic status predicts self-concept among learning disabled pupils, even though these factors taken separately did not make a useful prediction.

12 Tests of Significance

Chapter Preview

Two serious problems in establishing cause and effect relationships were mentioned near the beginning of Chapter 8. The first of these was that it is often very difficult to find groups that are equal in every respect except with regard to the treatment. Solutions to that problem were discussed in Chapters 9 and 10. The second problem was that it is often difficult to tell whether groups are the same or not after a treatment. This is the problem referred to as instability, and it is one of the major threats to internal validity.

The results of observations before and after a treatment are clouded by the fact that the unreliability of the tests or unique characteristics of the measurement occasion might introduce chance variations in scores derived from such observations. This threat to internal validity is controlled not by eliminating it, but rather by assessing in a mathematical fashion how likely it is that such instability occurred and then judging whether such instability is a critical factor. The basic strategies for estimating the likelihood of such chance fluctuations in scores are the topic of this chapter.

After reading this chapter you should be able to

- Describe the underlying theory of statistical tests of significance.
- Describe what is meant by level of significance, and interpret statements regarding levels of significance.
- Describe the purposes of each of the following statistical procedures:
  $-t$ test.
  –Analysis of variance.
  –Analysis of covariance.
- Identify situations in which each of the above statistical procedures would correctly be used.
- Given a statement in which each of the above statistical procedures is used, interpret the statement correctly.
- Use an appropriate table to identify the level of significance of a t statistic.

THE BASIS OF STATISTICAL REASONING

If you flipped a quarter ten times, and came up with six heads and four tails, would you be surprised? If you then flipped a half dollar and came up with five heads and five tails, would you be surprised? Comparing the two results, would you conclude that quarters are more likely to come up heads than half dollars? In the above cases, you would probably be unconvinced by the evidence. You would rightly point out that simply because a quarter comes out six heads and four tails one time, this does not mean that the result will always be that way. You know that the odds are that coin tosses will come out about half heads and half tails, and slight deviations from this norm are to be expected. The six heads represent a chance fluctuation–nothing to get excited about.

Similar problems arise in educational research. If the experimental class scores 80% on a test and the control class scores 70%, is this enough of a discrepancy to convince us that the treatment caused a difference? As we discussed in Chapter 3, neither educational tests nor the people who administer and score them are perfectly reliable; and the absence of reliability introduces an element of chance into educational research comparisons. Likewise, there is a certain amount of chance variation arising from random assignment. Because of this unreliability, we know that the scores of 80% and 70% are not precise measurements. These scores would probably have been different if we had measured the same students at a different time, under slightly different circumstances, or with a different form of the test. Therefore, it is possible that there is no more real difference between the experimental and control groups than there was between the quarter and the half dollar in the previous paragraph. The difference between the two coins was *probably due to chance*. Perhaps the difference between the experimental and control groups is also *probably due to chance*.

This is the problem dealt with by statistical tests of significance. Such tests provide an estimate of how likely it is that two or more observed outcomes are really merely chance fluctuations arising from attempts to measure an identical outcome. Such tests come with underlying mathematical theories and computational procedures, which will not be discussed here. By applying one of these tests to the coin tossing example, we can specify that the odds are about 75 in 100 that the quarter results (six heads) and the half dollar results (five heads) are really just chance variations of patterns which are likely to be identical in their long-range results. On the basis of this information, if you and a friend were flipping a coin to see who got a date with a certain bright, attractive person, you probably would not care whether the coin used for this purpose was a quarter or a half dollar. On the other hand, if the results of the statistical test would have shown that there was only 1 chance in 1000 that the results were chance variations from coins likely to be identical, then you *would* be concerned about which coin would be used.

This same logic can be applied to educational research. By applying statistical procedures we can make an estimate of how likely it is that two observed outcomes are really just chance variations arising from identical capabilities. Such information can be used to help us make judgments about educational experiments. In the educational example cited previously, we had an experimental group that scored 80% correct after a treatment, while the control group scored 70%. If we would apply a statistical test of significance to this problem, we might discover that the chances are about 75 in 100 that the scores of 80% (experimentals) and 70% (controls) on a grammar test are really just chance variations of identical grammatical ability influenced by unreliability. If we knew this, then we would conclude that the groups were probably not really different after the treatment. Furthermore, we would also conclude that the treatment had not produced an observed outcome greater than would be expected by mere chance. On the other hand, if our statistical test had shown that there was only 1 chance in 1000 that the scores of the two groups were likely to represent chance variations of an identical capability, then we would conclude that the groups probably were different after the treatment. Moreover, if we had previously ascertained that the groups were identical prior to the treatment, we would be justified in concluding that the treatment had produced an outcome greater than would have been expected by chance alone. This logic of statistical reasoning is schematically summarized in Figure 12–1.

Let us incorporate this statistical reasoning into the basic research strategy discussed earlier. If we found that the difference was one that was likely to have occurred by mere chance, then our reasoning would go like this:

- The two groups were identical to start with.
- The two groups were treated identically, except that one of them got the treatment.
- Afterwards, the groups still did not differ, except as would be expected by mere chance variations.
- Therefore, since the groups are still the same, the treatment must not have made a difference.

All this reasoning, of course, relies on our meeting the basic assumptions that the groups really were equal to begin with, that we really did treat them identically with regard to everything except the treatment, and that we really are validly measuring the outcome we think we are measuring. If we have failed to meet one of these assumptions (for example, if we have an invalid test measuring something other than what we intended to measure), then our conclusion would be wrong. *Statistical procedures cannot correct for faulty research procedures!*

If we would have found that the difference between the two groups was not likely to have occurred by mere chance, then our reasoning would go like this:

- The two groups were identical to start with.
- The two groups were treated identically, except that one of them got the treatment.
- Afterwards, the groups differed by a greater amount than would be expected as a result of mere chance variations.
- Therefore, since the groups are no longer identical, the treatment must have caused this difference.[1]

Note that the statistical reasoning discussed in the previous paragraphs is based on the assumption that the groups were *initially identical;* and this assumption, in turn, requires random assignment. Strictly speaking, therefore, many statistical tests of significance relying on this type of reasoning should be applied only to true

---

[1] Technically, the reasoning process discussed in the previous two paragraphs is referred to as *testing the null hypothesis*. References to the null hypothesis are included in the footnotes to Figure 12–1. Although the logic behind the null hypothesis is essential to educational research, the term itself is often confusing to students, and therefore it has been avoided in this text.

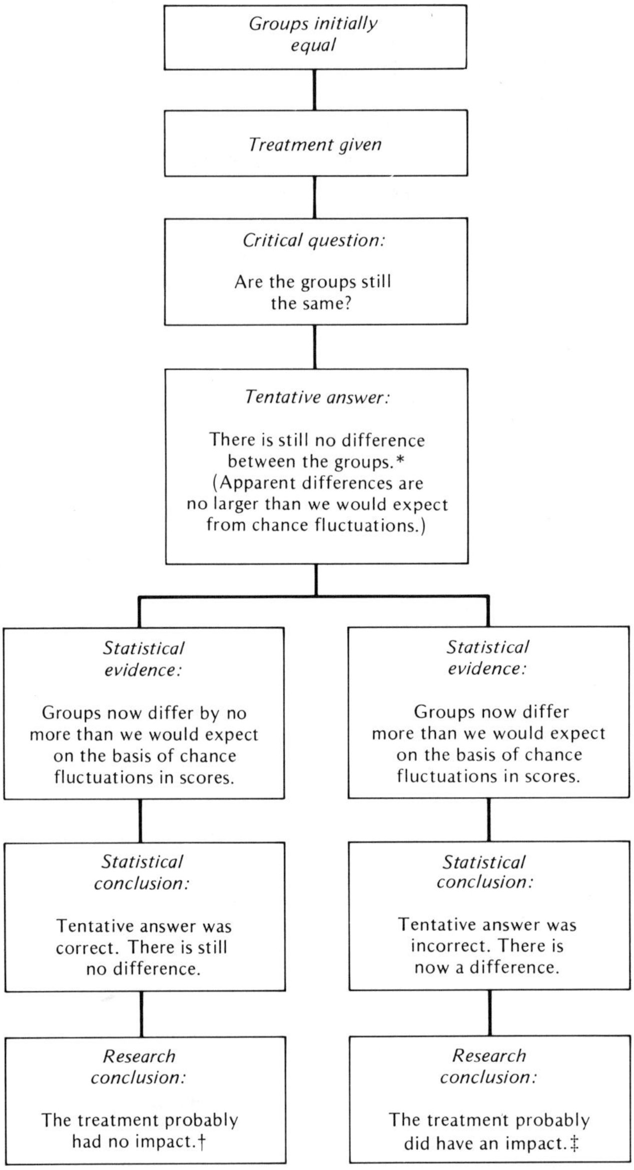
Groups initially equal
Treatment given
Critical question:
Are the groups still the same?
Tentative answer:
There is still no difference between the groups.* (Apparent differences are no larger than we would expect from chance fluctuations.)
Statistical evidence:
Groups now differ by no more than we would expect on the basis of chance fluctuations in scores.
Statistical conclusion:
Tentative answer was correct. There is still no difference.
Research conclusion:
The treatment probably had no impact.†
Statistical evidence:
Groups now differ more than we would expect on the basis of chance fluctuations in scores.
Statistical conclusion:
Tentative answer was incorrect. There is now a difference.
Research conclusion:
The treatment probably did have an impact.‡

Footnotes:

*The tentative answer is often called the *null hypothesis.* It is a hypothesis that there is *no* difference between the two groups.

†In other words, the null hypothesis is accepted.

‡In other words, the null hypothesis is rejected.

FIGURE 12–1. Summary Diagram of the Logic Behind the Statistical Tests of Significance.

experiments, where random assignment has been employed. Statisticians who have pursued the matter, however, have ascertained that within certain guidelines these same procedures can be applied—with much the same meaning—to situations in which random assignment was not used. The precise nature of these assumptions is beyond the scope of this book. Suffice it to say that to the extent that a quasi-experiment resembles a true experiment, the statistics become more valid.

Also note that it is not possible to make a sound judgment about how likely it is that the performance of the experimental and control groups differed by chance merely by examining the numbers 80% and 70%. To make such a judgment, additional information would be needed. At the very least, we would need the means and standard deviations of each group; but the easiest way would be to have the exact scores and plug them into a computer program, as Chapter 18 will describe. Some simple computational procedures are described in Appendix D, but for other procedures you should refer to more detailed texts.

The following sections of this chapter are intended to introduce you to some basic statistical tests of significance. Such an introduction will help you understand their use when you read about these statistics in professional journals and will enable you to know which procedures can help you solve a given problem in your own work. Before actually trying to use some of these statistical procedures, you will necessarily have to seek help regarding their computation and the basic assumptions underlying them.

STATISTICAL SIGNIFICANCE

A dictionary definition of the word *significant* would indicate that it means *important*. Using the logic described in the previous section of this chapter, we could say that the difference between two groups is significant (important) if the difference is unlikely to be a chance occurrence. Likewise, we could say that a difference is non-significant if the results *are* likely to have occurred by chance. This is the meaning which the word has in statistical usage. Statistical significance is a way of stating how likely it is that two or more observed outcomes are merely chance variations occurring from the measurement of an identical capacity.

Statistical significance should not be confused with such ideas as social significance, relevance for society, or educational importance. For example, my son has a dice baseball game. By applying methods similar to our earlier coin tossing analysis, I might discover that my son gets more 2s and 3s than could reasonably be expected by chance alone when he plays his dice baseball game. I might even conclude that there is only about one chance in a thousand that he could get 2s (home runs) as often as he does. This would be a statistically significant observation. However, in terms of what it reveals about my son's personality, what impact this finding will have on society, or what this means with regard to how he will grow up, the significance of this finding appears to be trivial. This would be an example of a statistically significant but practically inconsequential discovery. Thus, the term *significance* when used regarding a statistical test entails a very narrow, specific usage of the term.

When we make statements about statistical significance we do so in terms of a precise number. This number states the mathematical probability that the observed outcomes are merely chance variations arising from the measurement of identical capabilities. For example, if an experimental and a control group differ at the .01 level

of significance, this means that there is only 1 chance in 100 that the two groups are really equal on the observed outcome and that the observed scores are merely chance variations arising out of some sort of unreliability or instability. On the other hand, if the two groups differed at the .50 level of significance, this would mean that there are 50 chances in 100 that the observed outcome would occur if the groups were really equal and the observed outcomes were influenced by chance variations. Thus the *lower* the number included in the statement of significance, the *stronger* the degree of confidence we can have that the observed differences are not the result of chance fluctuations. In other words, the lower the level of significance, the stronger the differences.

This is a very important idea to understand. Some students confuse level of significance with correlation coefficients. Since a high number indicates a strong correlation, they assume that a high number indicates a strong difference between groups. This is not the case. It is easy to make the distinction, if you keep in mind the meaning of a statement of significance. A difference significant at the .001 level is stronger than a difference at the .05 level of significance, because it is better that there be only 1 chance in 1000 than that there be 5 chances in 100 that the differences arose out of random variations. Our confidence in an outcome would be greater if there were only 1 chance in 1000 that it occurred by chance than if there were 5 chances in 100 that it occurred by chance.

There are several ways of stating the level of significance. All of the following statements mean exactly the same thing.

- The two groups differed at the .01 level of significance.
- The two groups differed significantly (*p.* <.01).
- The two groups differed significantly (alpha level = .01).

The first statement employs terminology we have already discussed. In the second statement, "p. < .01" means that the probability of the results arising from chance fluctuations is less than 1 in 100. In the third statement, "alpha level = .01" means that when the person interpreted this result, he or she entered the statistical table under the .01 column. This usage of tables will be described in the next section of this chapter.

Prior to the widespread availability of computers for computing statistics, certain specific cut-off points were almost always used as levels of significance. A researcher would select a cut-off point and check a table to see whether the observed difference between means was more significant or less significant than would be indicated by that cut-off point. (An example of this usage of tables will be included later in this chapter.) Thus, if a researcher selected a cut-off point at the .05 level of significance and there were 6 chances in a hundred that the results were chance fluctuations, this outcome would be considered not significant. On the other hand, if there were only 4 chances in 100 that the difference represented a chance fluctuation, then this result was labeled significant.

Using this system, it is possible to develop a highly structured system of significance levels. We can label a result with less than 5 chances in 100 as being significant. A result at the .01 level of significance could be very significant, and one at the .001 level, extremely significant. Going the other direction, a result at the .10 level could be called nearly significant. Perhaps one above the .50 level of significance could be labeled not even remotely close to being significant. With the exception of the last, all of these labels have actually been in vogue at one time or another.

Currently, however, the trend seems to be toward reporting exact levels of significance whenever possible. If your computer tells you that a difference was significant at the .02 level, why convert this to "significant beyond the .05 level?" Just report the exact level, and let your readers have full access to this more precise information. The strategy of labeling levels of significance by these cut-off points arose out of an arbitrary consensus among researchers in the social sciences that if an event had a probability of greater than 1 in 20 of occurring by chance, this was too high a degree of probability to tolerate. Such reasoning has some validity behind it; and you can use this logic if you like, even if you present or deal with more precise levels of significance. If you have access to a computer that gives precise levels of probability (as in Chapter 14), then use the more precise information. On the other hand, if you have access only to a table (as in this Chapter), use the cut-off points— but use them intelligently, not as part of some sort of blind ritual.

t TESTS

If you want to determine how likely it is that two mean scores differ by more than chance, you can do this with a *t* test. If you have more than two means to compare, you cannot use a t test for your statistical analysis. Therefore, a t test could be used to test the significance of the following differences in means:

- The mean of a group prior to a treatment compared to the mean of the same group after the treatment.
- The mean of the experimental group on the posttest compared to the mean of the control group on the posttest.
- The gains made by the experimental group compared to the control group. (In this case, four scores would become two *gain scores*, because for each group pretest scores would be subtracted from posttest scores.)

A t test could *not* be used to test the significance of the following differences in means:

- Scores on pretest compared to performance on posttest and on a delayed posttest. (In this case, if you wanted to do two separate pretest-posttest comparisons, this would be possible with two t tests.)
- A comparison of the means of third graders, fourth graders, and fifth graders on an attention span test.
- A comparison of the performance of freshmen vs. sophomores, where the classes are further subdivided into boys vs. girls. (In this case, there are actually four groups.)

If you wish to compare the means of more than two groups, you have to use analysis of variance, which is discussed in the next section of this chapter.

A t test is performed by following an appropriate mathematical formula or by accessing an appropriate computer program. There are minor variations in the t test formulas, depending on the precise nature of your study. (The computational procedures for one of the basic t tests is included in Appendix D.) The output from the mathematical formula is a t statistic. To interpret a t statistic computed by hand, you have to refer to a table, like the one in Appendix B.

To use such a table, you have to determine your degrees of freedom and your alpha level. (No discussion will be provided here on why these apparently obscure labels exist.) The degree of freedom is associated with the number of subjects in the experiment minus one. The alpha level is the level of significance.

With this in mind, let us pursue an example. Suppose we run a t test with 30 subjects and come out with the result that t is equal to 2.30. Is this result significant at the .05 level? To answer this question, we look down the left-hand column (labeled *d.f.* for "degrees of freedom") until we find 29 (because $30 - 1 = 29$). We then look under the alpha level of .05. (Alpha levels are written across the top of the table.) Then we go down the .05 column to the point where .05 alpha level intersects with 29 degrees of freedom. The number appearing here is 2.045. The question we ask ourselves is this: "Is 2.30 greater than 2.045?" The answer is yes, and therefore our result *is* significant at the .05 level. To pursue this example further, let us see if this result is significant at the .01 level. To answer this question, we move over to the .01 alpha level column (at the top of the table). Then we look down this column until we find the intersection of .01 alpha level and 29 degrees of freedom. We then ask ourselves, "Is 2.30 greater than 2.756?" Since the answer is no, we can state that our result is *not* significant at the .01 level. From our use of the table, therefore, we can state that there is somewhere between 1 and 5 chances in 100 that the difference between the two means we are comparing is likely to have occurred if the two means had both been indications of the same level of performance. This is a relatively remote possibility; and in such a case, we would have pretty good confidence that the treatment had produced the desired outcome.

In general, most tables of significance are interpreted in this manner. Some are more complex, but the strategy of interpretation is about the same. No further examples (e.g., for analysis of variance or analysis of covariance) will be provided in this text. Once the level of significance is obtained from such a table, it is interpreted in the way described in the previous section.

Review Quiz

1. Which of the following questions could be answered using a *t* test?
   a. The boys averaged 4.5 answers correct. The girls averaged 5.1 correct. Is this difference likely to have arisen by chance?
   b. My students averaged 60.3% before I lectured to them and 75.1% after the lecture. Is this a real difference or a chance difference?
   c. What is the relationship between test anxiety and scores on the test? Do those with higher anxiety do worse than those with lower anxiety? As anxiety decreases, does that performance increase?
   d. I taught some students using computers and some with traditional methods. I want to find out if the computer worked differently at different levels of achievement orientation. Within each group, I had some high achievers, some medium achievers, and some low achievers.

Answers:
a and b would be tested with a *t* test, because each includes two (and only two) means for comparison.
Not c, because this is a comparison of two variables. It calls for a coefficient, a *t* test is used only when two *means* are being compared.
Not d, because this involves more than two groups. There are three different levels of achievement orientation using the computers, and three using the traditional method. That is six groups altogether.

----

2. Is each of the following significant at the .05 level? at the .01 level? at the .001 level?
   a. Pretest mean = 51.5.
      Posttest mean = 53.2.
      t = 2.70 (number of subjects = 60).
   b. Experimental group mean = 15.6.
      Control group mean = 23.7.
      t = 1.13 (number of subjects = 20).
   c. Boys average score = 34.9.
      Girls average score = 27.3.
      t = 2.99 (number of subjects = 100).
   d. *t* = 5.45.
      Number of subjects = 50.

Answers:
a. Significant at .05 level.
   Significant at .01 level.
   Significant at .001 level.
b. Not significant at any of these levels.

c. Significant at .05 level.
Significant at .01 level.
Significant at .001 level.
d. Significant at .05 level.
Significant at .01 level.
Significant at .001 level.

ANALYSIS OF VARIANCE

Analysis of variance tests the significance of differences among *two or more* groups. Thus, it can be employed in any situation in which a *t* test would be appropriate; and in addition it can be used when there are more than two groups. The output of an analysis of variance (called an *F* statistic) is evaluated in a way similar to the *t* statistic.

In dealing with two groups, therefore, we have an option of using either analysis of variance or a *t* test. The *t* test has the advantage of being somewhat easier to compute by hand. If both statistical procedures were used to evaluate the same set of data on two groups, the results of the analysis of variance would be identical to the results of the *t* test.

When we use analysis of variance with more than two groups, what the output tells us is the level of significance of the differences among the several groups. For example, if we compared the average performance of the Redbirds, Blackbirds, and Robins in music class an found a difference significant at the .01 level, all we would really know is that the highest group differed from the lowest group to a degree that would not be likely to occur by chance. To determine whether specific groups (e.g., Redbirds and Blackbirds) differed from one another, we would need further tests. These additional tests (which are not described further in this book) are interpreted in exactly the same way as *t* tests and analysis of variance.

Review Quiz

1. For each of the following, state whether the question could be examined by a *t* test, by analysis of variance, or by either a *t* test or analysis of variance.
    a. The football players were able to bench press only about 100 pounds at the beginning of the season. By the end of the season, they had advanced to 150 pounds.
    b. The experimental group gained more than the control group. Within the experimental group, those with high self-concepts did better than those with either medium or low self-concepts.
    c. The sets repaired by Mr. Kern's trainees lasted an average of 34.8 days before they needed further work. The sets repaired by Mrs. Foster's trainees lasted 63.2 days. Those repaired by members of the control group lasted an average of 28.3 days.

Answers:
a. Could use either (2 groups).
b. Analysis of variance (2 groups subdivided into three other self-concept groups; this makes six groups).
c. Analysis of variance (3 groups).

ANALYSIS OF COVARIANCE

Analysis of covariance can be described as an "adjusted" analysis of variance. It is useful when groups are initially unequal. It compares the means of two or more groups, while adjusting for initial differences among the groups. It answers the question,"How likely is it that these differences would have arisen by chance, if the groups would have been equal to begin with?" *The following are examples of questions that could be answered by analysis of covariance:*

- Would the posttest performance of these two groups still have been significantly different if their pretest performance would have been equal? (In other words, maybe the reason one group surpassed the other on the posttest was that that group had an initial edge. What would the results have been *if the groups would have been equal to begin with?*)
- Would the difference between boys and girls on the home economics test have been equal *if they would have been equal with regard to IQ?*
- Would girls be as interested as boys in scientific careers *if the amount of time indoctrinating them with regard to these careers would be the same?*

In each of the above questions, there is an attempt to make two groups equal in some respect and *then* to compare their mean scores to see if they differ more than would be expected by chance. An attempt is made to rule out some biasing factor before the comparison of group means is made. It should be noted that analysis of covariance does *not* replace random assignment. It always underadjusts for initial differences. Even though this procedure does not fully provide the same theoretical advantages as random assignment, it is a useful procedure, since it enables us to adjust at least partially for initial differences and to form an estimate of what the results would have been if the two groups had been equal in the first place. The best way to adjust for initial differences, of course, is to find two groups that have no initial differences.

The variable whose influence is controlled is called the covariate. Very commonly, pretest performance is used as a covariate in the analysis of posttest scores. For mathematical reasons which will not be discussed here, an analysis of covariance of this kind is usually superior to a *t* test or analysis of variance of gain scores obtained by subtracting the pretests from the posttests. In addition, it is possible to employ as covariates other variables that are thought to be the sources of selection bias. For example, if there is reason to believe that two groups differ in intellectual ability, then it would make sense to use IQ scores as a covariate in an analysis of covariance of the outcomes after a treatment. Finally, this procedure is often used in criterion group designs to adjust for some of the selection biases for which such designs are notorious. Such adjustments are useful, but they do not negate the fact that criterion group designs are still weak because of the lack of experimental manipulation in such designs.

Review Quiz

1. Which of the following questions would appropriately be answered by performing an analysis of covariance?
    a. What would be the relationship between test anxiety and test performance if the influence of creativity were removed?

b. If they would all have had the same amount of exposure to television newscasts, would the experimental and control subjects have differed in their knowledge of current events?

c. Did the boys differ from the girls on the pretest more than they did on the posttest with regard to their willingness to enter into a conversation with a person of the opposite sex?

Answers:

a. is an example of partial correlation. This is a correlation, not a comparison of means.

b. is a good example of analysis of covariance.

c. is an analysis of variance, not covariance. There is no covariate—nothing whose influence is being eliminated. This item *could* be converted to analysis of covariance, if it were rephrased like this:

> If they would have been equal before the treatment, were there any differences in the willingness of the boys and girls to enter into a conversation with a member of the opposite sex after the treatment?

However, this seems to be slightly different from the original question.

SELECTING A STATISTICAL PROCEDURE

The statistical procedures described in this and the previous chapter will help you solve many of the research problems you will encounter. In addition, a knowledge of these procedures will enable you to understand the usage of statistical procedures in many articles and reports you will read. It is important to note, however, that the treatment here has been very brief. Only a few of the most basic procedures have been introduced. Consulting the resources listed in the Annotated Bibliography will enable you both to learn more about the procedures described here and to learn about those that have not even been mentioned in the present text.

A problem that you may encounter when you first start using statistical procedures is how to decide what statistic to employ. You might understand everything that has been said in this and the last chapter, and you might be able to describe what is meant by a statistical statement when you see one written down; but how do you decide what statistic to use to solve a problem you wish to explore? How do you choose from the apparent maze of statistical procedures available to you? Figure 12–2 is an attempt to help you with this problem.

Figure 12–2 presents an algorithm designed in such a way as to take the statistical procedures discussed in this book and narrow the field as quickly as possible so that you can select the one that will help you investigate a given problem. The first question you should ask yourself, according to this diagram, is whether or not you plan to compare the means of two or more groups of subjects. If the answer is yes, then your search for a statistical procedure is immediately confined to the procedures described in the present chapter; and it is merely a matter of asking one or two more questions to find the exact statistic.

If your answer to the first question was no, then you should proceed to the second question, "Are you relating the performance of a group on one variable to the performance of that same group on another variable?" This is another way of saying, "Do you need a correlation?" and if your answer is yes, then you are directed to the correlational procedures described in the previous chapter. By answering a few more questions, you can select the exact statistic you need. Note that the algorithm arranges questions in such a way as to eliminate false possibilities as quickly as possible.

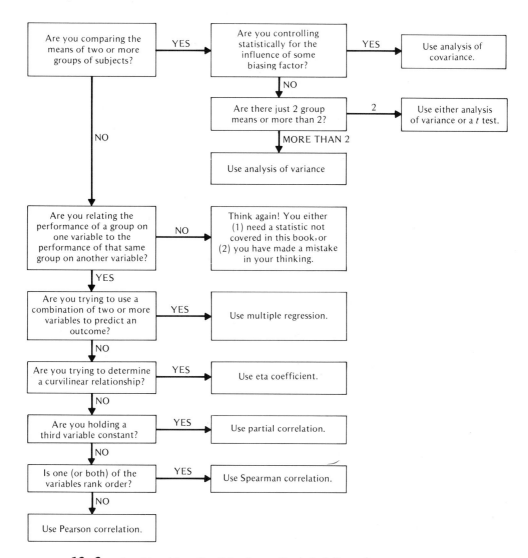

FIGURE **12–2.**   An Algorithm for Selecting a Statistical Procedure.

If you answered no to both of the above questions, then you either need a statistic not covered in the present text or you made a mistake in your answer to the first two questions. Unless you have already become fairly sophisticated, you should probably think things over again before you conclude that you have come up with a problem that goes beyond the present textbook. On the other hand, if you do think things over and discover that your answer to the first two questions is still no, then you might want to look elsewhere for statistical help. There are several relatively common techniques (such as chi square and factor analysis) that have not been covered in this book, and many of the more complicated procedures have likewise been avoided completely.

Figure 12–2 presents an oversimplified view of the process of selecting a statistical procedure. Were we to add even a few more procedures (such as chi square and factor analysis), it would become much more difficult to select a procedure merely by answering a few questions. The algorithm would expand quickly. Nevertheless, all users of statistics, no matter how sophisticated, actually use an algorithm something like that in Figure 12–2 when selecting statistical procedures. This is true even though some users may do this without realizing that they have such an algorithm in mind and even if the algorithms implicitly used by very sophisticated users are considerably more complex than this one. Therefore, some practice in using this algorithm will help you in two ways: (1) such practice will make you more familiar with the application of the statistics covered in this book; and (2) such practice will help you learn to think along appropriate lines so that if you would care to learn more about such statistical procedures you could fit new procedures into an expanded algorithm of your own.

Review Quiz—Selecting a Statistical Procedure

This quiz assumes that you will use the algorithm described in Figure 12–2. Choose the correct statistical procedure to help you answer each question. Then compare your answer to the answer provided in the text. The text answer is accompanied by the reasoning (based on the algorithm) upon which that answer is based.

In selecting your answers, choose from the following list:

Pearson correlation coefficient.
Spearman correlation coefficient.
Partial correlation coefficient.
Eta coefficient.
Multiple correlation coefficient.
T test.
Analysis of variance.
Analysis of covariance.

1. What is the relationship between the order in which tests are turned in and the scores on the test?

Answer:
Spearman correlation coefficient.
Reasoning:
(a) "Am I comparing the means of two groups. . .?" No.
(b) "Am I relating the performance of a group on one variable to the performance of that same group on another variable?" Yes. (One variable is *how soon a person turns the test in* and the other is *that person's score on the test.*)
(c) "Am I trying to use a combination of two or more variables to predict an outcome?" No.
(d) "Am I trying to determine a curvilinear relationship?" No. (Conceivably, your answer could have been yes at this point–if you expected that persons who finished either early or late on a test would do better than those who finished with in-between times. In this case, you would need an eta coefficient.)
(e) "Am I trying to hold constant a third variable?" No.
(f) "Are one or both of the variables rank order data?" Yes. (Order of tests is rank order.) Therefore, I need a Spearman correlation coefficient.

---

2. Do children with permissive parents become more open-minded thinkers than children with nonpermissive parents when they become adults?

Answer:

T test or analysis of variance.

Reasoning:

(a) "Am I comparing the means of two or more groups. . .?" Yes. (The two groups are *children with permissive parents* and *children with nonpermissive parents*.)

(b) "Am I controlling statistically for the influence of some biasing factor?" No.

(c) "Are there two groups or more than two?" Two groups. Therefore I can use either a t test or an analysis of variance.

---

3. Is it likely that the more familiar a word is the easier it will be to recognize it when its letters are scrambled, as in an anagram?

Answer:

Pearson correlation coefficient.

Reasoning:

(a) "Am I comparing the means of two groups...?" No.

(b) "Am I relating the performance of a group on one variable to the performance of the same group on another variable?" Yes. (You have a group of words. The two characteristics of the words with which you will be concerned are familiarity and ease of recognition.)

(c) "Am I trying to use a combination of two or more variables to predict some outcome?" No.

(d) "Am I trying to determine a curvilinear relationship?" No.

(e) "Am I trying to hold constant a third variable?" No.

(f) "Are one or both of the variables rank order data?" No. Therefore I need a Pearson correlation coefficient.

---

4. When the amount of time spent on a task is held constant, does discovery learning work better than teacher-centered learning?

Answer:

Analysis of covariance.

Reasoning:

(a) "Am I comparing the means of two or more groups. . .?" Yes. (The groups are *students taught through discovery learning* and *students taught through teacher-centered learning*.)

(b) "Am I controlling statistically for the influence of some biasing factor?" Yes. (The factor to be controlled is *amount of time on task*.) Therefore I need an analysis of covariance.

Additional examples are provided in the Workbook accompanying this text.

PUTTING IT ALL TOGETHER

After Mr. Anderson carried out the experiment outlined at the end of Chapter 10, it was necessary to analyze the results of the children's performance on the various tests. The results of the Fireman Tests are shown in Figure 12–3. The experimental group chose an average of 1.03 animals on the pretest and 2.24 on the posttest. The control group chose an average of 0.78 animals on the pretest and 0.83 animals on the posttest.

A t test for the pretest scores produced a t statistic of 1.12. With 48 degrees of freedom, this was not even close to being significant at the .05 level. However, on the posttest, the t statistic was 3.80. This difference was significant beyond the .001 level.

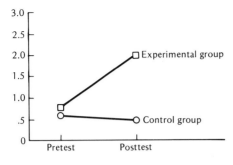

FIGURE 12–3. Average Number of Animals Chosen on Fireman Tests.

Mr. Anderson concluded that the groups had been initially equal, but that they differed at the posttest by more than would be expected by chance. Plugging this information into the Basic Strategy of Research Design, he concluded that the ALP had caused an improvement in attitude toward animal life.

Note that Mr. Anderson could have analyzed these results with an analysis of covariance. He could have compared posttest scores, using pretest scores as a covariate. However, since the groups were very close in their scores on the pretest, this more complex analysis would not seem necessary in this case. The results of an analysis of covariance would have been quite similar to the results of the t test.

Mr. Anderson also had supplementary data based on the number of good deeds and bad deeds reported to various agencies. These results are summarized in Figure 12–4. These results show that there was a low frequency of good deeds during the three years before the program was carried out and that the number of good deeds increased dramatically among the experimental students after the treatment was given. Likewise, bad deeds occurred at a high rate in both groups prior to the treatment; and after the treatment they maintained their high rate among the control students but dropped off among the ALP students.

To analyze these results, Mr. Anderson computed the average annual number of good deeds or bad deeds reported for each class prior to the experiment. He then compared the average number of good or bad deeds reported after the experiment for each group to this baseline information. The results are shown in Figure 12–4. The ALP students had averaged 5.33 reported good deeds per class per year during the three years prior to the ALP, and this average jumped to 14.33 after the ALP had

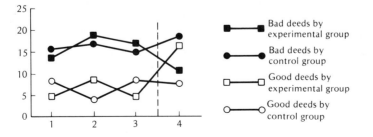

FIGURE 12–4.   Average Number of Good Deeds and Bad Deeds Reported per Class During Three Years Before Treatment and One Year After Treatment.

been introduced. The control group averaged 6.67 good deeds per class per year during the first three years, and this average stayed at 7.00 during the fourth year. This posttest difference between the ALP and non-ALP classes was statistically significant at the .01 level. The two groups had likewise been similar with regard to reported bad deeds in the three years prior to the ALP. After the experimental program, the number of bad deeds reported among the experimental classes dropped, whereas the number reported for the control classes stayed high. This difference between the two groups on the posttest was again significant at the .01 level.

Mr. Anderson knew that although the groups had not been randomly assigned, the pretest scores had shown that the experimental and control groups were about equal before the ALP was administered. This was true with regard to the supplementary variable (reported good deeds and bad deeds) as well as with regard to scores on the Fireman Tests. After the treatment, however, the ALP students surpassed the control students in their increases on the Fireman Tests, in their increase in the number of good deeds and in their reduction of bad deeds. Although he would have been happier with a true experimental design, Mr. Anderson was nevertheless satisfied that his quasi-experimental design had demonstrated a causal relationship. The ALP, he felt, had caused improved attitudes toward animal life.

SUMMARY

Statistical tests of significance are methods of assessing how likely it is that an observed difference between groups might have arisen as a result of mere chance fluctuations in group scores rather than as a result of the treatment under consideration. If there is a low degree of probability that the observed difference is one that could have arisen by chance, then this difference is referred to as a significant difference.

The simplest method for estimating the significance of the difference between the means of two groups is the *t* test. Analysis of variance is a slightly more complex but more versatile method, which can be applied to two or more groups. Finally, analysis of covariance gives us an estimate of how likely it is that the difference between two or more groups would have arisen out of chance if the two groups would have been initially equal with regard to some biasing factor.

In selecting an appropriate statistical procedure, it is essential to keep in mind the question you want answered by the statistic and the contribution that each statistical procedure can make. The algorithm in Figure 12–2 combines these factors in such a way as to help you quickly and easily determine what statistic will help you solve a specific problem.

Annotated Bibliography

BRADLEY, J.I. and McCLELLAND, J.N. *Basic Statistical Concepts* (2nd ed.) (Glenview, Ill: Scott, Foresman and Company, 1978). This is a programmed text which enables you to learn basic statistical concepts at your own speed.

BRUNING, J.L. and KINTZ, B.L. *Computational Handbook of Statistics* (2nd ed.) (Glenview, Ill.: Scott, Foresman and Company, 1977). This book provides a "cookbook" format for computing most of the important statistics that are used in educational research. If you know what statistic you need, know how to put numbers in columns, and have access to a calculator, it is easy to compute statistics with this book.

FREEDMAN, D., PISANI, R. and PURVES, R. *Statistics* (New York: W.W. Norton, 1978). This text covers the important, basic statistics in a detailed and comprehensive fashion. I consider this an advanced level book that could be easily comprehensible to the serious reader of the present text who wants to come to a better understanding of the important ideas of statistics.

HUFF, D. *How to Lie With Statistics* (New York: W.W. Norton, 1954). This is an old but good book. Huff teaches us to respect statistics by showing how easy it is to falsify data by misusing them. Reading this book will help you develop a healthy skepticism.

KIMBLE, G.A. *How to Use (and Misuse) Statistics* (Englewood Cliffs, N.J.: Prentice-Hall, 1978). This is a good introductory text. It differs from the Popham and Sirotnik text in that it is more informal in its presentation and goes well beyond the limits of education for its examples. This book could easily be read by a person who wants to learn about statistics without taking a stat course.

POPHAM, W.J. and SIROTNIK, K.A. *Educational Statistics: Use and Interpretation* (2nd ed.) (New York: Harper and Row, 1973). The choice of statistics texts depends largely upon the taste of the reader. I think this is a good book for beginners because it deals in simple terms and uses good, concrete examples. The computational chapters are presented separately from the conceptual chapters, and so a person who is not currently worried about computation can skip those chapters. This too is a useful book for a person who wants to learn about statistics without taking a course on the topic. This book does not go into the detail covered by the Freedman et al. book.

RUNYON, R.P. *Winning with Statistics* (Reading, Mass.: Addison-Wesley, 1977). This book covers the basic descriptive statistics and barely provides an introduction to tests of significance. It is a short and enjoyable book. It may be hard for you to imagine a statistics book which is hard to put down, but this and Huff's book fit that description.

Professional Journals

The following article uses a test of significance to test a hypothesis. In addition, nearly all the articles cited at the end of Chapters 9 to 11 and 13 through 15 include statistical procedures to test hypotheses. In many cases, these are statistical procedures which have been discussed in this text. In *every* case the statistical analyses are interpreted according to the guidelines provided in this chapter.

HOLMES, D.S., CURTRIGHT, C.A., McCAUL, K.D., and THISSEN, D. "Biorhythms: Their utility for predicting postoperative recuperative time, death, and athletic performance." *Journal of Applied Psychology* 65 (1980): 233–236. The authors examine whether the accuracy of predictions based on biorhythms is better than would be expected by chance guessing. Although the authors use a technique not discussed in the text (chi square), the results are easy to interpret.

13 External Validity

Chapter Preview

External validity deals with the question of whether or not the results of an experiment can be applied to other persons, in other settings, at other times than those involved in the original experiment. In other words, external validity deals with how far we can generalize the results of a study. Educators will often have less time to spend worrying about external validity than about internal validity; after all, their job is usually to solve their own problems, not to tell others how to solve theirs. Nevertheless, the question of external validity is still highly important to educators as consumers of educational research. Only if we can understand the limitations and restrictions that must be placed on generalizations can we make efficient use of the research of others in seeking solutions to our own problems.

After completing this chapter you should be able to

- Define external validity.
- Define and give examples of each of the threats to external validity.
- Describe how each of these threats operates to weaken the external validity of an experiment.
- Describe strategies for overcoming these threats to external validity.
- Define operational definitions and identify examples of correctly written operational definitions.
- Given a research variable, write an operational definition of it.

THE PROBLEM OF EXTERNAL VALIDITY

External validity deals with the question of whether a result obtained in one setting would be likely to occur in another setting. Internal validity was *internal* in the sense that it dealt with problems which occurred *within* the time span, *within* the research design and *within* the context of a particular experiment. In a similar way, external validity is *external* in the sense that it deals with considerations *outside* the time span, *outside* the design, and *outside* the context of a particular experiment. External validity deals with the question of how far we can generalize the results of a particular experiment beyond the original experimental setting. External validity deals with the question of whether the same result would occur with other persons, in other settings, and at other times.

To a certain extent, internal validity is a necessary prerequisite for external validity—much as reliability is a prerequisite for validity in test construction. In other words, it would be pointless to ask if a treatment would work in a setting beyond the experimental context unless it has previously been shown that it worked in the experimental setting.

As the previous chapters have indicated, teachers and other educators should be doing research on a regular basis. The kind of research they will most frequently find helpful is Level I research—employing the strategies that enable them to discover what outcomes are actually occurring in their educational settings. Although teachers are legitimately concerned about cause and effect relationships, they find that they have less time to devote to experimental and quasi-experimental research of Level II. This trend continues as we progress toward the higher levels of research. Higher levels depend on lower levels, but active professionals often find that they have less time and a lower inclination to engage in these higher levels. teachers are constantly concerned about what is happening in their classrooms, often about what is causing this to happen, but much less often about whether the same thing would happen elsewhere.

Although this relative lack of interest holds true for educators doing their own research, it does not hold true for educators reading the professional literature. When teachers pick up an article about an educational innovation, for example, one of the paramount concerns in their mind is, "Will it work in my classroom?" This question necessarily involves external validity. What we need to determine as we examine such an article is the likelihood that we can generalize the results of the experimental program to the learners in our own classroom. Even if the treatment worked as the article says, we need evidence that it will work for us. A closely related question is, "Are there specific types of learners in my classroom who would benefit from this program even though others may not?" These are the questions addressed by external validity.

THE THREATS TO EXTERNAL VALIDITY

Since external validity deals with the generalization of results to other persons, settings, and times, then anything that prevents or limits such generalizations is a threat to external validity. Therefore, it is easy to see that there are three basic threats to external validity:

1. Interactions of the treatment with *persons*.
2. Interactions of the treatment with the *setting*.
3. Interactions of the treatment with the historical context (*time*).

The term "interaction" means that it could be a *combination* of the treatment plus the unique persons, setting, or time that caused the observed outcome. We can strengthen the external validity of a study by demonstrating that there are no unique persons, settings, or historical events that were essential features of the study and that therefore limit the generalizability of the findings.

You have perhaps noticed that these same features can also influence the *internal* validity of an experiment. It will be useful at this point to demonstrate how these threats can have an impact on external validity that is different from their impact on internal validity. The difference can be seen in Figure 13–1. Diagram A presents an example of an uncontrolled experiment in which the unique features of the subjects, of the setting, and of the time interact in such a way as to threaten the internal validity of an experiment. In this diagram it is impossible to determine whether the higher performance of the experimental group is the result of the treatment or the result of one or more of the extraneous threats.

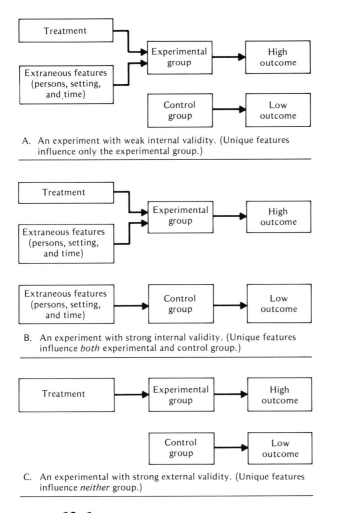

A. An experiment with weak internal validity. (Unique features influence only the experimental group.)

B. An experiment with strong internal validity. (Unique features influence *both* experimental and control group.)

C. An experimental with strong external validity. (Unique features influence *neither* group.)

FIGURE 13–1. Three Diagrams Showing the Impact of Unique Features of Persons, Setting, and Time on Internal and External Validity.

Diagram B shows the application of experimental design to control these threats to internal validity. From Diagram B it is possible to conclude that the treatment caused the improved performance, because the extraneous threats are the same for both groups. The treatment is the only variable that is different, and therefore it has to be the treatment that is responsible for the difference. However, in Diagram B we still do not know whether or not the same outcome would have occurred if the extraneous features were not present. This is the problem with regard to external validity: how do we know that it was not a combination of the treatment plus one or more of these extraneous factors that caused the difference? Diagram C presents a perfectly clear conclusion. The treatment, and only the treatment, can be said to be responsible for the outcome in this situation. The problem with Diagram C is that it is almost impossible to obtain this degree of clarity. To attain this degree of external validity, we should have to either (1) remove each of the extraneous factors completely, or (2) show that the extraneous factor is actually very much like the situation to which we wish to generalize and is therefore not a threat to generalization. Since the first course of action is a practical impossibility, the latter is the course of action to be followed.

The interaction of the treatment with persons is a threat to external validity to the extent that the subjects involved in the experimental situation are different from the persons to whom we wish to generalize the results. (This is a problem of external validity if the subjects in the whole experiment are atypical. If the problem is that the subjects in the experimental group are different from those in the control group, this is a problem of internal validity. Refer to Diagrams A and B of Figure 13–1 for a clarification of this distinction.) A frequent problem in research studies reported in educational journals is that the studies are based on volunteers, college sophomores, or even volunteer graduate students. When we try to generalize such results to our own settings, we are making the assumption that the people in our own setting are similar to these subjects. In many cases, this is an accurate assumption; but we should be aware that such groups sometimes have unique features—or perhaps it is *our* group that has the unique features which prevent accurate generalizations.

Likewise, it is not safe to make the automatic assumption that a school integration program that worked in a large city 2000 miles away will work in our own small town, that a program that teaches reading to highly motivated readers will work just as well with children of lower motivation, or that a method for teaching new teaching strategies to first-year teachers will be equally successful with teachers with ten years of experience. In each case, it is possible that there are unique features of the subjects who have derived demonstrable benefits from the treatment that make it improper to generalize the results to a second group with unique features of their own.

The *interaction of the treatment with the setting* can occur in several ways. The existence of a pretest sometimes provides an artificial setting that makes the results difficult to generalize. This can occur when the pretest sensitizes the subjects in such a way that it enables them to profit from the treatment. If such sensitization occurs, then it is by no means obvious that the treatment would have the same impact in the absence of a pretest. (Of course, if the pretest sensitizes the experimental group alone—and not the control group—this would be a threat to internal rather than external validity.) If our intention is to generalize the treatment to a situation in which we do not intend to use a pretest, then the existence of such a sensitizing pretest in the experimental situation would present a serious threat to external validity. An example of such pretest sensitization is presented in the box on page 239.

Mr. Weller wanted to find out if a new anti-smoking program would actually lead to a reduction of smoking among the persons to whom it was administered. He located 50 volunteers to take part in the experimental program. (The fact that these subjects volunteered for the program did not bother him, since he intended the program to be administered only to people who wanted to voluntarily quit smoking.) He randomly divided the 50 subjects into two groups and told 25 that they could start right away and the other 25 that they would have to wait for two weeks before they could receive the program. During the first interview, Mr. Weller also had all 50 subjects fill out a questionnaire regarding their attitudes toward smoking and indicating how many cigarettes they smoked each day. He then administered the program for two weeks to the first 25 subjects (the experimental group) and retested all 50 with the same measuring instrument at the end of the two-week period. He discovered that the experimental subjects smoked significantly fewer cigarettes and displayed attitudes more strongly opposed to smoking than the control subjects. He did a follow-up study six months later, and found that the experimental subjects maintained their antipathy toward tobacco. Mr. Weller was pleased with these results.

Did Mr. Weller demonstrate that his program worked? It sounds as though he did a good job. His treatment seems to have caused a reduction in smoking. Is it possible that the pretest rather than the treatment caused the reduction in smoking and the changed attitudes? Not really, because if the pretest had been responsible for the changes, then the same effect would have occurred in both groups, since both received the pretest. However, it is possible that a combination of the pretest and the treatment caused the changes. It is possible that the pretest might have sensitized both groups to profit from the treatment, but since only the experimental group received the treatment, only this group showed the improvement. A person taking the pretest might have said to herself, "I didn't realize that I smoked 34 cigarettes a day!" This and similar self-reflections might have developed a proclivity to benefit from the program. Without such predispositions, it is possible that the treatment might not have been so successful. Mr. Weller could eliminate this possibility by replicating his study without the pretest. (In fact, since he had relatively large, randomly assigned groups, the pretest was superfluous in this study. Mr. Weller should have omitted it to improve the external validity of the experiment.)

A similar problem occurs to the extent that the experimental situation is at all artificial. If the participants in both the experimental and control group know that they are part of an experiment, this knowledge is likely to affect their performance. Sometimes this artificial atmosphere leads to expectations of certain outcomes, such as success. (If this knowledge causes them to expect the treatment to work and the control condition to fail, then this is a threat to internal validity. If it provides a positive expectancy in both groups, then this would be a threat to external validity.) When such artificial expectations exist, it is possible that the treatment will work *only* when such positive anticipations are aroused; and if such expectations of success are not present in the situation to which the results are to be generalized, then there will be serious problems with external validity. Even if there is no widespread expectancy of success, it is still possible that the artificiality of an experimental setting will evoke features that will not appear in the situation to which the treatment is to be generalized. Such features could include greater attention than usual to record keeping, accidental additional attention to classroom details, the presence of additional teaching and supervisory personnel, and the availability of the research consultants to help the teachers. If such features are present in the experimental setting but not in the setting to which the results are to be generalized, then such factors pose a threat to external validity.

Even if there is no artificiality in the setting, there can be numerous unique features in the setting that could influence the degree of generalization that will be appropriate. Such obvious features as the size and atmosphere of the school, the size and atmosphere of the class, and whether or not the school employs such techniques as learning centers and team teaching would obviously influence the validity of generalizing to other settings. In addition, the exact way in which the treatment is actually implemented in the specific experimental setting is a crucial factor. For example, if a researcher reports using an open classroom technique quite effectively to enhance reading ability and self-concepts, it is of extreme importance to others interested in applying the same procedure elsewhere to know whether this researcher's definition of open classroom matches their own. Mismatches in operational definitions are a recurrent threat to external validity, and because of this importance, considerable emphasis will be given to methods for clarifying such definitions in a later section of this chapter.

The *interaction of the treatment with the historical context* is an important factor when there is anything unusual about either the experimental situation or about the situation to which we plan to generalize the results of the experiment. (If historical events occur to the experimental group but not to the control group, this is a threat to internal validity. If the historical events occur to both the experimental and the control group, such events may pose a threat to external validity, even if the threat to internal validity is controlled.) It seems obvious that some educational techniques that were demonstrated to be effective in 1910 may not be equally effective right now. On the other hand, very often historical events and historical context do not have a large impact on educational techniques. The point is that we have to be aware of such threats and look to see if these threats pose a problem for a particular generalization. This threat is particularly cogent when an experimental treatment is demonstrated to be successful on only one occasion and when that one occasion took place at a time when additional unusual events related to the treatment were simultaneously occurring.

CONTROLLING THE THREATS TO EXTERNAL VALIDITY

The threats to internal validity can largely be controlled through appropriate research design and experimental procedures. The same high degree of control is usually impossible to attain with regard to external validity. Research design plays a comparatively insignificant part in the control of external validity. A much heavier emphasis falls on the careful analysis of similarities and differences between the experimental and the target situation with regard to the persons, settings, and historical contexts involved. This analysis of similarities and differences is almost always imperfect, and for this reason there is almost always some doubt about the external validity of an experimental study.

The *threat of an interaction between the treatment and the persons involved in the study* can theoretically be brought under control by first randomly selecting the subjects for the whole study from the target population and then randomly assigning them to the experimental and control groups. In fact, this process is almost never actually followed. Almost always there is an attempt to generalize to a population from which subjects were not randomly selected. It is simply not often feasible to identify the entire population to which we wish to generalize and then randomly select subjects from this population. Try to imagine how you would derive a list from which you could randomly draw a sample for any of the following populations: the children you will teach in the next five years; learning disabled readers; American teachers; or students interested in learning drama. If you could define such a population, and draw a random sample from that population, you would be able to generalize your results to that population. However, you would find that you could accomplish this in only the most trivial cases. In real life, meaningful populations are either very large or change very often, and for these reasons an authentic random sample would be very difficult to capture.

Instead of random sampling, therefore, experts recommend a strategy called *purposive sampling for heterogeneity*. With this procedure, you do not try to get a random sample, but rather you try to make sure that the sample from which you will draw your experimental and control groups will include representatives of the whole variety of subjects to whom you wish to generalize your results. For example, if you intend to generalize your results to whites, blacks, Hispanics, learning disabled, non-learning disabled, motivated, and unmotivated learners, then you should be sure that your sample includes representatives of all these categories. If you plan to generalize your results to oriental students or to students with low self-concepts, but have included no subjects representing these classifications in your sample, then your generalization is weakened to the extent that there is any logical reason why such learners would be likely to respond differently than others to the treatment.

Even more useful than merely including representatives of each relevant category within your study is the strategy of *isolating relevant characteristics of subjects and analyzing their impact*. For example, if you included a sufficient number of white, black, and Hispanic subjects in your study, you could compute the average performance of each of these groups separately and see if the treatment affects the groups similarly or differently. With such information, you might find that the treatment works the same for all three groups, and this would lead you to believe that the results are generalizable across such groups. On the other hand, you might find that the treatment works for one group but not for the other two. Such information would not only limit your generalization but it would also tell you how to state your limits. Likewise, if you included a substantial number of both motivated and unmotivated learners, you could state whether the treatment worked equally well for both groups or whether one group benefited more than the other. (The process described in this paragraph consists of identifying interactions by analyzing moderator variables. This process will be described in detail in the next chapter.) Such information can be extremely useful either to a researcher or to a reader of research in determining the specific groups and subgroups to whom the results of a study can be generalized.

A similar aid to determining the limits for generalizations from a study can be found in *the careful statement of control variables*. These variables will be discussed in detail in the next chapter. At the present time, it is sufficient to point out that if we state clearly the exact nature of the subjects included in the study, this provides us with very useful information regarding populations to which the results can and cannot be generalized.

Finally, *replication* is an important way to increase the validity of generalizing results to varying populations. Replication is a term which refers to the repetition of an experimental study in a new setting (and often by a new researcher) to see if the same results will be obtained. To the extent that results are replicated on varying populations, it becomes increasingly likely that a generalization to other populations will be valid. By carefully specifying the nature of the population in each replication, it becomes possible to identify specific groups of subjects with whom a treatment is likely to work and other groups with whom it is unlikely to work.

The threat of an interaction between the treatment and the setting can be brought under partial control by making the experimental setting resemble as closely as possible the setting to which generalizations will be made. Basic research is often criticized on the basis of external validity, because human learning does not closely resemble either a rat maze or the memorization of nonsense syllables. The fact that a treatment has worked in an unrealistic, isolated situation does not immediately lead us to believe that it will work the same way in the real life situation to which we want to generalize. For this reason, quasi-experimental designs are often preferable to true experimental designs. A quasi-experimental design can allow us to retain the original setting undisturbed, and therefore the results will be more easily generalized to other situations that resemble this original setting.

In addition, generalizability can be increased by many other factors that reduce the artificiality of the experimental setting. If an experimental treatment is accepted as a routine part of the educational setting, then artificial behaviors and artificial expectations will be kept to a minimum. Since testing is often one of the most artificial aspects of an experiment, the use of unobtrusive measurements (discussed in Chapter 6) can be very helpful in this respect.

There are two design strategies that can reduce threats to generalizability arising from the experimental setting. First, it is possible to control some expectancy effects by employing a placebo control group. This additional control group can be added to the experiment in such a way that the artificial pressures of the experimental setting will influence both the experimental group and the placebo control group. If the experimental group thereafter out-performs both the control group and the placebo control group, then it is unlikely that the artificial pressures of the setting were the important factor.

A second design strategy helpful in overcoming threats arising from the setting involves the addition of two additional groups that are not pretested. For example, the randomized pretest-posttest control group design can be modified to take this form:

$$
\begin{array}{llll}
R & O_1 & X & O_2 \\
R & O_3 &   & O_4 \\
R &   & X & O_5 \\
R &   &   & O_6 \\
\end{array}
$$

Neither of the additional groups is pretested, and one of them receives the treatment. If the results arising from this design would indicate that scores at O_2 and O_5 were superior to those at O_4 and O_6, this would be strong evidence that the outcome was not a result of the interaction of the treatment with the pretest. As you may recall, however, when groups are randomly assigned, the pretest is not essential; and so in this case it would be simpler to retain two groups and omit the pretest. The four-group strategy can be adapted to situations in which the groups are not randomly assigned, and where the pretest is not optional. This adaptation is diagrammed below:

$$
\begin{array}{ccc}
O_{A1} & X & O_{A2} \\
O_{A3} & & O_{A4} \\
O_{B1} & X & O_{A5} \\
O_{B2} & & O_{A6}
\end{array}
$$

In this case, the performance of the first two groups is assessed with regard to the outcome of interest on all four testing occasions. However, on occasions B1 and B2 the two additional groups are pretested *on a different but related variable*. This additional variable could be an unobtrusive (but less valid) measurement of the desired outcome. Its purpose is to demonstrate that the two groups are initially equal. (Of course, if it would be feasible to do so, this additional pretest could be administered to the first two groups as well in order to strengthen the comparison.) The extra two groups are then measured on the real outcome variable (variable A) on occasions O_{A5} and O_{A6}. If the treatment is achieving its effect without an interaction with the pretest, then O_{A2} and O_{A5} will be superior to O_{A4} and O_{A6}.

An extremely important strategy to control threats to external validity arising from the experimental setting is the accurate operational definition of the treatment and of the other variables in the study. This strategy will be the detailed topic of the next section of this chapter.

Finally, replication is an important strategy for increasing the validity of generalizations to new settings. As a study is replicated with similar findings in different settings, there is a corresponding increase in the range of settings to which generalization would be appropriate. Likewise, if the results are replicated in certain settings but not in others, it becomes possible to systematically differentiate between appropriate and inappropriate settings in which to apply the results of the experiment.

The threat of an interaction between the treatment and the historical context can best be controlled by (1) carefully looking for and identifying extraneous events that might be the source of such interactions, and (2) replicating the study in different historical contexts. Remember that *historical context* does not refer merely to the passage of time as it appears in history books. If the results of a study performed on one occasion are to be applied on another occasion, then it is important to determine whether additional events are a prerequisite if the same outcome is to be expected. Such events as a successful football season, the airing of a successful novel for television, the assassination of a political leader, the death of a parent or classmate, and the awarding of scholarships within a school are part of the historical context. By identifying such events and by replicating the study in a variety of situations in which these events change, we can reduce the likelihood that generalizations are limited by interactions with the historical context.

OPERATIONAL DEFINITIONS

Operational definitions of a variable state the observable behaviors, events, or characteristics that we are willing to accept as evidence that the variable exists. Chapter 2 has discussed operational definitions of outcome variables. As you will recall, such operational definitions stated the observable behaviors we were willing to accept as evidence that an internal outcome (such as learning) has occurred. Just as operational definitions assisted us in measuring outcomes, the process of operational definition can assist us in determining what generalizations can be derived from an experiment.

All the major types of variables that have been introduced so far in this text can be operationally defined. The nature and functions of each of these types of variables will be the topic of the following chapter. The present section will focus on the important process of operational definition of the variables in a research study. Such operational definitions are important sources of control for external validity. Although they do not eliminate extraneous sources of bias, they assist us in the generalization process by specifying the exact nature of the persons, materials, and events involved in a study. Such specifications make it possible for us to identify more clearly the specific populations and settings to which we can generalize the results of a study.

The essential feature of an operational definition is that it must be stated in terms of *observable* events, behaviors, or characteristics. Such a definition differs from a conceptual definition. For example, we might conceptually define "positive self-concept" as a "feeling of self-worth in spite of temporary failings, based on previous reinforcing experiences." Although a conceptual definition such as this may be valuable in its own right, this is not an operational definition, because the definition does not state observable criteria by which we can classify a person as having a positive or negative self-concept. On the other hand, if we define *positive self-concept* as "the frequency with which a child utters spontaneous positive self-evaluations," then we have the beginning of an operational definition. By systematically observing a child, we can tell if he or she is uttering a positive self-evaluation. The reason this is the beginning of an operational definition is that it would still be necessary to specify how an observer would decide whether or not a self-evaluation was positive. Once this was accomplished, this would be a useful operational definition of *positive self-concept*. As Chapter 2 pointed out, however, it is important to remember that operational definitions are *only* evidence. A teacher trying to promote positive self-concepts among his students is really interested in having them develop a sense of self-worth— a concept that cannot be seen. The positive self-evaluations which the teacher will look for are merely the evidence to be accepted—for purposes of this assessment— that this feeling of self-worth exists.

In some respects, conceptual definitions are much more important than operational definitions. The concept contained in the conceptual definition is what we want to instill or theorize about. However, for purposes of understanding the limitations of our measurement or of our experimental study, it is the operational definitions that are important. This importance arises from the fact that only if we know how the variables have been operationally defined can we understand how far we can generalize the results of a study.

In many cases, *multiple* operational definitions are advisable. For example, when we are dealing with nebulous concepts such as frustration, aggression, or self-concept, it is often useful to devise more than one operational definition. Such multiple operational definitions are necessary to the extent that it is not obvious that any one operational definition is, in fact, nearly synonymous with the concept under consideration. The idea of multiple operational definitions of outcome variables has been discussed in Chapter 2. The same logic can be applied to all research variables.

The importance of multiple operational definitions of these other variables will become more obvious in Chapter 15, where theoretical research is discussed. For example, if a researcher wanted to examine the theory that "frustration leads to aggression and hurts the self-concept," it would be useful to devise multiple operational definitions of all these concepts.

The other variables in a study can be operationally defined in much the same way as the outcome variables. For example, the treatment is operationally defined through a specific statement of the observable behaviors, events, and characteristics that indicate that the treatment is occurring. In many cases, this is tantamount to providing a list of instructions regarding how someone else could replicate the study. In some cases, the operational definition of a treatment can be stated in a brief sentence or two, but in other cases a more detailed description is necessary. As in the case of outcome variables, conceptual definitions of treatments are possible, and quite useful in their own right. But in order to understand the scope of situations to which an experimental treatment can be generalized, operational definitions of treatments are essential. For example, an open classroom can be conceptually defined as "a classroom in which each learner learns according to his or her own needs." If you read that someone had demonstrated that an open classroom caused improved performance on science tests, would you be able to generalize this finding to the open classroom you might plan to set up in your own school? The answer is *no*—not unless you knew what the researcher did that enabled the students to learn according to their own needs. On the other hand, if the researcher defined the open classroom in terms of the exact activities the teacher and students performed during class sessions, then you could examine this definition to see if it matched what you had in mind as your own idea of an open classroom. This examination would enable your to estimate the likelihood that similar results would occur in your own open classroom.

Let us pause for a moment for a specific example of the value of such operational definitions. Let us say you read an article indicating that frustration leads to aggression among elementary school students. You might posses conceptual definitions of these two variables that would go something like this: "Frustration is the feeling that occurs when people are deprived of what they feel legitimately belongs to them. Aggression is a deliberate attempt to inflict pain on another person." These are rather widely accepted definitions of the terms, and you might even discover that they are shared by the author of the article. However, as you read the article, you might come across this sentence, "Frustration was induced by telling the children that they would not be able to see the movie that had previously been promised to them." This is, in fact, the author's operational definition of frustration. Later, your might read this sentence: "Aggression was assessed by administering a teacher evaluation form and counting the number of negative evaluations." This is the author's operational definition of aggression. Armed with these operational definitions, you can now see if you can generalize these results to your own situation. Perhaps you are interested in rearranging the seats in your classroom so that friends will no longer sit together. Does the research finding that "frustration leads to aggression among elementary school students" lead you to conclude that the pupils will be likely to fight with each other if you follow your plan of action? Based on the operational definitions given and looking at no other information, this conclusion would hardly seem warranted. The researcher's operational definition of frustration hardly seems to match the frustration you plan to inflict upon your pupils, and likewise the researcher's definition of aggression hardly matches your operational definition of aggression among your students. Only with this knowledge of the operational definitions can you determine the generalizability of such results.

Just as the outcomes and the treatment can be operationally defined, the other variables in the study can be defined in terms of the observable behaviors, events, and characteristics which provide evidence of their existence. For example, in the example cited in the previous paragraph, it would be useful if the researcher would operationally define *elementary school students*. Such a definition would consist of a simple description in observable terms of exactly who the elementary students were in the study. If they were predominantly white middle-class third graders, this would lead to different generalizations than if they were predominantly Hispanic inner-city fifth graders. Likewise, the setting can be operationally defined in terms of such variables as the size of the class, the physical construction of the school, the size of the school, the neighborhood in which the school is located, and many other variables. To the extent that any such factors can limit or extend the ability to generalize the results, the operational definition provides useful information for the external validity of the study.

Examine this detailed example. It provides an illustration of the use of operational definitions in drawing generalizations from a research report.

The following is a conclusion from a hypothetical research study:

Positive reinforcement of incompatible behaviors was found to be more effective than punishment in reducing aggressive behaviors amond elementary school children.

Mrs. Cox wanted to know whether the results of this study were applicable to her own classroom. She first examined the study and found that it was flawless with regard to internal validity. There was absolutely no question in her mind that within the study the results really did lead to the conclusion stated above. As she examined the study closely, she discovered that the operational definitions of the important variables were these:

Positive reinforcement consisted of the awarding of a point which could be turned in for material rewards or privileges at a designated time. (Mrs. Cox recognized this as a form of token reinforcement, which she had read about in professional publications.)

Punishment was defined as a spanking from the teacher administered in accordance with the guidelines of the school in the study. (She examined these guidelines and found that they were the same as those provided by her own school system.)

An aggressive behavior was defined as an overt attempt to inflict pain or injury on another pupil. The pain could be either physical or psychological; thus, insults would count as aggressive behavior. (The research report included a list of examples of aggressive behaviors, and Mrs. Cox agreed that each of the examples fit within her own personal definition of aggression.)

An incompatible behavior was defined as any nonaggressive and socially acceptable behavior that the child could perform instead of the aggressive behavior. A further qualification was that the behavior had to be one that could not be performed while the child was simultaneously performing an aggressive behavior. (Mrs. Cox again examined the list of examples and determined that all of these were examples of behaviors that she would consider to be socially acceptable, nonaggressive, and incompatible with aggressive activities.)

Elementary school children were operationally defined as third through sixth graders in a traditional school in a middle-class neighborhood. The children were 75% white, 20% black, and 5% Hispanic. These were about equal numbers of boys and girls. (After examining the brief paragraph that clarified what was meant by a traditional school, Mrs. Cox quickly recognized that these pupils were very much like the ones she taught.)

Mrs. Cox summarized the entire experiment for herself in operational terms:

In this study, consisting of children very much like my own, children who received token points for engaging in socially acceptable, nonaggressive behaviors that were incompatible with aggressive behaviors showed a greater reduction in frequency with which they inflicted deliberate pain or injury upon other pupils than children who were spanked for engaging in these aggressive behaviors. (In this summary, the word *aggressive* could be replaced with an operational definition each time it occurred, but that would make the sentence exceedingly cumbersome. Mrs. Cox felt uncomfortable with cumbersome sentences. So long as the word *aggressive* was operationally defined in her own mind, she was satisfied with this summary.)

Now Mrs. Cox turned to the problem of applying the results to her own classroom situation. Almost all the operational definitions matched her own setting. The one serious difficulty, however, was the operational definition of *punishment*. In her classroom, she punished her children, but she did not spank them. Rather, she punished them by taking away privileges. Keeping this difference in mind, she realized that the researcher had not provided evidence that rewarding an incompatible behavior *instead of punishing by removing a privilege* would result in a greater reduction in aggressive behaviors. Therefore, since there was a substantial difference in the operational definitions of punishment employed by Mrs. Cox and by the researcher who had performed the experiment, there was a serious question regarding the external validity of the study. In other words, it was not immediately obvious that the results could be generalized to Mrs. Cox's setting.

What should Mrs. Cox do? Should she ignore the results of this study? Or should she decide that the results were close enough and go ahead and apply the researcher's ideas in her own classroom? The answer is that Mrs. Cox should examine the situation on the basis of what she knows. What she knows is this: If the dominant method for controlling aggressive behavior in her classroom were spanking children for performing such behaviors, then replacing this method with the reinforcement of incompatible behaviors would lead to better results. However, Mrs. Cox does not use spanking in her classroom, but uses removal of privileges instead. Her immediate task is to determine how alike are her form of punishment and the form used in the study. If she concludes that both forms of punishment are quite similar, then she will conclude that the results are applicable to her own situation. On the other hand, if she concludes that her form of punishment is not even remotely similar to spanking, then she will conclude that the study has told her nothing useful for her own setting. Note that Mrs. Cox would not have to rely entirely on her own speculation or intuition in making this judgment. She might be able to look into the professional literature for other research on the different types of punishment. (If the article that she originally read was well written, it is possible that the author of that article might include references that will enable her to find these other sources.) By consulting such sources, she might, for example, find that the effects of her type of punishment are very similar to the effects of spanking, and this might lead her to give greater credence to the results under consideration.

After a close examination of the study and other related literature, Mrs. Cox might decide that the results of the original study cannot be directly generalized to her own situation. Nevertheless, she might decide that the idea is worth trying anyway. She would therefore implement the other researcher's ideas in her own classroom, using an appropriate experimental or quasi-experimental design to evaluate the results. If she would do this while using the same operational definitions as the previous researcher (with the exception that she would redefine punishment to fit her technique), then she would actually expand the state of knowledge on this topic. For example, if she discovered that the reinforcement of incompatible behaviors worked better than her form of punishment, this would lead to an increase in the range of generalization that could be based on the conclusion stated at the beginning of this example. On the other hand, if she would find that the same results would not occur with her redefinition of punishment, this would lead to a statement of specific situations to which the generalization could and could not be applied. In either case, Mrs. Cox's research would have led to an improvement in the quality of generalizations that could be based on this research. The range of generalizations could be further extended or refined in additional replications by systematically altering other operational definitions—for example, by altering the operational definition of elementary school children.

When you read research studies or listen to research reports, the operational definitions are not always clearly stated. It is safe to say that one of the most serious weaknesses in educational research is the absence of adequate operational definitions in such reports. Without operational definitions it is difficult to know what to make of the results. It is important, therefore, that you learn to look for the operational definitions. In some cases these will be clearly stated and all you will have to do is figure out where to look for them. In other cases the operational definitions are not at all clearly stated, and no matter how hard you look you will not be able to find them. You should develop a willingness to look for operational definitions and to ask about them when they are not obviously stated. You should likewise develop the ability to recognize weak and inadequate operational definitions and realize the threats to external validity posed by such inadequacies. When you are presenting your own results you should be willing to state clear operational definitions to help others determine how fully your results can be generalized to their settings.

The importance of operational definitions is not unique to educational research. They are just as necessary in most other areas of social science, and the operational definitions employed in other areas are often equally inadequate. Politicians have been know to run for office with promises of wonderful benefits to flow from their programs, but give no operational definitions of these programs. A colleague of mine once listened to a foreign diplomat speak of the peace and freedom in his country. At the end of the speech my friend mumbled to me, "I would like to hear his operational definition of peace and freedom." It would be similarly interesting to hear certain pop philosophers give their operational definitions of happiness and the good life. While such concepts are very usefully discussed on a purely conceptual level, an occasional operational definition can add insights to the discussions. Operational definitions can provide a valuable service to any thoughtful undertaking.

THE SUMMARY OF STRATEGIES FOR OVERCOMING THREATS

Table 13–1 on page 250 provides a summary of the principal strategies for overcoming the major threats to external validity. These strategies cannot provide the same high degree of control for external validity that we can provide for internal validity. Nevertheless, by following these guidelines we can (1) extend the range of situations to which generalizations can be made, and (2) identify specific restrictions that must be placed on generalizations.

One strategy that is common to attempts to control all three major threats to external validity is the careful examination of the experimental setting and of the setting to which generalization is to be made. This examination is undertaken in order to look for unique features of the subjects, setting, or historical context that might restrict generalizations. In our discussions of internal validity, this strategy of looking over the setting to see if anything unusual was happening was viewed as one of the *weakest* ways to control the threats to internal validity. And yet, this is one of the *strongest* ways to control the threats to external validity. Reliance on other-than-design strategies is the main reason why external validity is so much harder to establish than

TABLE **13–1.** Summary of the Major Strategies for Overcoming Threats to External Validity.

I. Threats arising from interactions of the treatment with *persons*.

    A. Examine the persons in the experimental setting and in the setting to which generalization will be made, and look for unique features.

    B. Use random sampling from an overall population.

    C. Use purposive sampling for heterogeneity.

    D. Isolate and identify important interactions within the study (moderator variables), and use these as a basis for stating precise generalizations.

    E. State any control variables focusing on persons.

    F. Operationally define all variables related to persons.

    G. Replicate the study with varying subjects.

II. Threats arising from interactions of the treatment with the *setting*.

    A. Examine the experimental setting and the setting to which generalization will be made, and look for unique features.

    B. Use a placebo design.

    C. Use designs without pretests.

        D. Use unobtrusive measurements on pretests.

    E. Use quasi-experimental rather than true experimental designs.

    F. Make the experimental setting as nonartificial as possible.

    G. State any control variables focusing on the setting.

    H. Operationally define all variables related to the setting.

    I. Replicate the study in varying settings.

III. Threats arising from interactions of the treatment with the *historical context*.

    A. Examine the historical context of the experimental setting and the setting to which generalization is to be made, and look for unique features.

    B. Replicate the study in varying historical contexts.

internal validity. We are forced to rely much more heavily on our observation and insight rather than on any more systematic procedure to control the extraneous variables. The resulting inferences are necessarily weakened.

The other strategy that is common to all three major threats is that of replicating the study in a different situation. If a study can be replicated in varying settings, the variety of persons, settings, and contexts to which generalization can be made will increase. Likewise, by being systematic in the way we vary the subjects, settings, and contexts for these replications, we can derive specific statements of the limits that must be imposed on the results arising from a research study.

In addition, the adequacy of operational definitions is a critical factor in establishing the external validity of a study. An operational definition states the observable events, behaviors, or characteristics that we are willing to accept as evidence that a variable exists. By stating clear and precise operational definitions, we provide guidelines regarding the limits that must be imposed on the results of a research study.

The other strategies are uniquely useful for specific problems. A specific strategy will not always be feasible or useful; but used in accordance with the guidelines described earlier in this chapter, these strategies can greatly enhance the validity of research studies. Random sampling, for example, is almost never possible; but in those situations where it *is* an appropriate strategy, it greatly improves the external validity of the study in which it is used. Likewise, while quasi-experimental settings are often more lifelike than true experimental settings, this will not always be the case. It is necessary to examine a specific situation to determine what guidelines are appropriate.

PUTTING IT ALL TOGETHER

As we left him at the end of the last chapter, Mr. Anderson was satisfied that he had demonstrated that his Animal Life Program (ALP) had actually caused the development of improved attitudes among the children to whom he had administered it. He realized his proof was not perfect, but he was at least temporarily satisfied. Now he wanted to know how far he could generalize his results. This was the question of external validity. Among what other persons, settings, and historical contexts could he expect similar results?

It was immediately obvious to him that such generalizations had to be restricted to children like those in his study, until additional evidence could be provided that the conclusions could be extended to children with varying characteristics. Therefore, since the children in his study came from mostly middle-class backgrounds, he was reluctant to offer any assurance to a colleague who taught in a very poor neighborhood that the ALP would work equally well in her school.

Likewise, generalizations were restricted by the fact that the school possessed unique characteristics. An obvious problem was that the school had volunteered itself for the program. Would a program that worked in a school where the humane educator had been warmly welcomed with open arms be equally effective in a school where the reception would be apathetic or even hostile? It was obvious that further information would be needed before this generalization would be warranted.

In addition, it was possible that other subtle characteristics of the setting could influence the external validity of generalizations, even though Mr. Anderson was not yet aware of what these other factors might be. To minimize this possibility, Mr. Anderson replicated the study on similar populations in two additional, geographically separated schools. The results were the same, and so these replications minimized the probability of accidental threats. Nevertheless, all three schools had volunteered and were located in middle-class neighborhoods and therefore the generalizations were still restricted.

Mr. Anderson saw little threat from the interaction of the treatment with the historical context. He had carefully watched for unusual events that might enhance attitudes toward animal life, and none had been obvious. In addition, the replications had been spread over a period of seven months, and this helped minimize the likelihood that some unique historical event or another was essential for the ALP to be successful.

The generalizations would be limited by the operational definitions of the variables. These will be explicitly discussed at the end of Chapter 14. At that time it will be obvious that the operational definition of the ALP will influence how far Mr. Anderson can generalize his results to additional similar programs. Likewise, it would be useful to estimate how closely his operational definition of a favorable attitude toward animal life matched the operational definitions possessed by others who might want to implement similar programs.

CHAPTER SUMMARY

This chapter has discussed the factors that influence the generalizability of the findings from a research study. The question of whether results can be generalized to other persons, to other settings, and to other historical contexts is the subject matter of external validity. Threats to external validity arise when unique characteristics of the persons, settings, or historical contexts restrict the generalizations that can be drawn from an experiment. This chapter has described each of these threats and has outlined strategies for overcoming or minimizing such threats. In addition to identifying overall populations to which generalizations can and cannot be made, the principles discussed in this chapter can help us identify specific subgroups *within* a larger group about whom it is or is not appropriate to generalize. In this way, results can be applied in a prescriptive manner.

Special attention has been given to the strategy of devising appropriate operational definitions. Such operational definitions state the observable behaviors, events, or characteristics that we are willing to accept as evidence that a variable exists. Conceptual definitions are important, but they are abstract and it is not always easy to identify what others mean when they are talking in conceptual terms. On the other hand, operational definitions are concrete and directly observable, and therefore it is possible to know exactly what others mean when they state their operational definitions. For this reason, operational definitions are extremely helpful in identifying the limits which must be applied to generalizations arising from an experiment.

Annotated Bibliography

AGNEW, N.M. and PYKE, S.W. *Science Game: An Introduction to Research in the Behavioral Sciences* (2nd ed.) (Englewood Cliffs, N.J.: Prentice-Hall, 1978). Chapter 7 provides a brief but good discussion of the problems of external validity.

COOK, T.D. and CAMPBELL, D.T. *Quasi-Experimentation: Design and Analysis Issues for Field Settings* (Chicago: Rand McNally, 1979). The index lists only about 15 pages from this book on external validity. But they are good.

Professional Journals

The following articles contain specific treatments of various threats to external validity.

AMAN, M.G. "Psychotropic drugs and learning problems: A selective review," *Journal of Learning Disabilities*, 13 (1980): 87–97. This author examines all the available research on the long-term and short-term effects of drug therapy for children with specific learning problems. He identifies discrepancies between the short-term and the long-term research and provides possible explanations for these discrepancies. This information helps the reader determine what conclusions can and cannot be drawn from currently available research and what research needs to be done to enhance generalizations.

KENDALL, J.R., MASON, J.M., and HUNTER, W. "Which comprehension? Artifacts in the measurement of reading comprehension," *Journal of Educational Research*, 73 (1980): 233–236. The authors examine four different tasks typically employed to measure reading comprehension and determine that the choice of any one of these methods confines the conclusions to a single operational definition that can severely limit the generalizations that arise from a study.

KNEEDLER, R.D. "The use of cognitive training to change social behaviors," *Exceptional Education Quarterly*, 1 (1980): 65–73. This article provides a good example of how a researcher can establish the extent to which results of research studies can be generalized by examining replications of a basic procedure in varying settings and with planned variations.

MATSON, J.L., MARCHETTI, A., and ADKINS, J.A. "Comparison of operant- and independence-training procedures for mentally retarded adults," *American Journal of Mental Deficiency*, 84 (1980): 487–494. These authors report specific steps they took to minimize the obtrusiveness of their experimental treatment. Such precautions enhanced both the internal and the external validity of the study.

SMITH, C.F., and WESTERN, R.D. "Passage independence: A neglected issue in the measurement of reading proficiency," *Reading World*, 19 (1980): 352–356. This study uses random selection of subjects in a study to examine the validity of a format for measuring reading comprehension. The random selection is useful not because it makes a direct inference possible, but because it extends external validity by assuring the inclusion of a wide variety of subjects to participate in the study.

STOKES, T.F., and KENNEDY, S.H. "Reducing child uncooperative behavior during dental treatment through modeling and reinforcement," *Journal of Applied Behavior Analysis*, 13 (1980): 41–49. The authors enhance the external validity of their findings by making the experimental as lifelike as possible, by using clear operational definitions, by using unobtrusive measurement, and by tying the results in with other research that ruled out specific threats to external validity.

14 Research Variables and the Research Hypothesis

Chapter Preview

This chapter will integrate many of the ideas discussed in previous chapters into a systematic framework for analyzing cause and effect relationships. This systematic framework is called the research hypothesis. There are several types of variables that go into such a hypothesis. All these variables have been at least briefly described in earlier chapters. The present chapter will describe the variables in greater detail and demonstrate how they fit into a research hypothesis and into a research prediction. Such research predictions lead directly to the research designs and statistical analyses discussed in the previous chapters. This process enables the researcher to answer important research questions.

After reading this chapter you should be able to

- Define and give examples of research hypotheses and research predictions.
- Define and give examples of each of the following types of variables:
  Independent variable.
  Dependent variable.
  Moderator variable.
  Control variable.
  Intervening variable.
  Extraneous variable.
- Given a set of variables, put them together into a correctly stated hypothesis or research prediction.
- Define and give examples of interactions and factorial designs.
- Given the results of a factorial design, describe the interactions shown by the data.

INTRODUCTION

The great majority of published educational research articles are intended as reports on Level III research. They provide evidence that a certain treatment causes a certain outcome and that the same outcome will occur elsewhere. Likewise, many of the papers written by students in research courses (including masters theses and doctoral dissertations) are expected to be examples of Level III research. Therefore, the present chapter will attempt to integrate the ideas from the previous chapters into a systematic presentation of the major components of a Level III research project.

STATING THE RESEARCH HYPOTHESIS

A *research question* asks about the relationship between two or more variables. A *research hypothesis* states the expected answer to the research question.

Both a research question and a research hypothesis contain at a minimum an independent and dependent variable. (There can be additional variables, but these will be introduced later in this chapter.) The research question asks about the relationship between the independent and the dependent variable. The research hypothesis states an expected relationship between the independent and the dependent variable.

The *dependent variable* is the outcome which is expected to arise from some treatment. Those variables that have been referred to as *outcome variables* in earlier chapters of this text were really dependent variables. Such variables are dependent in the sense that they *depend* on the treatment. For example, if the treatment has one effect, the dependent variable may have a low value; whereas if the treatment had a different effect, the dependent variable may have a high value.

The *independent* variable is the treatment that is expected to produce an outcome. *Independent variable* and *treatment* are used synonymously in this text. The independent variable is independent in the sense that it *does not depend* on the outcome (dependent) variable.

Another way to say this is that in experimental research the independent variable is the cause and the dependent variable is the effect. The independent variable is the treatment, the dependent variable the outcome.

Spot Quiz

Examine each of the following statements or questions and identify the independent and dependent variables:

1. Studying Shakespeare leads to a greater appreciation of Western culture.

2. Behavior modification leads to noncreative behavior among elementary school children.

3. Does watching "The Electric Company" on television really cause improvement in reading achievement?

4. Delaying reading instruction until the sixth grade will have no adverse impact on reading ability by the time the child reaches adolescence.

5. Do Halloween parties lessen the children's ability to learn during Halloween week?

Answers:
1. Dependent variable: appreciation of Western culture. Independent variable: studying Shakespeare.
2. Dependent variable: noncreative behavior. Independent variable: behavior modification.
3. Dependent variable: reading achievement. Independent variable: watching "The Electric Company."

4. Dependent variable: reading ability during adolescence. Independent variable: delaying reading instruction until the sixth grade.
5. Dependent variable: ability to learn during Halloween week. Independent variable: Halloween parties.

In each of the above cases, the independent variable produces an outcome; and this outcome is referred to as the dependent variable.

You may have noticed that some of the variables (such as noncreative behavior, studying Shakespeare, and appreciation of Western culture) are rather vaguely defined. You may have felt that they would require further operational definition. If you felt this way, you were right. Operational definitions of these variables will be discussed shortly.

When we undertake a research project (whether to serve our own personal needs or as part of a course assignment), we usually have some expectation of what the results will be. Such expectations are based either on our own hopes and experience or on a reading of previous research related to the question at hand. For this reason it is generally more desirable to state a research hypothesis than to state a mere question. This is not a major consideration; the important thing is that you need clearly specified dependent and independent variables.

In relatively rare cases it will be impossible to differentiate between the dependent and the independent variables. This will occasionally occur with research problems solved by correlation coefficients—problems that merely state a relationship with no implication that this is a causal relationship. For example, the following two statements both state a relationship, but the person noting the relationship probably sees no causal connection between the two:

- The students who did well in algebra were also the ones who did well in gym.
- People who arrived early for their therapy sessions were the same ones who arrive early for athletic events.

In such cases we have a choice. We can either (1) not label them at all or (2) arbitrarily declare one the dependent and the other the independent variable for purposes of stating the hypothesis.

In other correlational studies, however, there is an assumed causal relationship, even if the researcher is aware that mere correlational research does not prove causality. For example,

- There is a strong positive correlation between GRE scores and success in this course.

In this case, there appears to be a belief that the ability measured by GRE scores causes success in the course, even though the researcher may be aware that a correlation does not prove causality. At the very least, such statements involve a prediction. In such cases, the predictor is classified as the independent variable and the variable to be predicted is the dependent variable.

The *levels* of a variable are the different variations the variable can take. Every independent variable has at least two levels, and some can have more. For example, it is possible to identify two levels for each of the independent variables identified from the hypotheses and spot quiz on p. 255.

1. **Level 1:** Studying Shakespeare.
   Level 2: Not studying Shakespeare.

2. **Level 1:** Use of behavior modification.
   Level 2: No use of behavior modification.
3. **Level 1:** Watching "The Electric Company."
   Level 2: Not watching "The Electric Company."
4. **Level 1:** Delaying reading instruction until the sixth grade.
   Level 2: Starting reading instruction at the usual time.
5. **Level 1:** Halloween party.
   Level 2: No Halloween party.

In addition, several of these independent variables could have more than two levels (if the person doing the research would choose to have more than two levels). For example, Hypothesis 4 could easily be restructured to have three levels:

4. **Level 1:** Delaying reading instruction until sixth grade.
   Level 2: Delaying reading instruction until third grade.
   Level 3: Starting reading instruction at usual time (first grade).

In each of the above cases, it would not be correct to say that we have two or three independent variables. We rather have two or three levels (variations) of one treatment. When an experiment is conducted, each of the groups in the experiment receives one level of the treatment.

A *research prediction* is the same as a research hypothesis, except that it includes operational (rather than conceptual) definitions of the variables. In other words, a research prediction is a statement of the expected relationship between the dependent and independent variable, in which the conceptual terms used in the research hypothesis have been replaced by operational definitions. The following five statements have taken the questions and hypotheses from p. 255 and converted them to research predictions:

1. Reading *Julius Caesar* in accordance with our curriculum guidelines will cause students to make more references to a wider variety of aspects of Western civilization in an essay on Western culture at the end of the semester.
2. Pupils who receive a token reinforcement in which reinforcement is contingently given according to prescribed guidelines will score lower on the Torrance Tests of Creative Thinking than children who receive no such program.
3. The children who watch "The Electric Company" in a group for a half hour each school day will score higher on the standardized reading achievement test than the children who pursue their normal reading curriculum during this same period of time.
4. Children who are not required to learn to read until the sixth grade but are rather encouraged to read whenever they wish (according to guidelines discussed in the report) will score about the same on reading tests administered during the tenth grade as children who were required to start formal reading instruction in the first grade.
5. An hour-long Halloween party on the afternoon of October 31, during which children will wear costumes and have refreshments, will lower their scores on the math and spelling tests on the next class day.

Each of the above research predictions is stated in terms of operational definitions. In each case the operational definitions could be written more clearly, and such clarified operational definitions should be contained in the text of a research report. The brief statements contained in these predictions are satisfactory, provided they are backed up by more detailed definitions within the text. As you examined these predictions you may have been surprised, since a prediction may have stated something different from what you expected from the original question or hypothesis. This is not unusual, since only the person doing the research can determine his or her own operational definition of the variables in a study. If *you* were performing a study to examine each of these hypotheses, the operational definitions (and hence the predictions) might be different from those stated here.

The value of the research prediction is this: Once such a prediction is stated, then all the researcher has to do is find a way to see if the prediction is substantiated or not. Such predictions can be tested by finding an appropriate research design, conducting an experiment, and performing statistical tests on the results. If this endeavor shows the results that were anticipated by the prediction, then we have supported our research hypothesis. The strength of this support depends on the strength of our operational definitions and on the quality of the research design and procedures we used to test the prediction. On the other hand, if our experiment obtains results different from those anticipated by the research prediction, then we have evidence that our hypothesis was incorrect. Again, the strength of this evidence depends upon the strength of our operational definitions and upon the quality of the research design and procedures we used to test the prediction.

As you can see, there is a twofold advantage in a clear statement of a research prediction. First, it enables you *as a researcher* to specify for yourself exactly what it is that you need to do in order to determine whether your hypothesis is correct or not. Once you have reached this point, you know exactly what it is that you have to find out; and you can identify strategies that will or will not test this prediction. You may still have trouble actually carrying out a given design, and in some cases you may find that it is impossible to test a given prediction; but with a well-stated prediction you have reached a point where you know exactly what is required in order to test a research hypothesis.

The second advantage of a clear statement of a research prediction is that it enables you *as a consumer of research* to make a judgment about the relevance of someone else's research to your own needs. By reading another person's research prediction, you can make a tentative judgment about the external validity of that person's report and make a decision about whether you want to pursue the matter further. If the research prediction deals with something you are interested in, then you know that *if* the researcher has carried out the research design and other procedures appropriately, there may be something of value for you in the research. On the other hand, if the research prediction deals with something you do not even remotely care about, then you know that no matter how high the technical quality of the research may be there is little likelihood that it is going to tell you anything which you can generalize to your own needs. By knowing how to locate and make intelligent use of research predictions, consumers of research can greatly increase the efficiency with which they derive useful ideas from the professional literature.

MODERATOR VARIABLES

A moderator variable is a variable that influences (moderates) the impact of the independent variable upon the dependent variable. In the following hypothesis, for example, the sex of the child is a moderator variable:

- The use of popular music will increase the appreciation of poetry among elementary school children. The impact will be greater among girls than among boys.

In this example, the use of popular music is the independent variable and appreciation of poetry is the dependent variable. (Both of these could obviously benefit from operational definition.) The sex of the child is a moderator variable because it influences how effective the treatment will be with a given subject. If the subject is a girl, the independent variable tends to have one impact with regard to the dependent variable; whereas if the subject is a boy, the independent variable tends to have a different impact.

In the above example, the sex of the child was merely one of a myriad of variables that could have been chosen as a moderator variable. The following are two other variations of the same hypothesis, with a different moderator variable inserted in each case:

- The use of popular music will increase the appreciation of poetry among elementary school children. The impact will be greater among older children than among younger children.
- The use of popular music will increase the appreciation of poetry among elementary school students. The impact will be greater when the teacher is the same sex as the child than when the teacher is of the opposite sex.

You can easily see the advantage of using such moderator variables. The researcher (or reader) can discover not only *if* the treatment has the desired impact, but also *under what specific circumstances this impact is likely to vary.* This is extremely useful information for generalizing the results to other situations, as well as for selectively applying results to specific learners within a given educational setting.

The following hypotheses are restatements of the questions and hypotheses on p. 255. Moderator variables have been added to each hypothesis. In order to avoid stereotyped language and to show you a fuller range of how moderator variables can be introduced into research studies, the wording has been varied in each hypothesis.

1. Studying Shakespeare leads to a greater appreciation of Western culture among college-bound students, but not among non-college-bound students.
2. Behavior modification will reduce creative behavior among elementary school children in middle class schools, but will increase creative behavior in lower middle class schools.
3. Watching "The Electric Company" on television will cause substantial improvements in reading achievement among slow readers who are not classified as learning disabled. However, no such improvements will occur among slow readers who are classified as learning disabled.
4. Delaying reading instruction until the sixth grade will have no adverse impact on reading ability by the time the child reaches adolescence. This will be equally true among low IQ, medium IQ, and high IQ students.
5. Halloween parties will lessen the ability of high-anxiety children to learn during Halloween week. There will be no impact on medium-anxiety children, and low-anxiety children will actually have their ability to learn increased by attendance at Halloween parties.

In each of the above examples the original hypothesis has been changed by the addition of the moderator variable. In each case the moderator variable is a factor that could influence the impact of the independent variable upon the dependent variable. In each example there were other factors that could have been selected as moderator variables; the actual moderator variables selected in any study depend on what the researcher is interested in learning about the relationship between the independent and dependent variables.

The moderator variables in these examples were not operationally defined. It *is* possible and desirable to operationally define moderator variables. Such operational definitions can and should be included in the statement of the research prediction. For example, the third example from p. 259 can be further refined by the addition of an operationally-defined moderator variable:

   3. Among children who fall *outside* the classification of learning disabled according to the state guidelines, those who watch "The Electric Company" in a group for a half hour each school day will score higher on the standardized reading achievement test than the children who pursue the normal reading curriculum during this same period of time. However, among children who *are* classified as learning disabled according to the state guidelines, those who watch "The Electric Company" in a group for a half hour each school day will score no higher than those who pursue the normal curriculum.

Such a prediction is extremely precise and tells the researcher and reader exactly what must be done to verify or refute this prediction.

It is possible to have more than one moderator variable in the same study. When this occurs, it is best to avoid verbal complexity by using several sentences in the statment of the hypothesis, rather than trying to squeeze all the ideas into a single sentence. The following example adds a second moderator variable to the "The Electric Company" example:

   3. Watching "The Electric Company" on television will cause substantial improvements in reading achievement among slow readers who are not classified as learning disabled. However, no such improvements will occur among slow readers who are classified as learning disabled. Furthermore, high-anxiety learners will benefit substantially more from watching "The Electric Company" than will either medium- or low-anxiety learners.

In converting this to a research prediction with appropriate operational definitions, the best course of action would be to write separate predictions for each of the moderator variables. Although the above example contains two moderator variables, this is a fairly simple hypothesis because the hypothesis states that the moderator variables influence the independent variable *separately*, not *in combination with each other*. When moderator variables act in combination, they act not only upon the independent variable but also on each other and *then* on the independent variable. Such combinations are referred to as *higher order interactions*, and they are extremely difficult to conceptualize. In the above example, for instance, it could be hypothesized that low-anxiety learning-disabled learners and high-anxiety non-learning-disabled learners would benefit from the television program, whereas others would not benefit. It is also possible to have three or more moderator variables interacting with one another.

Predictions containing moderator variables are usually tested using *factorial designs*. An ideal factorial design is diagrammed as follows:

$$
\begin{array}{ccccc}
R & O_1 & X & Y_1 & O_2 \\
R & O_3 &   & Y_1 & O_4 \\
R & O_5 & X & Y_2 & O_6 \\
R & O_7 &   & Y_2 & O_8
\end{array}
$$

This diagram shows a true experimental design in which subjects are assigned at random to both the independent variable (X) and to the moderator variable $(Y_1$ and $Y_2)$. In actual practice, random assignment to the moderator variable is often impossible. (For example, how does one randomly assign subjects to sex, social class,

---

DEAR RESEARCHER:

My nephew was ferreting through a garret in an ancient parsonage in Stratford near Avon, when he came upon a tattered manuscript. Much of it was illegible. However, it seems that the scrawlings were the rough draft of a poem or play in iambic pentameter dedicated to the theme of educational research. It is my belief that this is the original version of Hamlet's third soliloquy. Is it possible that the enclosed lines were written by Shakespeare himself?

> To be, or not be to? that is the question:
> Whether 'tis nobler in the mind to suffer
> The slings and arrows of external invalidity,
> Or to take arms against a sea of threats,
> And with a moderator variable isolate and control them.

(Here some lines are lost . . . eaten by moths.)

> Thus conscience does make researchers of us all,
> And thus the native hue of true experimentation
> Is sicklied o'er with the pale cast of factorial design,
> And experiments of great pith and moment
> With this regard their generalizations expand
> And lose the name of irrelevance.—Soft you now:
> The fair Ophelia:

(The rest of the text is lost . . . eaten by moths.)

(signed) SCHOLARLY INQUIRER FROM PHOENIX.

DEAR SCHOLAR: No, this was not written by Shakespeare. It was written by Sir Francis Bacon. So were the rest of Shakespeare's plays.
(signed) THE LONELY RESEARCHER.*

---

*Reviewer A: "Ugh!"
Reviewer B: "Fantastic!"
Lucretius: "What is food to one man may be fierce poison to another." (*De rerum natura*, IV, 637)
Spinoza: "One and the same thing can at the same time be good, bad, and indifferent. . . ." (*Ethics*, Part IV, Preface) I'm obviously beginning to appreciate Spinoza a little more!

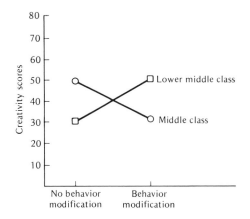

FIGURE 14–1. Results of a Hypothetical Study Testing the Hypothesis That Behavior Modification Will Reduce Creative Behavior Among Elementary School Children in the Middle Class Schools, but Will Increase Creative Behavior in Lower Middle Class Schools.

or grade level? The answer is that it cannot be done.) Therefore, such designs are often actually a combination of a true experimental or quasi-experimental design for the independent variable and criterion group design for the moderator variable. Nevertheless, there are good statistical procedures available to analyze these designs (usually analysis of variance or analysis of covariance), and the information derived from the moderator variables can be extremely valuable.

An *interaction* is said to occur when two variables act together to produce an effect. Chapter 8 discussed threats to internal validity as *interactions* which needed to be eliminated if possible. These threats were interactions because such threats to internal or external validity acted together with the treatment to produce an effect, and it was desirable to eliminate them because they clouded the issue of whether the treatment caused the observed outcome or not. Moderator variables also produce interactions. They act together with the treatment to produce an outcome. However, instead of trying to eliminate the interactions caused by moderator variables, the researcher tries to isolate these variables and measure the size and direction of the interaction. Instead of getting rid of the interaction, the researcher describes the interaction as precisely as possible and makes this description available for use in interpreting the results of the study.

The main reason for identifying moderator variables is to look for interactions.

Let us examine some diagrams showing the results of studies containing moderator variables.[1] Figure 14–1 shows the results of a study undertaken to test one of the sample hypotheses. These results show that middle class children who received *no* behavior modification averaged about 50 on the creativity test, whereas those middle class children who *did* receive the behavior modification program averaged about 30. This is what a prediction based on the hypothesis would expect. On the other hand, the lower middle class children without the behavior modification program averaged about 30, whereas those lower middle class children who received the program averaged about 50. Again, this is what the hypothesis would predict. The results summarized in the diagram, therefore, support the belief expressed in the hypothesis.

[1] These studies and results are fictional. They have been invented to provide clear examples.

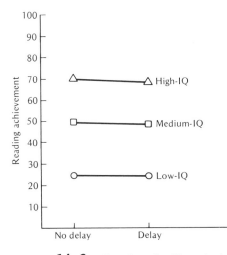

FIGURE **14–2.** Results of a Hypothetical Study Undertaken to Test the Hypothesis That Delaying Reading Instruction Until the Sixth Grade Will Have No Adverse Effect on Reading Ability by the Time the Student Reaches Adolescence. (The results show tenth-grade reading achievement tests, reported separately for low-, medium-, and high-IQ students.)

The hypothesized interaction of the moderator variable with the independent variable has been found to exist.

The fourth sample hypothesis (operationally stated on p. 259) states a moderator variable (IQ), but predicts no interaction. The results shown in Figure 14–2 support this hypothesis. Low-IQ subjects averaged about 25 in both the delay and no-delay condition. Likewise, medium-IQ subjects scored about the same in both conditions; and high-IQ subjects averaged about 70 in both conditions. These results show that there was no interaction between the treatment and the IQ level of the subjects. IQ did not influence the impact of the treatment on the subjects. It is important to point out that verifying the absence of an interaction can be just as useful as establishing the existence of an interaction.

There is an easy rule that will enable you to estimate whether or not there is an interaction through visual inspection of such diagrams. If the lines are parallel or nearly parallel, there is no interaction. If the lines cross or come toward each other so sharply that they would cross if they were allowed to continue a little further, then there is an interaction. This rule covers the obvious cases like Figures 14–1 and 14–2. In more subtle cases it is hard to ascertain by visual inspection whether or not the lines are nearly parallel, and in such cases it is necessary to rely on statistical procedures, such as analysis of variance, rather than the visual rule to interpret the results. Nevertheless, this is a useful rule that will help you to interpret research reports containing moderator variables and interactions.

Figure 14–3 shows the results of a study undertaken to examine another sample hypothesis. This diagram shows the results for a pretest and posttest for the learning-disabled and non-learning-disabled students who watched or did not watch "The Electric Company." There are three parallel lines and one sharply slanting line, and thus visual inspection informs us that there is an interaction. The nature of this interaction can be ascertained through a close examination of this diagram. However, since the pretest scores were nearly identical and the only differences were among the

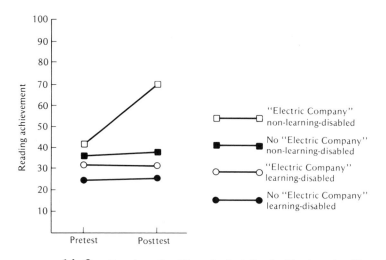

FIGURE 14–3. Results of a Hypothetical Study Testing the Hypothesis That Watching "The Electric Company" on Television Will Cause Substantial Improvements in Reading Achievement Among Slow Readers Who Are Not Classified as Learning Disabled, but No Such Improvements Among Those Slow Readers Who Are Classified as Learning Disabled. (The same results are more effectively presented in Figure 14–4.)

posttest scores, a better diagram can be drawn to focus more sharply on the interaction. Figure 14–4 accomplishes this sharper focus by omitting the pretest scores and zeroing in on the posttest scores, where the interaction actually occurs. Figure 14–4 shows that the learning-disabled pupils performed about the same in both experimental conditions, whereas the non-learning-disabled pupils performed much better when they viewed "The Electric Company."

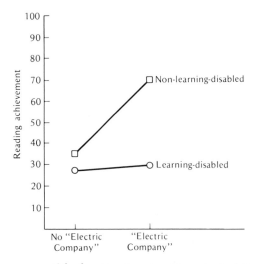

FIGURE 14–4. Results of a Hypothetical Study Testing the Hypothesis That Watching "The Electric Company" on Television Will Cause Substantial Improvements in Reading Achievement Among Slow Readers Who Are Not Classified as Learning Disabled, but No Such Improvements Among Those Slow Readers Who Are Classified as Learning Disabled. (These results are displayed better in this diagram than in Figure 14–3.)

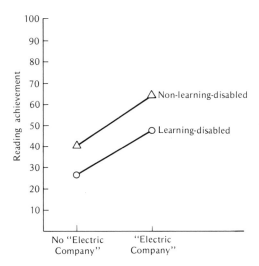

FIGURE 14–5. Results of a Hypothetical Study to Test the Hypothesis that Watching "The Electric Company" on Television Will Cause Substantial Improvements in Reading Achievement Among Slow Readers Who Are Not Classifed as Learning Disabled, but No Such Improvements Among Those Slow Readers Who Are Classified as Learning Disabled. (The results in this diagram do not support the stated hypothesis. Rather, they show that learning disabled students do worse than non-learning-disabled students in both treatment conditions. There is no interaction.)

The results shown in Figures 14–3 and 14–4 show that the experimental results supported the belief that the predicted interaction would occur. Of course, it would be possible that the hypothesized results might not be found in the experiment. For example, Figure 14–5 shows a different set of results of an experiment examining the same sample hypothesis. These results indicate that both learning-disabled and non-learning-disabled pupils performed better after watching "The Electric Company." The lines in the diagram are nearly parallel. This means that there is no interaction. Researchers interpreting results such as those shown in Figure 14–5 often state that there was an overall effect of both the treatment and the moderator variable, but there was no interaction between the two variables. In other words, the average score of those students who watched "The Electric Company" was higher than that of those who did not watch the show, and the average of the non-learning-disabled learners was superior to that of the learning-disabled learners. However, being in one or the other experimental condition did not have a different effect on learning-disabled than on non-learning-disabled pupils, as had been the case in Figure 14-4. These results do not support the belief that the hypothesized interaction exists.

Figure 14–6 presents results from a study examining another sample hypothesis. These results show that the low-anxiety students did poorly when there was no party, but did well when there was a party. The high-anxiety students, on the other hand, did well when there was no party and poorly when there was a party. The medium-anxiety students scored in between under both circumstances. These results show a strong interaction. The value of looking for such interactions can be seen from an examination of Figure 14–7. This hypothesis and diagram contains no moderator variables. A researcher undertaking a study to ascertain the effects of Halloween

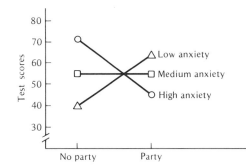

FIGURE **14–6.** The Results of a Hypothetical Study Testing the Hypothesis That a Halloween Party Will Have Different Effects upon Pupils at Different Levels of Arousal. (Figure 14–7 shows the results of the same study without taking into consideration the moderator variables.)

parties might obtain these results and conclude that parties make no difference. By looking for the appropriate interaction, however, the same researcher might find the rather dramatic interaction displayed in Figure 14–6. Identifying the correct moderator variables and integrating them into our research design can enable us to gain useful insights from experimental studies.

Is it better to hypothesize and discover interactions or to look for and verify the absence of interactions? The answer is that both interactions and verification of their absence provide useful information to the researcher and to the consumer of research. Figures 14–8 and 14–9 show the results of a sample study undertaken to examine related hypotheses which differ only because they predict a different interaction. Figure 14–8 shows an interaction, whereas Figure 14–9 shows no interaction. They both provide useful results. A researcher or reader examining the results in Figure 14–8 would conclude, "Spending time teaching Shakespeare achieves the desired impact among college-bound students but not among non-college-bound students. We should continue using Shakespeare for this purpose among the college-bound students, but maybe we should seek a different approach for our non-college-bound

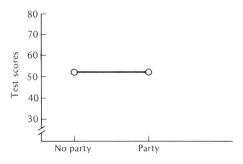

FIGURE **14–7.** Results of a Hypothetical Study Examining the Impact of Halloween Parties upon Test Scores. (No moderator variables are taken into consideration, and the results make it appear as if the parties had no effect on anyone. The same study is shown in Figure 14–6. In that diagram the moderator variable is shown, and the impact of the parties is more accurately portrayed.)

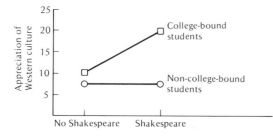

FIGURE 14–8. Results of a Study Testing the Hypothesis That Studying Shakespeare Leads to Greater Appreciation of Western Culture Among College-bound Students, but Not Among Non-college-bound Students.(These results show an interaction. Those in Figure 14–9 show no interaction.)

students." On the other hand, the same researcher or reader examining Figure 14–9 might conclude: "Spending time teaching Shakespeare achieves equally desirable benefits among both college-bound and non-college-bound students. Unless we find an approach which is even more successful, we should continue using Shakespeare for this purpose among both groups." Thus, either finding an interaction or finding the absence of an interaction can provide useful information for making decisions based upon the results of a research study.

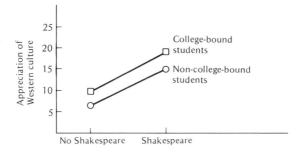

FIGURE 14–9. Results of a Study Testing the Hypothesis That Studying Shakespeare Leads to Greater Appreciation of Western Culture Among College-bound Students, but Not Among Non-college-bound Students. (These results show no interaction. Those in Figure 14–8 do show an interaction.)

CONTROL VARIABLES

A control variable is a factor that is controlled by the experimenter in order to cancel out or neutralize any impact this factor might otherwise have on the outcome variable. This control can be attained either through (1) equating across groups, (2) statistical manipulation, or (3) isolation and elimination. A control variable is identified because the researcher feels that this factor may influence the impact of the independent variable upon the dependent variable. Such an extraneous influence would make it difficult to determine the precise impact of the independent variable on the dependent variable. Therefore, the researcher controls this extraneous factor in order to remove its influence.

Let us examine the sample hypotheses that we have been following throughout this chapter, and this time we will add control variables.

1. Among high school seniors, studying Shakespeare leads to a greater appreciation of Western culture.
2. Behavior modification leads to noncreative behavior among elementary school children in public schools of Gotham City.

In the first hypothesis, high school seniors has been added as a control variable. It is possible that the effect of studying Shakespeare would be different at different age levels; the age or grade level of the students might influence how they will respond to Shakespeare. Therefore, the researcher has decided to include *only* high school seniors in the hypothesis. This rules out the extraneous factor, but of course it also limits the generalizations to high school seniors. In the second hypothesis, there are three control variables: grade level of children (elementary school, rather than middle school or high school), type of school (public, rather than private), and location (Gotham City). All three of these are factors that could influence how children will respond to behavior modification, and the researcher has controlled the threat of such extraneous interactions by including only elementary school children from one city. Of course, the generalizations that can be drawn from the study can no longer be extended to middle school, parochial school students in Milwaukee.

In the above examples we have added control variables to the original hypotheses before they were enriched by the addition of moderator variables. It is possible (and often desirable) to have both control variables and moderator variables within the same hypothesis. Each of the following examples contains independent, dependent, moderator, and control variables:

3. Among children between the ages of 9 and 11, watching "The Electric Company" on television will cause substantial improvements in reading achievement among slow readers who are not classified as learning disabled. However no such improvements will occur among 9 to 11 year old slow readers who are classified as learning disabled.
4. Among children who have no external pressure from their parents to persuade them to learn to read, delaying reading instruction until the sixth grade will have no adverse impact on reading ability by the time the child reaches adolescence. This will be equally true among low-IQ, medium-IQ, and high-IQ students.
5. Among fifth graders, Halloween parties will lessen the ability of high-anxiety children to learn during Halloween week. There will be no impact on medium-anxiety fifth graders, and low-anxiety fifth graders will actually have their ability to learn increased by attendance at Halloween parties.

In the third hypothesis, there are two control variables: age of child (9 to 11 years old) and level of reading difficulty (slow readers are included, but average and fast readers are excluded). The factors of age and level of ability are ruled out as threats to internal and external validity, but the researcher can no longer generalize the results to six-year-olds or to average readers. In the fourth hypothesis, a control variable has been added to rule out the likelihood that parental pressure will cloud the results of the experiment. However, the researcher can no longer generalize the results to children who do experience such pressure. In this case, this might be a severe constraint, since a very large number of children in American society probably *would* experience such pressure. In the fifth hypothesis the grade level is a control variable. It would also be possible to regard Halloween as a control variable if the researcher would be at all inclined to extend the results to such other occasions as Thanksgiving and Christmas. Unless someone can produce evidence to show that broader generalizations are warranted, the generalizations from this hypothesis are limited to fifth graders and to Halloween.

Like all other variables, control variables can benefit from operational definitions. While some control variables are quite easy to define operationally, others require considerable effort. For example, in the fourth hypothesis it would be extremely important (and probably difficult) to operationally define external pressure from parents. Such an operational definition would be of crucial importance in determining the limits to generalizations arising from a study based on this hypothesis. Once such operational definitions have been stated, they can and should be inserted into the research prediction. For example,

> Among children who receive a rating of 14 or less on the Parental Pressure Scale (PPS), those who are not required to learn to read until they reach the sixth grade but are rather encouraged to read whenever they wish to do so (according to guidelines discussed in the report) will score about the same on reading tests administered during the tenth grade as children who were required to start formal reading instruction in the first grade.

Readers of this prediction may not initially know what the PPS is, but they can find out by looking in the report. These readers can then judge for themeselves how closely the operational definition of children included in the study corresponds to the type of children they have in their own schools. They can use this information in deciding whether or not to examine the report more closely and in determining whether the results are applicable to their own schools. (This research prediction contains several terms that may seem not sufficiently clear to be considered acceptable in an operational definition. For example, the typical reader would not know what a PPS is or what is meant by "whenever they wish." However, these terms are acceptable so long as they are backed up by clear descriptions in the text of the report. The relatively vague terms are merely shorthand indicators that stand for lengthier descriptions that would be too bulky to include in a simple research prediction.)

You have probably noticed that there is a considerable similarity between moderator and control variables. This similarity arises from the fact that both take into account factors that may influence the impact of the independent variable upon the dependent variable. The difference is that the moderator variable both controls and examines this additional factor in such a way as to describe its precise impact. The control variable, on the other hand, merely controls this extraneous influence without providing any information about its precise relationship to the dependent and independent variables. Thus, while moderator variables have the potential to both restrict and refine generalizations, the role of the control variable is usually confined to merely restricting generalizations.

Because of this similarity, the same variables that can be used as moderator variables can also be used as control variables. A wise idea is to identify as many extraneous variables as possible that might influence the impact of the treatment on the outcome variable. Then make some of these into moderator variables, some into control variables, and leave some of them uncontrolled. At first thought, it might appear that since the moderator variable does everything the control variable does and more, then we should use moderator variables as often as possible. This would be true, except for a very important practical consideration. It is often difficult to obtain the variety or number of subjects that would be necessary for analyzing a factor as a moderator variable. In addition, an excessive number of moderator variables can make a study cumbersome. Similarly, it might at first seem that *no* extraneous factor should be left uncontrolled. Again, however, there is a practical consideration. There are so many factors that could conceivably influence the impact of the treatment on the outcome that it is not often possible to isolate all of them.

THE SEX OF THE SUBJECTS IN AN EXPERIMENT CAN BE EITHER A MODERATOR VARIABLE OR A CONTROL VARIABLE OR THE VARIABLE COULD BE IGNORED.

Let us examine a detailed example of how a researcher might decide what factors to treat as moderator variables and what factors to treat as control variables.

Assume that a researcher is interested in finding out whether the use of popular music will lead to greater appreciation of poetry among her students. She might start with this initial hypothesis:

The use of popular music will increase the appreciation of poetry among middle school children.

At this point she has already included one control variable—middle school children. She has done this because she is a middle school teacher and is not particularly interested in learning about what popular music will do for elementary or high school students. Next, she might ask herself, "What factors are likely to influence the impact of popular music upon the pupils?" Her answer might consist of a list like the following:

1. Sex of the child.
2. How recent the songs are.
3. Whether the popular music is instrumental or vocal.
4. The degree of familiarity the students show with regard to the music.
5. The child's attitude toward music.
6. The child's reading ability.
7. The attitudes of the child's parents toward poetry.
8. The type of poetry contained in the popular music.
9. The number of metaphors, similes, and other poetic devices used in the song.
10. Age of the child.

The researcher might decide to make items 1, 5, and 8, moderator variables. She might also decide to make items 2, 3, 4, and 10 control variables by including only specific levels of these variables within her study. She will do this by including only vocal songs familiar to the students that were played within the past month on a designated popular radio station. Her study will include only students between the ages of 13 and 14. She might also decide to use item 6 as a control variable—not by the process of isolation and elimination, as she had with the other variables, but rather through the process of statistical manipulation. She will do this by using reading ability as a covariate in analysis of covariance. This leaves uncontrolled variables 7 and 9. She might omit these from consideration because she considers them much too difficult for her to control. Based on these decisions, our researcher might derive the following hypothesis:

> Among 13 and 14 year old children, when the influence of reading ability is controlled, the use of current, popular vocal music with which the students are familiar will lead to an increased appreciation of poetry. This hypothesis will have the following restrictions:
>
> 1. The impact will be greater on girls than on boys.
> 2. Students with greater appreciation of music will benefit more than those with little appreciation of music. Those who actively dislike music will actually show a decrease in appreciation of poetry from this approach.
> 3. The impact will be greater when the popular music follows a ballad format than when it follows a different format.

The above hypothesis would still benefit from operational definitions of all the variables and from the statement of a research prediction. In an actual setting, the researcher might derive a list of extraneous variables quite different from the list shown here and may choose to treat the variables differently. The actual decisions would be based on what the researcher thinks she can and should do in order to make her study as useful as possible.

This discussion of control variables has focused on the technique of controlling extraneous factors through isolation and elimination. In each of the examples, an extraneous threat has been removed by excluding subjects or activities with certain characteristics from the study while including only those with more narrowly defined characteristics. This use of control variables is very widespread and important. The other two strategies for using control variables have been discussed previously in the text. Equating across groups can be accomplished by random assignment (p. 153), by random selection of subjects from a larger population (p. 240), and by purposive sampling for heterogeneity (p. 241). Random assignment controls such extraneous variables within the study, but serves no useful purpose with regard to generalizing beyond the scope of that study. Random selection from a target population would be an extremely strong control, but it is almost never used in practice. Generalizations based on purposive sampling for heterogeneity depend on the strength of the logical assertion that the subjects brought into the study are really similar to the population about which we wish to generalize. If this logical assertion is accurate, then this method has the advantage of controlling the extraneous bias without narrowing the field of generalization, as would the method of isolation and elimination. However, it is by no means obvious that purposive sampling for heterogeneity frequently provides such representative samples for the experimental treatment.

The method of statistical manipulation consists of the use of such techniques as analysis of covariance. These techniques cannot be discussed in detail in a text such as this. However, it will be helpful to point out that such statistical techniques cannot provide perfect adjustments for initial inequalities between groups. They often underadjust for differences. For this reason, control through the use of moderator variables or through the technique of isolation and elimination is often a more desirable strategy, especially for researchers who are not familiar with the complexities of such statistical procedures. Indeed, even experienced researchers frequently are unaware of these statistical subtleties, and therefore it is necessary to be careful in accepting some of the "results" in the professional literature.

INTERVENING VARIABLES

An intervening variable is a hypothetical variable that is assumed to be created by the operationally defined independent variable and that in turn is assumed to have an impact upon the dependent variable. The treatment produces the intervening variable, and the intervening variable in turn produces the outcome. This variable *intervenes* in the sense that the treatment does not produce the outcome directly but rather through the mediation (intervention) of this invisible, hypothetical, internalized process.

To take a brief example, a researcher might find that computer simulations cause students to do well on science tests. In fact, the computers themselves do not cause the improved performance on the science tests. Using the computers actually stimulates some internal change within the students (such as improved motivation, greater attention, perceived relevance, or something else) and this internal change is what eventually leads to the change.

In many cases, teachers—even when they are acting as researchers—do not particularly care what the intervening variable is. If using the computers results in improved performance, that is great. Who cares what internal process is causing the difference? Such an attitude may be appropriate in many instances, but in other cases the teacher/researcher will be interested in this underlying cause. The intervening variable is the basic subject matter of Level IV research, and it will be discussed in greater detail in the next chapter. At the present time, it will be sufficient merely to point out several examples of intervening variables derived from the hypotheses that we have been using as examples throughout this chapter. In the following examples the hypothesis is stated (without operational definitions, moderator variables, or control variables), and then a possible intervening variable is stated in parentheses.

1. Studying Shakespeare leads to a greater appreciation of Western culture. (Perception of important similarities within Elizabethan and contemporary society.)
2. Behavior modification leads to noncreative behavior among elementary school children. (An urge to conform in order to be reinforced as efficiently as possible.)
3. Watching "The Electric Company" on television causes improvements in reading achievement. (Improved attention to details arising out of the motivating format.)
4. Delaying reading instruction until the sixth grade will have no adverse impact on reading ability by the time the child reaches adolescence. (Self-motivation to acquire useful skills).
5. Halloween parties lessen children's ability to learn during Halloween week. (Increase in level of arousal.)

In the above examples the intervening variable has been appended to the barest possible statement of the hypothesis. This has been done for the sake of simplicity. In actual practice, the moderator variable should take into account all of the variables as they have been operationally defined. For instance, in the fifth example the increase in the level of arousal would interact with the moderator variable in such a way that those at a high level of anxiety would become ineffective learners as their arousal increased even further (because human learning does not take place effectively when arousal is excessively high). On the other hand, those at a low level of anxiety would find their ability to learn would be enhanced as arousal moved toward a more medium level (where human learning occurs most efficiently). Those already near a medium level would be unaffected by the change. In this way, the intervening variable explains all the results derived from the fully stated hypothesis.

Unlike the other variables, the intervening variable is usually not stated as part of the hypothesis. Rather, it is stated at the culmination of the review of the literature (prior to the hypothesis) as the specific statement of the rationale behind why the hypothesis is going to be stated in the form it will take. In addition, the intervening variable is often restated somewhere in the discussion or conclusions section of the report as an explanation of why the results turned out the way they did. In many cases, an article or research project focuses so completely on practical (as opposed to theoretical) concerns, that the intervening variable is either ignored completely or is only vaguely specified. This is not surprising, since the intervening variable is often of greater theoretical than practical importance. The full exploration of intervening variables is the goal of Level IV research.

EXTRANEOUS VARIABLES

An extraneous variable is a factor that produces an uncontrolled, unpredictable impact upon the dependent variable. Extraneous variables weaken experimental studies because they introduce ambiguity into the research process. To the extent that extraneous variables are prevalent, we are uncertain about the nature of the cause and effect relationship in an experimental setting and about the degree to which the results of an experiment can be generalized. The threats to internal and external validity are extraneous variables, and the whole purpose of the strategies discussed in the chapters on research design is to minimize the effect of such extraneous variables. To the extent that extraneous variables can be brought under control, the results of a study are strengthened.

THE RESEARCH VARIABLES COMBINED

Figure 14–10 summarizes the interactions of the various research variables. The independent, moderator, and control variables are under the researcher's control. They cause an impact within the subject. This impact is referred to as the intervening variable. In addition, the extraneous variables have an impact upon this intervening variable. Because such extraneous variables are not under the experimenter's control, their presence weakens a study. One of the goals of a researcher is to remove as many significant factors as possible from the extraneous variable category by bringing them into the categories of moderator and control variables. Such a process of removing extraneous variables strengthens a study.

The intervening variable is merely hypothesized; it cannot be visually observed. It is defined in conceptual terms. The intervening variable is produced by some combination of the causal variables in the left-hand column of Figure 14–10. The intervening variable produces the dependent variable. Thus the dependent variable is an *indirect* result of the variables in the left-hand column.

Figure 14–10 is a highly simplified diagram. One way that it has been simplified is that the independent, moderator, control, and extraneous variables could be

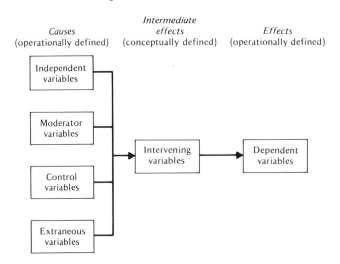

FIGURE **14–10.** Summary of the Variables in the Research Process.

pictured as interacting with one another, as well as having an impact upon the intervening variable. Arrows portraying such interactions have been omitted for the sake of simplicity. In addition, the role of the intervening variable has been oversimplified. In fact, there could be a whole string of boxes rather than a single box. For example, a certain set of causal variables might lead to improved motivation, which might lead to improved personal awareness, which might lead to enhanced attention, which might lead to new insights, which might lead (finally) to higher scores on a test. This whole chain has been compressed into a single box in Figure 14–10.

Every experimental study has at least one independent variable and one dependent variable. (There could be more than one of each of these in a given study.) Both of these variables should be explicitly stated in the hypothesis and in the research prediction. If either the treatment or the outcome variable is too complex to be stated succinctly, further operational definitions of these variables can be included in the methods section of a report. Every study also has an intervening variable, and often there can be more than one intervening variable. The intervening variable is not stated in operational terms, but rather is a conceptual explanation for the observed results. Intervening variables are normally not stated in the hypothesis or research prediction. Sometimes (perhaps because of the practical orientation of the researcher) intervening variables are only vaguely described or are not mentioned at all.

Not every study contains moderator and control variables. When such variables are contained in a study they should be operationally defined. Moderator and control variables are stated in the research hypothesis and in the research prediction. Often the operational definitions will require further explanation in the methods section of a report.

Review Quiz

1. Examine the following research hypothesis and identify each of the research variables requested below:

High school students who study Latin for two years will develop better English vocabulary skills than those who do not study Latin. This difference will occur both among those who are in advanced placement English classes and among those who are not in advanced placement English classes. This difference will occur because of an increased ability to break a word down into its component parts.

Identify the following variables:

• Independent:
• Dependent:
• Moderator:
• Control:
• Intervening:

Answers:
Independent: Studying Latin (vs. not studying it).
Dependent: Vocabulary skills.
Moderator: English class placement (advanced vs. nonadvanced).
Control: High school students.
Intervening: Increased ability to break a word into its component parts.

---

2. State the preceding hypothesis as a research prediction.

Answer:
Many answers would be possible, depending on the operational definitions you might invent. The following is a sample.

Students in grades 9 to 12 who complete two elective years of the Latin curriculum will score higher on a standardized vocabulary test than those who do not enroll in an elective Latin class at all. This difference will occur both among those students enrolled in advanced placement English at any time during their high school career and those never enrolled in advanced placement English.

---

3. The following are the results of a fictional study undertaken to test the above hypothesis and prediction. Do these results support the hypothesis or not?

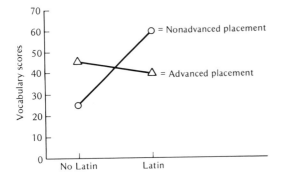

Answer:
No. These results show an interaction. They indicate that the Latin course helped the advanced placement students but that it helped the others more. This is not what the hypothesis and the prediction expected.

---

4. Examine the following research prediction and identify each of the research variables requested below:

Clients who enroll for counseling at the Roberts Psychiatric Clinic and are initially diagnosed as passive-aggressive will later show more assertiveness by resisting a mock telephone solicitor with cogent reasons after treatment employing Transductive Role Modeling (TRM) than similar clients receiving the traditional treatment. However, clients at the same clinic diagnosed as passive-withdrawn will show more assertiveness after receiving the traditional method of treatment than clients receiving the TRM treatment.

Identify the following variables:

- Independent:
- Dependent:
- Moderator:
- Control:
- Intervening:

Answers:

Independent: Type of treatment (TRM vs. traditional).

Dependent: Number of cogent responses given in resistence to the mock telephone solicitor (this is the operational definition of assertiveness).

Moderator: Initial diagnosis (passive-aggressive or passive-withdrawn).

Control: Clients who enroll for counseling at the Roberts Psychiatric Clinic.

Intervening: None is stated. A research prediction contains operationally defined variables. An intervening variable is defined in conceptual (not operational) terms, and therefore it has no place in a research prediction. If you found an intervening variable, you had to make it up.

5. The following are the results of a fictional study undertaken to test the above research prediction. Do these results support the prediction or not?

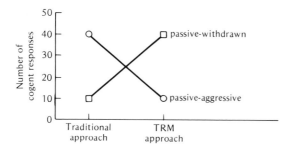

Answer:

No. They show exactly the opposite of what the prediction stated. Here, the passive-aggressive clients did better with the traditional approach, and the passive-withdrawn clients did better with the TRM approach. These results do not support the research prediction at all.

PUTTING IT ALL TOGETHER

One of the hypotheses which Eugene Anderson (our humane educator) tested can be stated as follows:

The Animal Life Program (ALP) will lead to improved attitudes toward animal life.

This is the hypothesis that Mr. Anderson tested with the experimental design in Chapters 10 and 12. Let us examine his hypothesis with relation to each of the research variables and their operational definitions:

Independent variable: The ALP. We know almost nothing about the ALP. If Mr. Anderson were writing a report on the ALP, it would be important for him to include a detailed description of the ALP, so that his readers would be able to formulate an idea of how closely the ALP resembled programs they might have in mind and so that they could replicate the study if they wished to do so.

Dependent variable: Attitudes toward animal life. This is operationally defined as the number of animals a child chooses to save on one or the other of the Fireman tests. A second dependent variable is the number of good deeds and bad deeds that are reported to the school, the police, or the humane society. These would be operationally defined in terms of whatever criteria these agencies use. It would be helpful to clarify this operational definition.

Control Variables: The study is confined to fourth, fifth, and sixth graders. It is likewise confined to a single school, and it would be useful to describe the school in terms of any unique characteristics of its size, its curriculum, its teaching philosophies, or its administrative orientation. Likewise, Mr. Anderson should specify demographic characteristics of the students (race, sex, etc.) and any other characteristics that might be relevant (how many owned pets, etc.). Finally, he should specify the nature of the community within which the school is located.

Moderator variables: Mr. Anderson has specified no moderator variables. He *could* have included such variables in his design by selecting one or more of the control variables and using such factors as moderator variables. It would still be possible for him to do this with regard to any variable about which he has data (such as sex, race, and pet ownership), provided he has a sufficient number of subjects to subdivide the subjects for factorial analysis.

Intervening variable: "Induced dissonance." There is no way you could have known this, because it is not discussed until Chapter 15. At that point, it will be explained that Mr. Anderson felt that his ALP worked because it caused the children to feel dissatisfied with the way their present actions related to an image they had of themselves as generally good persons. The treatment caused this dissonance; the dissonance caused changes in attitudes and behaviors; and one of the changes in behaviors was the tendency to choose more animals on the Fireman Tests.

These are the operational definitions of Mr. Anderson's research variables. He could state these in a research prediction as follows:

Among the fourth through sixth grade students in X school, the ALP humane education program described in this report will cause children to choose significantly more animals on the Fireman posttest than a group of similar children to whom the ALP has not been administered.

These operational definitions and this research prediction have been stated at this late point in the text. In actual practice, Mr. Anderson would have stated these definitions and this prediction near the *beginning* of his research project. By stating them in rough form at an early point in the project, he could use them to guide his selection of measurement devices and his choice of research designs. The earliest formulation would probably be changed several times as he encountered new ideas and new problems. The final product would be a guide for him in conducting the experiment, in analyzing the results, and in drawing conclusions. These operational definitions would also be an immense help to readers in evaluating the relevance of this research to their own problems.

SUMMARY

The research hypothesis states an anticipated relationship between the independent and the dependent variables. The independent variable is the term used to describe the treatment—the variable that is expected to cause an outcome. The dependent variable is the term used to describe the outcome that occurs as a result of a treatment. Both the independent and the dependent variable can and should be operationally defined. When these variables are operationally defined and inserted into the research hypothesis, the modified hypothesis is referred to as the research prediction. Once a research prediction is stated, the researcher can determine (by examining the components of this prediction) what steps need to be taken to verify or reject this prediction.

The moderator and control variables are factors that influence the impact of the independent variable upon the dependent variable. They differ in the respect that the moderator variable measures and describes its impact upon the treatment-outcome relationship. The control variable, on the other hand, is designed merely to eliminate (rather than measure and describe) its impact upon the relationship between the independent and dependent variables. Extraneous variables are factors that are uncontrolled and therefore threaten the internal or external validity of a study. The researcher gains greater control over a study by converting extraneous variables into moderator or control variables.

When moderator variables have an impact upon the relationship between the independent and dependent variables, this impact is referred to as an interaction. By establishing the precise nature of such interactions (and even by verifying the absence of them), the researcher is able to determine the precise populations about which results can be generalized. Analyzing such interactions can be a very fruitful research endeavor.

The intervening variable is the hypothesized factor that mediates between the independent and the dependent variables. The independent variable creates the intervening variable (an internal and invisible change); and the intervening variable in turn produces the impact on the dependent variable.

By clearly understanding and identifying these research variables, we can strengthen the quality of the research we perform. In addition, a thorough understanding of these variables and their interactions will enable us, as consumers of research, to make more effective use of research that is performed by others and then communicated to us in some fashion.

Annotated Bibliography

BAKER, R.L. and SCHUTZ, R.E. (EDS.) *Instructional Product Research* (New York: American Book Company, 1972). The second chapter of this book (written by Paul E. Resta and Robert L. Baker) is devoted to "Selecting Variables for Educational Research." The authors take an approach that is different from, but not incompatible with, that employed in the present text.

TUCKMAN, B.W. *Conducting Educational Research* (2nd ed.) (New York: Harcourt Brace Jovanovich, 1978). Chapter 4 focuses briefly on the topic covered by the present chapter.

MARTIN, D.W. *Doing Psychology Experiments* (Monterey, Cal.: Brooks/Cole, 1977). Chapter 6 provides good guidelines on how to select and define variables for formal research projects.

Professional Journals

Each of the following articles contains an explicit usage of at least one of the concepts discussed in this chapter. In addition, most of the articles provide an integration of many of the various concepts discussed up to this point in the text.

Bendell, D., Tollefson, N., and Fine, M. "Interaction of locus-of-control orientation and the performance of learning disabled adolescents," *Journal of Learning Disabilities* 13, (1980): 83–85. The authors use analysis of covariance to determine that learning-disabled adolescents with internal locus of control benefit from nonstructured learning settings, whereas those with external locus of control learn best in structured settings. This examination of locus of control as a moderator variable is extremely important, since the widespread practice is to provide all learning disabled students with structured settings.

McLeod, D.B., and Adams, V.M. "Aptitude-treatment interaction in mathematics instruction using expository and discovery methods," *Journal for Research in Mathematics Education* 11 (1980): 225–234. The authors show that college students with high general intellectual ability did better when they studied a math unit through an expository approach, whereas students with lower general intellectual ability learned better in a discovery setting.

Meyers, M.J. "The significance of learning modalities, modes of instruction, and verbal feedback for learning to recognize written words," *Learning Disabilities Quarterly* 3(3) (1980): 62–69. This article provides an extremely careful description of the operational definitions of the various research variables.

Mohr, K.G., Wyse, B.W., and Hansen, R.G. "Aiding consumer nutrition decisions: Comparison of a graphical nutrient density labeling format with the current food labeling system," *Home Economics Research Journal* 8 (1980): 162–172. this article uses level of education and family income as moderator variables in determining the effectiveness of a new labeling format for providing nutritional information on commercial food products.

Peterson, P.J., Janicki, T.C., and Swing, S.R. "Aptitude-treatment interaction effects of three social studies teaching approaches," *American Educational Research Journal* 17 (1980): 339–360. This study examines how students possessing different characteristics reacted differently to three separate strategies for teaching a social studies unit. The authors end the article by explaining why they think the moderator variables worked the way they did.

Richardson, E., DiBenedetto, B., Christ, A., and Press, M. "Relationship of auditory and visual skills to reading retardation," *Journal of Learning Disabilities* 13 (1980): 77–82. These authors use low reading ability as a control variable and state specific reasons for doing so.

Stevens, K. "The effect of topic interest on the reading comprehension of higher ability students," *Journal of Educational Research* 73 (1980): 365–368. This author introduces reading ability as a moderator variable to determine whether interest level is more important to readers at different levels of ability.

Wheeler, J. Ford, A., Nietupski, J., Loomis, R., and Brown, L. "Teaching moderately and severely handicapped adolescents to shop in supermarkets using pocket calculators," *Education and Training of the Mentally Retarded* 15 (1980): 105–112. This article contains a precise and clearly stated operational definition of the dependent and the independent variables.

Yarborough, B.H., and Johnson, R.A. "Research that questions the traditional elementary school marking system," *Phi Delta Kappan* 61 (April 1980): 527–528. This study reports that high-IQ students who received traditional grades during their elementary school years had more positive feelings toward self, peers, and school upon entering junior high school than those who received no marks. Among low-IQ students, however, those who received no marks scored higher. This interaction appeared on affective, but not cognitive, dependent variables.

15 Theoretical Research in Education

Chapter Preview

The focus in previous chapters has been on useful strategies for dealing with concrete, practical problems that educators are likely to encounter in performing their professional responsibilities. At times it is helpful to focus less on applied issues and more on theoretical issues. For example, in addition to knowing that discovery learning works, we might want to know *why* it works. The present chapter will discuss the basic strategies of theoretical research in education. The emphasis will be on helping you develop an understanding of the processes and an ability to interpret and to evaluate the theoretical research performed by others rather than on helping you prepare to do theoretical research yourself. The chapter will discuss ways in which theoretical and applied research are similar and how the methodologies discussed throughout this text provide a necessary foundation upon which theoretical research must be built if it is to be successful.

After reading this chapter you should be able to

- Describe the similarities and differences between theoretical and applied research.
- Describe strategies for identifying the intervening variables that are responsible for educational outcomes.
- Describe how the methodologies of applied research can be integrated into the process of theoretical research.

THE UNDERLYING PRINCIPLES BEHIND EDUCATIONAL OUTCOMES

Often it is important not only to know whether or not a particular treatment works, but also to know what underlying principle is at work to produce the observed outcome. In other words, we may be interested in knowing not only what outcomes are occurring (Level I research), what is causing those outcomes to occur (Level II), and whether the same events would cause the same outcomes in a different situation

(Level III), but also whether there are underlying principles that can be generalized to other treatments and to other outcomes. The search for such underlying principles is the essence of Level IV research.

The discussion of this type of research has been reserved to last, not because it is unimportant but for two reasons. First, the lower levels of research receive a priority in terms of how much time in-service educators can actually devote to research. Second, the other types of research are necessary prerequisites to successful higher level reseach. Higher level research is built upon sound foundations of lower level research.

It is important to stress that the fact that in-service educators often have little time for Level IV research does not mean that they should be unconcerned about such research. That suggestion would be an insult to professional educators. Just as we assume that physicians and surgeons are interested in the theoretical aspects of medical science and that engineers are interested in current scientific developments, it is safe to assume that educators are interested in the theoretical aspects and current developments in scientific fields related to education. While we do not assume that every physician is capable of performing a detailed chemical analysis that will lead to a new discovery or that every engineer can function as an abstract scientist, we do anticipate that most doctors and engineers spend some time thinking about such theoretical issues. We also presume that they are capable of reading and understanding the information provided to them by the theoretical researchers who are examining problems related to their fields of professional interest. It seems equally

appropriate to expect that professional educators will spend some time in theoretical speculations regarding the principles involved in their daily work. An emphasis on the practical should not prohibit attention to the theoretical aspects of our work.

How is theoretical research conducted? What does it mean to say that high level research builds upon lower level research? How does a person who is actively engaged in solving practical, concrete, daily problems find time to develop a simultaneous interest in abstract questions? Let me answer some of these questions by giving you an example from my own teaching experience.

Recently in a course I was teaching I tried a different way to teach a very difficult concept. I keep many of the tests I give to the students, and so I was able to use a cohort design to evaluate my new method. I usually asked three questions on the final exam dealing with this particular topic. By looking at my previous tests, I knew that in the past the students had consistently averaged between 70% and 75% correct on these questions. This had disturbed me, because on most concepts the students (who were dedicated people taking the course on a mastery basis) average in the range of 85% to 95% correct. After I tried my new way of teaching this concept, I continued to insert three perviously used items on that concept on the final exam. I discovered that the scores on these items jumped the next three semesters to 90%, 88%, and 90%. I was impressed. I had evaluated my new instructional method with a fairly sound research design and had pretty well proved to myself that this new method worked. In my elation, I even contacted a colleague who taught a similar course, and she tried the same approach and found it successful in her course too. I was impressed again, since I was now moving toward external as well as internal validity.

In a certain sense, it did not matter *why* this new method worked; all that really mattered was that it *did* work. Even if we could never figure out why the results came out the way they did, both my colleague and I intended to keep using this new method, because we had good evidence that it caused our students to master an important concept more effectively. But in another sense, it *did* matter why this new method worked the way it did. If I could find out what underlying principle was at work in making this new method produce its desirable outcome, I could apply that same principle to other appropriate instructional situations.

In identifying this underlying principle, I did not have to start from scratch or guess blindly in the dark. After all, when I had chosen my new method, I had made this choice for a reason. I had chosen the new method because I felt that the traditional way of teaching the concept had involved terminology that the students were likely to find confusing because they had used similar terminology in defining similar but distinct concepts. Therefore, I had decided to avoid the traditional terminology and had invented some new terms, which were not confusing because the students associated these terms with nothing at all. In using the new terms the students were able to examine the concept without confusion, and this enabled them to understand and apply it more easily.

In developing the new method, I had derived ideas from the concept that educational psychologists refer to as *proactive inhibition*. This concept refers to the fact that concepts we learn earlier are likely to interfere with our future attempt to learn concepts that are in any way similar to the earlier learning. My belief was that I could minimize proactive inhibition by using terms that did not remind students of earlier, unrelated concepts. When the new approach worked, therefore, I naturally took this as a verification of my belief that using terms that did not remind students of unrelated concepts reduced proactive inhibition and thereby enhanced learning of the new concept.

Had I really, at this point, proven that my theory was correct? Had I proven that this underlying principle had actually been at work in causing the beneficial outcomes that followed my new method? No, at this point, my proof regarding the underlying principle was actually quite weak—even though my proof regarding the success of the new method itself was very strong. My proof was weak because there were several other factors that could have caused the beneficial outcome. For example, maybe my new terms were more precise and descriptive than the traditional terms, and therefore the principle at work would be that more precise and descriptive terms lead more effectively to learning than terms that are not as precise and descriptive. Or perhaps when the traditional terms are taken away from teachers, they are forced to become more creative; and perhaps it was this increase in creativity on the part of my colleague and myself (rather than a decrease in proactive inhibition) that led to the improved performance of the students. These and similar alternative explanations could not be ruled out on the basis of this one experiment.

At this point my curiosity was temporarily satisfied. I knew my new method worked, and I had a suspicion that I knew what caused it to work. At the same time I was aware that I had not really provided solid evidence that it was this underlying principle that had been responsible for my improved outcomes. I was actually very interested in knowing whether I had successfully circumvented proactive inhibition; but I had important, practical things on my mind, such as teaching the next unit in that class and performing the rest of my teaching responsibilities. Therefore, I was able to devote no more time to the theoretical aspects of this problem. However, even though I had to put it out of my mind, I knew that a good way to pursue the issue further would be to replicate the process by trying to apply the same method to a new concept. I kept this in mind, and I looked for other situations in which I could apply the principle. Eventually, I did find other situations, and I discovered that the principle worked again. Such replications strengthened my belief that my principle was based on accurate generalizations. I have continued to pursue this issue, always on an informal basis while carrying out my professional responsibilities. In fact, in developing many of the concepts in this textbook, I have applied this principle by breaking with traditional approaches to a topic and using terminology that is less likely to invoke proactive inhibition among my readers.

If a researcher wanted to devote a greater portion of her life to examining the theory that proactive inhibition can be reduced by using terminology that does not remind students of unrelated concepts, what else could she do? There are two important steps that she could follow: (1) she could identify additional settings in which the principle should operate and then set up experiments to see if this hypothesis would be confirmed in these additional settings; and (2) she could draw up an exhaustive list of other plausible explanations of the outcomes and set up additional experiments to test these alternate explanations. She should set up these additional experiments in such a way that if her theory is correct, one result will occur; whereas if the alternative explanation is correct, then a different result will occur.

For example, I suggested earlier that perhaps my new terms were more precise and descriptive than the traditional terms and that it may have been this difference rather than the reduction of proactive inhibition that caused the improved learning. The researcher could check this possibility by setting up a situation in which the experimental group received the terms that reduced proactive inhibition but the control group received terms that were more precise and descriptive. If the experimental group still surpassed the control group under these circumstances, this would indicate that the alternative explanation was less plausible than the proactive inhibition theory. Such results would strengthen the theory.

Likewise, I suggested that the removal of the traditional terms might have forced the teachers to be more creative and that it might have been this increased creativity rather than the reduction of proactive inhibition that caused the improved learning. The researcher could check this possibility by giving an experimental teacher the new terms and a control teacher some placebo terms. If both sets of terms would arouse equal amounts of creativity (and she could check this through some system of observation) and if the experimental group still surpassed the control group in performance, then this would indicate that this alternative explanation was not as plausible as the proactive inhibition theory. This would further strengthen the hypothesis.

If the researcher could come up with a comprehensive list of alternative explanations and rule each of these out, and if she could apply the principle in a wide variety of situations with the expected outcomes, the theory would gain strength. Quite likely, she would not meet with unmitigated success in each test of the hypothesis. Occasionally she would find discrepant results. If she found enough discrepant results, she would abandon the theory. However, another very strong possibility is that when she encountered results which contradicted the theory, she would modify it rather than abandon it. For example, she might find that the principle works well when applied to abstract concepts but fails miserably when applied to concrete concepts. She would then change the theory to state that the use of terms that do not remind learners of unrelated concepts will minimize proactive inhibition and enhance the learning of abstract concepts. A lengthy series of tests of this theory would undoubtedly lead to a large number of revisions, and such revisions would make the theory more precise and resistant to subsequent refutation.

In this process of theory verification, she would not have to work alone. The theory is likely to be of interest to other professionals. Somebody else has undoubtedly done research at least indirectly relating to the topic, and she can find the results of such research by consulting appropriate library references. She could also publish the results of her own research. This would subject the theory to the professional scrutiny of her peers. Such publication might arouse considerable interest, and one result might be that ten or twenty others would test some of the alternative hypotheses or replicate the study in varying settings. The exchange of information resulting from such publication could spread valuable information to interested professionals and speed up the process of theory refinement by enlisting the aid of more researchers.

As the next section will show, whenever we pursue theoretical questions in the systematic manner described in this example, we are engaging in what can be called the science of educational research.

THE SCIENCE OF EDUCATIONAL RESEARCH

A dictionary will define science as a branch of study concerned with deriving verifiable general laws through the process of induction and hypothesis testing. A major thrust of this textbook has been to convince you that educational research is not *just* a science in this pure sense. It is also a very useful tool for identifying outcomes, establishing cause and effect relationships, and improving the quality of generalizations.

The statement that educational research is more than a science should not be interpreted as a denial that educational research can often be a scientific endeavor. As the previous section of this chapter has shown, there are many instances when educational research should be viewed as a science, even when science is defined in its purest sense. The attempt to identify verifiable general laws through the process of induction and hypothesis testing is an important part of the educational research process.

Science is not a quest for certainty. It is rather a process of seeking guidelines that enable us to make increasingly broad and accurate generalizations about the phenomena with which we are concerned. In logical parlance, there is a distinction between deductive and inductive reasoning. Deductive logic starts from a broad generalization and enables us to draw accurate conclusions about specific instances. If the broad generalizations are accurate, then properly applied deductive reasoning will provide accurate conclusions. Inductive logic, on the other hand, starts from specific instances and attempts to draw broad generalizations from these specific instances. The inductive process has the advantage over the deductive process of enabling knowledge to expand; we can derive new generalizations that are more comprehensive than our original generalizations. However, inductive logic has the disadvantage of losing the guarantee of accuracy that accompanied deductive reasoning. Since science attempts to derive *new* laws and generalizations and to expand our knowledge of a certain field, it relies heavily upon inductive logic. This reliance upon inductive logic provides the basis for the statement that science is not a quest for certainty. Certitude is an impossible goal for science, but by following appropriate guidelines we can substantially reduce the amount of uncertainty in our field of knowledge.

When educational researchers behave as scientists by pursuing increasingly broader generalizations and principles, they are faced with this same obstacle of incertitude that other scientists confront. This should not dissuade us from entering upon scientific research; rather it should make us aware of the limitations of educational research and emphasize the importance of doing as much as possible to reduce uncertainty. To return to the example from the previous section—no matter how hard she works at it, the researcher will never be certain that the theory is correct. There will always be the possibility that someone will think of another loophole and that a test of this alternative hypothesis will show that the theory is in some way lacking. This does not mean that the attempts at verification are futile; quite the contrary, they make the theory increasingly valuable. What this means is that a healthy skepticism is just as important in educational research as in any other science. Healthy skepticism does not imply contempt.

One of the most popular and comprehensive descriptions of how scientists successfully derive verifiable laws and generalizations has been provided by John Dewey, who identified the following steps in the scientific process:

1. *Identification of a problem.* At this first step, the problem is often vague and loosely defined. For example, the scientist might wonder, "Why do some children remember things longer than others?"
2. *Formulation of a hypothesis.* This is a conjectural statement that provides a solution to the problem. It is based on the scientist's insights into the problem. These insights are based on such processes as personal experience, reading, and thinking. For example, the scientist might hypothesize; "Children will

remember things longer if they organize the information themselves through discovery learning than if they receive the information in pre-organized form from the teacher."

3. *Reasoning and deduction.* The scientist analyzes the hypothesis and determines what observable events will follow as consequences if the hypothesis is correct. Usually, there are many observable phenomena that can be deduced from a single hypothesis. For example, the scientist might reason to the following deduction: "When high school students use computer simulations to learn about the principles of biology, they can either be informed about a principle ahead of time and use the simulation as an example clarifying the principle, or they can perform the simulation without any prior explanation and discover the principle for themselves. If the hypothesis is correct, students who follow the second approach should do better on test questions related to the principle six months later than those who followed the first approach."

4. *Verification, modification, or rejection of the hypothesis* by observing the results of an experiment set up to see if the predicted consequences actually do follow. For example, the scientist might assemble an experimental and control group, give one the discovery-oriented approach described above and the other the teacher-centered approach, and then see if the results verify the prediction that the discovery-oriented group will do better on a test six months later.

Steps 3 and 4 are performed repeatedly. If a prediction based on the hypothesis formulated at Step 2 is verified, this is taken as an indication that the hypothesis is a valid answer to the problem identified at Step 1. If a prediction based on the hypothesis is not confirmed by the results of the experiment, this is taken as an indication that either the prediction was based on an unsound deduction, the hypothesis needs to be modified, or the hypothesis needs to be rejected completely. Each time the scientist completes Step 4, it is necessary to return to one of the earlier steps. The exact reaction will depend on what the outcome was at Step 4. If the results supported the hypothesis by confirming the prediction, then the researcher will probably go to Step 3 and generate another prediction. If the results were contradictory to the prediction, then the researcher might return to Step 2 and modify the hypothesis before returning to Steps 3 and 4. If the results were so contradictory as to refute the entire hypothesis, then the scientist might return to Step 1, try to clarify the problem further, and eventually state a new hypothesis. By appropriately repeating the various steps in this process, the scientist is able to develop a useful theory that will serve as a solution to the problem.

Dewey's scientific method is not the only explanation of how scientists advance scientific knowledge. However, it has in common with the other explanations the emphasis on using objective, factual data in a hypothetical-deductive fashion to make inferences. Readers interested in additional aspects of scientific theory and its relationship to educational research should consult the references in the Annotated Bibliography at the end of this chapter.

THE RELATIONSHIP BETWEEN THEORETICAL AND APPLIED RESEARCH

The main difference between theoretical research and the more practical or applied research described throughout the earlier chapters lies in the fact that theoretical research focuses primarily on the intervening variable. It is important to note that

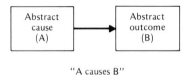

"A causes B"

FIGURE **15–1.** The Abstract Hypothesis Is Describing the Theoretical Relationship at Step 2 of the Scientific Method.

except for this focus, the methodologies employed at the different levels are quite similar. In fact, theoretical research is correctly viewed as an extension of the nontheoretical levels. Theoretical research must build upon the successful implementation of these applied levels in order to produce useful theoretical results. The kinship between theoretical research and the more applied levels can be seen in Figures 15–1 through 15–3.

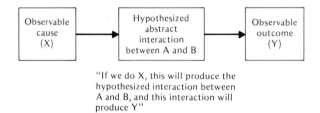

"If we do X, this will produce the hypothesized interaction between A and B, and this interaction will produce Y"

FIGURE **15–2.** The Deduced Prediction from Step 3 of the Scientific Method. (The components of Figure 15–1 have compressed into the middle box of this diagram.)

Figure 15–1 diagrams the statement of the theoretical hypothesis. This relationship is stated at Step 2 as the scientist pursues Dewey's scientific method. Figure 15–2 shows what happens to this abstract hypothesis when the scientist proceeds to Step 3 of the scientific method. At this step, the scientist asserts that if the hypothesis is correct, then a certain observable event will lead to a certain observable outcome. (The scientist has to resort to observable events and outcomes in this prediction; otherwise the prediction would merely be another unverifiable hypothesis.) What the prediction at Step 3 really states, therefore, is that a certain observable cause will produce the hypothesized interaction between the abstract cause and the abstract effect, and this interaction will in turn produce a specified observable outcome.

The interaction diagrammed in Figure 15–2 is really just another way of saying that the observable cause in the prediction is an independent variable which leads to an intervening variable (the interaction between the abstract cause and the abstract effect), and this intervening variable in turn leads to a dependent variable (which is really an operational definition of the abstract dependent variable). Figure 15–3 is a restatement of Figure 15–2 with the appropriate terms from the previous sentence inserted in the appropriate places. The diagram presented in Figure 15–3 is very similar to those we are already familiar with from the previous chapter. Once the research hypothesis is stated in these operational terms, it is tested by exactly the same procedures that are used to test the hypothesis described in the previous chapter.

Thus, one of the major ways in which theoretical research differs from applied

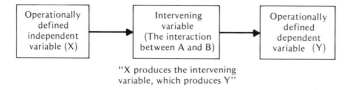

FIGURE **15–3.** The Relationship from Figure 15–2 Stated in Terms of Independent, Intervening, and Dependent Variables.

research is that the theoretical researcher must spend a large amount of time setting up the operationally defined hypothesis in Figure 15–2 in such a way as to make sure that it really is a prediction based on the abstract hypothesis of interest. Once this operationally stated hypothesis has been formulated, the methodologies employed by the theoretical researcher to verify or reject this hypothesis are exactly the same as those employed by nontheoretical researchers. A second difference between theoretical and applied research arises from the setting in which the hypothesis must be tested. In order to provide the most efficient and useful information relevant to the theoretical hypothesis, the prediction that emerges from Step 3 of the scientific method should be stated in such a way that insofar as possible the theoretical hypothesis *and only the theoretical hypothesis* will be able to explain the results obtained from the experiment. To accomplish this, the experimental setting has to be very carefully structured to isolate this one intervening variable. The difficulty or artificiality involved in careful structuring often makes practical researchers shy away from theoretical endeavors. Once such settings are set up, however, the procedures to carry out the experiment and to evaluate its outcomes are the same as those described in the earlier chapters of this book.

Applied research is undertaken to solve specific problems. Applied research enables us to find out what is happening in our educational settings, to find out what is causing these outcomes, and to find out how far such findings can be generalized. Applied research is not *per se* incompatible with theoretical research. In many cases applied researchers can help solve theoretical questions, and in many cases theoretical researchers can help solve practical problems. Such mutual helpfulness depends on planning and communication. A knowledge of the scientific processes involved in theoretical research will enable us to contribute more effectively to this process of planning and communication.

This textbook is written primarily for educators who are actively engaged in such processes as teaching, counseling, and administering educational programs. Because of this orientation, the text has focused on the practical and applied types of research that are most likely to be helpful to the readers in this audience. The present chapter has provided a brief introduction to how theoretical, nonapplied research is conducted. To a certain extent you may be able to do some of this theoretical research while you pursue more practical concerns. Readers who will need to do a great deal of theoretical research will almost certainly wish to acquire more information about the processes of theoretical research than is contained in this text. For example, most doctoral students take courses that deal with the philosophy of science and with the logical and statistical analysis of psychological constructs, and such courses would enable them to develop skills in those areas of theoretical research that do not overlap with the methodologies used in more applied research discussed in this textbook.

Although theoretical research has been treated only briefly and incompletely, the topic will be pursued no further in the present text. This brief introduction will enable you to do theoretical research on a minimal basis. In addition (and probably more importantly), this introduction will enable you to understand and formulate evaluations of the theoretical research that you will read as a professional educator. It should be obvious that much of the thinking you do requires focusing on abstract theories. This is often true even when you are neither reading research nor explicitly devoting your time to a research project. An understanding of how theoretical research works and an ability to focus the principles discussed in this text on theoretical problems will enable you to think more carefully and clearly about theoretical issues. Many thinkers and philosophers have defined science as organized common sense. To the extent that this is an accurate definition, an improved ability as a scientific thinker will make you a better thinker.

PUTTING IT ALL TOGETHER

In addition to being a practical man, Eugene Anderson prided himself on being a philosopher of sorts. He did not drink hemlock juice or suffer from existential *angst*, but he did like to speculate about such issues as why people act they way they do, what is meant by morality, and what it really means to be a humane person. Combining his educational vocation with his philosophical avocation, he wondered why some people are humane toward animals and others are hostile. He wondered why his Animal Life Program (ALP) worked with some children and not with others. He wondered what it was that made some programs work while others failed.

Mr. Anderson worked with organizations that wanted to imbue an appreciation of animal life in the American population. These organizations worked by promoting a love of animals in their programs. From his early work with his Fireman Tests, Mr. Anderson wondered if his colleagues might be barking up the wrong tree. He had noticed that about 25% of the children who took his tests chose to save no animals whatsoever. In their explanations for their choices, these children indicated no animosity toward animals. Rather, they simply ignored animals and chose material objects because the objects had monetary value. Moreover, he had noticed that he could predict with almost 100% accuracy that if a child chose a wallet, a credit card, or color television as his or her first choice, that child would *not* choose an animal for the second or third choice. Based on this information, Mr. Anderson had a hunch that it might make more sense to focus on fighting materialism than on trying to make children love animals.

Note that Mr. Anderson's hunch was based on very weak evidence. He had merely noticed an apparent correlation between choosing things with monetary value and rejecting animals. Such a correlation does not necessarily indicate a causal relationship. In addition, he has a poorly defined concept—materialism—which would have to be operationally defined before he could strengthen his conclusions. Mr. Anderson was aware of these shortcomings, but he still enjoyed his speculations.

The primary focus of Mr. Anderson's theoretical speculations was the question, "What was it that caused some programs to work while others failed?" The first programs he had evaluated had not succeeded in changing attitudes toward animal life. In discouragement, he had gone through the psychological literature on attitude change research and had discovered that an important principle was that attitudes were more likely to change if the participants in a program felt some sort of dissonance within their value systems. Applied to elementary school children, this meant that if children felt that they were basically decent and kind people, and could be convinced that some behaviors they engaged in were incompatible with this perception of themselves, then they would change these behaviors to bring them in accord with the image they wanted to have of themselves. When he developed the ALP, therefore, he designed the program in such a way that the early part of the program focused on creating this dissonance and the latter part of the program showed the children how to overcome the dissonance. When the ALP worked on repeated occasions, Mr. Anderson took this as evidence that this theory of induced dissonance was accurate. (Mr. Anderson's colleagues felt that he took delight in uttering the words "induced dissonance." Perhaps one of the rewards of seeing a theory work is being allowed to attach a name to it.)

The practical nature of Mr. Anderson's job prohibited him from exploring this theoretical question through additional research of his own. However, he took the liberty of sending a copy of his results to one of the leading researchers on attitude change research, and that author had responded by sending Mr. Anderson some additional information, which he found to be very helpful. Mr. Anderson made it a point to read each issue of the *Journal of Personality and Social Psychology*, for he found that this journal published high quality research that occasionally touched upon ideas of particular interest that could be incorporated into his humane education programs. In addition, he frequently consulted *Psychological Abstracts* to see what new ideas were published on topics of interest to him. Mr. Anderson discovered that whenever he integrated these new ideas into his ALP, the results seemed to improve.

Although Mr. Anderson was not doing a great deal of theoretical research of his own, he had become an intelligent consumer of such basic research. He had become successful at understanding theoretical research and had become adept at taking ideas from such theoretical research as a basis for shaping his applied research. Although he rarely isolated and manipulated the intervening variable, he let his awareness of the intervening variable generate new hypotheses and new operational definitions that led him to more successful results in his applied endeavors.

SUMMARY

Theoretical research focuses on the underlying causes behind the observed outcomes in an experiment. Although many educators do not have a great deal of time to spend performing research of a purely theoretical nature, it is important that educators become intelligent consumers of basic research. An educator who can understand theoretical research can use the findings of such research as an important source of ideas to attack the many practical problems that occur at the more applied levels of research.

Theoretical research focuses on the intervening variable. In addition, such research must often take place in a more artificial setting than applied research. Aside from these differences in focus and setting, however, theoretical research depends on the same methodologies as applied research. In fact, theoretical research can come to accurate conclusions only to the extent that it incorporates the strategies discussed in the earlier chapters to provide good internal and external validity. By applying what you have learned about educational research from the previous chapters to a critical reading of theoretical research, you can draw information more effectively from such research in order to find answers to the problems you need to solve.

Annotated Bibliography

AGNEW, N.M. and PYKE, S.W. *The Science Game: An Introduction to Research in the Behavioral Sciences*. 2nd ed. Englewood Cliffs, N.J.: Prentice-Hall, 1978. The first two chapters provide a novel and insightful approach to applying scientific methodology to behavioral sciences.

ANDERSON, B.F. *The Psychology Experiment*. 2nd ed. Belmont, Cal.: Brooks/Cole, 1971. The second chapter provides a very good introduction to the scientific method and the rules of science as they relate to the psychology experiment.

COOK, T.D. and CAMPBELL, D.T. *Quasi-Experimentation: Design and Analysis Issues for Field Settings*. Chicago: Rand McNally, 1979. A major portion of the first chapter deals with the concept of causality in scientific research.

KERLINGER, F.N. *Foundations of Behavioral Research*. 2nd ed. New York: Holt, Rinehart and Winston, 1973. The first chapter provides excellent insights into science and the scientific approach as it applies to research in the behavioral sciences.

Professional Journals

The following articles deal with theoretical research in education and in fields closely related to education.

CROSBY, F., BROMLEY, S., and SAXE, L. "Recent unobtrusive studies of black and white discrimination and prejudice: A literature review," *Psychological Bulletin* 87 (1980): 546–563. The authors compare the results of studies using unobtrusive measurement techniques (discussed in chapter 5) with the results of those studies using more obtrusive strategies. They then use the results of their analysis to examine the validity of three theoretical models of social attitudes and racial prejudice.

DANIEL, T.L., and ESSER, J.K. "Intrinsic motivation as influenced by rewards, task interest, and task structure," *Journal of Applied Psychology* 65 (1980): 566–573. The authors discovered that extrinsic rewards *lowered* intrinsic motivation when the task was one of high interest, but not when the task was of low interest. In addition, they found that extrinsic rewards tended to *increase* intrinsic motivation when the task was highly structured, but not when the task was more unstructured.

DAVIS, J.K., and RAND, D.C. "Self-grading versus instructor grading," *Journal of Educational Research* 73 (1980): 207–211. The authors start their article by reporting the results of someone else's research project and suggesting an alternative intervening variable. Then they set up their own research prediction and run their own study to see if their explanation is any better than the original.

16 Research Tools: The Library

Chapter Preview

It is not necessary (or advisable) to rely solely on our own skills and insights when we seek solutions to a research problem. Whatever problem we are interested in, someone else has probably dealt with one in some way similar to ours. We should bring such information to bear on our own problems so that we can benefit from the experience of others. A very large amount of the information in libraries can be helpful to us, if only we know how to find it. This chapter introduces many of the tools for researchers that can be found in libraries. An increasingly large number of services are becoming available in libraries throughout the country. By using these services effectively we can locate comprehensive sources of information that will enable us to deal effectively with our research problems.

After you read this chapter you should be able to:

- Identify the types of information that can be obtained from each of the following indexing and abstracting services:
  - *Current Index to Journals in Education.*
  - *Research in Education.*
  - *Psychological Abstracts.*
  - *Education Index.*
  - *Readers Guide to Periodical Literature.*
  - *Social Science Citation Index.*
- Use the above sources to locate a specific piece of information.
- Identify the types of information that can be obtained from journals, reviews, and books.
- Describe effective strategies for conducting a review of the literature on a specific problem.

USING THE LIBRARY TO SOLVE RESEARCH PROBLEMS

Every reader of this book has used the library, but most readers have not used it as effectively as they could. The library can be a valuable tool to help us solve educational problems. The value of the library is obvious for term papers and for formal research projects. Where else would we find enough citations to fill the required four to six pages? However, this is a very narrow perception of the role of the library in educational research. A more appropriate perception is to consider the library an important tool to help us keep abreast of what is going on in our field and to help us solve specific problems when they arise.

The resources of the library can be helpful even when we are doing something very informal, such as trying to devise a better way to measure attitudes toward music or looking for a better way to teach Johnny to divide by two-digit numbers. The library can be equally helpful when we are doing something very formal, such as writing a dissertation or preparing an article for professional publication in a national journal. In either case, our goal should be to use the library as a useful tool to help us clarify and solve our problem.

The following sections of this chapter will describe specific resources available in many libraries. The familiarity of readers with these different resources will vary considerably. In some cases you may already be aware of a resource and may use it frequently and successfully. In other cases you may be completely unfamiliar with a resource. Your goal should be to become aware of what is available and to know how to use each of these resources to help you solve the problems they are designed to solve.

When educators have a piece of information that they want to share with their colleagues, they often make this information available in professional journals or at professional meetings and conventions. Likewise, educators write down important pieces of information in the reports they submit to supervisors and to funding agencies. It would often be useful to have access to such information, and this chapter will describe the indexing and retrieval services that enable us to locate such information, whether it is distributed through a formal or an informal channel.

ERIC

The Educational Resources Information Center (ERIC) is a national information system comprised of clearing houses spread throughout the country. Each clearing house focuses on a specific area of educational interest, such as counseling or special education. The ERIC clearing houses collect documents that contain information relevant to their areas of interest. The specific clearing houses vary widely in the unique services they offer, and the easiest way to find out what is available in your area of interest is to contact the clearing houses that you think may provide information useful to your professional interests. A listing of the clearing houses and their mailing addresses can be found in many ERIC publications, including the two discussed in the following paragraphs.

The *Current Index to Journals in Education (CIJE)* is an ERIC publication that attempts to keep abreast of what is published in the many journals directly or indirectly related to education. *CIJE* is a published monthly, and a cumulative index is made available at the end of each six months. It publishes complete citations and brief abstracts for as many as possible of the thousands of articles on educational topics that are published each year. By examining the abstract, we can find out what the article is about; and if we are interested enough to want to know more, the citation tells us the exact page numbers in a specific journal where we can read the entire article.

To use *CIJE* we would start by referring to the index section. This might be the index of a monthly issue or the annual cumulative index. If we were starting our search with a specific topic in mind, we would begin by going to the subject index. To take a specific example, let us assume we are looking for information on how to teach moral values to emotionally disturbed children. We might begin by getting out the most recent cumulative index and looking under the subject headings of either "Emotionally Disturbed Children" or "Moral Values." If we entered the January–June 1979 *CIJE* Cumulative Index under the subject heading "Emotionally Disturbed Children," we would find 17 articles listed on page 672. One of these is listed as follows:

Television's Impact on Emotionally Disturbed Children's Value System. *Child Study Journal*. V. 8 n 3 p 187–202 1978
EJ 192 901

The references to EJ 192 901 tells us to look in the Main Entry Section where that number appears in sequence. There we would find the entry as follows:

EJ 192 901   PS 507 193
Television's Impact on Emotionally Disturbed Children's Value Systems. Donohue, Thomas R. *Child Study Journal;* v8 n3 p187-202 1978 (Reprint: UMI)
Descriptors: Elementary School Students; *Emotionally Disturbed Children; Identification (Psychological); *Modeling (Psychological); *Moral Values; Socialization; *Television Viewing

This investigation studied the influences of television's behavioral models on institutionalized, emotionally disturbed children between the ages of 6 and 11. Investigated were children's perceptions and judgments of right and wrong, appropriate and inappropriate behaviors. (SE)

FIGURE **16–1.**   An Entry from the Current Index to *Journals in Education (CIJE)*.

The first part of this entry tells us where to find the article, if we would want to pursue it further. In addition to being available in the *Child Study Journal*, the information in parentheses tells us that this article is also available as a reprint from University Microfilms. Next, there follows a list of descriptors. A descriptor is a heading under which an article is listed in the subject index. This information, which at first might sound superfluous, is often very helpful. By knowing what descriptors could be applied to the article we are currently examining, we can find out where similar articles are also likely to be found. For example, in this case, we know that "Modeling (Psychological)" is a descriptor that could apply to this article, and so we might want to look under that descriptor in the subject index to see if there are any other articles there that might be of interest to us. All the descriptors listed at this point are pertinent to the article in question, but the article was actually indexed only under the descriptors marked by an asterisk. Therefore, we would have found this article indexed under "Emotionally Disturbed Children," "Modeling (Psychological)," "Moral Values," and "Television Viewing." Finally, the abstract describes the contents of the article. By reading this abstract we can make a decision regarding whether or not we want to pursue the article any further. The initials in parentheses at the end of the abstract indicate who wrote the abstract. If the abstract would have been written by the author, it would say so at this point. In this case, the abstract was written by one of ERIC's professional reviewers.

Rather than merely plunging into *CIJE* to begin our search, we could be a bit more systematic by referring first to the *Thesaurus of ERIC Descriptors*. By looking in this book we can find out what descriptors are actually used in *CIJE*. Moreover, we can find related terms, broader terms, and more specific terms, which would enable us to make our search more efficient and thorough. In addition, the Thesaurus shows how many entries have been indexed under any descriptor in *RIE* and in *CIJE*, and this information can be helpful in determining how many citations we would be likely to get by looking under that descriptor.

Another important service offered by ERIC can be found in *Research in Education*. This publication performs a service similar to *CIJE*, but it focuses on non-journal sources of information. For example, doctoral dissertations and reports on government funded projects do not automatically get published in journals. These sources of information are often cited in *RIE*. Such a report or dissertation may, of course, later be converted to a journal article and subsequently be indexed in *CIJE*; but in such cases the information will be available much sooner through *RIE*. A sample entry from *RIE* is shown in Figure 16–2.

Most of the information contained in an *RIE* entry is either identical to that provided by a CIJE entry or is self-explanatory. A unique feature of the *RIE* entry is the EDRS price. This indicates how much it would cost to buy the document if you would wish to do so. In the example, the document can be purchased in microfiche for 83 cents or in hardcopy for $1.67 plus postage. Instructions on how to order such documents can be found in the ERIC volume in which you found the entry. Many libraries that subscribe to *RIE* also purchase all the accompanying microfiches, and in such cases you can find the document by locating the microfiche in an appropriate file drawer and reading it on a microfiche card reader.

In most cases, researchers using *CIJE* or *RIE* will use the subject index to locate an article or research report. However, it is also possible to locate information by using the author index. In fact, since there are likely to be fewer entries under the name of an author than under any given subject heading, it is easier to use the author index whenever the name of the author of the report is known. The author index is used in the same way as the subject index. Since many authors tend to find an area of interest and continue working in that area, it is often a good idea to look in the author index to find additional articles or reports by the same person who wrote a report that you found to be helpful.

ERIC can be searched by computer. Let us return to our *CIJE* example for a moment. In the January–June 1979 Cumulative Index there were 17 entries under "Emotionally Disturbed Children" and 15 entries under "Moral Values." Would it not be convenient to have immediate information about the articles that were indexed under both of these descriptors? This is exactly what the computer can do for us. Even better—the computer can do this for several years, and it can search *CIJE* and

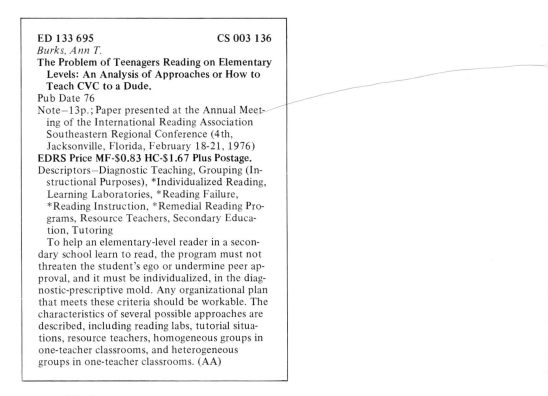

ED 133 695   CS 003 136
Burks, Ann T.
The Problem of Teenagers Reading on Elementary
    Levels: An Analysis of Approaches or How to
    Teach CVC to a Dude.
Pub Date 76
Note—13p.; Paper presented at the Annual Meet-
    ing of the International Reading Association
    Southeastern Regional Conference (4th,
    Jacksonville, Florida, February 18-21, 1976)
EDRS Price MF-$0.83 HC-$1.67 Plus Postage.
Descriptors—Diagnostic Teaching, Grouping (In-
    structional Purposes), *Individualized Reading,
    Learning Laboratories, *Reading Failure,
    *Reading Instruction, *Remedial Reading Pro-
    grams, Resource Teachers, Secondary Educa-
    tion, Tutoring
To help an elementary-level reader in a secon-
    dary school learn to read, the program must not
    threaten the student's ego or undermine peer ap-
    proval, and it must be individualized, in the diag-
    nostic-prescriptive mold. Any organizational plan
    that meets these criteria should be workable. The
    characteristics of several possible approaches are
    described, including reading labs, tutorial situa-
    tions, resource teachers, homogeneous groups in
    one-teacher classrooms, and heterogeneous
    groups in one-teacher classrooms. (AA)

FIGURE 16–2.   An Entry from *Research in Education (RIE).*

RIE for us simultaneously. In addition, we could add more descriptors to narrow our search even further. By doing a computer search of ERIC, therefore, we can obtain a set of abstracts that zero in precisely on what we are interested in. After reading the abstracts we may wish to choose for closer perusal the five or ten that would be of paramount interest to us.

Computer searches are performed from terminals located in the library, which are connected by telephone line to a large computer on which the citations and abstracts are stored. While it is theoretically possible for an individual researcher to do the search by himself or herself, this usually does not happen. Rather, a specialist who works for the library and has had training and practice in performing such searches is likely to do the actual search. Your role is to supply this specialist with the information needed to make an efficient and thorough search. Such preparation would probably include going to the *Thesaurus of ERIC Descriptors* to make sure that you have chosen terms that are actually employed by ERIC in its indexing system and to find out if there are additional terms that might help focus the search more appropriately. By providing your reference librarian with a good list of descriptors, you will provide the basis for a useful search. Besides using descriptors to include and exclude citations, limits can be set in other ways. For example you could request only those citations indexed since 1978 or only the 25 most recent citations. Fees for such services vary, but the general pattern seems to be to charge the user a fee based on computer time and the number of abstracts obtained. Most researchers prefer to have a copy of the abstracts mailed to them within a few days after the search is conducted. In addition to providing searches in response to specific requests, many libraries and indexing services are willing to provide a continuous updating with regard to research in an area of interest. In such a case, you would set up an initial search pattern, and then you would receive in the mail at appropriate times abstracts of whatever articles have recently appeared that meet your search requirements.

Notice that you do not have to be doing a term paper or writing an article for publication to benefit from these computerized search services. A researcher working at a theoretical level on teaching moral values to emotionally disturbed children might want to know everything that has been published related to this area, and therefore she might use a search strategy that would locate a large number of abstracts. On the other hand, a teacher in a public school classroom who is planning to implement a new program might enter a much narrower search to find out if anyone else has done anything similar to his program so that the ideas of others could be incorporated into his program.

An additional service provided by *CIJE* (but not *RIE*) is a listing within each monthly issue of the tables of contents of the journals abstracted in that issue. By looking through these tables of contents, you can find out what is being published in journals related to your field. This is an especially useful tactic for journals to which your library does not subscribe but to which you have access through interlibrary loans.

PSYCHOLOGICAL ABSTRACTS

The services provided by *Psychological Abstracts* are similar to those provided by ERIC. In general, this source indexes and abstracts the more formal pieces of information in the field of psychology, including journal articles, books, doctoral dissertations, and convention proceedings. It does not include such informal pieces of

> 14827. **Lorenz, Linda & Vockell, Edward.** (U Illinois Medical Ctr Disabled Children's Program, Chicago) **Using the Neurological Impress Method with learning disabled readers.** *Journal of Learning Disabilities,* 1979(Jan–Jul), Vol 12(6), 420–422. —Evaluated the ability of the Neurological Impress Method (NIM) of remediation (teacher and child read together in unison) to increase comprehension and word recognition skills among mildly learning disabled students. 44 2nd–5th graders with below-grade-level reading skills were tested on the Reading Comprehension subtest of the Peabody Individual Achievement Test and the Word Recognition subtest of the Wide Range Achievement Test before and after receiving remedial reading instruction using the NIM (experimental group) or traditional techniques (control group). An ANOVA showed no significant differences between pretest, posttest, and gain scores for the 2 groups. Students with auditory and nonauditory disabilities were equally unlikely to benefit. Despite subjective positive impressions of the method, it is concluded that further replications of NIM effectiveness are needed before its use becomes widespread. (6 ref) —S. Sieracki.

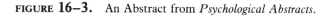

FIGURE 16–3. An Abstract from *Psychological Abstracts.*

```
AN  14827 62-6.
AU  LORENZ-LINDA.  VOCKELL-EDWARD.
IN  U ILLINOIS MEDICAL CTR DISABLED CHILDREN'S PROGRAM, CHICAGO.
TI  USING THE NEUROLOGICAL IMPRESS METHOD WITH LEARNING DISABLED READERS.
SO  JOURNAL OF LEARNING DISABILITIES. 1979 JUN-JUL VOL 12(6) 420-422.
CD  JLDIAD.
IS  022-2194.
LG  EN.
YR  79.
CC  3570.
PT  10.
MJ  READING-SKILLS.  REMEDIAL-READING.  LEARNING-DISABILITIES.
    READING-DISABILITIES.  READING-COMPREHENSION.
    ELEMENTARY-SCHOOL-STUDENTS.  RECOGNITION-LEARNING.  TEACHING-METHODS.
AB  EVALUATED THE ABILITY OF THE NEUROLOGICAL IMPRESS METHOD (NIM) OF
    REMEDIATION (TEACHER AND CHILD READ TOGETHER IN UNISON) TO INCREASE
    COMPREHENSION AND WORD RECOGNITION SKILLS AMONG MILDLY LEARNING
    DISABLED STUDENTS.  44 2ND-5TH GRADERS WITH BELOW-GRADE-LEVEL READING
    SKILLS WERE TESTED ON THE READING COMPREHENSION SUBTEST OF THE
    PEABODY INDIVIDUAL ACHIEVEMENT TEST AND THE WORD RECOGNITION SUBTEST
    OF THE WIDE RANGE ACHIEVEMENT TEST BEFORE AND AFTER RECEIVING
    REMEDIAL READING INSTRUCTION USING THE NIM (EXPERIMENTAL GROUP) OR
    TRADITIONAL TECHNIQUES (CONTROL GROUP).  AN ANOVA SHOWED NO
    SIGNIFICANT DIFFERENCES BETWEEN PRETEST, POSTTEST, AND GAIN SCORES
    FOR THE 2 GROUPS.  STUDENTS WITH AUDITORY AND NONAUDITORY
    DISABILITIES WERE EQUALLY UNLIKELY TO BENEFIT.  DESPITE SUBJECTIVE
    POSITIVE IMPRESSIONS OF THE METHOD, IT IS CONCLUDED THAT FURTHER
    REPLICATIONS OF NIM EFFECTIVENESS ARE NEEDED BEFORE ITS USE BECOMES
    WIDESPREAD.  (6 REF).
ID  NEUROLOGICAL IMPRESS METHOD, COMPREHENSION & WORD RECOGNITION SKILLS,
    MILDLY LEARNING DISABLED 2ND-5TH GRADERS WITH BELOW-GRADE-LEVEL
    READING SKILLS.
```

FIGURE 16–4. An Abstract from the Computerized Version of *Psychological Abstracts*. (This is the same abstract as that shown in Figure 16–5, but the computerized version contains some additional information.)

information as unpublished reports and curriculum guidelines, as would ERIC's *RIE*. *Psychological Abstracts* is published monthly, with semiannual cumulative indexes. An example of an abstract is shown in Figure 16–3.

As you can see, the information provided by *Psychological Abstracts* is very much like that found in *CIJE* or *RIE*. One difference is that *Psychological Abstracts* does indicate the institutional affiliation of the first author of the publication. Just as with the ERIC sources, information is found in *Psychological Abstracts* by first referring to a subject or author index and then looking up the abstract.

Like the other services, *Psychological Abstracts* can be accessed from a computer terminal for a computerized search. The output from the computer is slightly different from the hard copy information. The following is a computerized version of the entry cited on p. 298. An important addition is that the computerized version contains a list of descriptors (next to MJ in the twelfth through fourteenth lines). With this information we would know that we could find related articles under such descriptors as "Reading Skills," "Remedial Reading," and so on.

Although *Psychological Abstracts* focuses on psychology rather than on education, most researchers find that there is a large amount of overlap between educational methodology and psychological theory. Those researchers working at the theoretical level (as opposed to the concretely applied level) will find this to be an especially valuable source of information. The American Psychological Association provides many additional information dissemination services, and these can be identified by examining an issue of *Psychological Abstracts*.

EDUCATION INDEX

The *Education Index* covers many of the same sources as *CIJE*. It provides an index of titles and citations arranged according to topic headings and author headings, but it does not contain abstracts. The *Education Index* is published monthly, with an annual cumulative index. It cannot be accessed by computer at the present time. Because it contains simpler information, *Education Index* is often a bit faster in citing an article than is *CIJE*. Part of a page from *Education Index* is shown in Figure 16–5.

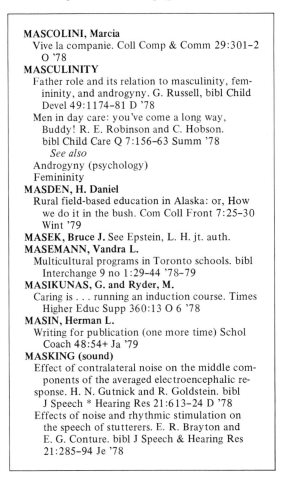

MASCOLINI, Marcia
  Vive la companie. Coll Comp & Comm 29:301-2
  O '78
MASCULINITY
  Father role and its relation to masculinity, fem-
  ininity, and androgyny. G. Russell, bibl Child
  Devel 49:1174-81 D '78
  Men in day care: you've come a long way,
  Buddy! R. E. Robinson and C. Hobson.
  bibl Child Care Q 7:156-63 Summ '78
    See also
  Androgyny (psychology)
  Femininity
MASDEN, H. Daniel
  Rural field-based education in Alaska: or, How
  we do it in the bush. Com Coll Front 7:25-30
  Wint '79
MASEK, Bruce J. See Epstein, L. H. jt. auth.
MASEMANN, Vandra L.
  Multicultural programs in Toronto schools. bibl
  Interchange 9 no 1:29-44 '78-79
MASIKUNAS, G. and Ryder, M.
  Caring is . . . running an induction course. Times
  Higher Educ Supp 360:13 O 6 '78
MASIN, Herman L.
  Writing for publication (one more time) Schol
  Coach 48:54+ Ja '79
MASKING (sound)
  Effect of contralateral noise on the middle com-
  ponents of the averaged electroencephalic re-
  sponse. H. N. Gutnick and R. Goldstein. bibl
  J Speech * Hearing Res 21:613-24 D '78
  Effects of noise and rhythmic stimulation on
  the speech of stutterers. E. R. Brayton and
  E. G. Conture. bibl J Speech & Hearing Res
  21:285-94 Je '78

FIGURE 16–5. Part of a Page from *Education Index*.

READERS GUIDE TO PERIODICAL LITERATURE

Like *Education Index, Readers Guide* contains titles and citations, but not abstracts. It does not cover the field of education in the great depth that *CIJE* or *Education Index* does, but it covers a wider variety of related topics than either of the other two. It comes out monthly, with an annual cumulative index. At present it is not accessible for computerized searches. A page from *Readers Guide* would look just like the page shown above from *Education Index*. (Figure 16–5).

OTHER ABSTRACTING SERVICES

There are several other abstracting services that meet specific needs, which are not mentioned here. You should check with your professional organizations to see what specific services may be available in your area of expertise.

The comparative advantages and disadvantages of the major indexing and abstracting services that have been described in this chapter are summarized in Table 16–1. This table indicates that there is much similarity and overlap among the various services, but each of them has unique characteristics that may help you solve specific problems.

TABLE 16–1. A Comparison of the Major Indexing and Abstracting Services.

	Psychological Abstracts	Education Index	Readers Guide	CIJE	RIE
Subject matter	Psychology	Education	General	Education	Education
Abstracts	Yes	No	No	Yes	Yes
Author index					
Monthly	Yes	Yes	Yes	Yes	Yes
Annual	Yes	Yes	Yes	Yes	Yes
Subject index					
Monthly	Yes	Yes	Yes	Yes	Yes
Annual	Yes	Yes	Yes	Yes	Yes
Table of contents of journals abstracted in each volume	No	No	No	Yes	No
Refereed journals	Yes	Yes	Yes	Yes	No
Thesaurus of descriptors	Yes	No	No	Yes	Yes
List of descriptors with each abstract	No	No	No	Yes	Yes
Computerized search available	Yes	No	No	Yes	Yes
Major advantage	Extremely thorough in field of psychology	Concise in field of education. Includes conference proceedings	Broad scope	Extremely thorough in field of education	Contains sources not in print elsewhere
Major disadvantage	Not many education journals. Comparatively long lag before indexing	No abstracts	Largely unrelated to education. No abstract	Not quite as recent as Education Index in printed format and conference proceedings	Lower quality control because of lack of refereeing. Microfiche inconvenient

```
AN 78-11-08757.
AU SCHWAB-M-R. LUNDGREN-D-C.
IN UNIV CINCINNATI, CINCINNATI, OH, 45221.
TI BIRTH-ORDER, PERCEIVED APPRAISALS BY SIGNIFICANT OTHERS, AND
   SELF-ESTEEM.
SO PSYCHOLOGICAL REPORTS 1978 V0043 #N2 P0443-0454.
RF 0036.
ON FX825.
LG EN.
YR 78.
CC VI.
CR ADAMS-B-N;1972;V0035;P0411;SOCIOMETRY.
   ADLER-A;1956;INDIVIDUAL-PSYCHOLOG.
   BERGER-E-M;1952;V0047;P0778;J-ABNORMAL-SOCIAL-PS.
   BURKE-H-L;1961;V0014;P0165;HUMAN-RELATIONS.
   COOLEY-C-H;1922;HUMAN-NATURE-SOCIAL.
   COOPERSMITH-S;1967;ANTECEDENTS-SELF-EST.
   CRONBACH-L-J;1951;V0016;P0297;PSYCHOMETRIKA.
   EISENMAN-R;1970;V0075;P0147;J-PSYCHOLOGY.
   FIEDLER-F-E;1967;THEORY-LEADERSHIP-EF.
   FLAMMER-D-P;1972;V0036;P0447;J-PERSONALITY-ASSESS.
   FORSLUND-M-A;1972;V0009;P0413;PSYCHOLOGY-SCH.
   GREENBERG-H;1963;V0060;P0221;J-SOCIAL-PSYCHOLOGY.
   HARTLEY-R-E;1959;V0005;P0457;PSYCHOLOGICAL-REPORT.
   LUNDGREN-D-C;1974;V0001;P0316;PERSONALITY-SOCIAL-P.
   MEAD-G-H;1934;MIND-SELF-SOC.
   MILEY-C-H;1969;V0025;P0064;J-INDIVIDUAL-PSYCHOL.
   MILLER-D-R;1963;V0005;P0639;PSYCHOLOGY-STUDY-SCI.
   MILLER-N;1976;V0033;P0123;J-PERSONAL-SOC-PSYCH.
   MIYAMOTO-S-F;1956;V0061;P0399;AM-J-SOCIOLOGY.
   NASH-J-C;1970;THESIS-OHIO-STATE-U.
   NORMAN-W-T;1963;V0066;P0574;J-ABNORMAL-SOCIAL-PS.
   NYSTUL-M-S;1974;V0030;P0211;J-INDIVIDUAL-PSYCHOL.
   PURPURA-P-A;1970;THESIS-FORDHAM-U. RICE-W-C;1971;THESIS-B-YOUNG-U.
   RING-K;1965;V0079;PSYCHOLOGICAL-MONOGR.
   ROSENBERG-B-G;1972;SEX-IDENTITY.
   ROSENBERG-M;1965;SOC-ADOLESCENT-SELF.
   SAMPSON-E-E;1972;P0086;PERSONALITY-SOCIALIZ.
   SCHACHTER-S;1959;PSYCHOLOGY-AFFILIATI.
   SCHOOLER-C;1972;V0078;P0161;PSYCHOL-B.
   SEARS-R-R;1970;V0041;P0267;CHILD-DEVELOPMENT.
   SHERWOOD-J-J;1965;V0028;P0066;SOCIOMETRY.
   STOTLAND-E;1962;V0064;P0183;J-ABNORMAL-SOCIAL-PS.
   STOTLAND-E;1962;V0076;PSYCHOLOGICAL-MONOGR.
   VOCKELL-E-L;1973;V0029;P0039;J-INDIV-PSY.
   ZIMBARDO-P;1963;V0031;P0141;J-PERSONALITY.
```

FIGURE **16—6.** A Sample Printout from a Computer Search of the *Social Science Citation Index (SSCI)*.

SOCIAL SCIENCE CITATION INDEX

A slightly different type of indexing and citation service is provided by the *Social Science Citation Index (SSCI)*. To use *SSCI*, we would first know of one article that supplied useful information on the topic we are interested in. By entering the pertinent information about this first article into a computer search, we can quickly find out what other journals have cited this same article. It stands to reason that if a second article cites this first article (which we already know to be relevant), then the second article may also be of interest to us. Pursuing this line of reasoning a bit further, we might want to know what additional books and articles (besides the one we already know about) were cited by this second article. We can obtain this information from *SSCI*. Below is an example of the sort of printout we can obtain from *SSCI*. By using *SSCI* in conjunction with ERIC, *Psychological Abstracts*, and the other indexing services, it is possible to compile a comprehensive bibliography that will enable us to zero in on the information needed to attack a research problem.

JOURNALS

In addition to knowing how to find information through indexes and abstracts, it is a good idea to be familiar with the research currently being reported in your field of professional expertise. One way to keep abreast of developments is to attend conventions or to read the summaries and proceedings of such conventions. Another way is to become a regular reader of the major journals in your field. Table 16–2 lists the 15 most frequently cited journals in education, according to a recent survey.

These are the most frequently cited journals in the *general* field of education. The journals cited most often in specific areas within this general field would vary from area to area. It would be a good idea to identify the major journals in your area and to read these frequently. Even if your library does not have access to certain journals, it is possible to monitor the contents through *CIJE* and to write for copies of important articles or to borrow the journals on interlibrary loan.

TABLE 16–2. The Fifteen Most Frequently Cited Journals in Educational Research.

	Date of Publication of Reference					
	Before 1945	1945– 1952	1953– 1960	1961– 1964	1965– 1969	Total
Journal of Educational Psychology	5	2	7	10	3	27
Educational and Psychological Measurement	0	0	7	2	4	13
Journal of Educational Research	3	0	2	4	3	12
Personnel and Guidance Journal	0	0	4	3	3	10
Journal of Counseling Psychology	0	0	1	3	6	10
Elementary English	1	0	0	3	5	9
Journal of Experimental Psychology	4	1	3	1	0	9
Teachers College Record	2	0	3	3	1	9
Elementary School Journal	0	0	4	3	1	8
Psychological Review	4	2	1	1	0	8
Review of Educational Research	0	0	3	3	2	8
Audiovisual Communications Review	0	0	1	4	2	7
Child Development	1	1	0	2	3	7
Harvard Educational Review	2	0	1	3	1	7
Journal of School Health	0	0	3	2	2	7

Source: a survey of the articles cited in the 1969 edition of the *Encyclopedia of Educational Research*. This table originally appeared in "Sources of Information in Educational Research Literature" by Edward L. Vockell and William Asher in *The Journal of Educational Research* 66 (1972): 181–183.

REVIEWS

It is helpful when someone gathers together and synthesizes all the current information on some topic of importance. This is a service performed by *reviews*. There are several reviews published on a regular basis. A few of the most popular related to the field of education are:

> *Mental Measurements Yearbook*
>
> *Encyclopedia of Educational Research*
>
> *The Encyclopedia of Education*
>
> *Encyclopedia of Educational Evaluation*
>
> *Review of Research in Education*
>
> *Yearbook of the National Society for the Study of Education*
>
> *Second Handbook of Research on Teaching*
>
> *Annual Review of Psychology*

Some of these reviews are issued annually, others are issued at longer intervals. In each issue important topics are identified, and the current information available on those topics is summarized and integrated in a scholarly fashion.

In addition to the above books, a large number of journals carry review articles. The *Review of Educational Research* specializes in integrative reviews. Likewise, *Psychological Bulletin* publishes a number of reviews on important topics in psychology. Many of the clearing houses of ERIC intermittently issue reviews of the literature in the areas for which they are responsible.

BOOKS

When research information is disseminated, it goes through informal channels, then to conventions, then to journals, and finally to books. The information contained in books published by reputable companies is likely to be of high quality, but this high quality is sometimes offset by the delay in getting it published. Nevertheless, books are an obviously important source of information to the researcher. Many books are indexed and abstracted by ERIC and the other abstracting services. Professional journals often provide book reviews on current books in the various areas of education.

Something that many researchers fail to do is to examine the entries in the library's card catalog carefully. An example of a card from such a catalog is shown below. Most readers are aware that each book is listed in the card catalog under the title, the author, and the subject heading. However, many readers are unaware of the other information that can be found on these cards. The card shown below, for example, tells when the book was published, indicates how many pages are in it, and states that it contains a bibliography on pages 167–168. This last piece of information would be helpful to you if you wanted to find more information on the topic covered by this book. Near the bottom of the card there are listed the three headings under which this

```
                    Punishment.

HQ       Vockell, Edward L
770.4        Whatever happened to punishment / Edward L. Vockell. –
V62          Muncie, IN: Accelerated Development, 1977

             xv, 175 p.: ill.; 23 cm.

             Bibliography: p. 167–168.
             Includes index.
             ISBN 0–915202–11–5 : $7.95



             1. Discipline of children.   2. Punishment.   3. Behavior modification.   I.
             Title.

         HQ770.4.V62                     649'.6                      77–80556
                                                                     MARC
```

FIGURE **16–7.**   A Sample Entry from a Card Catalog.

card is indexed in the subject file of the card catalog. By looking under these headings, you can find more books on the same topic. Both the Library of Congress number and the Dewey Decimal number are listed at the bottom of the card. Since books are arranged according to similarity of topics, it might be a good idea for you to wander off to that part of the library where this book is shelved to see what other books are located in this area. You may come across something that would otherwise not even enter your mind.

INTERLIBRARY LOANS

Computerization has made it increasingly easy to borrow books from libraries in distant cities. At a rapidly expanding number of libraries it is possible for a librarian to punch some simple information into a computer terminal and to be informed within seconds what libraries within a designated region of the country have a specified book or journal. By entering some additional information, the library is quickly and easily able to arrange to borrow the book on interlibrary loan. This means that even if your library does not have a book or journal, you can still have access to such publications. This can usually be accomplished at no cost to you or at only a minimal fee.

A number of library users are unaware of this resource. What this means in practice is that the card catalog in your own library may not be the best place for you to look to find information on a topic you are interested in. In many cases limiting yourself to the card catalog of a relatively small library will cause you to miss information to which you should have access. It is often better to look for sources of information in the indexing and abstracting services mentioned earlier in this chapter, in bibliographies to related publications, and in broader catalogs, and *then* to look for this specific information in your library. If it is not there, you can probably get it through an interlibrary loan. Check with your own library to see what services are available.

CONDUCTING A REVIEW OF THE LITERATURE

The sources of information mentioned in this chapter will enable you to carry out a successful search of the literature, provided you know what you are looking for. It is important that you define your problem as early as possible, and that you continue to refine the definition of your problem so that you can focus more and more closely on solutions to it. By drawing upon published sources you can avoid reinventing the wheel. You can take advantage of what is already known, and build upon the knowledge of others.

In addition to the structured procedures covered in this chapter for finding published sources of information, there is a further strategy that is less formal. Once you find an article (or book, or report) that is directly related to the topic you are interested in, carefully scrutinize the bibliography or list of references accompanying this piece of information. Then look up some of these articles in *CIJE* or *Psychological Abstracts* to see where they are indexed. In *CIJE*, examine the list of descriptors. This will enable you to get a good start; and once you are started, it often becomes easier to find more sources. A related idea is to look through the list of references accompanying an article you have found and then look up the names of the authors in the author indexes of a more recent issue of an appropriate indexing or abstracting service. Since authors who publish important ideas on one topic will often do so again, this can lead you to additional sources of information that you might not otherwise have found.

SUMMARY

The resources discussed in this chapter will help you find information that will enable you to attack your research problems more successfully. These library resources can be helpful at any level of research. Reading about these resources is not the best way to learn how to use them; the best strategy is to go into the library and actually try your hand at using each of the resources and services described. Even persons who think they know a great deal about using the library (and even authors of books like this) will discover that there is much to learn about how to get information from the library.

Several different indexing and abstracting services have been described here. Each service provides different advantages and disadvantages. Many of these services are computerized. Such services enable us to go directly to the information we need, rather than wading through a vast amount of irrelevant information before we find what is pertinent. In addition, a familiarity with the various journals, reviews, and books that present current research and ideas in our areas of specific interest will help us identify, clarify, and solve our educational problems. An important idea in this chapter is that we should not confine ourselves to the physical limits of any one library when we search for information. Systems of interlibrary loans are becoming increasingly efficient, and such systems enable us to obtain very quickly almost any information that we need.

Annotated Bibliography

BEST, J.W. *Research in Education* (2nd ed.) (Englewood Cliffs, N.J.: Prentice-Hall, 1970). Chapter 3 provides a comprehensive description of many of the resources available through the library.

MARTIN, D.W. *Doing Psychology Experiments* (Monterey, Cal.: Brooks/Cole, 1977). Chapter 3 provides creative guidelines on "How to Find Out What's Been Done" on a research problem of interest to you.

17 Research Tools: The Computer

Chapter Preview

The computer can be a valuable tool to a researcher. With the computer it is possible to perform statistical and mathematical calculations in a very short time. In addition, the computer enables a researcher to have a high degree of confidence that the calculations are accurate, provided the numbers given to the computer for analysis were accurate. All of the statistics that have been described in this text, as well as those covered in introductory statistics courses, can easily be performed by the computer. This chapter will show you how to put data into an appropriate format for analysis by computer and how to use the computer to perform statistical analyses.

After reading this chapter you should be able to

- Describe how to put data into an appropriate format for subsequent computer analysis.
- Interpret statements from a computer program designed to perform a statistical analysis.
- Perform a computer analysis of data.
- Interpret the output provided by a computerized statistical analysis.

THE ADVANTAGES OF THE COMPUTER

Computers are becoming increasingly more accessible to educators. They can make an important contribution to research tasks at any level of sophistication. All the statistical procedures described in this book (plus many more) can be performed by computer. Once the data have been correctly prepared and entered into the computer, a large number of analyses and subanalyses can be performed on the same set of data with only a minimum of additional effort.

Besides saving a great deal of time, the computer confers another advantage. Computer analysis enables researchers to be confident of the results of calculations. Many statistical procedures require complex mathematical computations, at many points of which errors can be made, and even minor errors can render the whole computational process inaccurate. With the computer, once the cards are correctly keypunched according to prescribed instructions, the possibility of errors is vastly reduced.

Even if you use the computer for analysis, however, there is still a possibility that you will get inaccurate results. This will usually occur not because of any error the computer will make, but rather because of errors you yourself may make as you are feeding the data into the computer. Computer programmers have a saying: "Garbage in, garbage out." This means that the computer just does what it is told to do. No matter how smart we view computers to be, they still are not smart enough to know when the programmer has made an error. Therefore, if you give the computer an order that the computer is capable of carrying out, the computer will carry out that command no matter how absurd it may be. This means that if you reverse the order of cards, instruct the computer to read the wrong columns, or simply keypunch data incorrectly, you will get erroneous results. The errors are your fault, not the computer's. Likewise, if you use the computer to perform a statistical analysis that should not appropriately be performed on a set of data (for example, if you instruct it to compute an analysis of variance rather than a correlation coefficient), the computer will have no way of knowing about your theoretical error and will just go ahead and perform the calculations. The result will be misleading; but again, this would be your fault, not the computer's.

Computers do in fact, occasionally make mistakes. (For example, electronic failures may cause the card reader or the printer to malfunction). However, the vast majority of errors that novices attribute to computers really occur because the person requesting a program from the computer made a mistake. This chapter is written to help you use the computer to obtain helpful and accurate results. It provides only a brief introduction; but by understanding this chapter and by following a few more instructions which will be unique to your own computer system, it will be possible for you to use the computer to compute all the statistics discussed in this book and in basic statistics books. In addition to the information provided here, you will find that most colleges and universities provide computer consultants who are familiar with such statistical programs and will help you analyze your data if you cooperate by organizing it correctly.

There are several sets of statistical programs available to researchers in education. Only one such set of programs will be discussed in this chapter. However, this set is typical of many of the others; and a reader who can understand how to use these programs will easily be able to shift to a different set of programs, if the need should arise. The statistical programs used as examples in this chapter are taken from the *Statistical Package for the Social Sciences* (SPSS). If you decide to use these programs yourself, you will certainly want more information about these programs; and you can obtain this information by consulting the book by Nie and his co-authors listed in the Annotated Bibliography at the end of this chapter. The SPSS programs were chosen as examples because they are well-designed programs, because they are widely available, and because their usage is easily understood by persons with no background whatsoever in computer programming.

This chapter will attempt no explanation of the electronic principles behind how the computer works. Only those principles of programming that are essential to understanding the use of the statistical programs will be discussed in this chapter. The cookbook approach which this chapter will follow will provide you with specific guidelines. If you know what you want and follow the guidelines, you will be able to get what you want from the computer.

PUTTING THE DATA INTO A PROPER FORMAT

In the programs which this chapter will describe, the data must be arranged in a systematic format. This requirement is typical of all computer programs. When the computer is ordered to calculate a statistic (for example, the mean of a set of IQ scores), it can accomplish this only by reading the information in specifically designated card columns and acting upon this information in a prescribed way. The computer does not know (or care) whether the contents of the designated card columns consist of IQ scores, bowling averages, or locker numbers; all it does is get the numbers and do what you tell it to do with them. Therefore, it is obviously important that you arrange the numbers appropriately, so that the computer can find the correct numbers and do the work you want it to do.

Figure 17–1 contains all the information needed about a hypothetical student to include him in a statistical analysis for a research project. However, this information is not arranged in a systematic manner that would make it ready for the computer to analyze.

> Jeff Jones is a 12-year-old boy. He attained a score on the I. Q. test of 104. He should be classified as coming from a high socioeconomic class, since his parents have an income of over $50,000 a year. He scored 14 correct on the pretest. At about the same time he scored 60 on the self-concept test. Later, he scored 34 on the posttest.

FIGURE 17–1.   An Example of Data that Must Be Put into a More Systematic Format Before It Can Be Analyzed by the Computer.

In Figure 17–2, the data available for analysis on eight similar students have been more systematically arranged. The haphazard, chain-of-thought approach has vanished, and now the data are arranged in systematic columns, with the same information placed in the same order for every student. The family income has been changed from "over $50,000" to "4" according to the following scale:

(1) = under $10,000
(2) = between $10,000 and $25,000
(3) = between $25,000 and $50,000
(4) = over $50,000

However, the information in Figure 17–2 is still not completely arranged for computer analysis. One of the remaining problems is that the computer programs in

	Sex	Age	Income	IQ	Pre.	Post.	Sc.
Jeff Jones	male	12	4	104	14	34	60
Mary Smith	Female	12	1	94	24	35	59
Albert Brown	male	13	2	100	4	14	42
Tom Williams	male	12	4	130	30	40	64
Bob Jamison	male	13	3	101	20	24	65
alice Wilson	Female	13	2	85	5	7	40
Teresa Smith	Female	12	3	80	15	15	65
Brenda Johnson	Female	13	4	120	30	40	65

FIGURE **17–2.** An Example of Data for Eight Students Which Have Been Partially Systematized for Computer Analysis.

the SPSS package deal only with numbers, not with words; and therefore "Jeff Jones" and "male" would be incomprehensible. This problem is easily solved by making Jeff Jones "01" and categorizing all males as "1" and all females as "2." (This decision was arbitrary. We could just as easily have made Jeff Jones "57149" and males "7." The key is to do something simple and to remember what you did.)

In Figure 17–3, the process of arranging the data for computer analysis has been completed. The only information that will be entered into the computer about Jeff Jones will be this:

011124104143460

As you can see, this is the first data line of Figure 17–3, with all the spaces omitted.

ID	Sex	age	Inc.	IQ	Pre.	Post.	Sc.
01	1	12	4	104	14	34	60
02	2	12	1	094	24	35	59
03	1	13	2	100	04	14	42
04	1	12	4	130	30	40	64
05	1	13	3	101	20	24	65
06	2	13	2	085	05	07	40
07	2	12	3	080	15	15	65
08	2	13	4	120	30	40	65

FIGURE **17–3.** The Data from Figure 17–3 Put Completely into a Format Ready for Computer Analysis.

A further change that has been made is that additional zeros have been added in front of such numbers as the IQ of Mary Smith (ID number 02) and the pretest score of Albert Brown (ID number 03). These additional zeros have been inserted to make it more likely that the correct scores will always appear in the correct columns for every student. Without the additional zero, for example, a keypuncher might put Mary Smith's IQ of 94 right next to her income of 1. This would cause everything from that point onward to be read erroneously, and such an error (an IQ of 942!) would seriously distort the results. The impact of such an error is shown in Figure17–4.

Line A   022121094243559
Line B   02212194243559
Line C   022121 94243559

Line A is the correct data for Mary Smith
Line B contains the error of omitting the zero and moving Mary's IQ and all following data one space to the left.
Line C is exactly the same as Line A, except that a blank space has been inserted before the IQ rather than a zero. This is a correct line; but keypunchers are very likely to omit spaces, whereas they are less likely to omit zeros.

If Line B were punched instead of Line A or C, the following errors would be fed into the computer:

		Mary's Real Data	What the Computer Would Read as Mary's Data
Col 1–2	ID	02	02
Col 3	Sex	2	2
Col 4–5	Age	12	12
Col 6	Income	1	1
Col 7–9	IQ	94	942 (The 9 & 4 have moved over) (The 2 from the pretest has moved over)
Col 10–11	Pretest	24	43
Col 12–13	Posttest	35	55
Col 14–15	Self-concept	59	90 (The computer would add the zero automatically)

FIGURE **17–4.**   An Example of What Happens When Data Are Arranged and Entered into the Computer in the Wrong Columns.

Once the data have been systematically arranged, the numbers are ready to be keypunched and analyzed by computer. The computer can read this information and compute means, standard deviations, correlation coefficients, analysis of variance, analysis of covariance, and many other statistics. The advantage of having access to a computer for computations regarding eight students is perhaps slight; but the same procedures that we shall apply to these eight subjects could be applied to hundreds or even thousands of subjects with no loss in accuracy and no increase in the complexity of the programs we would have to write.

Remember, any error that you have made up to this point is likely to go uncorrected by the computer. This applies not only to transcribing and keypunching errors, but also to errors of logic. For example, in Figure 17–2, the financial income data was converted to categories labeled 1 through 4. The researcher would probably consider the lowest category to be poor and the highest to be wealthy. If this is an incorrect or unsound classification, the computer will never correct the mistake; it will merrily go on comparing 1s to 4s, with no regard for what the researcher thinks the numbers stand for.

DEAR RESEARCHER: I've got you this time! Look how impersonal and degrading computers can be. In Figure 17-1, we had a nice, personal note about Jeff Jones. By the time he's ready to go into the computer, he's become not Jeff Jones, but "01." How impersonal can you get? I protest this dehumanizing process. What do you have to say about that? (signed) ANONYMOUS.

DEAR ANONYMOUS: Mathematics, by its very nature, is a bit impersonal. I don't see how putting a person's score on a card along with a code number is any more impersonal than writing the score in a column before you add the column, divide the result, or do whatever you want with it. Actually, the anonymity of the computer card can provide a valuable service by protecting the confidentiality of the person whose response is recorded. (signed) THE LONELY RESEARCHER.

PERFORMING A STATISTICAL ANALYSIS

Let us suppose we want to take the data from Figure 17–3 and compute a Pearson correlation coefficient between IQ and self-concept. This could be accomplished by writing the following program:

```
RUN NAME            SPSS PRACTICE DATA
VARIABLE LIST       SEX,AGE,INCOME,IQ,PRE,POST,SC
INPUT MEDIUM        CARD
INPUT FORMAT        FIXED (2X,F1.0,F2.0,F1.0,F3.0,3F2.0)
N OF CASES          8
PEARSON CORR        IQ,SC
STATISTICS          1
READ INPUT DATA
```

(Here we would insert the eight cards with each student's information on it.)

FINISH

The above is a partial listing of a program. When reading such listings, each line stands for a separate computer card. The following paragraphs will provide a brief description of each card.

The RUN NAME card gives a label that will be written at the top of each page of our output. If you run this same program, you will probably want to change the RUN NAME card to a description that will help you distinguish your printout from those of others running their programs or from the many other programs you yourself might run. For example, your card might read

RUN NAME   JANE DOE'S FOURTH TRY TO GET IT RIGHT

If the original RUN NAME card were removed and this one inserted in its place, the program would run the same way the original ran. The only exception is that "Jane Doe's Fourth Try to Get It Right" would appear at the top of each page in the printout instead of the original label.

The VARIABLE LIST card attaches labels to each variable for the computer's use. After the computer reads this card, it knows that it will be looking for seven variables. It will refer to the first one as "sex," the second as "age," and so on, until it finds all seven variables. There are some simple rules that must be followed in composing labels, and you can find these rules by referring to the SPSS manual.

The INPUT MEDIUM card merely informs the computer that our data will be provided from cards, as opposed to tape or some other method of putting information into the computer.

The INPUT FORMAT card tells the computer where to look to find the seven variables that we told it to look for. The word FIXED comes first, followed by a set of instructions in parentheses. The 2X means to skip the first two spaces on each data card. The F1.0 means that the first variable is one column long, and contains no decimal places. F2.0 means that the second variable is two columns long and contains no decimal places. F1.0 means that the third variable is one column long and has no decimal places. F3.0 means that the fourth variable is three columns long and has no decimal places. 3F2.0 means that the next three variables are each two columns long and each has no decimal places. If you re-read the preceding sentence while glancing back at the information within parentheses on the INPUT FORMAT card, you can see what the terms mean. An X means to skip whatever number of spaces is indicated by the number preceding the X. An F indicates a variable; and if there is a number before the F, this means that there are as many variables as indicated by the number. The number right after the F indicates how many columns the variable takes up, and the number after the decimal point indicates how many decimal places are in the variable. Try re-reading the INPUT FORMAT card and see if you can interpret it.

At this point the computer starts putting together what it has learned so far from our input. We had told it previously (on the VARIABLE LIST card) that the first variable would be called "sex." Now we have told it on the INPUT FORMAT card that the first variable is located in column 3. It now knows, therefore, that column 3 contains numerical information called "sex." Likewise, we had previously told the computer that the second variable would be called "age." From the INPUT FORMAT card it has learned that the second variable is found in columns 4 and 5. Therefore, it now knows that columns 4 and 5 contain numerical information that it will call "age." By this process the computer identifies and labels all seven variables. Notice that the computer does not know what "sex" means or what "age" means. All it knows is that there are variables with those names located at specified locations on the data cards it will read.

The N OF CASES card indicates how many subjects are in the analysis. This is important to the computer, because it needs to know how many cards to read.

The PEARSON CORR card tells the computer that we want to calculate a Pearson correlation. The terms IQ and SC on this card tell the computer which two variables we want to include in this calculation. The computer recognizes IQ and SC as terms from the VARIABLE LIST which it later matched with card columns based on information from the INPUT FORMAT card. It knows that IQ is the fourth variable, located in columns 7 through 9, and that SC is the seventh variable, located in columns 14 and 15.

The STATISTICS card lets us identify certain other statistics (besides the Pearson correlation coefficient) that we can have the computer calculate for us while it is computing the Pearson coefficient we have requested. The SPSS manual provides a list of the additional statistics that are available with each statistical procedure. By consulting this manual, you know that "1" means that you will get the mean and standard deviation for each of the variables; and so you have entered this on the STATISTICS card. This card is optional, it could be omitted, and the only effect would be that the mean and standard deviation would not be computed.

Requesting a calculation of the mean from the computer is often a good way to check your work. It would be possible that you might have mispunched some data, put it in the wrong column, or made some similar mistake. Since the mean is an extremely easy statistic to calculate by hand, you can check your work by comparing your own mean to that calculated by the computer. If they match, you know that the computer is reading the right data. In addition, if the mean is right, then it is likely that whatever other statistics the computer calculated based on the same numbers are also correct.

The READ INPUT DATA card informs the computer that the next cards will be the data cards—that is, those cards on which the student information is contained according to the designated format.

The FINISH card comes after the data cards and signifies that the run is over—that there are no more statistics to compute. It would be possible (and a later example will demonstrate this) to perform additional statistical procedures prior to the insertion of the FINISH card.

Figures 17–5 to 17–6 show the three pages of output that we would get from this input. Some of the information on these printouts is either of a technical nature or is unique to the computer system on which the program was run, and such information will be ignored here. If you look at the first page of the printout closely (Figure 17–5), you will notice that the first eight lines of our input are printed here. Immediately after the fourth line, you can see where the computer paused and summarized what it had learned about the names of the variables and where they were located.

Figure 17–6 shows the second and third pages. Page 2 is self-explanatory. Page 3 presents the Pearson correlation coefficient. Actually it presents four correlations: IQ correlated with IQ, IQ with SC, SC with IQ, and SC with SC. Most of this information is either redundant or useless, and the only thing we care about is that there is a correlation of .38 between SC and IQ. (The statement $p = 0.176$ means that there are about 18 chances in 100 that a correlation this high would occur by chance when the scores of 8 subjects are correlated.)

If we wished to do so, we could do further statistical analyses simply by inserting a few additional cards before the FINISH card. For example, the following card would get us a breakdown of mean IQ scores by sex to see if the boys or girls had the higher IQ scores.

BREAKDOWN   TABLES = IQ BY SEX

By adding the following additional card, we would get an analysis of variance, estimating the probability that the difference between mean IQs of boys and girls is merely a chance of variation:

STATISTICS   1

```
SPSS BATCH SYSTEM                                          10/03/80          PAGE    1

SPSS FOR DOS/360, VERSION H, RELEASE 8.0, NOVEMBER 1, 1979

DEFAULT SPACE ALLOCATION..     ALLOWS FOR..     274 TRANSFORMATIONS
WORKSPACE    192284 BYTES                      1098 RECODE VALUES + LAG VARIABLES
TRANSPACE    277468 BYTES                      4398 IF/COMPUTE OPERATIONS

       1 RUN NAME         SPSS HYPOTHETICAL PRACTICE DATA
       2 VARIABLE LIST    SEX,AGE,INCOME,IQ,PRE,POST,SC
       3 INPUT MEDIUM     CARD
       4 INPUT FORMAT     FIXED (2X,F1.0,F2.0,F1.0,F3.0,3F2.0)

          ACCORDING TO YOUR INPUT FORMAT, VARIABLES ARE TO BE READ AS FOLLOWS

          VARIABLE    FORMAT    RECORD    COLUMNS

          SEX         F  1.0       1        3-   3
          AGE         F F 2.0      1        4-   5
          INCOME      F F 1.0      1        6-   6
          IQ          F F 3.0      1        7-   9
          PRE         F F 2.0      1       10-  11
          POST        F F 2.0      1       12-  13
          SC          F  2.0       1       14-  15

THE INPUT FORMAT PROVIDES FOR  7 VARIABLES.     7 WILL BE READ
IT PROVIDES FOR  1 RECORDS ('CARDS') PER CASE.  A MAXIMUM OF   15 'COLUMNS' ARE USED ON A RECORD.

       5 N OF CASES          8
       6 PEARSON CORR        IQ,SC
       7 STATISTICS          1

***** PEARSON CORR PROBLEM REQUIRES          48 BYTES WORKSPACE *****

       8 READ INPUT DATA
```

FIGURE 17–5. The First Page of Output from the SPSS Program Described in "Performing a Statistical Analysis." (The actual deck of cards used to obtain this printout is shown in Figure 17–8.)

```
SPSS HYPOTHETICAL PRACTICE DATA                           10/03/80      PAGE   2

FILE   NONAME   (CREATION DATE = 10/03/80)

       VARIABLE      CASES          MEAN          STD DEV

         IQ            8          101.7500        16.7054
         SC            8           57.5000        10.4608


SPSS HYPOTHETICAL PRACTICE DATA                           10/03/80      PAGE   3

FILE   NONAME   (CREATION DATE = 10/03/80)

- - - - - - - P E A R S O N   C O R R E L A T I O N   C O E F F I C I E N T S - - - - - - - -

              IQ          SC

IQ          1.0000      0.3809
           (    8)     (    8)
           P=*****     P=0.176

SC          0.3809      1.0000
           (    8)     (    8)
           P=0.176     P=*****

(COEFFICIENT / (CASES) / SIGNIFICANCE)        (A VALUE OF 99.0000 IS PRINTED IF A COEFFICIENT CANNOT BE COMPUTED)
```

FIGURE 17–6. The Second and Third Pages of the Output from the SPSS Program Described in "Performing a Statistical Analysis."

317

We would know to use this STATISTICS card, because the manual tells us that analysis of variance is obtained as a supplementary statistic with the program BREAKDOWN by entering "1" on the STATISTICS card. Therefore, to get both the Pearson correlation, the mean, the standard deviation, the breakdown by sex, and an analysis of variance of this breakdown, we would enter the following cards into the computer:

RUN NAME	SPSS PRACTICE DATA
VARIABLE LIST	SEX,AGE,INCOME,IQ,PRE,POST,SC
INPUT MEDIUM	CARD
INPUT FORMAT	FIXED(2X,F1.0,F2.0,F1.0,F3.0,X3F2.0)
N OF CASES	8
PEARSON CORR	IQ,SC
STATISTICS	1
READ INPUT DATA	

(Next come the 8 data cards)

BREAKDOWN	TABLES = IQ BY SEX
STATISTICS	1
FINISH	

The output from the above deck would include that already shown in Figures 17–5 and 17–6. In addition, the results shown in Figure 17–7 would be provided as output. When you examine this printout, do not be overwhelmed by what appears to be a large amount of information with which you are not familiar. If you merely look at the information you do understand, this printout is comprehensible and useful. You probably do not care about the sum or the sum of squares at the top of the printout, but the mean and standard deviation provide useful information. Likewise, you probably are not familiar with terms like sum of squares, mean square, and between groups in the analysis of variance table; nor are you likely to be familiar with the usage of eta and eta squared at the bottom of that table. On the other hand, you do know that F is the output of an analysis of variance; and you know that *significance* refers to the likelihood of a difference between means occurring by chance. Here, the significance is .2657; and this would indicate that there is a high degree of probability that the differences between boys and girls arose by chance.

If you wanted to do so, you could keypunch these cards and run them through your own computer system (if it uses SPSS). You could compare your results to Figures 17–5 and 17–7 to see if you did it right. In order to do this, you would need to know a few further details.

First, there are actually three types of cards that go into a computer. One type is called a control card. The cards that we have been discussing here and that give instructions to the computer are examples of control cards. In the SPSS system, all control cards begin in the first column with the label of the card (RUN NAME, N OF CASES, etc.). Next it is necessary to skip to column 16 and to begin keypunching the rest of the information there.

The second type of card is the data card. These are the cards that contain the actual information about the subjects. With these, keypunching begins in the first column and continues as indicated by the designated format.

```
SPSS HYPOTHETICAL PRACTICE DATA                          10/03/80      PAGE   6
CRITERION VARIABLE IQ
- - - - - - - - - - A N A L Y S I S   O F   V A R I A N C E - - - - - - - - -
VARIABLE      CODE   VALUE LABEL        SUM        MEAN     STD DEV    SUM OF SQ      N
SEX            1.                    435.0000    108.7500   14.2683    610.7500     ( 4)
SEX            2.                    379.0000     94.7500   17.8022    950.7500     ( 4)
               WITHIN GROUPS TOTAL   814.0000    101.7500   16.1323   1561.5000     ( 8)

          A N A L Y S I S   O F   V A R I A N C E

     SOURCE          SUM OF SQUARES   D.F.   MEAN SQUARE      F       SIG.
     BETWEEN GROUPS     392.000        1       392.000      1.506    0.2657
     WITHIN GROUPS     1561.500        6       260.250

               ETA = 0.4480    ETA SQUARED = 0.2007
```

FIGURE 17-7. The Breakdown of Mean Scores by Sex and the Accompanying Analysis of Variance from the Program Described in "Performing a Statistical Analysis."

The third type of card is the system card. These have not been mentioned at all up to this point. System cards are the cards required by each computer system in order for a user to be allowed to use the computer and to request access to the SPSS programs.

Figure 17–8 shows the entire deck that generated the printouts used as examples in Figures 17–5 through 17–7. The first three and last two cards are system cards. The cards you would use to get onto your system and have access to the SPSS

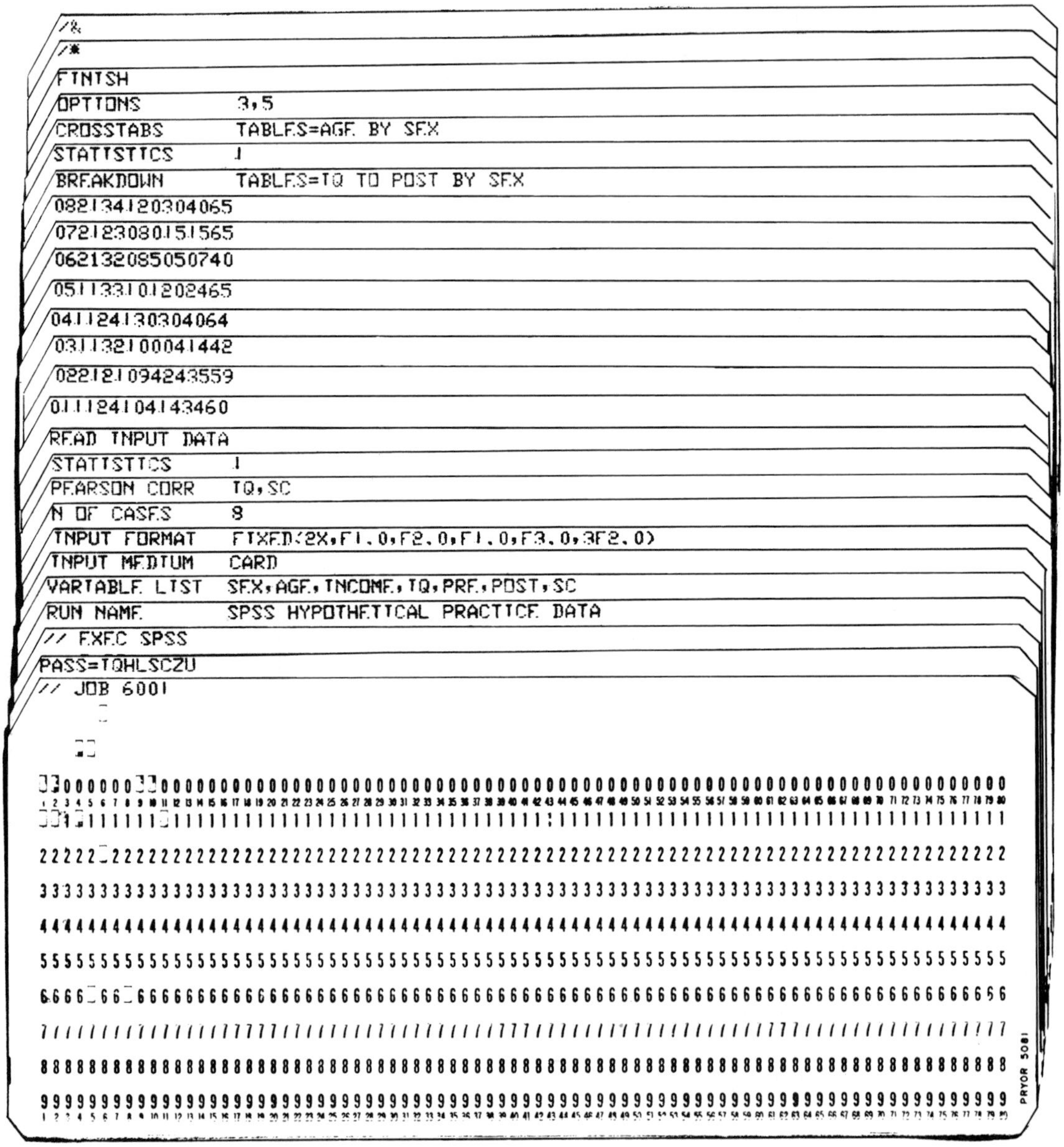

FIGURE 17–8. Sample Deck Used to Run the SPSS Programs Used as Examples in This Chapter.

programs would be different from these. However, the other 19 cards (11 control cards and 8 data cards) would be exactly the same as these on any system using the current version of SPSS.

An advantage of the SPSS programs is that they are designed in such a way as to help you correct many of the errors you make. Everything has to be entered into the computer according to a carefully selected format. If you wander from this format, it is likely that the computer will recognize your error and tell you what you did wrong. For example, if we would have mislabeled SC as SG by mistake, the computer would be unable to proceed, because it would not know what SG means. In this case, the printout would look like this:

PEARSON CORR   IQ,SG
THE FOLLOWING SYMBOL HAS CAUSED AN ERROR.."SG"
ERROR NUMBER..850.PROCESSING CEASES, ERROR SCAN CONTINUES.

This message would tell you that the computer cannot do what you told it to do (because it does not know what SG means), but it will examine the rest of the program to see whether there are any more errors to call to your attention. At the very end of the printout, there would be the following explanation:

ERRNO = 850
THE PEARSON CORR CARD CONTAINS AN INVALID VARIABLE LIST

The error messages are quite specific, and it is possible to use such messages to locate and remove errors quickly.

There are many statistical procedures that are possible through the SPSS, and there are similar systems that have not been discussed here. All the statistical procedures mentioned in this text and all those encountered in elementary statistics courses can be computed through the SPSS system. In addition, many more advanced statistics are available. Besides the statistical procedures, there are other functions that can be performed by the computer. It is possible, for instance, to have the computer do mathematical computations for us. For example, in the data we have been using for illustration, we might want to compute the amount of gain each student showed between pretest and posttest and correlate this with SC and IQ. This could be done by inserting the following card before the PEARSON CORR card:

COMPUTE   GAIN = POST-PRE

Then we would change the PEARSON CORR card as follows:

PEARSON CORR   IQ,SC,GAIN

By doing this, we would get a printout that would include the analysis we wanted. The many possibilities of what can be accomplished through the use of the computer can be explored by examining the manual for the SPSS programs or the manual for whatever system is available at your computer facility.

The use of the computer is by no means reserved to the more sophisticated levels of research. Even at Level I research, the computer can provide considerable advantages. Tests can be scored and item-analyzed by computer. Reliability coefficients, which are annoying or time consuming to compute by hand, are easy to calculate on the computer. Whatever your research needs may be, an important idea is to plan ahead so that you can take full advantage of what the computer has to offer. If you plan correctly, you can save steps when the time comes for analysis. Look ahead, figure out how you should format the information to make it most easily accessible to the computer, and then collect the data as much as possible in that format. Think ahead and eliminate, insofar as you can, the need for painstaking recopying and recoding of data before it can be keypunched. In some cases, it may even be possible to record the initial data on mark-sense cards or on optical scanning sheets that can be read by some computers, thus eliminating the need for you to do that portion of the keypunching.

The computer can save you time, and the amount of time you save will become greater as the number of subjects or the complexity of the analysis increases. Computers are available to almost every researcher. It is just a matter of knowing where to find them and how to access them. By becoming familiar with the computer, you can greatly expand your capabilities as a researcher.

PUTTING IT ALL TOGETHER

Early in his career in humane education, Eugene Anderson learned the advantages of using the computer. He discovered that he could use it to score his tests, to tabulate and compare means of various groups to whom he administered programs, and to compute correlations between scores on his tests and other characteristics that he expected to be either related or unrelated to performance on the tests.

One important use of the computer occurred in the process of validating his tests. As you may recall, such a process of validation would involve demonstrating that the tests correlate substantially with other measures of humane attitudes and that they correlate negligibly with characteristics theoretically unrelated to positive attitudes toward animal life. On one occasion, Mr. Anderson was able to administer his tests to 31 fourth graders, and he was able to obtain additional information regarding sex, reading ability, and IQ from this same group. To this group he gave not only two forms of the Fireman Test (Johnny and the Fireman and Janet and the Fireman), but also a TV test, which gave children a chance to hypothetically choose to watch current TV shows that either did or did not feature animals.

Mr. Anderson had previously decided to use a standardized format for data tabulation. By using the same format every time he administered his tests, he could eventually combine the data from several different administrations and make more complete comparisons. The form on which he tabulated his data is shown in Figure 17–9.

The program that Mr. Anderson used to analyze his data is listed in Figure 17–10. Let us briefly examine the listing for this program. The VARIABLE LIST card tells the computer that there will be twelve variables, and the INPUT FORMAT card tells the computer where to find the twelve variables. Notice that the computer has been instructed to ignore the first seven columns. These columns contain information

										Johnny			Janet								
School	Year	cl. D.					Sex	Gr.	Pat	1	2	3	1	2	3	TV	cl. Q.		Read		
1	4	7	9	0	0	1	1	4	2	2	4	8	2	4	8	3	1	0	6	6	0
1	4	7	9	0	0	2	2	4	1	9	2	5	0	3	1	1	1	1	0	4	9
1	4	7	9	0	0	3	2	4	1	2	9	1	2	3	5	1	0	9	5	4	0
1	4	7	9	0	0	4															
1	4	7	9	0	0	4															
1	4	7	9	0	0	5															
1	4	7	9	0	0	6															
1	4	7	9	0	0	7															
1	4	7	9	0	0	8															

FIGURE **17–9.** The Data Tabulation Sheet from Which Mr. Anderson Keypunched His Humane Education Data.

that Mr. Anderson may be interested in on some other occasion (for example, if he would combine the data from several administrations of the tests); but at present he was not interested in any analysis using this information.

The sixth card in this listing is a RECODE card, instructing the computer to change all blanks to a value of minus nine. Mr. Anderson made this change because several of the variables have a possible value of zero, and the computer would treat zeros and blanks the same way in computations. Thus a person who did not take a test would get the same score as a person who scored zero on it. By changing a blank to a minus nine, he has eliminated this problem. Later, he inserted a MISSING VALUES card to instruct the computer to omit from specific analyses the scores of subjects who have a score of minus nine. (The usage of RECODE and MISSING VALUES cards is explained in the SPSS manual.)

By using a series of COMPUTE and IF cards (the seventh through sixteenth cards), Mr. Anderson arranged to have the computer score the Fireman Tests. On the data tabulation sheet (Figure 17–9) he entered not scores but rather the first, second, and third choices for each student on the Johnny test and on the Janet test. He then instructed the computer to examine each choice and give the student one point for any number (2,4, or 8) that corresponds to the choice of an animal. The computer obtains a separate score for Johnny, a separate score for Janet, and a Fireman score that combines the Johnny and Janet scores. If you examine lines seven through sixteen closely, you can probably figure out the logic of this computerized scoring process.

With the SELECT IF cards, Mr. Anderson instructed the computer to include in the analysis only those students who completed both a Johnny and a Janet test. The other students may be used for another analysis some other time, but at the present time he wished to exclude them from the computations.

Mr. Anderson requested his first statistical analysis on the PEARSON CORR card. This is a card that you have seen previously. The output from this analysis is shown in Figure 17–11. Notice that although there were 31 subjects listed on the N OF CASES card, the number of subjects in each actual calculation ranged from 23 to 26. This reduction in numbers occurred because of selections the computer made based on the SELECT IF and MISSING VALUES cards.

```
RUN NAME        HUMANE EDUCATION TEST VALIDATION                                   PAGE 0001

RUN NAME        HUMANE EDUCATION TEST VALIDATION
VARIABLE LIST   SEX,GRADE,PET,JOHN1,JOHN2,JOHN3,JANET1,JANET2,JANET3,TV,IQ,READ
INPUT MEDIUM    CARD
INPUT FORMAT    FIXED(7X,10F1.0,F3.0,F2.0)
N OF CASES      31
RECODE          SEX TO READ(BLANK=-9)
COMPUTE         JOHNNY=0
COMPUTE         JANET=0
COMPUTE         FIREMAN=0
IF              (JOHN1 EQ 2 OR JOHN1 EQ 4 OR JOHN1 EQ 8)JOHNNY=JOHNNY+1
IF              (JOHN2 EQ 2 OR JOHN2 EQ 4 OR JOHN2 EQ 8)JOHNNY=JOHNNY+1
IF              (JOHN3 EQ 2 OR JOHN3 EQ 4 OR JOHN3 EQ 8)JOHNNY=JOHNNY+1
IF              (JANET1 EQ 2 OR JANET1 EQ 4 OR JANET1 EQ 8)JANET=JANET+1
IF              (JANET2 EQ 2 OR JANET2 EQ 4 OR JANET2 EQ 8)JANET=JANET+1
IF              (JANET3 EQ 2 OR JANET3 EQ 4 OR JANET3 EQ 8)JANET=JANET+1
COMPUTE         FIREMAN=JOHNNY+JANET
MISSING VALUES  SEX TO READ(-9)
IF              (JOHN1 GE 0)
IF              (JANET1 GE 0)
PEARSON CORR    JOHNNY,JANET,FIREMAN,TV,IQ,READ
READ INPUT DATA

BREAKDOWN       TABLES=JOHNNY,JANET,FIREMAN BY SEX,PET
STATISTICS      1
FREQUENCIES     INTEGER=JOHNNY,JANET,FIREMAN(0,6)
OPTIONS         8
CROSSTABS       JOHNNY,JANET,FIREMAN BY SEX(1,2) WITH IQ/
                TABLES=JOHNNY,JANET BY SEX
OPTIONS         3,5
FINISH
```

FIGURE 17–10. Mr. Anderson's Computer Program. (*Note:* The system cards and a few of the cards which put labels on the printouts have been omitted from this listing.)

```
HUMANE EDUCATION TEST VALIDATAION                               10/02/80        PAGE   4
FILE   NONAME    (CREATION DATE = 10/02/80)
- - - - - - - P E A R S O N   C O R R E L A T I O N   C O E F F I C I E N T S - - - - - - -

             JOHNNY       JANET      FIREMAN        TV1         TV2          IQ         READ

JOHNNY       1.0000      0.7584      0.9377       0.2660      0.1060      0.2531      0.2565
             ( 26)       ( 26)       ( 26)        ( 25)       ( 25)       ( 24)       ( 24)
             P=*****     P=0.000     P=0.000      P=0.099     P=0.307     P=0.116     P=0.113

JANET        0.7584      1.0000      0.9377       0.1715      0.0846      0.3180      0.2077
             ( 26)       ( 26)       ( 26)        ( 25)       ( 25)       ( 24)       ( 24)
             P=0.000     P=*****     P=0.000      P=0.206     P=0.344     P=0.065     P=0.165

FIREMAN      0.9377      0.9377      1.0000       0.2322      0.1012      0.3020      0.2464
             ( 26)       ( 26)       ( 26)        ( 25)       ( 25)       ( 24)       ( 24)
             P=0.000     P=0.000     P=*****      P=0.132     P=0.315     P=0.076     P=0.123

TV1          0.2660      0.1715      0.2322       1.0000      0.9269      0.1677      0.2956
             ( 25)       ( 25)       ( 25)        ( 25)       ( 25)       ( 23)       ( 23)
             P=0.099     P=0.206     P=0.132      P=*****     P=0.000     P=0.222     P=0.085

TV2          0.1060      0.0846      0.1012       0.9269      1.0000      0.1871      0.2278
             ( 25)       ( 25)       ( 25)        ( 25)       ( 25)       ( 23)       ( 23)
             P=0.307     P=0.344     P=0.315      P=0.000     P=*****     P=0.196     P=0.148

IQ           0.2531      0.3180      0.3020       0.1677      0.1871      1.0000      0.7435
             ( 24)       ( 24)       ( 24)        ( 23)       ( 23)       ( 24)       ( 24)
             P=0.116     P=0.065     P=0.076      P=0.222     P=0.196     P=*****     P=0.000

READ         0.2565      0.2077      0.2464       0.2956      0.2278      0.7435      1.0000
             ( 24)       ( 24)       ( 24)        ( 23)       ( 23)       ( 24)       ( 24)
             P=0.113     P=0.165     P=0.123      P=0.085     P=0.148     P=0.000     P=*****

(COEFFICIENT / (CASES) / SIGNIFICANCE)        (A VALUE OF 99.0000 IS PRINTED IF A COEFFICIENT CANNOT BE COMPUTED)
```

FIGURE 17-11. The Correlation Matrix Resulting from Mr. Anderson's PEARSON CORR Card. (The number of cases in parentheses varies, because some students were excluded from specific analyses by the MISSING VALUES card.)

325

```
HUMANE EDUCATION TEST VALIDATAION
CRITERION VARIABLE FIREMAN
                                                        10/02/80        PAGE  9
- - - - - - - - - - A N A L Y S I S   O F   V A R I A N C E - - - - - - - - - -
VARIABLE    CODE   VALUE LABEL        SUM       MEAN    STD DEV    SUM OF SQ    N

PET          0.                     37.0000    2.8462   2.5445     77.6923  ( 13)
PET          1.                     29.0000    2.2308   1.7394     36.3077  ( 13)
                                   ---------                     ---------
       WITHIN GROUPS TOTAL          66.0000    2.5385   2.1794    114.0000  ( 26)

*****************************************************
**                                                 **
**       A N A L Y S I S   O F   V A R I A N C E    **
**                                                 **
**  SOURCE          SUM OF SQUARES  D.F.  MEAN SQUARE    F      SIG.  **
**                                                 **
**  BETWEEN GROUPS      2.462        1      2.462     0.518   0.4786  **
**                                                 **
**  WITHIN GROUPS     114.000       24      4.750                    **
**                                                 **
**        ETA = 0.1454    ETA SQUARED = 0.0211                       **
**                                                 **
*****************************************************
```

FIGURE 17-12 The Breakdown of Mean Scores by Pet Ownership and the Accompanying Analysis of Variance Resulting from Mr. Anderson's Breakdown and Statistics Cards.

HUMANE EDUCATION TEST VALIDATAION

FILE   NONAME   (CREATION DATE = 10/02/80)   10/02/80   PAGE   19

FIREMAN

```
CODE
   0  I
      ******************************************  (   8)
      I
      I
   1  I
      ****************  (   4)
      I
      I
   2  I
      ************************  (   6)
      I
      I
   3  I
      ************************  (   6)
      I
      I
   4  I
      ********  (   2)
      I
      I
   6  I
      ********************  (   5)
      I
      I....I....I....I....I....I
      0    2    4    6    8   10
      FREQUENCY
```

VALID CASES   31   MISSING CASES   0
```

FIGURE 17–13. The Frequency Histogram Resulting from Mr. Anderson's FREQUEN-
CIES and OPTIONS Card. (The numbers 0 through 6 under the word "Code" on the left-hand
side of the printout indicate scores on the combined Fireman tests.)

327
```

328

```
HUMANE EDUCATION TEST VALIDATAION                              PAGE   27
FILE   NONAME    (CREATION DATE = 10/02/80)            10/02/80
* * JOHNNY  * * * * * * * * * *  C R O S S T A B U L A T I O N  O F  * * * * * * * * * * * * * * * * * *
* *        * * * * * * * * * *                    B Y  SEX        * * * * * * * * * * * * * *  PAGE  1 OF  1

                     SEX
        COUNT  I
        COL PCT IMALE        FEMALE                ROW
                I       1. I       2. I           TOTAL
JOHNNY          I--------I--------I
        0. I      4    I      4    I              8
CHOSE NO ANIMALS I   28.6  I   33.3  I           30.8
                I--------I--------I
        1. I      5    I      4    I              9
CHOSE ONE ANIMAL I   35.7  I   33.3  I           34.6
                I--------I--------I
        2. I      2    I      1    I              3
CHOSE TWO ANIMAL I   14.3  I    8.3  I           11.5
                I--------I--------I
        3. I      3    I      3    I              6
CHOSE THREE ANIM I   21.4  I   25.0  I           23.1
                I--------I--------I
         COLUMN        14        12               26
         TOTAL       53.8      46.2            100.0

CHI SQUARE =   0.29233 WITH   3 DEGREES OF FREEDOM   SIGNIFICANCE =  0.9615
```

FIGURE 17-14. The Cross Tabulation of Males and Females According to How Many Animals They Chose on the Johnny Test.

Next he requested a breakdown comparing the means of boys to those of girls and the means of pet owners to those of non-pet-owners. This breakdown was accompanied by an analysis of variance (signified by a "1" on the STATISTICS card that follows the BREAKDOWN card). This BREAKDOWN card actually yielded six analyses of variance, and one of them is shown in Figure 17–12. You have already seen a printout like this, and you can tell from examining it that the difference between pet owners and non-pet-owners is quite small and is very likely to have arisen by chance.

Next, he requested a simple frequency count with a FREQUENCIES card. The selection of "8" on the OPTIONS card accompanying this FREQUENCIES card enables him to obtain the frequency histogram shown in Figure 17–13. (Mr. Anderson learned this from the SPSS manual.)

With the ANOVA card, Mr. Anderson requested an analysis of covariance, comparing the means on the Johnny, Janet, and combined Fireman Tests of the boys and girls with IQ as the covariate. The results of this analysis are not shown in this text. Finally, he used a CROSSTABS card to get an exact count of how many boys compared to girls chose zero, one, two, or three animals on the Johnny and on the Janet test. This cross tabulation is shown in Figure 17–14. The second number in each block is the percentage of males or females falling into each category. This percentage was obtained by entering "3" and "5" on the accompanying OPTIONS card.

Mr. Anderson found these results to be useful. He also found it impressive that the computation of all these statistics (including the many shown in the listing but not shown in the figures) took only 39.16 seconds of computer time.

SUMMARY

The computer can be a great help to researchers at any level of sophistication. If you put accurate information and correct instructions into the computer, it will provide you with accurate statistical analyses in a remarkably short time. On the other hand, if you enter faulty data or provide incorrect instructions, it will provide you with inaccurate and possibly misleading information. This chapter has provided guidelines on how to put data into an appropriate format for keypunching and submission to the computer. It has also provided basic guidelines for performing some statistical analyses. Additional information can be obtained by consulting manuals and more detailed resources dealing with computers.

Annotated Bibliography

NIE, N.H., HULL, C.H., JENKINS, J.G., STEINBRENNER, K., and BENT, D.H. *Statistical Package for the Social Sciences* (2nd ed.) (New York: McGraw-Hill, 1975). This is the manual for the SPSS programs. It provides comprehensive and detailed instructions on how to write the control cards and format the data to perform statistical analyses using the SPSS programs. This manual should enable you to do most of your own programming; but if you need additional help, there is probably a consultant available at your computing center.

18 Carrying Out a Research Project and Writing the Report

Chapter Preview

This chapter provides some basic guidelines for carrying out a formal research project and for writing a report on such a project. It is assumed that the reader is already familiar with the principles discussed in previous chapters. The information in this chapter will be useful to readers who are required to do a research project as part of their course work or thesis requirements. It will also be useful to those professionals who wish to perform formal research for their own satisfaction or because of the professional requirements of their jobs. It will be helpful to those readers who want to write research proposals to submit to funding agencies to obtain grants of various kinds or who have to write any kind of reports.

After finishing this chapter you should be able to

- Identify and describe the major steps in conducting a research study.
- Identify and describe the major components of a research report.
- Conduct a formal research study.
- Write a research report.

INTRODUCTION

This chapter will discuss conducting and reporting upon formal research projects. This term is used to distinguish formal undertakings from the more informal research of educators who will use the strategies discussed in this text as a regular part of evaluating and improving their educational efforts without disrupting their ordinary routine to conduct a separate study.

SELECTING AND CLASSIFYING A PROBLEM

This book is based on the premise that educators need basic research skills to solve daily problems and to perform their professional responsibilities effectively. With this in mind, it should be obvious that it should not be difficult for you to find a problem to do research on. Your world is probably full of such problems. If you do not have a problem that requires research skills for its solution, this is probably because you are not actively engaged in teaching, in administration, or in counseling. All educators have problems that they can attack through educational research methodology. Just identify an outcome which you want to encourage or discourage. This is your dependent variable. Then identify ways to increase or prevent this outcome. These methods are your independent variable. State a research problem and use the strategies described in Chapter 14 to refine it. The problems you face on your job are important, and if you are asked to do a research project to demonstrate your research capability, then certainly you should channel your energies into an area of relevance to your professional career.

Finding a problem on which to do research, therefore, should not be difficult. A realistic approach is to narrow the field of prospects to a single problem. This has to be left to your judgment. Certainly, the means to attack some problems in an effective manner may be beyond your control, and you would hardly want to tackle them as a course assignment; but all educators are beset with problems that can be successfully attacked and better understood (if not solved) through experimental, quasi-experimental, criterion group, or correlational research. Identify one of them and state it in rough form. Then clarify this problem through such procedures as operational definition and the strategies described in Chapter 14. Often, the nature of the problem changes as it is clarified. For example, a teacher may start out trying to solve the problem of how to make children sit still and eventually shift to researching

---

DEAR RESEARCHER: I am taking a course in which I have been given an assignment to do an educational research report. I have to select a problem by Wednesday evening. I am a very busy person, and I don't have time to look for research problems. I find this very irritating, because I have three learning disabled children that have been mainstreamed and I don't know what to do with them. In addition, I'm trying to develop a new method for teaching math which I think will help my pupils apply mathematics principles to their daily lives. Besides that, I'm trying to find out what causes so much anxiety when we watch the films in our new science series. How am I supposed to have time to find a research problem? Please help me. Tell me: What is the Great Unanswered Question of Educational Research? I need your help. (signed) OVERWHELMED WITH PROBLEMS

DEAR OVERWHELMED: The Great Unanswered Question of Educational Research is this: Why do teachers who spend all day dealing with problems have trouble finding a problem to do research on? In your letter you stated three different educational problems which have kept you from thinking of a problem. Do your research on one of them. (signed) THE LONELY RESEARCHER

new methods for teaching math to learning disabled pupils. An assigned research project can be beneficial not only because you will learn how to do such assignments, but more importantly because it will encourage you to attack your problems in a more scientific and effective manner.

REVIEW OF THE LITERATURE

Once you have decided on a problem to attack, find out what is already known about it. Look for what others have said about defining the real nature of the problem and about solutions to it. You may decide to stay on a purely practical level and simply verify that a specific treatment can produce a specific effect in your own educational setting. This is itself a valuable outcome. On the other hand, you may decide to become at least a little bit theoretical and develop a hypothesis that will expand upon someone else's theory. You may even grow bold and develop a theory of your own.

In reviewing the literature, a good idea is to look for moderator variables that are applicable to your problem. Even if you choose to operate at a very applied and nontheoretical level, the knowledge that a certain treatment will work differently with some subjects than with others can be a valuable discovery for your own professional use. In addition, if you choose to go a more theoretical route, the identification and testing of new moderator variables while replicating another researcher's experiment can provide valuable expansions of existing theoretical knowledge.

The review of the literature should be conducted in accordance with the guidelines

described in Chapter 16. Even while you are conducting this literature search, you can start organizing it into the portion of your paper that will be called the "review of the literature." A useful approach is to write down on cards specific ideas from various sources as you accumulate them and to modify and merge these cards in an appropriate order as the review of the literature leads to a clarified statement of the problem. Let your literature search be guided by the question, "What do I still need to know before I can take some reasonable action?" Then look for answers to this question. Do not let the review of the literature be a mere formality.

STATEMENT OF THE HYPOTHESIS

When you think you have a solution to the problem (no matter how tentative) write this down as your hypothesis. Then go about refining your hypothesis until you feel a degree of satisfaction with it. Include appropriate control and moderator variables, as well as the dependent and independent variables. After you have devised a clearly stated hypothesis, write out a research prediction in which all the terms of the hypothesis are operationally defined. Most researchers find that this process forces them to clarify the problem into a much clearer formulation. It is perfectly legitimate (and quite desirable) to go back to earlier steps by modifying the statement of the problem, looking for more information in the professional literature, and restating the hypothesis as often as necessary. Avoid making changes in your statement of the problem and hypothesis just to make the problem easier to solve. Your changes should be directed toward helping you solve as thoroughly as possible the problem you want to solve.

It is legitimate to change the hypothesis as often as you wish, up until you put the actual experiment into practice and collect data. After that, it is scientifically unsound and disreputable to change the hypothesis. Science (and educational research) would not make noteworthy progress if the researcher were allowed to look at the results first and then decide what the hypothesis should be. This would allow chance factors to play an important part and render the research meaningless. The scientific method depends on first stating a prediction and then conducting an experiment and collecting data to verify or refute the prediction. It is important that you adhere to this convention.

PLANNING THE EXPERIMENTAL PROCEDURES

Once you have satisfactorily stated your hypothesis and research prediction, then it is time to plan and carry out an experiment to verify or refute this research prediction. By looking at the research prediction that you derived from your research hypothesis, you should be able to determine exactly what information you will need to test this prediction. The knowledge you have gained from previous chapters will help you decide what research design and other experimental procedures will help you acquire this information.

Since most research in education involves human beings as subjects, it would be possible that someone doing research could either intentionally or accidentally do something during a research project that would be harmful to the participants.

Researchers should take careful precautions to see to it that no such harmful effects occur. Most school systems, universities, government agencies, and professional organizations have specific guidelines for research involving human subjects. If you adhere to the guidelines, you can be fairly certain that harmful effects will be ruled out. These guidelines are designed to prevent subjects from being hurt, embarrassed, frightened, or in any other way imposed upon or negatively affected by experimental procedures.

In many cases, such guidelines indicate that subjects have a right to refuse to participate in a research study, to remain anonymous if they wish to, and to have responses kept confidential. Subjects also have the right to expect that researchers behave in a responsible manner in all respects during the experiment. Ethical guidelines merely mean that we have to behave responsibly when we collect data. The guidelines do not by any means prohibit useful educational research. In most cases, these guidelines will make you behave no differently than you would wish to behave in performing responsible research even if there were no guidelines. They simply make sure that common sense is observed in research on human subjects. The guidelines are most likely to restrict the activity of researchers who use measuring instruments that are not normally part of the school's testing program or who require the students to do something that is not part of the school curriculum. In such cases, the researcher should obtain the approval of appropriate administrative officials or curriculum committees in the schools before introducing the test or altering the curriculum.

Extraordinary measures may be essential in research of a major theoretical nature, but the research projects conducted by many of the readers of this text will involve no more than measuring student performance to assess the effectiveness of teaching techniques. In such cases the educators will often do what they normally do, but do it more effectively and analyze the results. There is usually no threat at all to the welfare of the participants, provided the data is handled confidentially. Specific permission from administrative sources or from a curriculum committee is probably not even necessary. For example, my university has a policy that if a professor merely examines course examinations and compares two groups (for example) to see if the method used in one group is superior to that used in the other, then no specific permission is required. On the other hand, if the professor would introduce a treatment that is not an actual part of the curriculum or provide a type of measuring instrument that would not routinely be used as part of student evaluation, then specific permission has to be obtained from the university's Committee on the Use of Human Subjects. Even if no permission is required, of course, it is expected and required that the professor be acting responsibly and ethically. Similar guidelines probably apply in your educational setting. If you are in doubt, err on the side of safety, and ask permission.

In addition to what is ethical, it is important to be concerned about what is possible and what is practical. For example, it might seem obvious that the best way to test your research prediction would be by having randomly assigned experimental and control groups whose performance would be measured by a carefully validated battery of tests. However, you might quickly discover that randomly assigned groups are not going to be available to you or that the desired battery of tests would be both too costly and too time consuming to warrant its use. Therefore, you might have to settle for a quasi-experimental design using a less than perfect measuring device. However, although it is important to be aware of what is practical, it is equally important not to be too quick to abandon the search for the ideal. In many cases it is possible to cooperate with educational administrators in such a way as to achieve random assignment, and it is likewise possible to obtain or develop measuring instruments that provide a high degree of validity.

It is important to obtain or develop and field test all the instruments and materials that will be needed for the study. An appropriate research design must be selected that will provide the control necessary to maximize internal and external validity. Appropriate scheduling must be arranged so that unusual events will not ruin the timing of the treatments or observations. Insofar as possible, all problems should be anticipated, so that emergency adjustments do not have to be made as the study is being carried out.

You should plan the statistical analysis at this point, before any data are collected. By doing this, you can make sure that you will obtain all the data you need to test your hypothesis. You will be able to ascertain that you will know what to do with the data after you have obtained your results. Once you have conducted the study, it will be too late to go back and collect a piece of data that you really should have collected in the first place.

If you plan to use the computer for data analysis, make plans to do this before you collect the data. It may be possible to devise measuring instruments so that data can be initially recorded in a fashion that is easily compatible with keypunching and analysis. If you fail to plan ahead, you will at the very least have a more difficult task when it comes time to turn the data over to the computer, and at the worst you may discover that your data are simply not compatible with the types of computer analysis which would be most appropriate.

CARRYING OUT THE STUDY

After appropriate planning, you should implement the experimental strategy according to the prescribed plan. Stick to the proposed plans as closely as possible. Even the most noble plans, however, sometimes go awry; and when something surprising comes up or something just plain goes wrong, adjustments of some sort have to be made. When it is necessary to make changes in plans, do so as much as possible within the guidelines of sound educational research procedures. Modify your original plan; do not abandon it. Come as close as you possibly can to getting a full test of your research prediction. In some cases, of course, the changes will be positive rather than negative. For example, you may discover an additional group for comparison or an extra opportunity for measurement that would strengthen the findings. By all means, take advantage of such opportunities if they actually strengthen your research design. Keep a close record of whatever changes you make, so that you can analyze the impact of these changes upon your study.

ANALYZING THE DATA

If you have planned appropriately, analyzing the data is not a difficult problem. You simply do what you said you would do. The real problems occur if you fail to plan your analysis ahead of time. Students who wait until after they have collected their data to decide how to analyze their results often discover that there is no acceptable way to do the analysis for their inappropriately collected data.

While doing your analysis, you may discover that there are additional analyses that would be helpful. It might be that you had forgotten or not known about a certain analysis. Or it might be that a certain result might be surprising and a further analysis (perhaps taking into consideration a new moderator variable) would be helpful to clarify this confusion. In such cases, it is appropriate to do the additional analyses and to report on them.

DRAWING CONCLUSIONS

After you have conducted your study and analyzed the results, it is necessary to look back and see how the results relate to your research prediction and to your research hypothesis. You may be forced to conclude that your results are ambiguous, perhaps because of some error you made in the experimental procedures. In such a case, admit the ambiguity and recommend ways to clarify the results in the future. Even the best researchers will occasionally come up with ambiguous results. The embarrassment lies not in attaining ambiguous results, but in failing to recognize them as ambiguous.

TABLE 18–1. The Major Steps in Carrying Out a Research Study.

Step	*Chapter in This Book Where You Can Seek Guidelines*
Select a problem.	
Determine which of many to focus on.	
Clarify the problem so that you know what your real problem is.	Chapters 13 & 14
Review the literature to seek solutions.	Chapter 16
State your hypothesis.	
Identify all variables (dependent, independent, moderator, control).	Chapter 14
State research prediction.	Chapter 14
Plan experimental procedures.	
Check ethical considerations.	Chapter 18
Select a design.	Chapters 9, 10, & 11
Develop, obtain, and field test all instruments.	Chapters 2 to 4, 6
Anticipate any problems that may arise.	
Plan for statistical analysis.	Chapters 5, 11, & 12
Plan for computer usage.	Chapter 17
Carry out the study.	Chapters 9, 10, 11, & 15
Stick to your plan.	
Note modifications.	
Analyze the data.	Chapters 11 & 12
Do all analyses that were planned.	
Do supplementary analyses, if any.	
Draw conclusions.	Chapters 8 & 15
Write report.	Chapter 18

WRITING THE REPORT

Once you have completed the study and drawn your own conclusions, you will want to convey the results to someone else. This need not be an onerous task. Even though this step is listed here after drawing the conclusions, much of the writing can be accomplished long before the study is completed. As you read the following sections about the contents of the research report, it should be noted that everything in the main body of the report up to the results section can actually be written before the experiment is conducted. The rest is merely a matter of writing down what happened, analyzing these happenings, and drawing conclusions.

At this point, it may be useful to summarize the major steps in carrying out a research project. Table 18–1 provides such a summary. In examining this table, recall that although these steps are listed sequentially, there may be alterations in the order. For example, although writing the report is listed as the last step, a major portion of the report can (and should) be written before the study is carried out. Dissatisfaction with a hypothesis might mandate a return to a new statement of the problem. The second column in Table 18–1 provides a brief listing of chapters in which each of the guidelines (or sub-guidelines) is discussed. Such a listing of chapters is necessarily an oversimplification, since many topics are covered in more than one chapter. Nevertheless, even a tentative list may be helpful to a researcher who needs to know where to look for more information.

THE PARTS OF A RESEARCH REPORT

The parts of a research report will now be described in the order in which the parts normally appear. In many cases, the actual time at which the parts are written would vary from the order described here. For example, although the title and abstract are described first and come at the beginning of the report, they should be written last, after the rest of the report has been compiled. Otherwise it may be difficult for the title and the abstract to catch the full sense of what the report is actually about. In addition, even though each part is labeled separately here, sometimes labels are omitted and sometimes parts are combined. For example, the "statement of the problem" is often directly attached to the end of the review of the literature rather than comprising a separate section all to itself. Many reports merge certain sections into such combinations as "Results and Discussion" or "Discussion and Conclusions." The important thing is to use a style that will convey the information clearly to the reader; and if departing from these guidelines will enable you to do a better job, then you should certainly let your own wisdom guide you.

THE TITLE OF THE REPORT

Always make your title succinct and meaningful. Avoid lengthy titles. When I wrote my doctoral dissertation, the original title was "The Relationship Between the Perceived Quality of Educational Research Reports as Viewed by Educational Researchers and by Educational Decision Makers." After my major professor got finished talking to me, the title had become "Information Quality and Educational Decision Making." The reduction from 20 to 6 words in the title had lost little information, had forced me to communicate more precisely, and made it more likely that people would bother to read the title without annoyance.

The word "relationship" can almost always be deleted from a title. Words describing the nature of the subjects or the type of instrument used to collect data can usually be omitted unless this information is likely to be of use to the reader. Your title should communicate as briefly and directly as possible the precise nature of what your report is about.

It is useful if your title contains key words that will be recognized by others who might be interested in your research. This is important because your report may be picked up by an abstracting service, and such services index reports by key words in the titles. With this in mind, for example, you may want to be sure that your title contains the relevant key words from the ERIC *Thesaurus*, if you expect your report to be indexed in any of the ERIC dissemination services.

The title should be written *after* the report is written. Of course, the title may occur to you during the project, while you are writing the report, or even before you have begun the research. In such cases, do not throw the title away. But be sure to examine it carefully after the report is written to make sure it conveys what it is expected to convey.

THE AUTHORS AND AFFILIATION

The statement of authorship tells readers who is responsible for the research. If there is only one author, it is easy to place the name in this slot. When there are multiple authors, it becomes a problem to determine the order in which the authors are to be listed. Being first author is somewhat more prestigious. When people refer to a research article, they often refer to it as "So-and-so's work"; and in doing so, they often use the name of only the first author. The decision regarding the order of authors has to be made among the persons involved in the project, of course; but the basic guideline should be that the person who bore the major share of the responsibility in performing the research should be listed as first author.

One area where assignment of authorship sometimes becomes a problem is when a student works on a paper in cooperation with a professor. There is a possibility that the student will do all the work and the professor will merely read it at the very end, but that the professor will expect to be first author. This is an obviously improper practice. If a professor is going to be first author, then the professor should bear the major share of the responsibility. This does not mean that the professor should spend more hours actively working on the project than the student, but rather that the professor's contribution be the essential component of the project. For example, a professor may have spent ten years developing a certain theory and then guide a student in the careful collection of data related to this theory. If the professor's contribution is such that the student would never have been able to perform the research without the professor's guidance, then it would certainly be appropriate for the professor to be first author, even though 90% of the actual work performed on the project was done by the student. On the other hand, if a student does a Master's thesis on a topic of only remote interest to the professor and the professor merely reads the paper and verifies that it is well done, then it would seem that the student should be first author. I find that a safe guideline is to ask who will be responsible for the authenticity of the report if someone criticizes it after its release. If the professor is going to be held responsible, then the professor should take major responsibility and be first author. If the student is going to be held responsible, then the student should assume the primary responsibility and the first authorship.

It is worth noting that many journals currently permit the authors to add a footnote indicating that the article was written under conditions of co-authorship. If there are more than two authors, the same guidelines apply; whoever assumes a greater deal of responsibility should receive greater recognition.

The statement of institutional affiliation should show the reader what institution supported the research activity. This serves two purposes. It gives the institution credit for performing a useful service, and it informs readers about the location of an institution where there is likely to be some interest in this area of research. A minor problem arises if the researcher completed the research at one institution but then moved to another before the research was published. In such cases, the author has the option of listing the institutional affiliation at either the original or the current location. The best idea seems to be to indicate the original institution along with the author's name accompanying the title and to put the new institution in a footnote together with a mailing address indicating where the author can currently be reached.

Many journals request additional information about the author and include this information in a footnote or in a separate section of the journal where all the authors for a given issue are described. Make this information brief and accurate. If you make it too lengthy, someone may edit it; editing may result in a different impression than you would want to give of yourself.

THE ABSTRACT

The abstract should include a brief summary of the key points of the report. It is usually limited to 100 or 150 words, and so you have to be concise. The abstract should be written in such a way that a person can read it and have a good idea of what the report is about. An abstract should contain as its essential ingredients the statement of the hypothesis, the statement of the research prediction, and a brief statement of the results. In addition, a very brief statement of why the research is worth doing may sometimes be important. It is not necessary (or even advisable) to write each of these ingredients as a separate part and to chain them together. Rather, they should be integrated in a meaningful fashion. It might be possible to write a clear passage of 50 words briefly stating why the research is important, and this passage could end with a succinct statement of the hypothesis. Then the rest of the abstract could contain a statement of the results inserted into the format of the operationally defined research prediction. The reader can then tell by reading this abstract why the research should be of interest, what the specific problem is, and what the results are. As stated above, it is usually a good idea to write the abstract after the rest of the report has been written. It is an easy task to go through a well written report and pull out the material needed for a concise abstract.

A well written abstract is a great service to everyone concerned. I would recommend always including an abstract, even if the person or organization to whom you are submitting the report does not ask for one or will not publish it. Abstracts are the main method you have to put your ideas in front of the people you want to read them. The importance of abstracts can be seen in writing grant proposals. When reviewers are reading several grant proposals to decide which ones they will fund, the main thing they often focus on immediately prior to the decision is the abstract. There is no time to reread the whole proposal at such a time, and the decision is going to be based largely on what you said (or failed to say) in your abstract. The situation is the same with published articles and even term papers. Decisions regarding whether to read an article or what grade to give a paper are often based on an assessment of the abstract.

It is also important to note that your abstract may be picked up by an indexing and abstracting service. If an article is not accompanied by an abstract, someone else who works for the indexing and abstracting service will have to write one for you, or else the report will merely be indexed without an abstract. Both of these alternatives are undesirable. In addition, such services index the report under key words. They often allow you to suggest key words for indexing. You can often identify key words beyond your title by underlining up to ten important words throughout the abstract. In choosing such words, you should use terms that are taken insofar as possible from the thesaurus of the organization that you expect to index your report. The idea is to make your report as readily available as possible to persons who will want to find it.

Some journals, conventions, and funding organizations follow a process of blind review. This means that the paper will be reviewed in such a way that the reviewers will not know who wrote the report and therefore cannot let information about authorship influence their judgments regarding the quality of the report. If you are submitting a report to blind review, follow the guidelines indicated by the journal or other organization. You will usually include the same information described here, but you will arrange it in a slightly different format.

THE REVIEW OF THE LITERATURE

Contrary to popular belief, the purpose of the review of the literature is not to overwhelm the reader with a large number of impressive citations. Quite the contrary, the main purpose of this review is to put the hypothesis to be examined in the research report into its proper context. Secondary purposes of this part of the report are to provide readers with guidelines regarding where they can look to find more information and to establish the author's credentials by letting readers know that the researcher is aware of what has been going on with regard to the current and related topics. These secondary aspects should not be emphasized to the neglect of the primary purpose.

The exact length and the precise contents of the review of the literature will vary depending on whom the researcher expects to read the report. If the target audience consists of readers who have no knowledge whatsoever about a topic and who will want background information, then time will have to be spent explaining each of the sources that are cited. At the other extreme, if the intended audience consists of persons who will already be very familiar with the background research, then a simple reference to four or five authors in a single sentence may provide a satisfactory perspective on how their research relates to the problem at hand. Decide what your audience needs, and then provide that information. Confine yourself to the relevant aspects of the sources you cite. If a source has an elaborate theory that relates to many aspects of education, focus only on how that theory relates to the problem at hand. If a few readers want more information, they can always look it up.

The best and easiest method of citation is the style advocated by the publication manual of the American Psychological Association. This style is also widely used in educational journals. A sample citation to one of my articles in a review of literature might look like this:

> Kosmoski and Vockell (1978) found that learning centers stimulated both cognitive and affective growth among elementary school students.

This citation format immediately tells the reader who wrote the article and how recent it is. This is accomplished without any bothersome footnote. If readers want to find out more about the article, they can look in the list of references at the end of the article and find the article by Kosmoski and Vockell. At that point there will be an indication of the exact title of the article, the name of the journal, and the issue and pages upon which the article appeared. This method conveys useful information without disrupting the reader's attention needlessly. Almost all other methods are more distracting.

THE STATEMENT OF THE PROBLEM

The review of the literature should lead clearly and naturally to a statement of the problem. In most cases the statement need not even be a separate section of the report. It can simply be part of the concluding paragraph of the review of the literature. The train of thought should go something like this: "These various sources have shown that. . . . All this leads us to wonder about the relationship between X and Y." Such a statement of the problem leads to a natural transition to the statement of the hypothesis.

THE STATEMENT OF THE HYPOTHESIS

The hypothesis should be clearly stated immediately before the methods section of the report. This statement can be couched in purely conceptual terms at this point; or if it seems natural to do so, it can employ operationally defined terms. In general, a more specific and thorough operationally stated prediction should be reserved for a later point in the methods section, immediately prior to the presentation of the results that will confirm or reject this prediction.

If the hypothesis is a complex one, do not be afraid to state it in several sentences instead of trying to compress too many ideas into a single, complicated sentence. In certain instances, it might seem more natural to state a question at this point and then to follow this up with an operationally defined research prediction that answers this question in the methods section. This is an acceptable practice, so long as the question clearly and unambiguously asks about the relationship that would be contained in the hypothesis if it were stated in that form.

In dissertations and formal research papers, the statement of the hypothesis is often contained in a separate section of the report. In most journal articles and less academic situations, the hypothesis fits easily and naturally at the very end of the review of literature. The last paragraph of the review of literature could summarize the review by stating a concise problem, and then the hypothesis could provide a tentative answer to this problem.

THE METHODS SECTION

Within the methods section, all the important variables in the study should be operationally defined. This will include control and moderator variables as well as the dependent and independent variables. This operational definition process should be so complete that another researcher could duplicate the process by simply doing what you said you did in the methods section. In fact, few readers will actually wish to duplicate the process, but only such a precise description will enable them to make judgments regarding the internal and external validity of the research.

A detailed description of the subjects and the setting should be provided. It should be clear to the reader which variables were treated as moderator and which as control variables. The independent variable should be described in precise detail so that a reader can duplicate the treatment. An exact description should be given of any instruments used to measure the dependent variable. In providing these operational definitions, you can use a certain amount of brevity. For example, if you employ a commercially developed product with which your readers are almost certain to be familiar, you can get by with merely mentioning the exact label attached to this product and indicating where readers can get further information. If you use the Stanford-Binet IQ test or some other standardized test about which the readers are probably already well informed or can easily obtain additional information, then a detailed operational description of such dependent variables would be unnecessary. On the other hand, whenever there is any ambiguity, provide additional specific information. Sometimes it will be necessary to state that you used an instrument developed by yourself, describe it as fully as possible, and then tell the readers to contact you if they want more details.

The methods section should also include a statement of the research design and of the statistical procedures used in the analysis of the data. This should be stated in such a way that the readers could replicate your analysis if they had access to your data. (In fact, if some other competent researcher should ask to see your data, you should be willing to permit this, if this can be done without infringing on the rights of your subjects.) At this point you should be aware of the wide variety in levels of expertise that will exist among your readers. For example, some will be qualified statisticians, whereas others will not even know what a t test is. You yourself may not be highly proficient in research design or statistics. You may have used a certain statistical procedure, for instance, simply because a textbook specified that you should do so. In such cases, a good idea is to provide a brief description of the research design or the statistical procedure and then insert a bibliographic citation indicating where the reader can find more information about the topic. If you used a computer to perform your analysis, it is often helpful to specify the nature of your computer programs and cite the source in which the reader can learn more about these programs.

It is often useful to conclude the methods section with an operationally stated research prediction. Such a prediction should follow a format similar to that shown in the examples in Chapter 14. A statement of this prediction in operational terms at this point will enable the reader to have clearly in mind what the results would look like if they supported the hypothesis, and this will make more meaningful the examination of the results that follow immediately thereafter.

THE RESULTS SECTION

The results section makes the results of the study available for the reader to examine. All the results that the previous sections led the readers to believe they would see should be presented in this section. In many cases, researchers combine this and the following section into a "Results and Discussion" section. This is an especially good idea if the discussion is brief and is most appropriately presented when the results are fresh in the mind of the reader. At the very least, you should point out to the reader what hypothesis or aspect of the hypothesis a given piece of data refers to and whether or not this result verifies or rejects that aspect of the hypothesis.

It is advisable to make use of tables and figures in presenting your results. In doing so, refer to these as tables and figures, not as charts, graphs or diagrams. The table and figure terminology is the more standardized. Number your tables and figures consecutively, sequencing your tables and figures separately. (For example, the first figure is Figure 1, even if it comes after Table 3.) When you write your report, it is good to put all the figures and tables on separate pages rather than in the actual text and then to make a notation like the following in the actual text:

(Insert Figure 5 about here)

One advantage of this approach is that it is considerably easier for the typist. Another advantage is that the readers can set the tables and figures in a separate pile and refer to them whenever necessary, even moving them along as they proceed to new pages in the text that continue to refer to the same figure. Another advantage is that journal editors prefer it this way, because it is much easier to make arrangements for printing if they do not have to adjust to the idiosyncrasies of your typing format. In some cases, journals merely photocopy what you give them and insert the results into the journal. If this is the case, there may be specific guidelines for you to follow in order to provide photo-ready copy.

Organize your information in such a way as to give a clear and accurate impression of what your results show. Badly organized tables create confusion and encourage readers to ignore them. For example, Tables 18–1 and 18–2 both present the same

TABLE **18–2.** Mean Performance and Gains of Experimental and Control Groups on Critical Thinking Test and Analysis of Variance of Posttest Scores with Pretest Scores as the Covariate.

Experimental group pretest	(n = 25)	Mean = 18.0	S.D. = 3.0
Control group pretest	(n = 13)	Mean = 18.5	S.D. = 3.4
Experimental group posttest	(n = 25)	Mean = 20.0	S.D. = 2.5
Control group posttest	(n = 13)	Mean = 18.4	S.D. = 4.4
Gain by experimental group	(n = 25)	Mean = 2.0	S.D. = 3.4
Gain by control group	(n = 13)	Mean = 0.1	S.D. = 2.5

F ratio for analysis of covariance of posttest scores using pretest as covariate: $F = 3.97$ (d.f. = 2.35). Level of significance = .05.

TABLE **18–3.** Mean Performance and Gains of Experimental and Control Groups on Critical Thinking Test.

	Pretest	*Posttest*	*Gain*
Experimental (n = 25)	18.0 (3.0)	20.0 (2.5)	2.0 (3.4)
Control (n = 13)	18.5 (3.4)	18.4 (4.4)	− 0.1 (2.5)
F ratio (d.f.)		3.97 (2.35)	
Level of significance		.05	

Standard deviations in parentheses. The *F* ratio is a result of an analysis of covariance in the posttest scores with pretest scores as the covariate.

results of an experiment in which an attempt was made to teach critical thinking skills to an experimental group of college students. Both tables show the number of subjects in the experimental and control groups, and both show the means and standard deviations of both groups on both testing occasions. Both tables show the gains made by each group, the F Ratio obtained from an analysis of covariance, the degrees of freedom, and the exact level of significance. This information is completely obscured in Table 18–2, but the same information is quite clear in Table 18–3. The difference lies in the fact that the data in Figure 18–3 are arranged in such a way as to allow easy comparisons between the numbers.

As an additional visual aid, it would be useful to accompany the results shown in Table 18–3 with a graph showing the results. Figures 18–1 and 18–2 present the results shown in Table 18–3. A reader looking at Figure 18–1 is given no clear impression from the data. What is there to conclude? This figure shows four columns of about equal height with one edging slightly above the others. This would not show a reader that the treatment had produced an impact. On the other hand, Figure 18–2 presents the same data in such a way as to show that the treatment did produce an

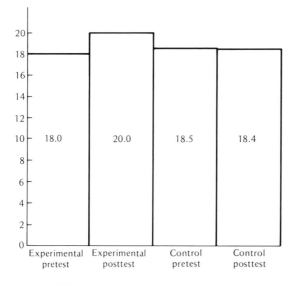

FIGURE **18–1.** Mean Critical Thinking Performance of Experimental and Control Groups on Pretest and Posttest.

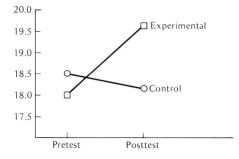

FIGURE **18–2.** Mean Critical Thinking Performance of Experimental and Control Groups on Pretest and Posttest.

impact. The sharply crossing lines give an impression that the treatment made a difference.

It is impossible in this brief and general text to explain in detail how to draw good diagrams and tables. The important point is to organize the information in a logical fashion and to present it so that it conveys the information you want to convey. Make it easy for readers to focus their attention where you want them to and to make the comparisons you want them to make. In addition to presenting the data in tables and figures, of course, it is necessary to provide a brief narrative description interpreting each of the tables and figures.

Tables and figures are most effectively designed when it is possible for the reader to understand them without referring constantly to the text. You should consider a table or figure well done when you can show it to someone who has not seen the narrative accompanying it, and that person can make a correct interpretation of the results.

The number of tables and figures and the amount of results presented will vary, depending on the nature of the report and the audience for which it is intended. In general, a doctoral dissertation or Master's thesis will contain a much lengthier results section than a journal article based on the same research. The idea is that the dissertation or thesis contains a superabundance of details, whereas the article reports only those results that are necessary to demonstrate to readers what they need to know. Interested readers can always consult the original report for more details, if they want more specific information. Include all the results that your readers will need to formulate a decision of their own concerning whether or not the results support the research hypothesis.

THE DISCUSSION SECTION

As its name states, the purpose of this section is to discuss the results of the experiment. The discussion should focus on how the results have confirmed or rejected the research prediction and thereby confirmed or rejected the research hypothesis. It is appropriate at this time to show how expectations from the review of the literature have been verified or rendered suspect by the research from the current study. It is likewise appropriate at this time to point out how results may have failed to support the research predictions and to suggest reasons for any failures. New results are not introduced here. Rather, this section explains what has been demonstrated by the results already presented.

This section is the place where limitations should be clearly recognized. Do not artificially deride your research, but honestly admit its limitations. State what shortcomings there were with regard to internal validity, and specify how these weaknesses affect the inferences about the cause and effect relationships emerging from your study. If the research of others cited in your review of the literature has some bearing (for example by providing evidence that a certain threat was probably not a significant factor), then cite such evidence at this point. This is the place to state as accurately as possible the limitations regarding the external validity of your study. No study has perfect external validity; and by stating the specific limitations of your study and bringing to bear whatever other researchers have had to say about factors related to external validity, you will help your readers draw useful generalizations from your research.

This section is often combined with either the results or the conclusions section of the report.

THE CONCLUSIONS SECTION

This section returns to the conceptual level. Previously, the results have been discussed in terms of operational definitions. Now this section devotes its attention to what the results really mean—to what they have to say about the concepts involved in the research. This section is where the operation of the intervening variable is discussed. At this time you should help your readers determine what conclusions they can actually draw based on the research you have presented. This section is often combined with either the discussion or summary section of the report.

THE SUMMARY

The summary restates the hypothesis and major findings of the study, pointing out how the findings have confirmed or rejected the hypothesis. In many respects the summary looks a lot like the abstract. The major difference is that when writing the summary you can assume that the reader has read the rest of the report. This is often a very short section, but it can be lengthened considerably by being combined with the conclusions section of the report.

THE REFERENCES

Any source that you cited in the report should be listed in the references at the end of the report. The APA style of listing references (compatible with the citation style mentioned in the Review of Literature section) provides the best format. Avoid the temptation to cite impressive references without valid reason. List in the reference section only those sources to which you actually made a reference in the text of the report. Some research reports have an additional bibliography section for additional sources not specifically cited in the report. The list of references can be a valuable resource to others who might want to pursue your line of research beyond where you have led them. Proofread the references as carefully as you do the text of the report. Proofreading lists of reference for errors is more difficult than proofreading the text, because volume and page numbers are not very exciting. However, errors at this point can be a serious disservice to the avid reader whom you would most like to serve by providing a lead toward further information.

SOME GENERAL COMMENTS ON THE WRITTEN REPORT

The main point of writing a report is to convey meaningful information to other persons. This should be done in an objective manner, but objectivity does not necessitate boredom or lack of creativity. By following the guidelines provided here you can write a good report, provided you have good information to convey. On the other hand, it may be wise under certain circumstances to modify some of the guidelines to fit your specific needs.

Since most writers have a tendency toward verbosity, I hesitate to give the following advice. When you are submitting a report it is often better to provide more information than necessary, with the assumption that readers can ignore what they do not want. If you include too much information in an article submitted to a journal, the editor can always tell you that the article will be acceptable if you revise and shorten it. On the other hand, if you err on the side of brevity the reader or editor has no way of knowing whether you could add further information if given a chance to do so. Under such circumstances editors tend to reject manuscripts instead of asking authors to add more information. This advice means that when in doubt you may prefer to add additional, relevant, cogent ideas. It does not mean that you should pad the report with irrelevancy or speak in circumlocutions in order to consume enough space to appear impressive. In general, the more concisely you can state your point, the more your readers will appreciate you.

If you perform a piece of research with good internal validity and well defined limits with regard to external validity, you should consider submitting it to a professional journal. Publishing your research will enable your to benefit from the comments of your peers, will advance the state of knowledge on a given topic, and will provide readers with concrete information that can lead to solutions to some of their own problems. If you follow the guidelines described in this chapter, you should be able to write a presentable report. To submit an article, first find a journal that is likely to be interested in your work. A good way to identify such a journal is to select one which you cited in your own review of the literature. Your research will be viewed as a follow-up to the research already followed in that journal. Then look for the "Guidelines for Manuscript Submission" in that journal. These are often inside the front or back cover or somewhere around the Table of Contents. Follow the guidelines carefully. Submit the required number of copies together with a letter briefly stating that you want to submit the manuscript for possible publication and that you have not already published the same article in another journal.

Normally, you will receive an acknowledgment that the article has been received within a week or two, but then there follows a period of two to three months (or more) during which the article is reviewed. Sometimes your article will be accepted. Often, however, it will be rejected on the first submission, but the editors may suggest some modifications and recommend possible resubmission with revision. If you receive a request for modifications, take the editor's suggestions seriously. Resubmitting very often leads to acceptance of the article for publication. Even after the article has been accepted, there will be a publication lag of four months to a year, since the journal is likely to have a backlog of articles already accepted for future issues. Once the article appears, you will be pleasantly surprised on how many comments you will receive from colleagues you do not even know, asking for further information or offering you ideas of their own on the same topic. This exchange of professional information can be a fruitful and enjoyable enterprise.

SUMMARY

This chapter has provided a summary in Table 18–1 of the major steps in carrying out a formal research project. In addition to restating and integrating the important points from previous chapters, these guidelines have focused on ethical and practical considerations in carrying out such a project. The chapter discussed the major components of a research paper and provided practical suggestions on how to submit a report to a journal for publication. By following these guidelines, you will find that the pursuit of formal educational research projects can be a fruitful enterprise.

Annotated Bibliography

American Psychological Association. *Ethical Principles in the Conduct of Research with Human Participants* (Washington, D.C., 1973). These guidelines are widely accepted as appropriate for protecting the rights of subjects involved in experimental studies.

American Psychological Association. *Publication Manual of the American Psychological Association* (2nd ed.) (Washington, D.C., 1974). These guidelines for writing research reports are acceptable to an ever increasing number of schools, conventions, journals, and funding organizations. Your library should have a copy.

Anderson, B.F. *The Psychology Experiment* (Belmont, Cal.: Brooks/Cole, 1971). Chapter 10 provides clear and straightforward guidelines for writing a research report.

Martin, D.W. *Doing Psychology Experiments* (Monterey, Cal.: Brooks/Cole, 1977). Chapter 10 provides very good guidelines on how to write a report based on psychological research.

Strunk, W. and White, E.B. *The Elements of Style* (3rd ed.) (New York: Macmillan, 1979). This brief book provides valuable information on how to express yourself briefly and cogently. It provides guidelines that will help you write your report without sounding like the stereotypic social scientist.

Professional Journals

The following articles provide good examples of how to deal with issues that arise in conducting and reporting upon research projects.

Baker, B.L., Heifetz, L.J., and Murphy, D.M. "Behavioral training for parents of mentally retarded children: One-year follow-up," *American Journal of Mental Deficiency* 85 (1980): 31–38. This article provides a good example of summarizing a very large amount of additional information with a single citation (at the top of p. 32).

Bryant, J., Comisky, P.W., Crane, J.S., and Zillmann, D. "Relationship between college teachers' use of humor in the classroom and students' evaluations of their teachers," *Journal of Educational Psychology*, 72 (1980): 511–519. This article cites 36 sources in its review of the literature. It is interesting to note how the authors cite a large number of authors extremely briefly (e.g. 16 citations in one sentence and 10 in another) and a few authors in specific detail. All of these sources are synthesized in such a way as to give the reader a clear focus on the research problem.

ZILBERGELD, B., and EVANS, M. "The inadequacy of Masters and Johnson," *Psychology Today*, August 1980: 29–43. Although this report deals with several methodological problems in the sex therapy research of Masters and Johnson, its focus on the reporting of data is most relevant for this chapter. The authors argue that because of ambiguity in the reporting of the data, it is almost impossible to draw sensible conclusions from the research.

Appendix A
Glossary

Achievement Test An instrument designed to measure the degree of mastery of academic skills.

Affective Outcomes Events or behaviors which arise out of changes in attitudes, personality traits, etc. within a subject.

Alpha Level The statistical probability that an observed result (such as a difference between two means) is likely to be a chance occurrence.

Analysis of Covariance A statistical procedure for determining whether two or more groups would have differed on a criterion variable by more than chance if they would have been more nearly equal with regard to some variable in the first place.

Analysis of Variance A statistical procedure for determining the likelihood that the observed difference on a criterion variable between means occurred by chance. This procedure can be used with two or more groups.

Applied Research The use of research strategies to establish cause and effect relationships and to make generalizations about such relationships in order to solve specific, practical problems. The term overlaps with what some textbooks refer to as action research or evaluative research. Applied research is to be distinguished from theoretical research.

Attitude Test A measuring instrument designed to assess the attitude a respondent possesses toward people, places, events, etc.

Behavioral Objective The observable behavior which the teacher is willing to accept as evidence that learning has occurred. A behavioral objective is a specific type of operational definition.

C A symbol used in diagrams of research designs to indicate that the members of a group were selected on the basis of possessing a certain characteristic (criterion group design) rather than through assignment to experimental and control groups.

Cluster Sampling The type of sampling procedure in which the researcher selects the sample in "clusters"— i.e., groups of subjects rather than single subjects one at a time. The resulting sample is likely to contain members more similar to one another than separately selected subjects would be.

Coefficient Alpha A statistical procedure for estimating the internal consistency reliability of a test. It is interpreted in the same way as the Kuder-Richardson coefficient, but it can be used in more widespread situations.

Cognitive Outcome A change in behavior that arises out of new learning in the areas of knowledge, concept-formation, understanding of principles, problem-solving, etc.

Cohort Design   A quasi-experimental design in which a group of subjects is compared to another group of subjects which has preceded or will follow it through an institution. The institution can be either narrowly defined (such as a school) or broadly defined (such as American society). For example, sociologists might compare current adolescents to their pre-Vietnam-era cohorts.

Comparison Group   A group of subjects that does not receive the treatment and whose performance is compared to that of the experimental group. Sometimes the comparison group receives an alternate treatment.

Concurrent Validity   This type of validity deals with the question of whether a certain measurement technique correlates highly with another technique that is supposed to measure the same thing.

Confidence Interval   The boundaries within which a score most likely falls. The term is used when a score is estimated, as through sampling procedures. Confidence intervals are placed around the statistic obtained from the sample to indicate the range within which the real score of the population probably lies.

Construct Validity   This type of validity deals with the question of whether or not a measurement technique is actually providing an assessment of some underlying characteristic that can be given a specific label.

Content Validity   This type of validity deals with the question of whether a certain measurement technique measures the whole range of topics it is supposed to measure (rather than a restricted, nonrepresentative range of such topics).

Continuous Behavior   A behavior that cannot be meaningfully counted by merely enumerating specific instances of the behavior, but rather occurs over a prolonged period of time. (Contrasted with discrete behavior.)

Control Card   In computerized statistical programs, one of the cards designated by the statistical package to give instructions to the computer (as opposed to a data or system card).

Control Group   The group of subjects from whom the treatment is withheld in an experiment. The performance of this group is compared to that of the experimental group.

Control Variable   A factor whose extraneous impact upon an experiment is eliminated either through randomization, statistical control, or isolation and removal.

Correlation   The degree to which two or more events are related. A high correlation means that two events are strongly related—the occurrence of one event is associated with a predictable pattern in the other. A low correlation means that two events or characteristics are unrelated.

Correlation Coefficient   A statistical procedure for estimating the strength of a relationship. Such coefficients range from $+1.00$ to -1.00. A high absolute value (whether positive or negative) indicates a strong relationship. A low absolute value indicates a weak relationship.

Criterion Group Research   A nonexperimental approach to ascertaining the nature of relationships between variables. A group which possesses a certain characteristic (the independent variable) is compared to a group that does not possess that characteristic with regard to some outcome (the dependent variable). Although the results of such research often look like the results of experimental research, it is not possible to draw causal inferences directly from such results.

Criterion Referenced Test   A test with which a respondent's performance is judged by comparison to some pre-established standard (the criterion), rather than by comparison to the performance of other respondents who took the same test.

Criterion Related Validity   This term refers to those methods of establishing the validity of a measuring technique which rely on computing correlations between the test being validated and some other test. This other test is referred to as the "criterion." Specifically, concurrent and predictive validity are examples of criterion related validity.

Curvilinear Relationship   A relationship that is not linear. That is, the relationship follows a certain pattern for a while, then follows a different pattern. However, the overall pattern of the relationship is predictable.

Data A term used throughout this text to refer to the results obtained from an observation or measuring instrument.

Data Card In computerized statistical programs, one of the cards on which the information (data) about the subjects is actually listed (as opposed to a control or system card).

Degrees of Freedom A term derived from theoretical statistics and related to the number of subjects in a study. The term is important because it refers to the point at which a researcher enters a statistical table to determine the level of significance of a statistical analysis (as in the use of the *t* statistic). (In this book, instructions accompanying the computation of statistics in Appendix D indicate how to determine the degrees of freedom.)

Dependent Variable The outcome that is measured after an experimental treatment has been administered to determine if the treatment had the expected effect. The dependent variable has been referred to throughout this text as the outcome variable. It is *dependent* in the sense that it depends on the treatment for its value.

Design *See* Research Design.

Discrete Behavior A behavior which can be counted by enumerating specific instances of it. (Contrasted with continuous behavior.)

Equivalent Forms Reliability The form of reliability that estimates the degree of similarity between two forms of the same test. Statistically, equivalent forms reliability is estimated by computing the correlation coefficient between scores by the same persons on both forms of the test.

Eta Coefficient A statistical procedure for estimating the strength of curvilinear relationships. Eta coefficients are always positive and must be accompanied by a diagram to show the nature of the relationship.

Expectancy Effects The threat to internal and/or external validity that arises from the fact that it could be the attitudes the subject or experimenter has toward the experimental situation rather than the treatment itself which caused an observed outcome.

Experiment An attempt to establish a cause and effect relationship by administering a treatment to one group of subjects and withholding the treatment from another group of subjects.

Experimental Group The group of subjects to whom the treatment is administered in an experiment.

Experimental Mortality The threat to internal validity that arises from the fact that observed differences in the outcome variable might occur because of changes in the group composition (because of subjects dropping out) rather than because of an effect of the treatment.

External Validity The degree to which the conclusions from an experiment can be generalized to other subjects, other situations, and other times.

Extraneous Variable A factor whose influence upon an attempt at measurement or upon an experimental design is uncontrolled and therefore unknown. Extraneous variables introduce error and uncertainty into measurement and experimental processes.

***F* Ratio** The result of analysis of variance or analysis of covariance. To interpret an *F* ratio, it is necessary to refer to a table. However, computer printouts normally give the exact level of significance accompanying an *F* ratio.

Factorial Design A research design that takes into account moderator variables and examines their precise impact upon the relationship between the independent and dependent variables.

History Extraneous events occurring in the environment at the same time the experimental variable (the treatment) is being tested. Such events can pose a threat to either internal or external validity.

Hypothesis A statement of the relationship between the independent and the dependent variables, together with whatever moderator and control variables are being taken into account. The research hypothesis is a tentative answer to the research question or research problem, and the purpose of an experiment is to support or reject this hypothesis. Because of the nature of the inferential logic that forms the basis of the scientific method, the hypothesis can never really fully be confirmed, since there is always the possibility of a subsequent rejection. Clear evidence contradicting a hypothesis, however, can refute a hypothesis. In such cases, the hypothesis must be rejected or modified.

Independent Variable   The treatment that is administered to the experimental group and withheld from the control group in an experimental study. In a more general sense, it is the treatment that leads to the outcome—the cause that produces the effect. It is *independent* in the sense that it does not depend upon the dependent variable for its value.

Instability   The threat to internal validity that arises from the fact that chance fluctuations in test scores rather than the actual treatment might have caused observed differences in an outcome variable.

Instrument   *See* Measuring Instrument.

Instrumentation   The threat to internal validity that arises from the fact that observed differences in an outcome variable could be the result of changes in the instrument (or in the way the instrument is administered) rather than the result of the treatment itself.

Intact Groups   A group of subjects in an experiment that was already formed prior to the experiment or that was assembled on some basis other than random assignment. This absence of randomization is the essential characteristic of an intact group.

Interaction   An interaction occurs whenever one variable has an effect upon another. Some interactions are "good," in the sense that we deliberately look for them and make them the focus of our study. For example, whenever a treatment has an effect, this can be referred to as an interaction of the independent with the dependent variable. If the moderator variable has an impact on the way the treatment influences the dependent variable, this is referred to as an interaction. However, some interactions are "bad," in the sense that they introduce ambiguity into a study that is focusing on something else. For example, when extraneous variables (such as selection bias) have an effect on the relationship between the independent and dependent variables, this is an interaction that leads to *threats* to either internal or external validity.

Internal Consistency   The degree to which all the items on a test tend to measure the same characteristic. The term is often used in association with discussions of reliability.

Internal Validity   The degree to which conclusions about cause and effect relationships within an experiment are accurate.

Interobserver Reliability   The degree to which two or more different observers tend to agree that an event does or does not occur during a series of observations. Unlike other forms of reliability (which are estimated with correlation coefficients), this one is usually determined by calculating the percentage of instances in which the observers agree on the occurrence or nonoccurrence of a behavior.

Interscorer Reliability   The degree to which two or more different scorers tend to give the same scores to the same set of responses to a measuring instrument.

Interval Data   The results of a measurement process that do more than merely rank the respondents—they actually assign exact scores. The intervals between the scores are meaningful, and are constant in their meaning throughout the entire range of scores. (In the present text, no important distinction is made between interval and ratio scores.)

Intervening Variable   The hypothetical factor that is responsible for the interaction observed in an experiment. This variable *intervenes* in the sense that the independent variable produces the intervening variable, and the intervening variable in turn produces the impact upon the dependent variable.

Interview   A data collection format in which an interviewer asks the respondents questions and records their answers for tabulation, rather than requiring the respondent to answer the questions directly (as would be the case with a questionnaire).

Item   A question statement, or other opportunity for a respondent to provide information or for an observer to record such information. A series of items makes up a test.

Item Analysis   A set of statistical procedures that can be used to estimate the quality of test items. In general, item analysis tends to select items that are of about medium difficulty and that tend to measure the same thing as the other items on the same test.

Kuder-Richardson Reliability Coefficient   A statistical procedure for estimating the internal consistency of a measuring instrument.

Learning   An internal change in the organization of knowledge that results from some insight or reinforced practice. Learning cannot be directly observed, but its existence has to be inferred from observed behaviors.

Likert Scale   A technique of measurement where a respondent is given a statement and is asked to place his or her response into one of these five categories: "strongly agree," "agree," "uncertain," "disagree," and "strongly disagree."

Linear Relationship   A relationship that follows a very specific pattern (which can be diagrammed by drawing a straight line).

Level of Significance   *See* Statistical Significance.

Manipulation   An artificial contrivance to provide an experimental treatment to one group of subjects while withholding it from another.

Matching   A system of pairing subjects for an experiment on the basis of some similarity and assigning one to the experimental and the other to a control group. The *only* permissible use of matching occurs when it is followed by random assignment to treatments. Other uses present problems of regression toward the mean.

Maturation   The threat to internal validity that arises from the fact that changes in an outcome variable may occur routinely as a result of the passage of time rather than as a result of the treatment that occurred while time was passing.

Measurement   An attempt to assign numerical values to characteristics possessed by the subjects. This is done through the process of operational definition and then in some way tabulating the subjects' performance with regard to the operational definition.

Measurement Instrument   A device or plan of action for carrying out the measurement process. The instrument is usually software (e.g., a test or questionnaire), rather than hardware, as the name may imply. In this text, the terms "measurement instrument" and "test" are used synonymously and interchangeably.

Moderator Variable   A variable that influences (moderates) the impact of the independent variable upon the dependent variable.

Mortality   *See* Experimental Mortality.

Multiple Correlation Coefficient   A statistical procedure for estimating the strength of the relationship between one variable and some combination of two or more other variables.

Negative Correlation   A relationship between two variables such that as the scores on one increase, the scores on the other *decrease*.

Nominal Data   Results of a measurement process that are purely categorical in nature; that is, all they do is *classify* subjects. There is no meaning (such as an implication that "2" is higher than "1") beyond the mere process of classification. Nominal data is a step below ordinal data.

Norm Referenced Test   A test with which a respondent's performance is judged by comparison to the performance of other respondents (the norms) rather than with regard to some pre-established standard.

Norms   A set of scores that provide a basis for comparing the performance of a respondent or group of respondents to the performance of other respondents on the same instrument.

O A symbol used in diagrams of research designs to indicate the occurrence of an "observation" or testing occasion.

Observable Behavior A behavior of a person that is external to the extent that two or more observers could easily agree that the behavior is or is not occurring.

Observation The act of collecting data about the performance of a subject.

Observational Technique The label given to those types of measurement techniques where an observer watches someone else's behavior, judges that behavior in some way, and then records this judgment.

Open Ended Question An item on a questionnaire or in an interview on which the respondent is given a great deal of freedom to compose his or her own answer. (Contrasted with a structured question.)

Operational Definition The observable behavior or events that a researcher is willing to accept as evidence that a variable exists.

Ordinal Data Results of a measurement process that do more than classifying (nominal data) but do not yet give real meaning to the size of intervals (as would interval data). Such results merely rank the respondents, but do not assign exact scores. The normal usage of the word "ordinal" as opposed to "cardinal" numbers should enable you to remember this, since all ordinal data contain a ranking of first, second, etc.

Outcome Variable The outcome that occurs as a result of some treatment or activity. In formally defined hypotheses, the outcome variable is referred to as the dependent variable.

Partial Correlation A statistical method for estimating what the relationship between two variables *would* have been if the influence of some third variable would have been reduced or held constant.

Pearson Correlation Coefficient The most frequent procedure for computing the correlation coefficient between two variables. It requires interval or ratio data for its computation.

Percentile Rank The percentage of scores equal to or below a respondent's score on a test.

Population In sampling theory, the larger group from which the sample is drawn is referred to as the population.

Positive Correlation A relationship between two characteristics such that as the score on one increases, the score on the other also increases.

Posttest An observation or measurement of the subjects in an experiment that is conducted after the treatment has been administered to the experimental group.

Predictive Validity That type of validity that deals with the question of whether a certain measurement technique accurately predicts the respondent's performance on some future task.

Pretest An observation or measurement of the subjects in an experiment that is conducted before the treatment is administered to any of the subjects.

Pretesting The threat to internal validity that arises from the fact that it might be the benefits derived from taking the pretest rather than from the treatment which resulted in changes observed in an experiment.

Quasi-Experiment An experiment which is not based on random assignment of subjects to groups, but which attempts to overcome this shortcoming by various compensatory strategies.

Questionnaire Any data collecting instrument, other than an achievement or ability test, on which the respondents directly supply their own answers to a set of questions.

Quota Sampling The sampling procedure in which the researcher identifies a set of important characteristics of the population and then selects the sample in a nonrandom way so that the sample will match the population with regard to this set of characteristics.

R A symbol used in diagrams of research designs to symbolize that the subjects have been assigned to a group at random.

Random Assignment   The process of placing subjects into groups in such a way that chance is the only factor that determines which subjects go into which groups.

Randomization   A term used interchangeably with random assignment.

Random Sampling   The sampling procedure by which the decision regarding who will be taken from the population and included in the sample depends on chance alone.

Ratio Data   Results of a measurement process that are expressed not only in terms of meaningful intervals but also in relation to an absolute zero. (There is no meaningful importance between interval and ratio data in the present text.)

Regression Toward the Mean   *See* Statistical Regression.

Reliability   The degree of consistency with which a test (or alternate forms of the same test) will produce similar results on occasions when it theoretically should produce the same result.

Reliability Coefficient   A numerical indicator of the degree of consistency displayed by a measuring instrument. In many cases, the reliability coefficient is a correlation coefficient and is interpreted in the same way as a correlation coefficient.

Research Design   The systematic scheduling of the times at which treatments are to be administered to subjects and at which observations are to be made of the performance of the subjects.

Research Prediction   A logical consequence derived from the research hypothesis and stated in operationally defined terms.

Respondent   A person who gives responses to a measuring instrument.

Sample   A subgroup taken from a larger group in such a way as to make it similar to the larger group with regard to important characteristics. (The larger group is called the population.)

Sampling   The process by which a smaller group (a sample) is selected from among the members of a larger group (a population) so that the characteristics of the smaller group can be used to estimate the characteristics of the larger group.

Scattergram   A type of diagram used to display correlations between two variables.

Scientific Method   The process of advancing theoretical knowledge by drawing inferences based on the careful and objective observation of facts. A popular formulation of the scientific method was stated by John Dewey. This formulation focuses on (1) the perception of a problem, (2) the statement of a hypothesis as a tentative answer to the problem, (3) the deduction of predicted consequences based on that hypothesis, (4) conducting an experiment to verify or reject that prediction, and (5) drawing conclusions about the hypothesis based on an analysis of the results of the experiment.

Selection   The threat to internal validity that arises from the fact that a group's performance on an outcome variable may arise from the composition of the group itself rather than from the treatment that is supposed to have produced the outcome.

Significance   *See* Statistical Significance.

Spearman-Brown Formula   A mathematical correction procedure that is applied to split-half reliability estimates to provide an accurate estimate of test reliability.

Spearman Correlation Coefficient   The statistical method for estimating the strength of a relationship when one or both of the variables is rank order (ordinal) rather than interval or ratio data.

Split-Half Reliability   The type of reliability that can be computed by correlating a randomly selected half of the test with the other half of the test. The result is corrected by the Spearman-Brown formula.

Stability   The tendency for the same result to occur on different measuring occasions. The stability of a test is statistically estimated by a test-retest reliability coefficient.

Standardized Instrument   A data collection instrument with highly structured instructions for administration and scoring and which has norms available to provide comparisons with other persons who have responded to the same instrument.

Statistical Procedures   Mathematical tools for summarizing and making judgments about the results obtained from some sort of measurement process.

Statistical Regression   The threat to internal validity that arises from the tendency of subgroups that have been selected on the basis of extreme scores to have a mean score closer to the mean on subsequent retests.

Statistical Significance   The statistical probability that an observed result (such as the difference between two means) is likely to be a chance occurrence.

Stratified Sampling   A strategy for selecting samples in such a way that specific subgroups (strata) will have a sufficient number of representatives within the sample to provide ample numbers for subanalysis of the members of those subgroups.

Structured Question   A question on a questionnaire or in an interview where the respondent merely selects one of several possible answers rather than creating his or her own answer. (Contrasted with open ended questions)

Subject   A person who takes part in an experiment by either receiving the treatment or having it withheld from him or her.

Systematic Sampling   A strategy for selecting the members of a sample that allows only chance and a "system" to determine membership in the sample. The "system" is a planned strategy for selecting members after a starting point is selected at random, such as every tenth subject, every fourth subject, etc.

System Card   In computerized statistical analysis, one of the cards (unique to each specific computer system) that enables a user to enter cards into the computer and have access to the statistical programs (as opposed to a data or control card).

t **Statistic**   The result of a *t* test. A *t* statistic is compared to an appropriate table to determine the level of significance of the result.

t **Test**   A statistical procedure for determining the likelihood that an observed difference between the means of two groups occurred by chance.

Table of Random Numbers   A list of numbers whose content is determined purely by chance. Such a table can be used to select subjects at random or to assign subjects at random to treatments.

Test   A set of items for measuring some characteristic of a respondent. In this book the word refers to any measuring instrument, not merely to academic tests.

Test-retest Reliability   The type of reliability that is estimated by computing the correlation between the same people's performance on two administrations of the same test.

Theoretical Research   Research that focuses primarily at the conceptual level, as distinguished from Applied Research, which focuses on the use of research methods to solve practical problems. The methodologies of the two types of research are quite similar, but theoretical research gives primary attention to the intervening variable, whereas applied research gives only minimal attention to this variable.

Treatment   An event or activity that is expected to produce an outcome. Determining whether or not this outcome occurs is the purpose of an experiment.

True Experiment   An experiment based upon random assignment of subjects to groups and the appropriate timing of treatments and observations.

Unobtrusive Measurement   A data collection technique that enables the researcher to collect data in such a way that the respondent is unlikely to be aware that data is being collected and is therefore unlikely to "react" to this measurement process.

Validity   In research, this term refers to whether or not the results of some measurement or experiment really show what they claim to show. For example, the various types of test validity (cf. Content, Criterion Related, Construct, Concurrent, and Predictive Validity) all deal with whether a test measures what someone claims the test measures. Likewise, the forms of experimental validity (cf. Internal and External Validity) deal with the question of whether or not an experimental treatment has really shown what someone claims it has shown.

Variable   Anything to which different numerical values can be assigned for purposes of analysis or comparison. The term is usually synonymous with the terms "factor" or "characteristic," as these terms are used in normal usage. The specific types of variables that can be identified in a formal research project are the independent, dependent, moderator, control, and intervening variables.

X   A symbol used in diagramming research designs to signify the administration of an independent variable.

Appendix B
Statistical Tables

TABLE 1. Critical Values of t.

d.f.	Level of Significance					
	.20	.10	.05	.02	.01	.001
1	3.078	6.314	12.706	31.821	63.657	636.619
2	1.886	2.920	4.303	6.965	9.925	31.598
3	1.638	2.353	3.182	4.541	5.841	12.941
4	1.533	2.132	2.776	3.747	4.604	8.610
5	1.476	2.015	2.571	3.365	4.032	6.859
6	1.440	1.943	2.447	3.143	3.707	5.959
7	1.415	1.895	2.365	2.998	3.499	5.405
8	1.397	1.860	2.306	2.896	3.355	5.041
9	1.383	1.833	2.262	2.821	3.250	4.781
10	1.372	1.812	2.228	2.764	3.169	4.587
11	1.363	1.796	2.201	2.718	3.106	4.437
12	1.356	1.782	2.179	2.681	3.055	4.318
13	1.350	1.771	2.160	2.650	3.012	4.221
14	1.345	1.761	2.145	2.624	2.977	4.140
15	1.341	1.753	2.131	2.602	2.947	4.073
16	1.337	1.746	2.120	2.583	2.921	4.015
17	1.333	1.740	2.110	2.567	2.898	3.965
18	1.330	1.734	2.101	2.552	2.878	3.922
19	1.328	1.729	2.093	2.539	2.861	3.883
20	1.325	1.725	2.086	2.528	2.845	3.850
21	1.323	1.721	2.080	2.518	2.831	3.819
22	1.321	1.717	2.074	2.508	2.819	3.792
23	1.319	1.714	2.069	2.500	2.807	3.767
24	1.318	1.711	2.064	2.492	2.797	3.745
25	1.316	1.708	2.060	2.485	2.787	3.725
26	1.315	1.706	2.056	2.479	2.779	3.707
27	1.314	1.703	2.052	2.473	2.771	3.690
28	1.313	1.701	2.048	2.467	2.763	3.674
29	1.311	1.699	2.045	2.462	2.756	3.659
30	1.310	1.697	2.042	2.457	2.750	3.646
40	1.303	1.684	2.021	2.423	2.704	3.551
60	1.296	1.671	2.000	2.390	2.660	3.460
120	1.289	1.658	1.980	2.358	2.617	3.373
∞	1.282	1.645	1.960	2.326	2.576	3.291

TABLE 2. A table of random numbers.

33	60	43	33	62	85	62	50	12	32
48	34	14	98	42	73	94	95	32	14
44	59	72	63	99	70	63	81	20	70
94	70	33	25	95	10	41	42	23	54
89	17	95	88	29	34	87	20	48	10
63	62	06	34	41	67	17	36	50	51
65	37	37	29	84	30	17	13	77	41
58	12	47	01	33	18	93	60	21	38
14	16	02	95	59	24	45	77	78	97
29	12	64	11	16	93	87	53	23	76
16	13	72	58	23	28	62	99	45	25
16	18	73	57	30	16	96	38	31	78
91	50	65	27	37	11	37	46	30	63
79	92	23	09	50	42	46	03	86	38
20	78	92	34	91	04	97	32	72	01
05	82	48	68	46	99	25	46	76	32
61	26	45	86	42	59	24	10	89	12
21	04	62	69	87	28	21	97	37	34
35	79	55	62	06	04	14	21	62	68
22	47	87	38	87	32	09	44	88	25
36	09	55	06	91	13	20	41	36	90
45	14	15	34	54	55	83	15	29	42
58	84	34	52	00	21	11	46	26	38
08	84	19	78	78	00	99	52	10	44
07	39	32	41	68	48	80	43	66	96
39	73	72	75	37	14	58	10	44	90
70	20	39	40	94	87	26	13	00	56
59	37	20	90	75	71	13	76	90	45
68	84	30	36	46	32	08	57	45	74
65	57	41	63	80	80	59	23	81	76
16	39	72	85	22	38	56	01	94	30
03	74	09	42	16	21	21	55	44	91
82	21	60	43	97	03	79	85	18	08
38	29	40	02	99	37	46	46	25	20
65	25	96	25	80	94	24	60	42	38
43	06	85	00	76	21	36	16	48	16
27	21	42	26	02	98	34	60	72	53
39	86	64	69	17	17	97	76	88	77
15	38	71	28	56	66	22	73	83	58
58	05	25	01	31	71	29	33	39	84

Lengthier tables of random numbers can be found in most books of statistical tables.

Appendix **C**
Sample Research Reports

This appendix contains two published research reports. You can examine them to see the principles discussed in this book at work. Both of the studies upon which these reports were based took place in applied educational settings, and both supplied information that was directly useful to educational practitioners. However, the two reports differ considerably in the level of control they were able to provide for the threats to internal and external validity.

After each of the reports, a brief analysis will provide the following information:

- Statement of the hypothesis.
- Listing of the research variables:
  - Independent variable.
  - Dependent variables.
  - Moderator variables.
  - Control variables.
  - Intervening variables.
- Operational definitions of the research variables.
- Statement of the research prediction.
- Research design.
- Uncontrolled threats to internal validity.
- Uncontrolled threats to external validity.
- Statistics employed and their purpose.
- Validity of the conclusions.

If you wish to do so, you can jot down the above information as you read each article. Then you can compare your answers with those provided in the analysis afterward. (Note that in some cases the correct answer will be "none stated.")

The Learning Center: Stimulus to Cognitive and Affective Growth

Georgia J. Kosmoski
Public School System
Hammond, Indiana

Edward L. Vockell
Purdue University
Calumet Campus
Hammond, Indiana

Open education has been described as child-centered. In open-education programs the child has freedom of choice, opportunities to interact with peers and teachers, and freedom from fear of errors. The child experiences freedom to explore his own interests in depth. The child is given a wide selection of materials and is exposed to problem-solving situations and interdisciplinary units (1).

Succinctly stated, open education emphasizes the interaction of the child with the total environment (2).

Some educators feel that the results of open education are not measurably different from those of traditional teaching (3). Yet, several studies have shown significant differences. Joanna Sullivan (4) found that open education, through individualization of classwork, enhanced self-concept and increased cooperation among pupils. Pupils in this open situation were more free to express opinions and were more communicative than pupils in traditional settings.

It is relatively easy to describe open education, but Katz (5) has shown that it has no standard practices or methods. It has been suggested that the learning center (not to be confused with a resource center) might be one way of achieving open education. However, no research has been completed to date to show that learning centers encourage improved self-concepts, attitudes, or academic skills. If the effectiveness of learning centers could be demonstrated, a major problem of implementing open education would be alleviated. According to George (6), learning centers are suited to easy implementation and present a setting desirable for open education. If George's assertions are true, the teacher should be able to use learning centers in the classroom easily and effectively.

The present study examines the effect that an open-concept program using a learning-center complex had on pupils' academic achievement and attitudes. It was hypothesized that pupils in an open-space program using a learning-center complex would show greater gains than those resulting from mere growth or maturation. Increased gains, it was hypothesized, would occur in verbal skills as measured by the Iowa Tests of Basic Skills, in attitudes toward self as measured by the Piers-Harris

The Elementary School Journal, Volume 79, Number 1. © 1978 by The University of Chicago.

Children's Self-Concept Scale, and in attitudes toward peers, educational institutions, and educational authority figures as measured by a semantic differential.

METHOD

Subjects and Setting

The study was conducted at an open-space elementary school in an urban, multiethnic, and multiracial neighborhood. Annual enrollment is about eight hundred pupils. The subjects were pupils in Grades 3, 4 and 5, 72 percent of whom were caucasian, 26 percent black, and 2 percent of other racial groups. Socioeconomically the subjects ranged from lower class to middle class. The subjects varied widely in recorded school performance and in previously recorded intelligence quotient scores.

For two years, a team of six teachers at the school had provided, for some of the subjects, daily contact with an individualized learning-center complex.

The learning-center complex can be described as an area where pupils can pursue a series of individualized learning modules. Each module was self-paced, designed for mastery learning, and included appropriate audiovisual aids, module-specific objectives, and activities. Evaluation procedures had been set up. The themes of the individual modules dealt with topics generally accepted in the elementary-school curriculum. Modules were continually changed, and the center was constantly supervised by a professional teacher.

Seven guidelines were set up for pupils' participation in the learning-center program:

1. They could choose to use or not to use the center as they deemed appropriate.
2. They could use the center daily for about one-half to three-quarters of an hour.
3. They selected the particular module they wished to work with.
4. They were encouraged to complete, whenever possible, any module they had begun.
5. They could work independently or with others.
6. They used the center simultaneously with other pupils in their first through fifth years in school.
7. They used the supervising teacher as a guide, resource, and facilitator.

INSTRUMENTS

To obtain a sample of academic growth, the Vocabulary section of the Iowa Tests of Basic Skills (7) was administered. Alternate forms 1 and 2 were administered as pre- and posttests.

Self-concept was measured by the Piers-Harris Children's Self-Concept Scale (8). The identical form was used for the pre- and posttest. The entire test was read orally to all subjects.

Finally, to measure each subject's attitudes toward his peers, toward the school, and toward school authority figures, Osgood's Semantic Differential Scale (9) was adapted. The scale was revised to make it appropriate for the comprehension levels of elementary-school children. DiVesta and Walls (10) made a similar adaption for pupils in elementary school.

PROCEDURE

The pretest was administered the first week of the school year. All three instruments were administered in one sitting to all the subjects simultaneously. Subjects were intructed to work alone, to be honest, and not to affix their signature to the semantic differential scale or to the Piers-Harris test. Each test packet was coded to make it possible to match pretest and posttest scores. The confidentiality of these anonymous results was permanently assured.

SUBJECT SELECTION

Four major groups were identified—three experimental and one control:

Group A was made up of subjects who were continuing in the treatment, having completed at least one school year in the program before the research.

Group B was made up of subjects who were entering the learning-complex program for the first time at the beginning of this study.

Group C was made up of subjects who had participated in the treatment for at least one school year before the research but were no longer participating at the beginning of this study.

Group D, the Control Group, was made up of subjects who were not, and never had been, participants in the learning complex.

Subjects were assigned to each of these four conditions at random. This unusual opportunity for random assignment arose because of administrative considerations. For reasons unrelated to the learning-center program, it became necessary to reschedule all the pupils in Grades 1 through 5. It was decided that the fairest way to do so would be to assign the pupils to each of the various teachers at random. After this random assignment was completed, all the pupils who were assigned to the six teachers in the learning-center program were classified as members of Group A or Group B. Pupils assigned to teachers other than these six became members of Group C and Group D. A random subsample was drawn from each of these groups for analysis in this study.

Campbell (11) recommends this procedure for carrying out scientific research on curriculum changes without disrupting social processes.

The data from this study, then, can test two hypotheses that replicate each other. The first hypothesis is that, if the program has been effective, pupils who were in the program previously (Groups A and C) should surpass pupils who had not been in the program (Groups B and D) on all the dependent variables at the time of pretesting. Because no deliberate attempt had been made to assign these pupils at random to these pre-experimental treatments, the data to test this hypothesis would represent a somewhat imperfect quasi-experimental design (12).

The second hypothesis is that, if the program is effective, pupils either entering or remaining in the program (Groups B and A) should outgain pupils leaving or remaining out of the program (Groups C and D) on all variables. The gain scores on all dependent variables should represent a linear progression along a continuum. Group B should gain most, Group A should come next, Group C should come third, and Group D should gain least. This analysis of gain scores is contaminated by upper-limit ceiling effects on Group A and by similar lower-limit effects on Group D. Still, the design to test this second hypothesis would more closely resemble a true experiment (12). If both hypotheses received support, the evidence would be extremely compelling that the program was effective.

RESULTS

The results are summarized in Table 1 and Figures 1 through 6. An analysis of variance and Duncan Multiple Range Tests showed that on all three variables the scores of the pupils who had taken part in the program exceeded those of the pupils who had not taken part ($p < .05$). In other words, the pupils who had previously used the learning centers had more positive self-concepts, felt better about school, and learned more than the pupils who had not.

As the gain scores in Column 3 of Table 1 show, the results closely follow the hypothesized pattern. (These results are summarized in Figures 4 through 6.) On all three variables, the pupils who had not been in the program but were entering it for the first time (Group B) scored the greatest gain. The pupils who continued in the program (Group A) scored the next highest gain. The pupils who had been participants but had left the program (Group C) scored losses on the self-concept and the attitude scales and showed a much smaller gain in achievement than either Group

TABLE 1. Mean Scores on Pretest and Posttest and Mean Gains for Each Experimental Group.

	Self Concept		
Group	*Pretest*	*Posttest*	*Gain*
A (Staying in)	55.38	60.67	5.29
B (Entering)	36.38	52.04	15.66
C (Leaving)	56.33	55.88	− 0.45
D (Never in)	40.88	42.75	1.87

	Semantic Differential		
	Pretest	*Posttest*	*Gain*
A (Staying in)	30.91	34.83	3.92
B (Entering)	11.95	30.75	18.80
C (Leaving)	31.54	28.71	− 2.83
D (Never in)	15.46	11.67	− 3.79

	Iowa Tests of Basic Skills Vocabulary		
	Pretest	*Posttest*	*Gain*
A (Staying in)	18.17	23.46	5.29
B (Entering)	11.42	18.88	7.46
C (Leaving)	16.00	20.58	4.58
D (Never in)	11.29	12.67	1.38

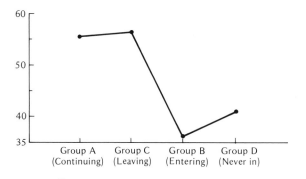

FIGURE 1. Mean scores on pretest: self-concept

A or Group C. Finally, the pupils who had never been in the program (Group D) scored about the same on the pretest and the posttest of the self-concept scale. They also showed the greatest losses on the attitude score and the smallest gain in achievement of all four groups. In these analyses, the gain scores of Group A and Group D are influenced by ceiling effects. However, such statistical artifacts do not contaminate the results, but rather make them a conservative test of the hypothesis. If there had been no ceiling effects, the scores of Group A might have been slightly higher and those of Group D even lower.

Another way to examine the data is to regard the study as containing two subexperiments, testing two subhypotheses: Do pupils who join a learning-center program for the first time score higher than pupils who do not join (Group B vs. Group D)? Do pupils who have been in a learning-center program and continue in it score higher than pupils who have been in the program but leave (Group A vs. Group C)? Analysis of variance of the data presented in Table 1 shows that pupils who joined scored significantly greater gains ($p < .05$) on all three variables than pupils who stayed out (Subhypothesis 1). However, the differences between pupils who stayed and pupils who left were not significant at the .05 level (Subhypothesis 2). Although these conclusions would be moderated by the ceiling effects, the results still strongly suggest that the advantages of entering such a program outweigh the disadvantages of leaving it.

An analysis of the results classified by sex of subjects revealed no significant differences. Therefore these results are not tabulated here.

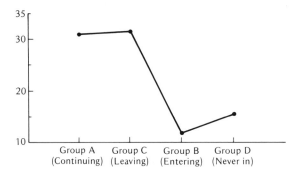

FIGURE 2. Mean scores on pretest: semantic differential

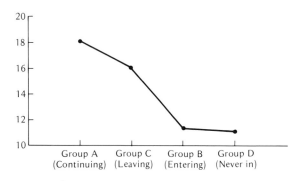

FIGURE 3. Mean scores on pretest: vocabulary

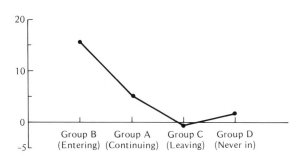

FIGURE 4. Mean gains on self-concept

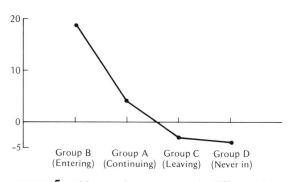

FIGURE 5. Mean gains on semantic differential

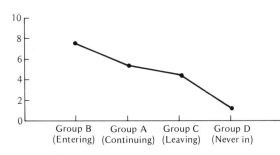

FIGURE 6. Mean gains on vocabulary test

DISCUSSION AND CONCLUSIONS

This study provides the most solid evidence to date that learning centers do accomplish goals, both affective and cognitive. The random-assignment technique used in this study suggests that the observed differences resulted from the treatment itself, not from some extraneous factor such as maturation, pretesting, or selection bias.

The results strongly indicate that pupils who used the learning centers learned more than pupils who did not. In addition the pupils who had participated in the learning centers felt better about themselves and about their learning environment than pupils who had not participated. While theoretical arguments concerning learning centers have suggested that either cognitive or affective improvements would occur, this is the first reported empirical proof that both of these favorable outcomes can result from such a program. Affective outcomes did not have to be sacrificed to achieve accelerated academic development, nor did academic goals have to be watered down to make the pupils feel good.

One concern has frequently been expressed about programs that offer comparative freedom and individualization. Will the pupils inadvertently suffer if they are exposed to the program for only a short time and then compelled to return to their more ordinary routines? If a child is placed in a learning-center environment and has to leave it for some reason, might he not learn less and feel worse than if he had never been exposed to the learning center? The results of this study allay this fear. On all three variables the pupils who left the program scored significantly higher than the pupils who had never used the centers. Even though the pupils who had to leave the program (Group C) showed losses on the affective variables on the posttest, their scores in these areas were still significantly higher than those of Group D. Thus, the slight drop of Group C, which occurred near the ceiling of the scores, would best be interpreted as the failure of good attitudes to continue to get better, while the drop in the scores of Group D would indicate undesirable attitudes getting worse. The pupils who left the program still scored a gain on the achievement test, a gain comparable to that of pupils who had never used the centers.

The best interpretation of these results seems to be that pupils who used the centers developed skills and attitudes that enabled them to work effectively in the learning-center environment or outside it. The pupils who left would have done even better if they had stayed in the program, but those pupils had acquired experiences that enabled them to interact effectively even in less favorable environments.

Freedom from boredom seems to be the main reason for the success of the program. Because of individualization, pupils could work as a group when group work was important but could work alone when individual work seemed a better idea. Thus, pupils could either surge ahead or work at a remedial level without fear of frustration or embarrassment. The atmosphere was conducive to improved attitudes and more effective learning.

The description of the learning centers suggests that their structure caused the gains. However, it is possible that learning centers of this kind would not be equally effective elsewhere. Some unique element may account for the gains in the study—perhaps the skill of the teachers. Two factors enhance the generalizability of the results. First, the teachers in the study were similar to other teachers in the school and in the city—similar in age, level of education, and professional experience. There is no evidence that the teachers in the study were atypical and therefore unusually qualified to make the program effective. Second, the teachers were unaware that an evaluative experiment was being carried out. The testing was made a routine part of the program.

Although these factors increase the generalizability of the results, the only way to rule out such threats to external validity is to replicate the study elsewhere.

In summary, this study has provided strong evidence that learning centers can produce cognitive and affective benefits in elementary-school children. The study suggests that learning centers teach skills and attitudes that are useful even after the children leave the learning center. The study provides empirical support for the belief that learning centers are useful.

This study has shown that a learning-center program can fulfill many of the goals of open education. Such centers are easy to establish and supervise, and they lead to measurable benefits to the pupils. It would seem, therefore, that such programs merit serious consideration as important ways of implementing open education in today's classrooms.

References

1. V.M. Howes *Informal Teaching in the Open Concept*. New York, New York: Macmillan, 1974.
2. R. Barth. *Open Education and the American School*. New York, New York: Agathon Press, 1972.
3. J. Ruedi and C. West *Pupil Self-Concept in an Open School and in a Traditional School*. Urbana, Illinois: University of Illinois, 1972. ERIC ED 066–217.
4. J. Sullivan. "Open-Traditional: What Is the Difference?" *The Elementary School Journal, 74* (May, 1974), 493–500.
5. L. Katz. *Research on Open Education: Problems and Issues*. Washington, D.C.: ERIC Clearinghouse on Early Childhood Education, 1973. ERIC ED 068–166.
6. P.S. George. *Learning Centers Approach to Instruction*. Gainesville, Florida: Florida Educational Research and Development Council, 1973. ERIC ED 080–518.
7. E.F. Lindquist and A.M. Hieronymous. *Teacher's Manual: Iowa Tests of Basic Skills*. Boston, Massachusetts: Houghton Mifflin Company, 1964.
8. E.V. Piers and D.B. Harris. Piers-Harris Children's Self-Concept Scale (The Way I Feel About Myself). Nashville, Tennessee: Counselor Recordings and Tests, 1969.
9. C.E. Osgood and J.G. Snider. *Semantic Differential Technique: A Sourcebook*. Chicago, Illinois: Aldine Publishing Company, 1963.
10. F. DiVesta and R. Walls. "Factor Analysis of the Semantic Attributes of 487 Words and Some Relationships to the Conceptual Behavior of Fifth Grade Children," *Journal of Educational Psychology* (Vol. 61, No. 6, Part 2), (December, 1970).
11. D.T. Campbell."Reforms as Experiments," *American Psychologist*, 24 (April, 1969), 409–29.
12. D.T. Campbell and J.C. Stanley. *Experimental and Quasi-Experimental Designs for Research*. Chicago, Illinois: Rand McNally, 1963.

Analysis of
"The Learning Center: Stimulus
to Cognitive and Affective Growth"

Statement of Hypothesis

Children participating in the learning centers will show improvements in verbal skills, in self-concept, and in attitudes toward school compared to children who do not participate in the learning center. (Stated on p. 362)

Independent Variable

Learning centers vs. traditional program. The learning centers are operationally defined in specific detail on page 363, in the paragraph beginning with "The learning center....". The seven guidelines in the subsequent paragraph are also an important part of the operational definition.

Dependent Variables

There are three dependent variables, and all are operationally defined in the section labeled "Instruments." First, "verbal skills" or "academic growth" were defined as performance on the Vocabulary section of the Iowa Tests of Basic Skills. A citation in the list of references indicates where readers can obtain more information about this test. Second, "self-concept" was defined as performance on the Piers-Harris Children's Self-Concept Scale. Again, readers can obtain more specific information about this test by checking the reference cited in parentheses. Third, "Attitude toward peers, toward school, and toward authority" was measured by a semantic differential scale. The two citations accompanying this definition indicate where readers can find out what a semantic differential scale is and how it was adapted to elementary-school children. (Note that this journal does *not* use the APA citation style which I have recommended. I personally find this inconvenient.)

Moderator Variables

Sex of subjects. You can tell this from the sentences on page 366 that state, "An analysis of the results classified by sex of subjects revealed no significant differences. Therefore these results are not tabulated here." In other words, the researchers

370

checked and verified that the treatment worked about equally well for boys and for girls.

It would also be possible to consider "learning centers" the independent variable and "previous experience with learning centers" a moderator variable. This line of reasoning is not pursued here, because no detailed analysis was undertaken to identify the precise interaction of these two variables (as through a factorial analysis). If you listed this as a moderator variable, however, you should not consider yourself wrong. The distinction is not crucial.

Control Variables

The subjects were first through third graders (p. 363). In addition, the first paragraph under "Subjects and setting" (p. 363) specifies pieces of information about the school, and these should be considered control variables. In addition, this was a school in which the learning centers had previously been in operation for two years.

Intervening Variables

"Freedom from boredom," which caused the pupils who used the centers to develop "skills and attitudes that enabled them to work effectively in the learning center environment or outside it" (p. 368).

Statement of the Research Prediction

The original hypothesis on page 362 contains some of the operational definitions, and therefore it is a partial statement of the research prediction. More specifically, on page 364 the predicted results that would support the hypothesis are spelled out in precise detail.

Research Design

There are two designs here. Actually, the study can be viewed as two separate studies, which replicate one another. The first is a quasi-experimental design (described on page 364). Subjects had not been assigned at random to the groups for this design, but neither had they been deliberately assigned in a biased fashion. Therefore, an analysis of the data comparing those who had been in the program previously to those who had never been in the program seems appropriate. The second design is a true experimental design (described on page 364). The subjects were assigned to the groups at random in this design. These designs may appear somewhat more complex in this report than they did when they were presented in the textbook. This is because there are *four* separate groups of subjects ("continuing," "leaving," "entering," and "never in.") If you look closely, however, you will see that the principles discussed in the textbook are directly applicable.

Uncontrolled Threats to Internal Validity

All the threats to internal validity seemed to be well controlled. This research seems to have demonstrated that the learning centers *did* cause the expected outcomes *in the experimental setting*.

Uncontrolled Threats to External Validity

The authors point out the major problems with regard to external validity on page 368. The clear operational definitions of the research variables will make it easy for readers to examine this report to see if it applies to their own interests. The major difficulty seems to be that from this one study we cannot be certain that we can rule out the probability that some unique characteristics of the school or teachers caused the learning centers to work. (For example, maybe the teachers in this school were exceptionally talented, and perhaps the same treatment would not work as effectively if implemented by less able teachers.)

Statistics Employed and Their Purpose

The procedures used in the analysis were analysis of variance and the Duncan Multiple Range tests. The analysis of variance showed that the groups in each analysis differed by more than would be expected by mere chance. The Duncan Multiple Range tests is a procedure used as a follow-up for analysis of variance. The analysis of variance shows that there is a difference *among* the four groups, and then the Duncan test identifies specific groups that differ from one another by more than chance. In principle, the Duncan test is similar to a *t* test or analysis of variance. The statistical tests indicate that the results followed the hypothesized pattern.

Validity of the Conclusions

The conclusions drawn by the authors were valid. The study had some limitations, but the authors stated their awareness of them. The conclusions are also tied in with the statement of the problem from the review of the literature.

Sex Education for EMR Adolescent Girls: An Evaluation and Some Suggestions

BLAIR BENNETT

Graduate Teaching Assistant - Special Education
Purdue University, West Lafayette, Indiana

EDWARD VOCKELL

Assistant Professor of Education
Purdue University, Calumet Campus
Hammond, Indiana

KAREN VOCKELL

Instructor of Education
Purdue University, Calumet Campus
Hammond, Indiana

Providing appropriate sex education for mentally retarded adolescents presents some unique problems. Although their physical development often takes place at a normal pace, their ability to understand and interpret this development to themselves is often quite markedly retarded. Although both parents and educators express concerns over such problems, an extensive review of the literature (Vockell & Mattick, in press) indicates that little empirical research has been reported. The present study was undertaken to implement a program of sex education for EMR girls and to evaluate it in such a way as to provide guidelines for others interested in implementing such programs.

The girls available for the program were female young adults classified as educable mentally retarded by the staff of a day center for the retarded in a midwestern

This report is based on a pilot program completed in May, 1972. Appreciation is expressed to Dr. Audry Riker, psychologist at Wabash Center for the Mentally Retarded, for her advice and cooperation in conducting this program. It was originally published in *The Journal for Special Educators*, Volume 9, 1972, pages 1–6. Reprinted with permission.

metropolitan area. Ten girls between 17 and 23 years of age were recommended for the sex education course by the staff, and all received parental permission to attend. One multiply handicapped girl voluntarily dropped from the class because she felt it made her "think about sex too much" and thus frustrated her because she felt she had no hope of marriage. Two other girls missed parts of the class because of conflicts with jobs and vacations. Thus nine girls were available for the pretest and seven for the posttest IQ (WAIS) ranged from 58 to 81, with a mean of 69.1. Socioeconomic status ranged from lower class to upper-middle class. All the girls were Caucasian.

Although the girls had not previously had a sex education program, they had all attended group therapy sessions with a female psychologist who answered questions as they arose. One of the girls had been sterilized prior to the beginning of the program because of promiscuous sexual behavior and another was sterilized while the program was in progress. Another girl at the center who was not in the program was married and pregnant. Six of the ten girls had "steady boyfriends". One girl was suspended for one week from the center during the study for her continuing inappropriate display of affection during working hours with her boyfriend, who was also a client at the center. She returned to the program when she returned to the center. Thus the group consisted of girls who were interested in acquiring information about sex and were willing to interact in a group situation. The girls as a group stated that they were unable to communicate with their parents about sex and expressed eagerness to learn.

The girls were administered the Sex Information Inventory for Girls (Vockell, Schmidt, Mattick, & Vockell, 1972) as a pretest and postest. This instrument is based on the behaviorally stated objectives from *Social and Sexual Development*, a curriculum outline and guide developed by the Special Education Curriculum Center of the University of Iowa (Myers, Walden, Moran, Gardner, Showalter, Levi, and Phillips, 1971). The class instructor was not shown the test nor the results of the pretest.

Classes met three times a week (Monday, Wednesday, and Friday) from 3:00 till 4:00 at the day center for a period of four weeks. The program covered the topics of menstrual hygiene, body hair and acne, human reproduction, sexual feelings, masturbation, premarital sexual intercourse, sexual deviance, contraception, and venereal disease. The lesson plans in *Social and Sexual Development* were used as a basis for the discussions. These lesson plans were supplemented by two films, *Boy to Man* and *Girl to Woman*, which were obtained from the state center of educational films. The class was conducted by a female graduate student in special education. The material was presented through lecture and group discussion.

At the beginning of the course the girls showed an inability to distinguish between pictures of males and of females when such cues as hair length and sex-related clothing were unavailable. On the posttest, although there were still deficiencies, visual discrimination between the sexes increased considerably. Errors in discrimination which did occur on the posttest were largely the result of classifying prepubescent girls as boys. (Anything without breasts was often classified as a male picture.) This might be taken as a tendency on the part of the girls to focus on breast as the distinguishing female characteristic without differentiating effectively between different physical stages of development.

Information about sexual terminology and the biological facts of menstruation increased considerably as a result of the course. Knowledge about venereal diseases was somewhat unclear on both the pretest and posttest. The difference was that girls who knew anything at all about VD on the pretest seemed to know more about symptoms and medical tests after the course, whereas those who knew nothing on the pretest continued to know nothing on the posttest. Although the students knew a great deal about the general aspects of sexual intercourse on the pretest (e.g., the penis goes into the vagina), knowledge of specific aspects (e.g., the penis must become erect) increased considerably on the posttest. Knowledge about the general and specific aspects of birth control increased considerably on the posttest.

When asked whether they would keep it a secret or tell an adult if a strange man put his hand on her breast, the girls showed a greater willingness to discuss this with a teacher or other adult on the posttest. However, over half the girls stated that they would still keep this a secret.

Awareness that sex was possible before marriage increased on the posttest. Contrary to intentions and expectations, however, the girls showed a greater permissiveness on the posttest towards engaging in premarital sex, especially if a girl were in love or hoped to get married. One reason for this might be that when the instuctor attempted to handle this on a somewhat open discussion basis, one of the girls voiced strongly the opinion that sexual intercourse was a good idea for two people who were in love.

Another surprising result was the girls' attitudes towards touching the vaginal area. The intention of the instructor was to teach that this area should be touched only in private, not in public places. However, the girls showed a greater reluctance to touch the vaginal area even in private places on the posttest. This could have been the result of focusing attention during the course on a problem that had previously not even occurred to them.

In general, then, although the girls came into the program with relatively high entering behavior, nevertheless measurable improvements took place in many areas. This was especially true in the case of one girl who appeared extremely confused on the pretest. For example, she seriously maintained that the reason girls had menstrual periods was that the Bible says that Johnny Appleseed chopped down the cherry tree. Such confusion disappeared on the posttest.

There are specific suggestions for implementing such programs which can be drawn from the results of this exploratory program. First, teaching basic facts to the class as a whole is not an effective way to teach these facts to those who do not already know them. It might be a better idea to give a pretest and merely to provide specific instructions for those who show shortcomings in specific areas on such a pretest. For example, such a procedure might have been useful in dealing with information about basic facts about VD in our program.

Second, while the course was successful in teaching girls not to key on irrelevant cues such as hair length and clothing, a further recommendation would be to avoid over-emphasis on a single characteristic, such as female breasts, when there are additional cues available. If the intention is to teach a student to make accurate discriminations, the best policy would seem to be to provide examples of as many positive and negative distinguishing characteristics as possible. Appropriate discrimination training would also be valuable in dealing with the problem of touching the vaginal area. Emphasis should be given to examples both of situations when this is appropriate and of situations when it is inappropriate.

Finally, since a primary purpose of a program like this is to prevent sexual exploitation of the girls, the problems of sexual abuse and premarital sex are especially important. Apparently a more intensive program would be necessary to make the girls more willing to discuss even minor sexual molestations with an adult rather than keeping them secret. With regard to premarital sex, the more permissive attitude expressed by the students at the end of the course might be in large part an indication of greater frankness on the part of the girls. The fact that the problems had been openly discussed during the program might have caused them to give their real opinion rather than "what they were supposed to say." On the other hand, their responses might reflect a real attitude change resulting largely from the permissive position taken by one of the girls during the open discussion. The peer status held by this girl and the fact that she would continue to exert influence over the girls even after the instructor of the course was no longer present would enhance her importance as an agent of attitude and behavior change. Perhaps a way to counteract this would be to introduce other prestigious models who would verbalize and exhibit the desired attitudinal and behavioral outcomes in contradiction to the girl in the class.

There is little point in discussing whether or not sex education should be provided to the mentally retarded: sex education takes place automatically. The fact that six of the girls were going steady, that many of them had already engaged in sexual activity, and that they naturally had sought information about their own developing bodies are indications that informal sex education was taking place in this group. The question is not whether sex education should be provided or not, but rather who will be the educator—the girl who will encourage sexual experimentation to enhance her own peer status or a trained professional. In other words, will sex education proceed haphazardly or systematically? It is our hope that the suggestions made on the basis of our exploratory program will benefit other professionals in systematic attempts to help retarded adolescents deal with their feelings and with their developing bodies.

References

MEYERS, R., WALDEN, S.B., MORAN, S., GARDENER, S., SHOWALTER, R., LEVI, K.S., PHILLIPS, D., Social and Sexual Development. Iowa City, Iowa: Special Curriculum Development Center, 1971.

VOCKELL, E.L., and MATTICK, P., Sex education of the mentally retarded: An analysis of the problems, programs, and research. Education and Training of the Mentally Retarded, 1972, in press.

VOCKELL, K., SCHMIDT, L., MATTICK, P., and VOCKELL, E.L., Sex information inventory for girls. Purdue University, mimeographed, 1972.

Analysis of
"Sex Education for EMR Adolescent Girls:
An Evaluation and Some Suggestions"

Statement of Hypothesis

The sex education program described in this report will cause improved attitudes among EMR girls. (This hypothesis is not clearly stated, but it is easily surmised from the last sentence in the first parapgraph of the article.)

Independent Variable

The sex education program. The independent variable is briefly described on page 374. It is then intermittently described in further detail throughout the report.

Dependent Variable

Performance on the Sex Information Inventory for Girls. The contents of this instrument are briefly described on page 374. Additional indications of the contents of this instrument occur throughout the article as specific results are discussed.

Moderator Variables

None is mentioned

Control Variables

Educable Mentally Retarded (EMR) females between the ages of 17 and 23 who volunteered for the program and had their parents' permission to participate. They were all noninstitutionalized. Additional details about the subjects are mentioned in the second paragraph.

Intervening Variables

None is clearly specified.

Statement of the Research Prediction

The sex education program described in this report will cause the EMR Girls in the program to get more correct answers on the posttest than on the pretest of the Sex Information Inventory for Girls. (This research prediction is not clearly stated, but it can easily be inferred.)

Research Design

This is the One-Group Pretest-Posttest "nondesign."

Uncontrolled Threats to Internal Validity

The only threat which *is* controlled *by the design* is simple selection. All the other threats (including the interaction of selection with other factors) are unaffected by the design. It is necessary to find other information to rule out the other threats. Some major possibilities will be mentioned here.

1. *Maturation* is probably not a serious problem. Girls who have not acquired this knowledge by the time they are 17–23 years old probably will not acquire it through mere maturation during the short period involved in this study.
2. *History* could be a threat, but the researchers reported no obvious threats in this regard. Perhaps the report should include an indication that this threat was ruled out.
3. *Pretesting* could be a problem. Since the same test was used as a pretest and posttest, it seems possible that information was acquired by taking the pretest or by thinking about the pretest rather than from the program itself.
4. *Instrumentation* could be a problem, if the tester became more experienced as the testing went on. For example, if the tester was a beginner at administering such a test to EMR girls, then it is possible that she would have done a weaker job of administering the test the first few times and gotten better as time went on. Therefore, improvements on the posttest could have occurred because of the improved skills of the tester.
5. *Experimental mortality* was not a problem since no one dropped out.
6. *Expectancy* could have been a problem. The persons who evaluated the program were the same ones who ran it, and they certainly expected positive results. The fact that they actually reported some negative findings tends to mitigate this problem.

The researchers who carried out this experiment were satisfied *themselves* that they had ruled out the major threats to internal validity, but they have not included sufficient information in the report to convince their readers of this.

Uncontrolled Threats to External Validity

None of the major threats to external validity is controlled. The most obvious problems are that the subjects and the setting may possess unique characteristics that would make the results hard to generalize elsewhere.

Statistics Employed

No statistical analyses are reported. We really do not know how likely it is that the observed differences could be attributed to chance variations in scores.

Validity of the Conclusions

This is obviously a weaker study than the first. However, the authors recognize this, and they advance their conclusions very tentatively. The research design was very weak, but it was better than nothing at all.

As the authors state in their opening paragraph, there is very little evidence of any sort on this topic; and therefore a humble start is better than no start. So as long as the research is presented and understood in the context of the apparent limitations, then it seems useful to perform and publish such research; even though it would obviously be better to have a stronger design. Additional researchers can build upon this research, and the publication of repeated findings could strengthen the state of knowledge on this topic.

Appendix **D**
Computational Procedures for Statistics

This appendix contains a cookbook approach to computing the Pearson correlation coefficient and the *t* test. The data included in the sample computations are taken from Figure 17–2.

Note that to compute either of these statistics, you have to compute a square root (for Step 21 of the Pearson computation and Step 23 of the *t* test computation). Be sure you can accomplish this before you start. It is very disheartening to get that far along and discover that you cannot go any further. If the square root is the only thing preventing you from performing these calculations, do not overlook the possibility of dialing up a friend on the telephone and having your friend calculate square root for you from a more sophisticated electronic calculator than you have access to.

Even with this cookbook approach, the computer is usually an easier way to obtain your results.

The following pages contain a list of steps for each procedure, plus an example of how to perform the computation. If you follow the steps carefully, you will get the right answer.

t TEST

Step 1. Arrange the scores according to the two groups. The order of the scores within each group is irrelevant.

Step 2. Add together all the scores in the first group.

Step 3. Square each of the scores in the first group.

Step 4. Add together all the squared scores from Step 3.

Step 5. Square the number obtained in Step 2.

Step 6. Count the number of scores in the first group.

Step 7. Divide the result of Step 5 by the result of Step 6.

Step 8. Subtract the result of Step 7 from the result of Step 4.

Step 9. Add together all the scores in second group.

Step 10. Square each of the scores in the second group.

Step 11. Add together all the squared scores from Step 10.

Step 12. Square the number obtained in Step 9.

Step 13. Count the number of scores in the second group.

Step 14. Divide the result of Step 12 by the result of Step 13.

Step 15. Subtract the result of Step 14 from the result of Step 10.

Step 16. Add together the results of Step 8 and Step 15.

Step 17. Add together the results of Step 6 and Step 13 and subtract 2.

Step 18. Divide the result of Step 16 by the result of Step 17.

Step 19. Divide the result of Step 6 *into* 1.

Step 20. Divide the result of Step 13 *into* 1.

Step 21. Add together the results of Step 19 and Step 20.

Step 22. Multiply the result of Step 18 by the result of Step 21.

Step 23. Take the square root of the result of Step 22.

Step 24. Divide the result of Step 2 by the result of Step 6.

Step 25. Divide the result of Step 9 by the result of Step 13.

Step 26. Subtract the result of Step 24 from the result of Step 25. If the result is negative, drop the minus sign.

Step 27. Divide the result of Step 26 by the result of Step 23. The result is your *t* value.

Step 28. Make the result of Step 17 your degrees of freedom.

Step 29. Read the table for *t* values. If your *t* value is higher than the *t* value in the table for the correct degrees of freedom, your result is significant at the designated level.

Sample Computation

Step 1.

Males	Females
34	35
14	7
40	15
24	40

Step 2. $34 + 14 + 40 + 24 = 112$

Step 3. $34 \times 34 = 1156$
$14 \times 14 = 196$
$40 \times 40 = 1600$
$24 \times 24 = \underline{576}$

Step 4. 3528

Step 5. $112 \times 112 = 12{,}544$

Step 6. Number of scores $= 4$

Step 7. $12{,}544 \div 4 = 3136$

Step 8. $3528 - 3136 = 392$

Step 9. $35 + 7 + 15 + 40 = 97$

Step 10. $35 \times 35 = 1225$
$7 \times 7 = 49$
$15 \times 15 = 225$
$40 \times 40 = \underline{1600}$

Step 11. 3099

Step 12. $97 \times 97 = 9409$

Step 13. Number of scores $= 4$

Step 14. $9409 \div 4 = 2352.25$

Step 15. $3099 - 2352.25 = 746.75$

Step 16. $392 + 746.75 = 1138.75$

Step 17. $4 + 4 = 8 \quad 8 - 2 = \underline{\underline{6}}$

Step 18. $1138.75 \div 6 = 189.79$

Step 19. $1 \div 4 = .25$

Step 20. $1 \div 4 = .25$

Step 21. $.25 + .25 = .50$

Step 22. $189.79 \times .50 = 94.895$

Step 23. $\sqrt{94.895} = 9.74$

Step 24. $112 \div 4 = 28$

Step 25. $97 \div 4 = 24.25$

Step 26. $24.25 - 28 = -3.75 = 3.75$

Step 27. $3.75 \div 9.74 = 0.38$

Step 28. $df = 6$

Step 29. 0.38 is not even close to 2.571, and therefore the difference is not significant at the .05 level.

PEARSON CORRELATION COEFFICIENT

Step 1. Arrange the scores in matching columns. Pair each of the scores that belong together in adjacent columns.

Step 2. Count the number of pairs.

Step 3. Multiply the two numbers in each pair times each other.

Step 4. Add the products obtained in Step 3.

Step 5. Multiply the number obtained in Step 4 by the number obtained in Step 2.

Step 6. Square each number in the first column.

Step 7. Add the squared values found in Step 6.

Step 8. Multiply the number from Step 7 by the number from Step 2.

Step 9. Add together all the scores in the first column.

Step 10. Square the number obtained in Step 9.

Step 11. Square each number in the second column.

Step 12. Add the squared values found in Step 11.

Step 13. Multiply the number from Step 12 by the number in Step 2.

Step 14. Add together all the scores in the second column.

Step 15. Square the number obtained in Step 14.

Step 16. Multiply the number obtained in Step 9 by the number obtained in Step 14.

Step 17. Subtract the result of Step 16 from the result of Step 5. Note that the result of Step 17 can be either positive or negative.

Step 18. Subtract the number obtained in Step 10 from the number obtained in Step 8.

Step 19. Subtract the result of Step 15 from the result of Step 13.

Step 20. Multiply the result of Step 18 by the result of step 19.

Step 21. Take the square root of the number obtained in Step 20.

Step 22. Divide the result of Step 17 by the result of Step 21. Unless you are computing a split-half reliability coefficient, you are finished. The result of Step 22 is the Pearson Correlation Coefficient.

If you are computing a split-half reliability coefficient, continue below. (These steps provide the Spearman-Brown Correction Factor.)

Step 23. Multiply the result of Step 22 times 2.

Step 24. Add 1.00 to the result of Step 22.

Step 25. Divide the result of Step 23 by the result of Step 24. The result of Step 25 is the *corrected* split-half reliability coefficient.

Sample Computation

Step 1. *Column A*   *Column B*

Column A	Column B
104	60
94	59
100	42
130	64
101	65
85	40
80	65
120	65

Step 2. Number of pairs = 8

Step 3.
$104 \times 60 = 6240$
$94 \times 59 = 5546$
$100 \times 42 = 4200$
$130 \times 64 = 8320$
$101 \times 65 = 6565$
$85 \times 40 = 3400$
$80 \times 65 = 5200$
$120 \times 65 = \underline{7800}$

Step 4.   47,271

Step 5. $47,271 \times 8 = 378,168$

Step 6.
$104 \times 104 = 10,816$
$94 \times 94 = 8,836$
$100 \times 100 = 10,000$
$130 \times 130 = 16,900$
$101 \times 101 = 10,201$
$85 \times 85 = 7,225$
$80 \times 80 = 6,400$
$120 \times 120 = \underline{14,400}$

Step 7.   84,778

Step 8. $84,778 \times 8 = 678,224$

Step 9. $104 + 94 + 100 + 130 + 101 + 85 + 80 + 120 = 814$

Step 10. $814 \times 814 = 662,596$

Step 11. $60 \times 60 = 3600$
$\phantom{\text{Step 11.}}\ 59 \times 59 = 3481$
$\phantom{\text{Step 11.}}\ 42 \times 42 = 1764$
$\phantom{\text{Step 11.}}\ 64 \times 64 = 4096$
$\phantom{\text{Step 11.}}\ 65 \times 65 = 4225$
$\phantom{\text{Step 11.}}\ 40 \times 40 = 1600$
$\phantom{\text{Step 11.}}\ 65 \times 65 = 4225$
$\phantom{\text{Step 11.}}\ 65 \times 65 = \underline{4225}$

Step 12. $ 27{,}216$

Step 13. $27{,}216 \times 8 = 217{,}728$

Step 14. $60 + 59 + 42 + 64 + 65 + 40 + 65 + 65 = 460$

Step 15. $460 \times 460 = 211{,}600$

Step 16. $814 \times 460 = 374{,}440$

Step 17. $378{,}168 - 374{,}440 = 3728$

Step 18. $678{,}224 - 662{,}596 = 15{,}628$

Step 19. $217{,}728 - 211{,}600 = 6128$

Step 20. $15{,}628 \times 6128 = 95{,}768{,}384$

Step 21. $\sqrt{95{,}768{,}384} = 9786.13$

Step 22. $3728 \div 9786 = .38$

The rest of the steps are unnecessary, because this is not a split-half reliability coefficient.

Index of Names

Index